EDGECRUSHER

Komm mit!

Holt German
Level 1

HOLT, RINEHART AND WINSTON
Harcourt Brace & Company

Austin • New York • Orlando • Chicago • Atlanta • San Francisco • Boston • Dallas • Toronto • London

ISBN 0-03-032519-6

3 4 5 6 7 041 99 98 97 96 95

Director: Lawrence Haley

Executive Editor: Barbara Kristof

Editorial Staff: Helen Becker, Frank Dietz, Francine Ducharme Hartman, Steven Hayes, Christian Hiltenbrand, Cindy Reinke-Presnall, Robyn Stuart, Beth Goerner, *Department Secretary*

Editorial Permissions: Janet Harrington

Design and Production: Pun Nio, *Senior Art Director;* Candace Moore, *Designer;* Frances Kerr, *Design Coordinator;* Robin Bouvette, Leslie Kell, Carol Colbath, Jane Thurmond, *Design Staff;* Donna McKennon, *Media Designer;* Bob Bretz, Rebecca Byrd Bretz, *Marketing Designers;* Debra Saleny, *Photo Research Manager;* Mavournea Hay, Shelley Boyd, *Photo Researchers;* Carol Martin, *Electronic Publishing Manager;* Kristy Sprott, *Electronic Publishing Supervisor;* Deborah Fey, Maria Homic, Denise Haney, *Electronic Publishing Staff;* Gene Rumann, *Senior Production Coordinator*

For permission to reprint copyrighted material, grateful acknowledgment is made to the following sources:

allmilmö Corporation: Advertisement, "Best in Germany-Best in America," from *Metropolitan Home,* Special Edition, The Best of Winners!: Fall 1991, p. 9.

Baars Marketing GmbH: Advertisement, "Leerdammer Light: Das haben Sie jetzt davon," from *Stern,* June 25, 1992, no. 27.

Bauconcept: Advertisement, "Die Oase in der City!," from *Südwest Presse: Schwäbisches Tagblatt,* Tübingen, July 14,1990.

Bertelsmann Club: Advertisement and front cover, "Die Firma," from *Bertelsmann Club,* March 1993, p. 9.

Bundesverband der Phonographischen Wirtschaft E. V.: "Singles" from *Bravo,* 40/1993, p. 75, September 30, 1993. MUSIKMARKT TOP-Single-Charts, put together at the request of the Federal Sound Association of Media Control (Bundesverbandes Phono von Media Control).

C & A Mode: Advertisement, "C & A: SCHNUPPER PREISE," March 1992, p. 18.

CMA: Advertisement, "Milch/Coffeins," from *Stern,* June 25, 1992, no. 27, p. 35.

Columbia Tristar Home Video GmbH & Co. KG: Advertisement, "Groundhog Day," from *K-Tips,* June, 1993, p. 8.

Commerzbank: Logo and "Umrechnungstabelle: Stand: Febr. '93" (exchange rate card).

Crash Discothek: Advertisement, "Crash," from *in münchen,* July 25–August 8, 1991, no. 30/31.

Deike-Press-Bilderdienst: Game, "Skat," from *Südwest Presse: Schwäbisches Tagblatt,* Tübingen, July 1990.

Deutscher Wetterdienst: "Das Wetter" from *Frankfurter Allgemeine: Zeitung für Deutschland,* June 9, 1993, no. 131/23D.

EMI April Music Inc.: "Kino" by Rolf Brendel. Copyright © 1984 by Edition Hate/EMI Songs Musikverlag. All Rights Controlled and Adminstered by EMI April Music Inc. All Rights Reserved. International Copyright Secured.

Winfried Epple: Advertisement, "Gute Laune," by Wertobjekte Immobilien Epple (Wie) from *Südwest Presse: Schwäbisches Tagblatt,* Tübingen, July 14, 1990.

Frankfurter Allgemeine: "Das Wetter" from *Frankfurter Allgemeine: Zeitung für Deutschland,* June 9, 1993, no. 131/23D.

Die Gilde Werbeagentur GmbH: Advertisement, "Butaris," from *Petra,* June 1992, p. 197.

Dr. Rudolf Goette GmbH: Advertisements, "Dienstag, 26. Januar" and "Dienstag, 25, Mai," from *Pro-Arte: Konzerte '93.*

Gräfe und Unzer Verlag GmbH, München: Recipe, "Pikanter Quark," from *Das große Vollkorn Kochbuch,* p. 126. Copyright © by Gräfe und Unzer GmbH, München. "Dallmayr," and photograph of "Münchens ältestes 'Schlaraffenland': Feinkost Dallmayr," "Das Wetter" (weather chart), "Der Besondere Tip," and photograph of "Feuchtfröhliche Gaudi ohnegleichen: Isarfloßfahrten" from "Englischer Garten," and photograph "Der Englische Garten ist Europas größte Großstadt-Grünanlage" from "Januar Fasching," "Ludwig Beck," "Medizinische Versorgung," from "Olympiapark," and photograph "Olympiapark: Der Schauplatz der XX." and from "Peterskirche, St. Peter" from *MERIAN live!: München,* pp. 30, 31, 39, 42, 80, 95, 112, 119, and 120.

Hamburg Tourist Board: Advertisement, "Tag u. Nacht," from *Hotels und Restaurants 93/94,* Hamburg Das Tor zur Welt.

ACKNOWLEDGMENTS continued on page 365, which is an extension of the copyright page.

AUTHOR

George Winkler
Austin, TX

Mr. Winkler developed the scope and sequence and framework for the chapters, created the basic material, selected realia, and wrote activities.

CONTRIBUTING WRITERS

Margrit Meinel Diehl
Syracuse, NY

Mrs. Diehl wrote activities to practice basic material, functions, grammar, and vocabulary.

Carolyn Roberts Thompson
Abilene, TX

Mrs. Thompson was responsible for the selection of realia for readings and for developing reading activities.

CONSULTANTS

The consultants conferred on a regular basis with the editorial staff and reviewed all the chapters of the Level 1 textbook.

Maria Beck
University of North Texas
Denton, TX

Dorothea Bruschke
Parkway School District
Chesterfield, MO

Ingeborg R. McCoy
Southwest Texas State University
San Marcos, TX

Patrick T. Raven
School District of Waukesha
Waukesha, WI

REVIEWERS

The following educators reviewed one or more chapters of the Pupil's Edition.

Jerome Baker
Columbus East High School
Columbus, IN

Angela Breidenstein
Robert Lee High School
San Antonio, TX

Nancy Butt
Washington and Lee High School
Arlington, VA

Frank Dietz
University of Texas at Austin
Austin, TX

Connie Frank
John F. Kennedy High School
Sacramento, CA

Don Goetz
West High School
Davenport, IA

Joan Gosenheimer
Franklin High School
Franklin, WI

Jacqueline Hastay
Lyndon Baines Johnson High School
Austin, TX

Leroy Larson
John Marshall High School
Rochester, MN

Diane E. Laumer
San Marcos High School
San Marcos, TX

Carol Masters
Edison High School
Tulsa, OK

Linnea Maulding
Fife High School
Tacoma, WA

Linda Miller
Craig High School
Janesville, WI

Doug Mills
Greensburg Central Catholic
High School
Greensburg, PA

John Scanlan
Arlington High School
Arlington, OR

Rolf Schwägermann
Stuyvesant High School
New York, NY

Mary Ann Verkamp
Hamilton South Eastern High School
Indianapolis, IN

Jim Witt
Grand Junction High School
Grand Junction, CO

FIELD TEST PARTICIPANTS

We express our appreciation to the teachers and students who participated in the field test. Their comments were instrumental in the development of this book.

Eva-Marie Adolphi
Indian Hills Middle School
Sandy, UT

Connie Allison
MacArthur High School
Lawton, OK

Dennis Bergren
West High School
Madison, WI

Linda Brummett
Redmond High School
Redmond, WA

M. Beatrice Brusstar
Lincoln Northeast High School
Lincoln, NE

Jane Bungartz
Southwest High School
Fort Worth, TX

Devora D. Diller
Lovejoy High School
Lovejoy, GA

Margaret Draheim
Wilson Junior High School
Appleton, WI

Kay DuBois
Kennewick High School
Kennewick, WA

Elfriede A. Gabbert
Capital High School
Boise, ID

Petra A. Hansen
Redmond High School
Redmond, WA

Christa Hary
Brien McMahon High School
Norwalk, CT

Ingrid S. Kinner
Weaver Education Center
Greensboro, NC

Diane E. Laumer
San Marcos High School
San Marcos, TX

J. Lewinsohn
Redmond High School
Redmond, WA

Linnea Maulding
Fife High School
Tacoma, WA

Judith A. Nimtz
Central High School
West Allis, WI

Jane Reinkordt
Lincoln Southeast High School
Lincoln, NE

Elizabeth A. Smith
Plano Senior High School
Plano, TX

Elizabeth L. Webb
Sandy Creek High School
Tyrone, GA

ACKNOWLEDGMENTS

We are very grateful to the German students who participated in our program and are pictured in this textbook. We wish to express our thanks also to the parents who allowed us to photograph these young people in their homes and in other places. There are a number of teachers, school administrators, and merchants whose cooperation and patience made an enormous difference in the quality of these pages; we are grateful to them as well.

MAIN CHARACTERS

Brandenburg: Daniel Hartmann, Handan Hasbolat, Timo Krause, Cordula Nowak, Hannelore Tehrani, Taraneh Tehrani, Constantin Trettler

Schleswig-Holstein: Sigried Becker, Marc Duncker, Will Roger Föll, Julianne Grimm, Johan-Michel Menke, Holger Müller, Constanze Russek, Nalan Sönmez

München: Benedict Böhm, Veronika Böhm, Mark Ikusz, Marianne Kramel, Stefan Seyboth, Sandra Zlinac

Baden-Württemberg: Gesa Grossekathöfer, Cordula von Hinüber, Astrid Junius, Kai Katuric, Oliver Meyer, Darius Schabasian, Gisela Simon, Karl-Heinz Simon

TEACHERS AND FAMILIES

Cordula and Eduard Böhm, Monika and Eckhard von Hinüber, Anke Kjer-Peters, Heidi Reich, Helena and Herbert Russek, Gisela and Karl-Heinz Simon, Renate and Dieter Sprick, Jutta and Jochen Thassler, Bärbel and Johann Trettler

SCHOOLS

Bismarck-Gymnasium, Hamburg; Drei Linden Oberschule, Berlin; Ellental-Gymnasium, Bietigheim-Bissingen; Helene-Lange-Gymnasium, Hamburg; Johann-Rist-Gymnasium, Wedel

Komm mit!

Contents

Come along—to a world of new experiences!

Komm mit! offers you the opportunity to learn the language spoken by millions of people in several European countries and around the world. Let's find out about the countries, the people, and the German language.

Vorschau

Komm mit nach
Brandenburg!

KAPITEL 1
Wer bist du? 16

Komm mit nach
Schleswig-Holstein!
LOCATION FOR KAPITEL 4,5,6.....88

**VISIT THE NORTHERNMOST STATE IN GERMANY
WITH FIVE GERMAN TEENAGERS AND—**

Talk about school and school subjects • KAPITEL 4

Shop for clothes for a party • KAPITEL 5

Meet with friends in a cafe • KAPITEL 6

KAPITEL 4
Alles für die Schule!.....92

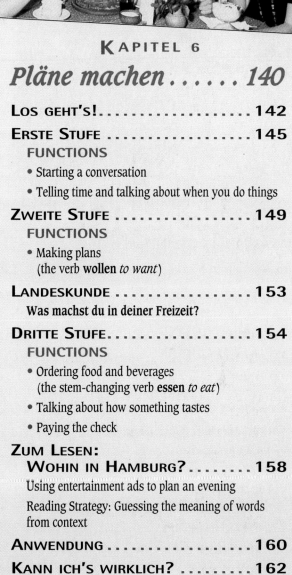

Komm mit nach
München!

VISIT THE HISTORIC AND MODERN
CITY OF MUNICH AND—

Help a friend with chores • KAPITEL 7

Go shopping for groceries • KAPITEL 8

Visit Munich with some
American students • KAPITEL 9

KAPITEL 7
Zu Hause helfen 168

Komm mit nach
Baden-Württemberg!

LOCATION FOR KAPITEL 10,11,12....240

VISIT THE BEAUTIFUL STATE OF BADEN-WÜRTTEMBERG IN THE SOUTHWESTERN PART OF GERMANY AND—

Talk about movies and concerts • KAPITEL 10

Shop for birthday gifts • KAPITEL 11

Prepare for and go to a birthday party • KAPITEL 12

KAPITEL 10
Kino und Konzerte 244

CULTURAL REFERENCES

Vorschau

German is the native language of nearly 100 million people in Austria, Germany, Switzerland, Liechtenstein, and parts of France and Italy. It is an official language of Luxembourg and is used as a second language by many other people in central Europe.

DÄNEMARK

Nordsee

Ostsee

• Hamburg

• Bremen

Elbe

Weser

Havel

Oder

POLEN

Ems

NIEDER-
LANDE

BUNDESREPUBLIK

☆ Berlin

Potsdam •

Rhein

• Düsseldorf

DEUTSCHLAND

Elbe

Oder

Spree

Neisse

Bonn •

RUHRGEBIET

• Leipzig

Saale

Dresden •

BELGIEN

Mosel

• Frankfurt

Main

TSCHECHISCHE REPUBLIK

Rhein

Neckar

LUXEM-
BURG

Rhein

SCHWARZWALD

• Stuttgart

Donau

FRANKREICH

Isar

• Linz

Donau

SLOWAKEI

Inn

Traun

München •

A L P E N

Salzburg •

Wien ☆

Rhein

Zugspitze ▲

Eisenstadt •

Salzach

ÖSTERREICH

Basel Zürich

Aare

• St.Gallen

Bregenz •

⊙ Vaduz

Innsbruck •

A L P E N

* Enns*

Graz •

Luzern •

Chur •

Großglockner ▲

UNGARN

Bern •

SCHWEIZ

A L P E N

Davos •

Großvenediger ▲

Rhône

Interlaken •

St.Moritz •

Klagenfurt •

Eiger ▲

ITALIEN

Zermatt •

LIECHTENSTEIN

SLOWENIEN

▲ Matterhorn

KROATIEN

② Matterhorn, Schweiz

① Innsbruck, Österreich

③ Wartburg, Deutschland

1 Komm mit! *Come along!*

You are now going to take a trip to the German-speaking countries of **Deutschland, Österreich, Schweiz,** and **Liechtenstein.** As you listen to a description of these countries, try to locate on the map the places mentioned. When you have finished, do the following activities.

1. Find and identify:
   a. a non-German-speaking country west of Germany
   b. a river that runs through Germany, Austria, and Hungary
   c. a city in northern Germany; in Austria; in Liechtenstein
2. **a.** Look at the map on page 2. What three German cities have the status of city-states?
   b. Look at the map on page 3. What is the name of the mountain peak southwest of Zermatt, Switzerland?

EUROPA
NORWEGEN
SCHWEDEN LETTLAND
DÄNEMARK LITAUEN
GROSSBRITANNIEN
IRLAND
NIEDER-LANDE POLEN
BEL. DEUTSCHLAND
LUX.
TSCHECH. REP.
SLOWAKISCHE REP.
SCHWEIZ ÖSTERREICH UNGARN
FRANKREICH LIECH. SLOWENIEN
KROATIEN BOSNIEN-HERZEGOWINA
SERBIEN
ITALIEN
SPANIEN AND.
PORTUGAL ALB.

Map of the Federal Republic of Germany

DÄNEMARK

Nordsee

Ostsee

Kiel

SCHLESWIG-HOLSTEIN
Lübeck

Rostock

MECKLENBURG-VORPOMMERN
Neubrandenburg

HAMBURG

Schwerin

Ems

BREMEN

NIEDERSACHSEN

BRANDENBURG

POLEN

Weser

BUNDESREPUBLIK

Havel

Oder

BERLIN

Hannover

Potsdam

Frankfurt a.d. O.

TEUTOBURGER WALD

NIEDERLANDE

Rhein

Münster

Braunschweig

Magdeburg

Spree

NORDRHEIN-WESTFALEN

SACHSEN-ANHALT

Essen   Dortmund

HARZ

Cottbus

RUHRGEBIET

DEUTSCHLAND

Halle

Neuss

Kassel

Leipzig

SACHSEN

Neisse

Düsseldorf

Erfurt

Köln

Dresden

Aachen

THÜRINGER WALD

THÜRINGEN

Chemnitz

Elbe

Bonn

WESTERWALD

HESSEN

Saale   Gera

ERZGEBIRGE

EIFEL

Koblenz

TAUNUS

Suhl

BELGIEN

LUXEM-
BURG

RHEINLAND-PFALZ

Frankfurt a. M.

OBERPFÄLZER WALD

TSCHECHISCHE
REPUBLIK

Mosel

Wiesbaden

Main

Mainz

BÖHMERWALD

Würzburg

SAARLAND

Mannheim

Nürnberg

BAYERISCHER WALD

Saarbrücken

Heidelberg

BADEN-
WÜRTTEMBERG

BAYERN

FRANKREICH

Karlsruhe

Donau

Regensburg

Stuttgart

Neckar

SCHWÄBISCHE ALB

Rhein

Ulm

Augsburg

Isar

Inn

SCHWARZWALD

München

Freiburg

BAYERISCHE
ALPEN

SALZBURGER
ALPEN

Rhein

SCHWEIZ

Rhein

Zugspitze

ÖSTERREICH

Map of Liechtenstein, Switzerland, and Austria

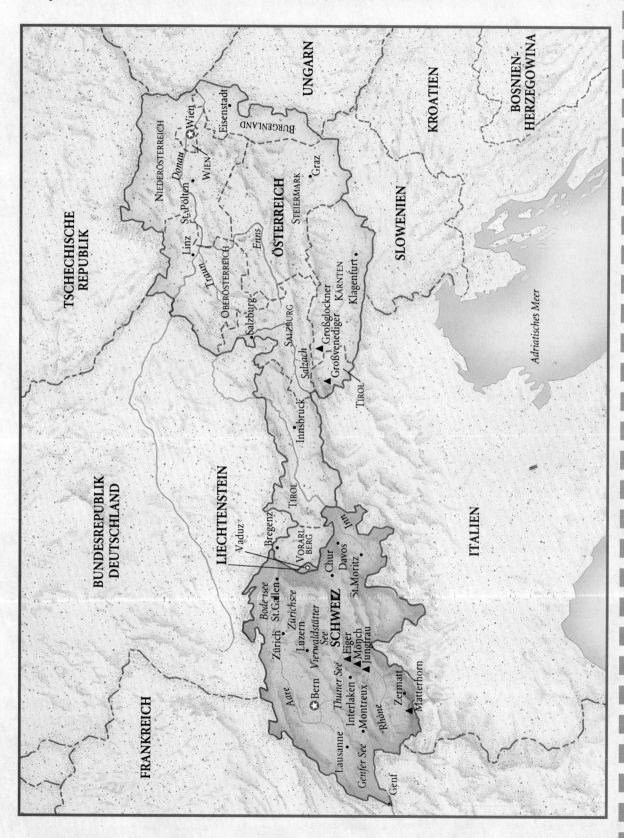

There are many things that may come to mind when you hear of places like Germany, Switzerland, Austria, and Liechtenstein. As you can see from these photos, life in these countries ranges from the very traditional to the super modern.

1 *ICE, Intercity-Express*

2 *Brandenburg Gate in Berlin*

3 *Liechtenstein*

4 *State Opera in Vienna*

5 *Matterhorn, southwest of Zermatt*

Through the centuries, in areas as diverse as science and sports, literature and psychology, German-speaking women and men have made invaluable contributions, both in their own countries and abroad.

Albert Einstein

Albert Einstein (1879-1955) revolutionized physics with his theory of relativity. In 1933 he emigrated to the United States and began a lifetime teaching career at the Institute for Advanced Study in Princeton, New Jersey.

(1)

Steffi Graf

(2)

Steffi Graf (1969-), one of the top-ranked tennis players in the world, has won a number of major tournaments, including the Grand Slam Championship in 1988.

Ludwig van Beethoven (1770-1827) is perhaps the best known composer of classical music. Though his hearing grew increasingly impaired, he composed his greatest masterpieces during the last years of his life.

Ludwig Van Beethoven

(3)

Annette von Droste-Hülshoff

(4)

Günter Grass (1927-) is a major figure in contemporary German literature. Many of his works are controversial and deal with such issues as Germany's struggle with its Nazi past. Two well-known works are **Die Blechtrommel** and **Katz und Maus**.

Günter Grass

(5)

Annette von Droste-Hülshoff (1797-1848) was one of the leading women writers of nineteenth-century Germany. She is remembered for both her poetry and her prose, her best-known work being the novella **Die Judenbuche**.

Sigmund & Anna Freud

(6)

Sigmund Freud (1856-1939) is the founder of modern psychoanalysis. His theories of the unconscious, neuroses, and dreams have had a lasting impact on psychology. His daughter, **Anna Freud** (1895-1982), helped develop the study of child psychology.

Das Alphabet

2 Richtig aussprechen *Pronounce correctly*

The letters of the German alphabet are almost the same as those in English but the pronunciation is different. Listen to the rhyme, and learn the alphabet the way many children in German-speaking countries learn it. Then pronounce each letter after your teacher or after the recording.

a b c d e,
der Kopf tut mir weh,

f g h i j k,
der Doktor ist da,

l m n o,
jetzt bin ich froh,

p q r s t,
es ist wieder gut, juchhe!

u v w x,
jetzt fehlt mir nix,

y z,
jetzt geh' ich ins Bett.

There are a few more things you should remember about German spelling and pronunciation.
  a. The letter **ß** (Eszett) is often used in place of the "double s" (ss) in German spelling. However, the **ß** cannot always be substituted for the "double s", so it is important that as you build your German vocabulary you remember which words are spelled with **ß**.
  b. Many German words are spelled and pronounced with an umlaut (¨) over the **a, o,** or **u** (**ä, ö, ü**). The umlaut changes the sound of the vowels, as in **Käse, Österreich,** and **grün.** You will learn more about the use of the umlaut in the **Aussprache** sections of the book.

3 Deutsche Abkürzungen *German abbreviations*

Listen to how these common abbreviations are pronounced in German.

VW BMW USA BRD ADAC BASF

VORSCHAU

Wie heißt du?

4 Hör gut zu! *Listen carefully*

a. Listen and try to figure out what these students are saying.

> Hallo! Wie heißt du?

> Ich heiße Robert. Und du? Wie heißt du?

> Ich heiße Monika.

b. Below are some popular first names of German girls and boys. Listen to how they are pronounced.

Vornamen für Mädchen

Daniela
Marina   Michaela   Nicole
Ute   Silke   Ulrike   Karin
Birgit   Christine   Julia   Inge
Christiane   Claudia   Gisela
Antje   Kristin   Katja
Sara

Vornamen für Jungen

Mark   Sven   Jörg
Holger   Stefan   Jochen
Christof   Michael   Jens   Benjamin
Peter   Daniel   Andreas   Manfred
Uwe   Christian   Alexander
Sebastian

c. Pick a German name for yourself and practice pronouncing it.

5 Namenkette *Name chain*

One student begins the "name chain" by asking the name of the person next to him or her. That student answers and then asks the next person until everyone has had a turn. Students who wish to do so may use the German name they chose in Activity 4c above.

BEISPIEL   *EXAMPLE*   **Ich heiße Antje. Wie heißt du?**

6 Wie heißt mein Partner? *What's my partner's name?*

In this book you will be asked many times to work with a partner to find out new information and to practice the new things you are learning. Find a partner who sits near you and ask that person his or her name. Then he or she will ask you.

Im Klassenzimmer *In the classroom*

7 Was ist das? *What's that?*

a. As you look at the picture to the right, listen to the way the names of the classroom objects are pronounced.

b. Pick one of the objects in the illustration and write the German word for it on an index card. When your teacher calls out that object, place your card next to the correct object in your classroom.

c. Take turns asking a partner what the different objects in the classroom are called. As you point to something, you will ask: **Was ist das?** and your partner will answer in German.

Ausdrücke fürs Klassenzimmer

Expressions for the classroom

Here are some common expressions your teacher might use in the classroom:

Öffnet eure Bücher auf Seite ... ! *Open your books to page...*
Nehmt ein Stück Papier! *Take out a piece of paper.*
      einen Bleistift! *a pencil.*
      einen Kuli! *a pen.*
Steht auf! *Stand up.*
Setzt euch! *Sit down.*
Hört zu! *Listen.*
Schreibt euren Namen! *Write down your names.*
Paßt auf! *Pay attention.*
Geht an die Tafel! *Go to the chalkboard.*

Here are some phrases you might want to use when talking to your teacher.

Wie sagt man ... auf deutsch? *How do you say... in German?*
Was bedeutet ...? *What does...mean?*
Wie bitte? *Excuse me?*

8 Simon sagt ... *Simon says...*

Look over the classroom expressions for a few minutes. Now your teacher will give everyone in the class instructions in German, but you should do only what your teacher says if he or she first says **Simon sagt ...**

BEISPIEL   LEHRER(IN) Simon sagt, steht auf!
                    Everyone in the class stands up.

Die Zahlen von 0 bis 20

9 Hör gut zu! *Listen carefully!*

Listen to how the numbers below are pronounced. Then read each number.

0	1	2	3	4	5	6	7	8
null	eins	zwei	drei	vier	fünf	sechs	sieben	acht

9	10	11	12	13	14	15
neun	zehn	elf	zwölf	dreizehn	vierzehn	fünfzehn

16	17	18	19	20
sechzehn	siebzehn	achtzehn	neunzehn	zwanzig

EIN WENIG LANDESKUNDE
(About the country and the people)

Look again at how the numbers are written in German. Pay particular attention to the numbers 1 and 7.

When using hand signals to indicate numbers or when counting on their fingers, Germans use the thumb to indicate one, the thumb and the index finger to indicate two, and so on. How do you indicate numbers with your fingers?

10 Wir üben mit Zahlen! *Practicing with numbers*

a. Each person in the class will count off in sequence: first student **eins**, second student **zwei**, etc. When you reach 20, start again with number one.
b. With a partner, count aloud the girls, then the boys in your class.
c. Tell your partner your phone number one digit at a time. Your partner will write it down, say it back to you, and then tell you his or her telephone number.

11 Zahlenlotto *Number Game*

Draw a rectangle and divide it into sixteen squares as shown. Number the squares randomly, using numbers between 0 and 20. Use each number only once. Your teacher will call numbers in random order. As you hear each number, mark the corresponding square. The winner is the first person to mark off four numbers in a vertical, horizontal, or diagonal row.

8	2	5	13
7	1	6	4
9	10	3	19
18	11	16	12

Why Study German?

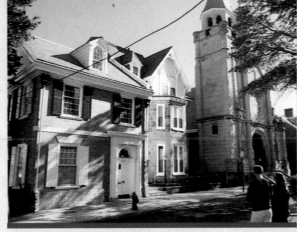
Germantown, Pennsylvania

*C*an you guess how many Americans trace all or part of their ethnic background to Germany, Austria, or Switzerland? — 10 million? 30 million? 50 million? If you guessed 50 million, you were close! Forty-nine million people, or about 20% of the population, reported that they were at least partly of German, Swiss, or Austrian descent.

Germans were among the earliest settlers in the United States. In 1683, the first group arrived from Krefeld and founded Germantown, Pennsylvania. Since 1683 more than seven million German-speaking immigrants have come to this country.

United Nations General Assembly

Everywhere, there are reminders of those early settlers: towns such as Hanover, North Dakota; Berlin, Wisconsin; and Potsdam, New York; and German family names such as Klein, Meyer, and Schneider are very common. Many traditions, such as the Christmas tree and the Easter bunny, as well as many words and phrases, like *pumpernickel, noodle, wurst, dachshund,* and *kindergarten*, and those "typically American" foods such as hamburgers, pretzels, and frankfurters were brought over by German-speaking immigrants and have become part of our everyday life and language.

Perhaps German will play an important role in your future. Many exciting jobs and careers require knowledge of a foreign language, and many employers consider it to be a great asset. You could use German in many ways in your future — as a teacher, librarian, lawyer, buyer for a large company, economist, writer, publisher, financial expert, reporter, translator, sportscaster — and, of course, tour guide, to name just a few possibilities. More than 1,200 American companies have offices in the German-speaking countries, and over 140,000 Americans live and work there. German is particularly useful in technological fields. Many high-tech companies name German as the language they would prefer prospective employees to have studied.

Above all, NOW is a great time to discover German. Dramatic changes are taking place all over Europe. With the disappearance of the "iron curtain" you can now travel freely in the former German Democratic Republic (East Germany), where travel was

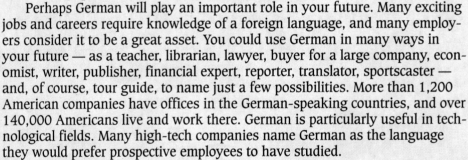

greatly restricted for over 40 years. History-making events, like the fall of the Berlin Wall and the reunification of Germany, make this an exciting and interesting time to be learning the language and learning more about the people of the German-speaking countries. So, **komm mit** (*come along*), and let's learn German!

November, 1989: The Fall of the Berlin Wall

Tips for Studying German

Most likely, you decided to study German so that you can learn to *speak* the language. This book is designed around conversational expressions (in the **SO SAGT MAN DAS!** boxes), that will help you do just that. The vocabulary (**WORTSCHATZ**) and grammar (**Grammatik**) are intended to expand your language skills so that you can say what you really want to say.

Speak

To get the best results from instruction in German, practice speaking aloud every day. Talking with classmates and your teacher is an easy and fun way to practice. Don't be afraid to experiment! And remember: It's okay to make mistakes! It's a natural part of learning a language.

Practice

Studying for short periods each day is the best way to keep on top of things. As with most subjects, it is much easier to remember things in small pieces than in large ones. Cramming for hours the night before a test will not work. Remember, you did not learn English by staying up all night once when you were two years old!

Listen

Listening to a new language is one of the best ways to learn it. You probably won't be able to understand everything you hear, but don't be frustrated. You are actually absorbing many things even though you don't realize it. When you are asked to listen for certain information, think of it as a detective game. Listen for possible clues, catch what you can, and enjoy it!

Expand

You will need to get a notebook for your German class. In this **Notizbuch** you will be asked periodically to write information that pertains to you personally. You can use this information when you are asked to say or write something about yourself. There are also many ways to increase your contact with German outside of class. You might be able to find someone living near you who speaks German or find German programs on TV. There are also many German magazines and newspapers in stores and libraries in the United States. Don't be afraid to try to read them! You will not understand every word you read, but that's okay—you don't need to. You can usually tell what a story or article is about from the words you do recognize.

Connect

When you study vocabulary, use the new words in a sentence or phrase. When you are trying to learn whole phrases or sentences, use them in a conversation. For example, if the phrase is a question, supply an answer, and if the phrase is a statement, think of a question that would fit with it. When you are learning new grammar points, always use them in sentences as part of a larger conversation.

Have fun!

Above all, remember to have fun! The more you try, the more you will learn. By studying German you are opening the door to many exciting discoveries about the German-speaking countries and the people who live there.

KOMM MIT NACH

Brandenburg!

Brandenburg

Population: 2.64 million

Area: 29,056 square kilometers (11,216 square miles), approximately as large as the state of Maryland

Capital: Potsdam (140,000 inhabitants)

Cities: Cottbus, Brandenburg, Frankfurt an der Oder

Rivers: Oder, Havel, Spree

Canals: Oder-Spreekanal, Rhinkanal, Oder-Havelkanal

Lakes: Ruppiner See, Werbellinsee, Schwielochsee, Plauer See

Industries: Textiles, machinery, cement, porcelain, farming, forestry, petroleum, coal

Favorite local dishes: Lentil soup, chicken fricassee

Photo ①: Die Terrassen von Schloß Sanssouci in Potsdam

Brandenburg

Brandenburg, the heartland of former Prussia, is a state characterized by vast flat sandy lands, hundreds of beautiful lakes, and large wooded areas consisting mostly of fir trees. A trip through the towns in Brandenburg reveals stately buildings and churches in characteristic red brick, waiting to be restored to their former beauty.

② Castle Branitz in Cottbus, built in 1772, now a museum, is situated in a magnificient nineteenth-century park.

③ A marble statue of Frederick the Great, sculpted by Joseph Uphues.

④ The new wing of Sanssouci Palace, built in 1747 and remodeled between 1771 and 1775. In the background the recently renovated **Historische Mühle**.

⑤ Cecilienhof Palace, built between 1913 and 1917. Here the Allied powers signed the Potsdam Agreement in 1945.

⑥ A ship hoist at Niederfinow on the **Oder-Havel-Kanal.** Canal barges, like the one pictured here, transport bulk goods, such as coal, sand, or gravel.

The students in the following three chapters live in the Potsdam area. Potsdam is the capital of Brandenburg. In 1993, Potsdam celebrated its 1000th birthday. The city became famous when Frederick the Great decided to establish his summer residence there and built Sanssouci Palace.

⑦ Ahmet, Jens, Handan, Tara, Holger, and Steffi invite you to Potsdam.

1 Wer bist du?

wieder
Ich ruf' Dich
gleich an.
Viele Grüße
Uli

Schülerausweis I | POTSDAM

gültig bis: **31. 7. 93**

(93)

gültig bis: **31. 7. 94**

(94)

gültig bis: **31. 7. 95**

(95)

Schulstempel/Unterschrift

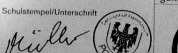

① Guten Tag! Wie heißt du?

When summer vacation is over and school begins, students look forward to seeing old friends and meeting new ones. What is the first day of school like for you? What do you look forward to?

In this chapter you will learn

- to say hello and goodbye; to ask someone's name and give yours; to ask who someone is
- to ask someone's age and give yours
- to talk about where people are from; to talk about how someone gets to school

And you will

- listen to some students introduce themselves telling their names, ages, and where they are from
- read a letter from a pen pal
- write a short letter introducing yourself to a pen pal
- learn where the German states and their capitals are located; find out how students in German-speaking countries get to school

② Ich komme mit dem Moped zur Schule.

③ Ich bin 16 Jahre alt. Und du?

Los geht's!

Jens   Tara

Holger   Ahmet

Vor der Schule

Look at the photos that accompany the story.
Where and when do you think these scenes
are taking place? What clues tell you this?

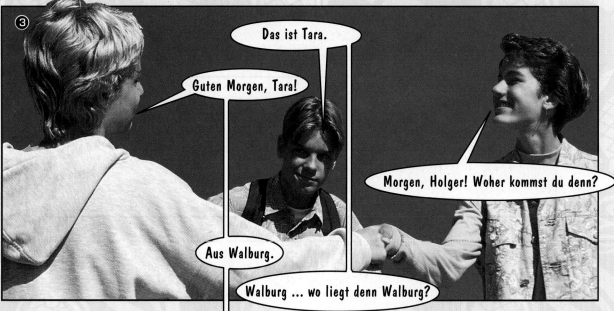

④

Schau mal! Da kommt Ahmet. Hallo, Ahmet!

Hallo, Tara! Hallo, Jens! Was gibt's?

Sag mal, Ahmet, ist morgen Training?

Ja, klar! Um 3 Uhr.

Ach so!

⑤

Ich bin Holger. Wie heißt du?

Ahmet. Ahmet Özkan.

Wie bitte? Öz …

Ich buchstabier' für dich: Ö-Z-K-A-N. Stimmt doch, oder?

Ja, das stimmt!

Also, einfach! Und woher bist du?

Aus der Türkei.

⑥

Ahmet ist der beste Mann bei uns im Team. Die Nummer „Eins"!

Ja, prima!

Schon gut, tschüs!

Tschüs, Ahmet!

1 Was passiert hier? *What's happening here?*

Do you understand what is happening in the **Foto-Roman**? Check your comprehension by answering these questions. Don't be afraid to guess.

1. What happens at the beginning of the story?
2. Why is Jens' age important?
3. What do you learn about the new student?
4. What information does Ahmet have for Jens? What "team" do you think they are talking about?

2 Genauer lesen *Reading for detail*

Reread the conversations. Which words or phrases do the characters in the **Foto-Roman** use to

1. greet each other
2. ask someone's name
3. ask where someone is from
4. ask where a place is
5. say goodbye

3 Stimmt oder stimmt nicht? *Right or wrong?*

Are these statements right or wrong? Answer each one with either **stimmt** or **stimmt nicht**. If a statement is wrong, try to state it correctly.

1. Jens ist jetzt sechzehn und kommt mit dem Moped zur Schule.
2. Ahmet ist neu in der Schule.
3. Walburg ist in Bayern.
4. Tara und Holger haben morgen Training.
5. Ahmet kommt aus der Türkei.

4 Wer macht was? *Who is doing what?*

What have you learned about each of these students? Match the descriptions on the right with the names on the left, then read each completed sentence.

1. Holger
2. Tara
3. Jens
4. Ahmet

a. ...ist jetzt sechzehn und kommt mit dem Moped zur Schule.
b. ...ist der beste Mann im Team.
c. ...buchstabiert den Namen von Ahmet.
d. ...ist neu in der Schule.

5 Wer bist du denn? *Who are you?*

Using words from the box, complete this conversation between two new students.

ULRIKE Hallo! Ich __1__ Ulrike. Wer bist __2__ denn? Bist du __3__ hier?

GUPSE Ja, ich heiße Gupse. Ich __4__ aus der Türkei. __5__ kommst du?

ULRIKE __6__ Hessen.

GUPSE Schau mal! __7__ ist das?

ULRIKE Das ist die Birgit. Sie __8__ sechzehn und kommt __9__ dem Moped zur Schule. Toll, was?

> mit Woher
> heiße ist
> Wer Aus
> du
> neu
> komme

ERSTE STUFE

Saying hello and goodbye; asking someone's name and giving yours; asking who someone is

SO SAGT MAN DAS! *Here's how you say it!*

Saying hello and goodbye

Saying hello:

Guten Morgen!	*Good morning!*
Morgen!	*Morning!*
Guten Tag!	*Hello!*
Tag!	
Hallo!	} *Hi!*
Grüß dich!	

Saying goodbye:

Auf Wiedersehen!	*Goodbye!*
Wiedersehen!	*Bye!*
Tschüs!	
Tschau!	} *Bye!*
Bis dann!	*See you later!*

6 Hör gut zu! *Listen carefully*

Listen to the following people greet each other or say goodbye. For each exchange you hear, write whether it is a **hello** or a **goodbye**.

EIN WENIG LANDESKUNDE
(About the country and the people)

Guten Morgen! and **Guten Tag!** are standard greetings and can be used in almost any social situation. With whom do you think you might use the abbreviated forms **Morgen!** and **Tag!**? The phrases **Hallo!** and **Grüß dich!** are casual and are generally used with friends and family. **Grüß dich!** is heard more in southern Germany and Austria. **Auf Wiedersehen!**, **Wiedersehen!**, and **Tschüs!** are all ways of saying goodbye. Which of the three do you think would be the most formal? If you were going to greet a fellow student and good friend, and then say goodbye, which phrases would you use?

Grüß dich, Klaus!

Guten Tag, Frau Müller!

Auf Wiedersehen, Herr Kießling!

Tschau, Silvia!

7 Hallo!

Here you see some friends greeting each other and saying goodbye. Match the exchanges with the appropriate pictures.

 a.
 b.
 c.
 d.

1. —Tschüs, Lisa!
   —Tschau, Christian!
2. —Wiedersehen, Frau Weber!
   —Auf Wiedersehen, Peter!

3. —Tag, Alexander! Sebastian!
   —Tag, Julia!
4. —Guten Morgen, Herr Koschizki!
   —Morgen, Elisabeth!

8 Freunde begrüßen

Greeting friends

Make a name tag for yourself, using your own name or one chosen from the list in the **Vorschau.** Get together with a few of your classmates. For more German first names, turn to page 325 in the back of your book. Greet and say goodbye to each other, using the names on the tags. Don't forget to greet and say goodbye to your teacher.

Was sagt Anna zum Monster mit den drei Köpfen?

SO SAGT MAN DAS! *Here's how you say it!*

Asking someone's name and giving yours

When you meet a new student you'll want to find out his or her name.

You ask:
Wie heißt du?

The student responds:
Ich heiße Holger.

You might also ask:
Heißt du Holger? *Is your name Holger?*

Ja, ich heiße Holger.

To ask a boy's name:
Wie heißt der Junge?
Heißt der Junge Ahmet?
   Is that boy's name Ahmet?

Der Junge heißt Ahmet.
Ja, er heißt Ahmet.

To ask a girl's name:
Wie heißt das Mädchen?
Heißt das Mädchen Ulrike?

Das Mädchen heißt Steffi.
Nein, sie heißt Steffi.

9 Hör gut zu! *Listen carefully*

To complete these conversations, match each exchange you hear with the correct illustration.

a.

b.

c.

d.

Grammatik Forming questions

There are several ways of asking questions in German. One way is to begin with a question word (interrogative) such as **wie** *(how)*. Some other question words are: **wer** *(who)*, **wo** *(where)*, and **woher** *(from where)*.

Look at the questions below. How are they different from questions such as **Wie heißt der Junge?**[1] What is the position of the verb in these questions?[2]

Heißt du Holger?   Ja, ich heiße Holger.
Heißt das Mädchen Kristin?   Nein, sie heißt Antje.

10 Wie heißt er? Wie heißt sie?

How well do you remember the names of your classmates? When someone asks you: **Wie heißt das Mädchen?** or **Wie heißt der Junge?**, give the name of the person referred to. For practice, use complete sentences.

SO SAGT MAN DAS!

Asking who someone is

To find out someone else's name you ask: **Wer ist das?**
The response might be:

Das ist die Moni.

Das ist der Stefan.

Das ist Herr Gärtner, der Deutschlehrer.

Das ist Frau Weigel, die Biologielehrerin.

1. These questions anticipate *yes* or *no* as a response. 2. The verb will always be at the beginning of a *yes/no* question.

Grammatik — The definite articles der, die, and das

German has three words for *the:* **der, die,** and **das,** called *definite articles.* These words tell us to which class or group a German noun belongs. Words that have **der** as the article, such as **der Junge** *(the boy),* are masculine nouns. Words that have the article **die,** such as **die Lehrerin** *(the female teacher),* are feminine nouns. The third group of nouns have the article **das,** as in **das Mädchen** *(the girl),* and are neuter nouns. You will learn more about this in **Kapitel 3.**

der—words (masculine)	die—words (feminine)	das—words (neuter)
der Junge		das Mädchen
der Lehrer	die Lehrerin	
der Deutschlehrer	die Deutschlehrerin	

11 Hör gut zu! *Listen carefully!*

Holger is asking Jens and Tara about various people in the class. Listen and decide whether the person they are talking about is male or female.

12 Wie heißt der Junge?

Holger is trying to learn the names of everyone in his class. He asks Tara for help. Rewrite the conversation, filling in the missing definite articles **der, die,** or **das.**

HOLGER Wie heißt der Junge?
TARA __1__ Junge heißt Uwe. __2__ Uwe kommt aus München.
HOLGER Und __3__ Mädchen?
TARA __4__ Mädchen heißt Katja. __5__ Katja kommt aus Hamburg.
HOLGER Und wie heißt __6__ Lehrerin?
TARA __7__ Lehrerin heißt Frau Möller.

EIN WENIG LANDESKUNDE

In casual speech, the definite articles **der** and **die** are often used with first names (**Das ist die Tara. Das ist der Jens.**). This practice occurs more often in southern Germany, Austria, and Switzerland than in northern Germany. **Der** and **die** are also often used with the last names of celebrities and other well-known people. How would you refer to **Steffi Graf**?

LERNTRICK

In English, we know that the word "the" signals a noun. In German, we use **der, die,** and **das** in much the same way. Remember that in German, every time you learn a new noun, you must also learn the definite article (**der, die,** or **das**) that goes with it.

13 Wer sind meine Mitschüler?

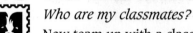

Who are my classmates?

Now team up with a classmate and ask each other the names of other students in the class. Be sure to use all of the ways of asking you have learned.

14 Ratespiel *Guessing Game*

Bring in pictures of well-known people and ask your classmates to identify them.

ZWEITE STUFE

Asking someone's age and giving yours

SO SAGT MAN DAS!
Asking someone's age and giving yours

To find out how old someone is, you might ask:

You might get responses like these:

Wie alt bist du?

Ich bin vierzehn Jahre alt.
I am 14 years old.
Ich bin vierzehn.
Vierzehn.
Nein, ich bin vierzehn.

Bist du schon fünfzehn?
Are you already 15?
Wie alt ist der Peter?
**Und die Monika? Ist sie auch
fünfzehn?**

Er ist fünfzehn.

Ja, sie ist auch fünfzehn.

Can you identify the verbs in the different examples?[1] Why do you think the verbs change?[2]

WORTSCHATZ

Do you remember the numbers you learned in the Vorschau?

0	null	1	eins	2	zwei	3	drei	4	vier	5	fünf
6	sechs	7	sieben	8	acht	9	neun	10	zehn	11	elf
12	zwölf	13	dreizehn	14	vierzehn	15	fünfzehn	16	sechzehn	17	siebzehn
18	achtzehn	19	neunzehn	20	zwanzig							

---

15 Hör gut zu!

Holger wants to get to know his new classmates, so he asks Ahmet how old everyone is. Listen to their conversation and write down the ages of the students below.

Handan: ═══   Ahmet: ═══   Renate: ═══   Jens: ═══

16 Wir stellen vor *Introducing*

Ask your partner's name and age and then introduce him or her to the rest of the class.

---

1. The verbs are **bist, bin, ist**. 2. The verbs change because the subjects of the sentences change.

Grammatik Subject pronouns and the verb **sein** *(to be)*

The phrases **ich bin, du bist, er ist, sie ist,** and **sie sind** each contain a subject pronoun corresponding to the English *I, you, he, she,* and *they*, and a form of the verb **sein** *(to be)*: *I am, you are, he is, she is, they are.* **Sein** is one of the most frequently used verbs in German.*

Ich	**bin**	dreizehn.
Du	**bist**	auch dreizehn.
Karola Sie }	**ist**	vierzehn.
Jens Er }	**ist**	sechzehn.
Ahmet und Holger Sie }	**sind**	sechzehn.

17 Hör gut zu!

Listen to the following sentences and determine if Ulrike is talking about herself, about one other person, or about more than one person.

	about self	about one person	about more than one person
1			
2			

18 Wie alt sind sie?

Fill in the missing forms of **sein** in this conversation between Ahmet and Holger.

HOLGER Sag mal, wie alt __1__ du?
AHMET Ich __2__ 16.
HOLGER Du __3__ 16? Ich auch. Und wie alt __4__ Tara und Jens?
AHMET Tara __5__ 14, und Jens __6__ 16.

19 Wie alt sind die Jungen und Mädchen?

Say who these people are and how old they are.

Steffi, 15

Melanie und Katja, 16

Björn, 16

Karola, 14

20 Zum Schreiben *Writing*

You are preparing for a conversation with an exchange student from Germany. Write in German the questions you want to ask in order to find out the student's name and age. Then write how you would answer those questions yourself.

*There are three other forms of **sein** you will learn about and practice later: **wir sind** *(we are)*, **ihr seid** *(you are, plural)* and **Sie sind** *(you are, formal)*.

21

The **Bundesrepublik Deutschland** (*Federal Republic of Germany*) is made up of **Bundesländer** (*federal states*). Each **Bundesland** has a **Hauptstadt** (*capital*) and its own regional government. The **Bundesrepublik Deutschland** is abbreviated **BRD**.

a. How many **Bundesländer** are there? Make a list of them.
b. Write the **Hauptstadt** beside the name of each **Bundesland**.
c. Which **Bundesland** borders Switzerland? Austria?
d. What are the **Hauptstädte** of Switzerland and Austria?

Kiel • SCHLESWIG-HOLSTEIN

MECKLENBURG-VORPOMMERN
Schwerin •

HAMBURG
BREMEN
NIEDERSACHSEN

BRANDENBURG
Potsdam • BERLIN

Wiebke Jansen, 16

Jörg Schulze, 19

Hannover

Magdeburg •
SACHSEN-ANHALT

Kemal Acar, 15

NORDRHEIN-WESTFALEN
• Düsseldorf

Dresden •
Erfurt •
THÜRINGEN
SACHSEN

HESSEN
• Wiesbaden

RHEINLAND-PFALZ
Mainz •

SAAR-LAND
Saar-brücken •

Stuttgart •
BAYERN

Melina Kiritsis, 18

München •

Brigitte Dennhöffer, 19

Wien ✪

BADEN-WÜRTTEMBERG

Zürich •
Bern ✪ SCHWEIZ

LIECHTENSTEIN
✪ Vaduz

ÖSTERREICH

SO SAGT MAN DAS!

Talking about where people are from

To find out where someone is from you might ask:

Woher kommst du? *or*
Woher bist du?
Bist du aus Deutschland?

The other person might respond:

Ich komme aus Texas.
Ich bin aus Texas.
Nein, ich bin aus Wisconsin.

To find out where someone else is from you ask:

Und Herr Gärtner, der Deutschlehrer, woher ist er?
Kommt die Inge auch aus Österreich?

Er ist aus Österreich.
Nein, sie kommt aus Thüringen.

What do you think the question word **woher** is equivalent to in English?[1]

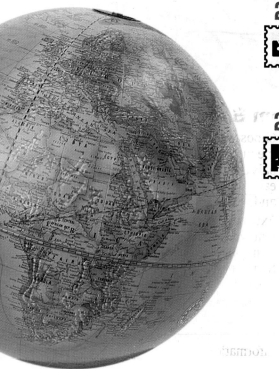

22 Hör gut zu!

Look at the map on page 27 as you listen to the five students introducing themselves. For each introduction, write the name of the student who is speaking and where he or she is from.

23 Woher sind sie?

a. Look at the photos of the people on page 27. Take turns asking and telling your partner about each person pictured, mentioning name, age, and where that person is from.

b. Ask your partner where he or she is from, and your partner will ask you. Be prepared to share your partner's answer with the class.

c. One student begins by calling on a classmate. That person says his or her name, age, and where he or she is from, then calls on someone else.

---

1. **Woher?** asks the question *From where?*

24 Rate mal

Choose one of the **Landeshauptstädte** from the box below and write it down. The city you choose is your imaginary hometown. Your partner will try to guess where you are from. If he or she guesses incorrectly, you can say **Nein, ich komme nicht aus ...** After your partner guesses correctly, switch roles and guess where your partner is from.

Erfurt   Magdeburg   Mainz   Dresden   Berlin

Düsseldorf   Saarbrücken   Hannover   Wiesbaden
                        Hamburg   Bremen
Kiel   Stuttgart   Potsdam   Schwerin   München

25 Woher kommst du?

A classmate, Birgit, slips Holger the following note in class.

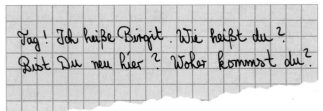

Tag! Ich heiße Birgit. Wie heißt du?
Bist Du neu hier? Woher kommst du?

What does Holger write back to her? Write his note.

SPRACHTIP

There are many short words in German that you can use to connect your ideas and to make your German sound more natural. Some of these words are: **und** *(and),* **auch** *(also),* **jetzt** *(now),* and **schon** *(already).*

The teenagers in the **Foto-Roman** also used some other expressions: **Also, einfach!** *(That's easy!);* **Ach ja!** *(Oh, yeah!);* **Ja klar!** *(Of course.);* and **Prima!** *(Great!).* Look back at the conversations in the **Foto-Roman** and see how these words were used.

26 Zum Schreiben   *Writing*

a. Choose three of the students shown on the map on page 27 as possible pen pals and write three sentences about each of them, telling their names, ages, and where they are from.

b. Exchange papers with a partner and read your partner's sentences. Is everything written correctly? Make corrections on your partner's paper and he or she will do the same on your paper.

c. Now write a few sentences about yourself that you might use in a letter to one of these people, giving the same information.

Wie kommen die Mädchen und Jungen zur Schule?

Annette kommt **mit dem Bus.**

Michael kommt **mit der U-Bahn.**

Philipp kommt **mit dem Rad.**

Sara kommt **zu Fuß.**

Meine Mutter bringt mich **mit dem Auto.**

Und Heike kommt **mit dem Moped.**

27 Hör gut zu!

Based on the information given in the **Wortschatz**, determine whether the statements you hear are right or not. List the names you hear and write beside the name **stimmt** if the information is correct or **stimmt nicht** if it is incorrect.

SO SAGT MAN DAS!

Talking about how someone gets to school

To find out how someone
gets to school you ask:

    Wie kommst du zur Schule?
    **Kommt Ahmet zu Fuß zur
      Schule?**
    Wie kommt Ayla zur Schule?
    **Und wie kommt der Wolfgang zur
      Schule?**

The responses might be:

    Ich komme mit dem Rad.

    Nein, er kommt auch mit dem Rad.
    Sie kommt mit dem Bus.

    Er kommt mit der U-Bahn.

Wie kommst du zur Schule?

LANDESKUNDE

In Germany, many people of all ages ride bicycles—to school, to work, even to do their shopping. Why do you think this might be so? In addition to bicycles, there are a number of other possibilities available to German students for getting to and from school. Students who are at least 16 can drive a **Moped**, 14-year-olds can ride **Mofas**, and students 18 or over can get a driver's license for a car. We asked several students around Germany about how they get to school; here are their responses.

Christina, *Bietigheim*

„Ich heiße Christina, bin 17 Jahre alt und komme mit dem Leichtkraftrad zur Schule."

Johannes, *Bietigheim*

„Also, ich heiße Johannes Hennicke, bin 12 Jahre alt und fahre jeden Morgen mit dem Fahrrad zur Schule."

Sonja, *Berlin*

„Ich heiße Sonja Wegener. Ich bin 17 Jahre alt. Ich fahre meistens mit der U-Bahn zur Schule, aber im Sommer fahr' ich mit dem Fahrrad."

Tim, *Berlin*

„Ich heiße Tim Wiesbach und komme mit meinem Moped jeden Tag, wenn das Wetter mitspielt, zur Schule."

Sandra, *Berlin*

„Ich heiße Sandra Krabbel. Ich geh' auf die Max-Beckmann-Oberschule, und meistens fahr' ich mit dem Bus, ganz selten auch mit dem Fahrrad, und jetzt neuerdings auch manchmal mit dem Auto, aber nur sehr selten."

A. 1. How do these students get to school? List the names of the students that were interviewed, then beside each name write the way that each student gets to school.

2. Look at the list you made, and try to determine where these students might live: in a large city? in a suburb? etc. First discuss this question with a partner, then together explain to the rest of the class how you came to the conclusions that you did.

3. The photo above is fairly typical for a German city. What do you notice about it? Is the German city in the photo similar to or different from a city in the United States? What conclusions can you draw about possible differences in transportation in Germany and in the United States?

B. Ask several of your classmates how they get to school, and decide together if there are differences between the way American students get to school and the way German students get to school. Write a brief essay discussing this question.

28 Versteckte Sätze *Hidden sentences*

How many questions and answers can you form?

a. Viele Fragen *A lot of questions*

Wie	kommst kommen kommt	die Sonja der Jens du Ahmet und Holger	zur Schule?

b. Viele Antworten *A lot of answers*

Der Johannes Der Tim Ich Ahmet und Holger	komme kommen kommt	mit dem Rad. mit dem Bus. zu Fuß. mit dem Moped. mit dem Auto. mit der U-Bahn.

29 Wer ist neu?

Can you complete this conversation between Susanne and Manfred, two students at Tara's school? (More than one question may be possible!)

SUSANNE   Tag! ═══?
MANFRED   Ja, ich bin neu hier.
SUSANNE   ═══?
MANFRED   Ich heiße Manfred.
SUSANNE   Und ═══?
MANFRED   Aus Saarbrücken.

Inge kommt mit dem Moped.

MANFRED   ═══?
SUSANNE   Das ist Inge.
MANFRED   ═══?
SUSANNE   Ja, Inge ist sechzehn und kommt immer mit dem Moped zur Schule. ═══?
MANFRED   Nein, ich komme mit dem Rad zur Schule.

Which one is the new student? How does he or she get to school?

30 Interview

Write eight questions like the ones you came up with in Activity 29. Be sure to use questions beginning with question words, as well as yes/no questions. Then, working with a partner, use the questions you wrote to interview each other.

31 Eine Umfrage *A survey*

a. Form small groups. Each of you will take a turn asking the person to your right how he or she gets to school.

b. Now take turns reporting to the whole class on how the classmate you asked gets to school. As everyone reports, one person will make a chart on the board. Discuss the survey results with the class.

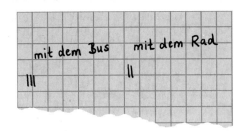

32 Für mein Notizbuch *For my notebook*

As your first entry in your **Notizbuch**, write something about yourself. Include your name (or your German name), your age, where you are from, and how you get to school.

A U S S P R A C H E

Richtig aussprechen / Richtig lesen
Pronounce correctly / Read correctly

A. To practice the following sounds, say the words and sentences below after your teacher or after the recording.

1. The letters **ä** and **e**: The long **ä** and **e** are pronounced much like the long *a* in the English word *gate*.
   Mädchen, dem, zehn / Das Mädchen kommt mit dem Bus.

2. The letter **ü**: To pronounce the long **ü,** round your lips as if you were going to whistle. Without moving your lips from this position, try to say the vowel sound in the English word *bee*.
   Grüß, begrüßen, Tschüs / Grüß dich, Klaus! Tschüs, Ahmet!

3. The letter **ö**: To pronounce the long **ö**, round your lips, then without moving your lips from this position, try to say the vowel sound in the English word *bay*.
   Hör, Österreich / Inge kommt aus Österreich.

4. The letter **w**: The letter w is pronounced like the *v* in the English word *viper*.
   wer, wo, woher, wie / Woher kommt Uwe? Aus Walburg?

5. The letter **v**: The letter v is usually pronounced like the *f* in the English word *fish*.
   vier, vor, von, viele / Er ist vierzehn, und Volker ist fünfzehn.

Richtig schreiben / Diktat *Write correctly / Dictation*

B. Write down the sentences that you hear.

ZUM LESEN

Postkarten aus den Ferien

LESETRICK

When you read the German texts in this book, you do not need to understand every word. As you progress, you will learn to pay attention to certain things—and you'll be amazed at how much you understand.

Using Visual Clues Certain clues will help you determine in advance what the reading might be about. Before you try to read a text, look at the title and at any visual clues, such as photos or illustrations, as well as at the format of the text. Very often these clues provide you with enough information to figure out what the text is about.

1. Look at the pictures as well as the format of these texts. What kinds of texts are they?

2. What do you think **Postkarten aus den Ferien** means? The format of the texts should help you guess what the word **Postkarten** means. Once you know that, ask yourself: When do people usually write texts like this? How does the answer to this question help you understand what the words **aus den Ferien** mean?

3. Have you ever written to someone while you were on vacation? What did you write about?

4. With a friend, write down some phrases you use when you write to friends on vacation.

5. Which **Postkarte** mentions a lot of activities?

Schwarzwald

Hallo Rita!
Herzliche Grüße aus dem Schwarzwald! Das Wetter ist prima – warm und sonnig. Wir schwimmen, wandern, und spielen Tennis, Volleyball, Minigolf.
Bis bald!
Monika

Rita Meyer
Gartenstraße 21
14482 Potsdam

London

Liebe Frau Polgert!
How do you do? Ich bin in London und finde die Stadt und die Engländer ganz phantastisch! Ich lerne viel Englisch.
Herzliche Grüße!
Ihre Claudia Bach

Fr. Anja Polgert
Vogelsangstr. 39
14478 Potsdam
Germany

Brandenburger Tor, Berlin

Liebe Omi! Lieber Opi!

Ich bin mit meiner
Schulklasse in Berlin
– eine tolle Stadt, echt
super!
Wir kommen am Freitag
wieder zurück.
Liebe Grüße
Euer Bernhard

Gerhart u. Friede Schnitzler
Eichenstr. 7
14489 Potsdam

6. Which words in these texts are types of greetings or farewells?

7. To whom are these texts written? What clues tell you how well the writers know the people to whom they are writing? Which **Postkarte** is probably written to a teacher? How can you tell?

8. Where is each person writing from? Why are they there? If they do not state the reason directly, what phrases help you infer why they are there?

9. What is the weather like where Monika is?

10. Why does Claudia use an English expression in her **Postkarte?** Do you think she is enjoying herself? How do you know?

11. Write a postcard in German based on one of the following activities:

   a. You and a friend have stayed with a German family while on vacation. After you leave, write a postcard to your host family, telling them where you are and how you like it.

   b. Assume you are in Germany for the first time. Write a postcard to a friend who knows some German.

Liebe(r) ...

Ich bin in ___.
Hier ___ es sehr
schön. ___ ist eine
interessante Stadt.

Herzliche ___

ANWENDUNG

1 Listen to four people talking about themselves. Write their names on a piece of paper, then beside each name write the person's age and where he or she is from.

2 **a.** Say hello to a classmate. Ask his or her name, age, and where he or she is from.

b. Introduce yourself to the class, giving your name, age, and where you are from. Then introduce the classmate you just met.

3 Read the letter below and complete the activities that follow.

> *Eisenach, den 10. Februar 1994*
>
> *Lieber Ralph!*
>
> *Ich heiße Mandy Gerber. Ich bin aus Eisenach. Das ist in Thüringen. Ich bin vierzehn Jahre alt. Wie alt bist Du? Bist Du auch vierzehn? Bitte, schreib mir und schick auch ein Foto von Dir! Viele Grüße*
>
> *Mandy*

a. Make a list of things Mandy tells about herself.

b. What does Mandy want to know? Make a list of her questions.

4 Look at the **Schülerausweis** (*school identification card*) to the right and answer the questions that follow.

a. To whom does this **Schülerausweis** belong?

b. When was this person born?

c. Where does this person live?

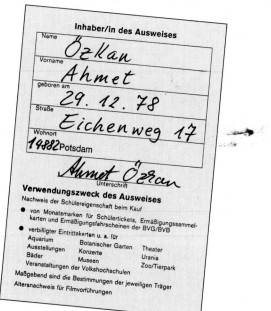

5 If you were an exchange student in one of the German-speaking countries, you would receive a **Schülerausweis.** Using the example to the right as a model, create a **Schülerausweis** for yourself, filling in all the required information.

6 Look at the picture below with a partner and take turns with your class-mates telling how the people in the illustration get to school.

 7 Write a letter to a pen pal in Germany like the one Mandy wrote to Ralph on page 36. Use the information you wrote about yourself from Activity 26c to help you.

8

R O L L E N S P I E L

You and some of your friends have been designated to introduce the "exchange students" on page 31.

a. Working as a group, prepare statements that you can use in your introductions. Remember to give as much information as possible about each student, including name, age, where he or she is from and how he or she gets to school. Include anything else that might be of interest to the class.

b. Using the pictures, present the visiting exchange students to the class.

Can you greet people and say goodbye? (p. 21)

Can you give your name and ask someone else's? (p. 22)

Can you ask and say who someone is? (p. 23)

1 How would you say hello and goodbye to the following people?

a. a classmate   b. your principal

2 How would you introduce yourself to a new student and ask his or her name?

3 a. How would you ask who someone is? Say who these students are.

Tara

Jens

Holger

Ahmet

Can you supply the correct definite articles (der, die, das) for the nouns you have learned in this chapter? (p. 24)

4 Complete Birgit's explanation to Holger about who everyone is, using the articles **der, die,** and **das.**

════Junge da? Er heißt Helmut. Und ════ Mädchen heißt Monika. ════ Lehrer heißt Herr Becker. Und ════ Deutschlehrerin heißt Frau Hörster.

Can you ask someone's age and tell yours? (p. 25)

5 a. How would you ask a classmate his or her age and say how old you are?

b. Say how old the following students are.
Silke, 15   Dirk, 13   Marina und Susi, 14

Can you ask where someone is from and tell where you are from? (p. 28)

6 How would you ask a classmate where he or she is from?

7 Say where the following students are from. Make statements with both **kommen** and **sein.**

a. Nicole, Brandenburg   c. Mark, Niedersachsen
b. Britte und Andreas, Sachsen-Anhalt

8 How would you tell someone where you are from?

Can you say how someone gets to school? (p. 30)

9 How would you ask a classmate how he or she gets to school? How might he or she respond?

Say how these people get to school:

a. Steffi, bicycle   b. Petra and Ali, moped   c. Anna, subway

ERSTE STUFE

SAYING HELLO AND GOODBYE

Guten Morgen!   *Good morning!*
Morgen!   *Morning!*
Guten Tag!   *Hello!*
Tag!
Hallo! } *Hi!*
Grüß dich!
Auf Wiedersehen!   *Goodbye!*
Wiedersehen!   *Bye!*
Tschüs! }
Tschau! } *Bye!*
Bis dann!   *See you later!*

ASKING SOMEONE'S NAME AND GIVING YOURS

heißen   *to be called*
Wie heißt du?   *What's your name?*
Ich heiße ...   *My name is....*
Wie heißt das Mädchen?
  What's the girl's name?

Sie heißt ...   *Her name is...*
Wie heißt der Junge?   *What's the boy's name?*
Er heißt ...   *His name is...*
Heißt sie ...?   *Is her name ...?*
ja   *yes*
nein   *no*

ASKING WHO SOMEONE IS

Wer ist das?   *Who is that?*
Das ist ...   *That's...*
Herr ...   *Mr...*
Frau ...   *Mrs...*
der Lehrer   *teacher (male)*
die Lehrerin   *teacher (female)*
der Deutschlehrer   *German teacher (male)*
die Deutschlehrerin   *German teacher (female)*
die Biologielehrerin   *biology teacher (female)*

der Junge   *boy*
das Mädchen   *girl*

DEFINITE ARTICLES

der
die } *the*
das

OTHER USEFUL WORDS

und   *and*
jetzt   *now*
auch   *also*
schon   *already*
Also, einfach!   *That's easy!*
Ach ja!   *Oh, yeah!*
Ja, klar!   *Of course!*
Prima!   *Great!*

ZWEITE STUFE

ASKING SOMEONE'S AGE AND GIVING YOURS

sein   *to be*
Wie alt bist du?   *How old are you?*
Ich bin 14 Jahre alt.   *I am 14 years old.*

Du bist ...   *you are (sing)*
Er ist ...   *He is...*
Sie ist ...   *She is...*
Sie sind ...   *They are...*

DIE ZAHLEN VON 0 BIS 20.

See page 25.

OTHER USEFUL WORDS

Bundesland, ̈er   *federal state (German)*
Hauptstadt, ̈e   *capital*

DRITTE STUFE

TALKING ABOUT WHERE PEOPLE ARE FROM

kommen   *to come*
Woher bist (kommst) du?
  Where are you from?
Ich bin (komme) aus ...
  I'm from....
Sie ist (kommt) aus ...
  She's from....
Er ist (kommt) aus ...
  He's from....

Sie sind (kommen) aus ...
  They're from....

TALKING ABOUT HOW SOME-ONE GETS TO SCHOOL

Wie kommst du zur Schule?
  How do you get to school?
Ich komme ...   *I come...*
  mit dem Bus   *by bus*
  mit dem Rad   *by bike*
  mit dem Auto   *by car*

  mit dem Moped   *by moped*
  mit der U-Bahn   *by subway*
  zu Fuß   *on foot (I walk)*

ASKING QUESTIONS

Wer?   *Who?*
Wie?   *How?*
Wo?   *Where?*
Woher?   *From where?*

KAPITEL

2
Spiel und Spaß

1 Was machst du denn in deiner Freizeit?

Teenagers in German-speaking countries enjoy their spare time in many ways. They play sports and games, pursue various interests and hobbies, listen to music, and get together with their friends. Does this sound like what you and your friends do in your free time? How are the leisure time activities you like to do similar to the ones mentioned above? How are they different?

In this chapter you will learn

- to talk about interests
- to express likes and dislikes
- to say when you do various activities; to ask for an opinion and express yours; to agree and disagree

And you will

- listen to German students talk about sports and other activities
- read excerpts from German newspapers and magazines
- write a brief introduction for a visiting student from Germany
- find out what people in German-speaking countries do in their free time

② Fußball finde ich super!

③ Ich sammle gern Briefmarken.

Los geht's!

Was machst du in deiner Freizeit?

Look at the photos that accompany the story. What are the people in each picture doing? What do you think Holger might be telling them about himself?

Holger

Jens

Tara

Steffi

Ahmet

①

Was spielt ihr denn da?

Was fragst du?

Ich frage, was ihr da spielt.

Karten.

Ja, das sehe ich. Aber was spielt ihr?

Wir spielen Mau-Mau.

Wer gewinnt?

Tara und Ahmet, wie immer!

②

Du gewinnst auch manchmal.

Aber ihr mogelt oft.

Was? Wir mogeln nicht.

Du bist nur sauer, weil du verlierst.

Spielst du auch Karten, Holger?

Ja, aber nicht so gern.

Was machst du denn sonst in deiner Freizeit?

Tja, hm ... Fußball, ich geh'* oft schwimmen, im Winter lauf' ich Ski, ich ...

③

④

Was noch? Hast du andere Interessen?

Na, klar! Ich sammle Briefmarken. Und ich höre gern Musik.

Spielst du ein Instrument?

Ja, ich spiele Gitarre.

* Frequently in spoken German, the e-ending on the ich-form of the verb is omitted. In writing this is indicated by an apostrophe.

1 Was passiert hier?

Do you understand what is happening in the **Foto-Roman**? Check your comprehension by answering these questions. Don't be afraid to guess!

1. What are Ahmet, Tara, and Jens doing at the beginning of the story?
2. Which sports does Holger play? What other interests does Holger mention?
3. Why is Tara teasing Holger? What does she say to him?
4. How does Holger feel at the end of the story? What does he say that lets you know how he feels?

2 Genauer lesen

Reread the conversations. Which words or phrases do the characters use to

1. ask what someone likes to do in his or her free time
2. say they like to listen to music
3. ask if someone plays an instrument
4. ask if someone has other interests
5. tell what their favorite sport is
6. say that they do something often
7. say that they find something boring

3 Was paßt zusammen?   *What goes together?*

Jens and Tara ask Holger what he does in his free time. Match each question on the left with an appropriate response on the right.

1. Spielst du Karten?
2. Was machst du in deiner Freizeit?
3. Hast du auch andere Interessen?
4. Spielst du ein Instrument?
5. Spielst du auch Tennis?

a. Nein, Tennis finde ich langweilig.
b. Ja, ich sammle Briefmarken und höre gern Musik.
c. Ja, aber ich spiele Karten nicht so gern.
d. Ich spiele Fußball, ich geh' schwimmen, und im Winter lauf' ich Ski.
e. Ja, ich spiele Gitarre.

4 Welches Wort paßt?   *Which word fits?*

Based on the story you just read and heard, complete each of the sentences below with an appropriate word from the box.

> Karten   Musik   sammelt
> langweilig   spielen   Tennis

Tara, Ahmet und Jens spielen gern __1__. Holger __2__ lieber Briefmarken und hört auch gern __3__. Holger findet Tennis __4__, aber Tara findet den Sport super. __5__ ist Taras Lieblingssport. Tara und Steffi __6__ oft Tennis.

5 Wer macht was?

What have you learned about these students? Match the statements with the people they describe.

1. Tara
2. Ahmet
3. Holger
4. Jens
5. Steffi

a. verliert oft beim Kartenspielen.
b. spielt Karten nicht gern.
c. findet Holger nett.
d. spielt oft mit Tara Tennis.
e. gewinnt oft beim Kartenspielen.

WORTSCHATZ

JENS Was machst du in deiner Freizeit?
UTE   Ich mache viel Sport. Ich spiele ...

Fußball

Basketball

Volleyball

Tennis

JENS Spielst du auch Golf?
UTE   Nein, ich spiele nicht Golf.
JENS Spielst du ein Instrument?
UTE   Ja klar! Ich spiele ...

JENS Hast du auch andere Interessen?
UTE   Ja, ich spiele auch...

Gitarre

Klavier

Karten

Schach

Und dann noch . . .

Schlagzeug

Flöte

Trompete

LERNTRICK

Look for cognates when you read. Cognates are words that look similar and have the same meaning in German and English. Some are identical, for example, *tennis* and **Tennis**. Others differ slightly in spelling, such as *trumpet* and **Trompete**. How many cognates can you find in the **Wortschatz**?

6 Hör gut zu!

Using the drawings above as a guide, listen as Holger asks what his classmates do in their free time. First write the name of any activity you hear mentioned. Then, listen again for the students' names. This time, write each student's name beside the activity he or she does.

7 Bildertext

Complete the following description of Ahmet's free time activities, using the pictures as cues.

Ahmet spielt oft __1__ ⚽ . Mit Tara und Jens spielt er oft __2__ 🂡 , aber

__3__ ♟ spielt er nicht so gern. Er spielt auch zwei Instrumente: er spielt

__4__ 🎸 , und er spielt auch __5__ 🎹 , aber das spielt er nicht so gut.

SO SAGT MAN DAS!

Talking about interests

If you want to know what a friend does in his or her free time, you might ask:

Was machst du in deiner Freizeit?
Spielst du Volleyball?
Do you play volleyball?
Was macht Steffi?
Spielt sie auch Volleyball?

Toll! Und Jens? Spielt er auch Volleyball?

You might get these responses:

Ich spiele Gitarre.
Ja, ich spiele Volleyball. *or*
Nein, ich spiele nicht Volleyball.
Sie spielt Tennis und Basketball.
Ja, ich glaube, sie spielt oft Volleyball.

Nein, er spielt nicht Volleyball.

Ein wenig Grammatik

In the sentences above that use **spielen,** the subject pronouns change as different people are addressed or talked about. A question addressed to one person uses **du.** The response to such a question uses **ich.** What pronouns do you use in German when you talk about a female? a male?[1] As the subject pronoun changes, the forms of the verb also change: **ich spiele, du spielst, er/sie spielt.** The part of the verb that does not change is the *stem*. What is the stem of **spielen?**[2] In the two boxes below, match the verb endings with the pronouns.[3]

du   ich   er   sie

-t   -st   -t   -e

---

8 Was fehlt hier?

Holger wants to know what some of his classmates do in their free time. Supply the correct endings of the verbs.

1. HOLGER   Mach═══ du oft Sport?
   HEIKE   Ja, ich mach═══ viel Sport!
   HOLGER   Was spiel═══ du denn alles?
   HEIKE   Ich spiel═══ Fußball, Volleyball und auch Tennis.

2. HOLGER   Und Werner? Was mach═══ er gern?
   HEIKE   Er spiel═══ gern Klavier.
   HOLGER   Spiel═══ Gabi auch Klavier?
   HEIKE   Nein. Sie spiel═══ Gitarre.

---

1. **sie; er** 2. **spiel-** 3. **du:st ich:e er:t sie:t**

9 Fragen und Antworten *Questions and answers*

Steffi is trying to find people to play a game with her. Complete her conversation with Tara by filling in the missing lines with an appropriate question or answer from the boxes. Which game do they decide to play? Do all the girls like that game?

Spielt die Elisabeth auch?

Na klar! Basketball ist Klasse!

Nein, aber sie spielt Volleyball.

Spielst du auch Volleyball?

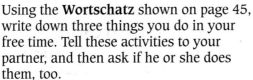

STEFFI	Hallo, Tara! Sag mal, spielst du Basketball?
TARA	══
STEFFI	══
TARA	Ja, Elisabeth spielt auch.
STEFFI	Und die Sybille?
TARA	══
STEFFI	Und du? ══
TARA	Ja, ich spiele auch Volleyball. Und Elisabeth auch.
STEFFI	Prima! Also spielen wir heute Volleyball!

10 In meiner Freizeit ...

Using the **Wortschatz** shown on page 45, write down three things you do in your free time. Tell these activities to your partner, and then ask if he or she does them, too.

BEISPIEL DU **Ich spiele ...**
Und du?

PARTNER **Ja, ich spiele auch ...** *or*
Nein, ich spiele nicht ...

11 Ein Interview

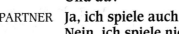

a. You are a reporter for the school newspaper and are interviewing students about their interests. Get together with two other classmates and ask them questions in German to find out what they do in their free time. Then switch roles.

b. After you talk to two classmates, write what you learned, so that your article can be ready for the next edition.

BEISPIEL DU **Was ...?**
(JOHN) **Ich spiele Fußball und Basketball, und ...**
YOU WRITE **John spielt Fußball und Basketball, und ...**

Und dann noch...

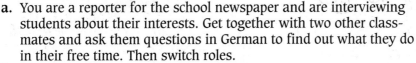

Baseball
Handball
Videospiele
Tischtennis
Brettspiele

ZWEITE STUFE

Expressing likes and dislikes

SO SAGT MAN DAS!

Expressing likes and dislikes

To find out what someone likes
or doesn't like to do, you ask:

Was machst du gern, Ahmet?
Schwimmst du gern?
Do you like to swim?
Steffi, Tara, was macht ihr gern?

The responses might be:

Ich spiele gern Fußball.
Nein, nicht so gern.

Wir schwimmen sehr gern.
We like to swim very much.

To talk about what others like to do,
you say:

Tara und Steffi schwimmen gern. *or*
Sie schwimmen gern.

Ein wenig *Grammatik*

In the question **Was macht ihr gern?** two people are addressed directly; the subject pronoun is **ihr**. The response to this question is also plural and uses **wir**: **Wir schwimmen gern.** The endings added to the verb stem with **ihr** and **wir** are -**t** and -**en**: **Schwimmt ihr? Ja, wir schwimmen gern.**

When you are talking *about* two or more people, use the plural pronoun **sie**. What ending is added to the verb stem when the pronoun **sie** is used?[1]

In the two boxes below, can you match the verbs and pronouns correctly?[2]

bist schwimmt machen
spielen komme

sie (pl) **du ich wir ihr**

12 Hör gut zu!

Gabi is trying to find someone to do something with her. Listen as she talks with her friends and determine if she is speaking to one person or more than one. Then figure out what game Gabi wants to play and who finally plays it with her.

	one	more than one
1		
2		

1. -**en** 2. Answers will vary. Possible answers: **sie machen, du bist, ich komme, wir spielen, ihr schwimmt**

13 Was fehlt hier? *What's missing?*

Complete the following conversation between Ahmet and Holger with **ihr**, **wir**, or **sie** (pl).

HOLGER	Tag Jens, Ahmet! Was macht __1__ jetzt?
JENS UND AHMET	__2__ spielen jetzt Fußball. Was machst du?
HOLGER	Steffi, Uwe und ich hören Musik. __3__ hören Country sehr gern. Ich glaube, Tara und Stefan kommen auch. __4__ hören Country auch gern. Und __5__? Hört __6__ das gern?
JENS UND AHMET	Na klar!

UWE   Sag mal, was machst du gern?
STEFAN   Oh, ich ...

sammle Briefmarken und Comics

zeichne

bastle viel

UWE   Und ihr, Christiane und Ulrike?
CHRISTIANE   Tja, wir ...

besuchen Freunde

schauen Fernsehen

hören Musik

UWE   Und deine Freunde, Katharina und Sven? Was machen sie?
CHRISTIANE   Sie ...

schwimmen

tanzen

wandern

Und dann noch ...

Wir ...

lesen   malen

kochen   schreiben

fahren Rad   laufen Ski

laufen Rollschuh   joggen

segeln   reiten

14 Mix-Match: Viele Interessen *A lot of interests*

Complete Jutta's description of her and her friends' free time activities by matching the following phrases to form complete sentences.

1. Ich besuche ...
2. Und ich spiele ...
3. Uwe und ich schauen ...
4. Christiane hört ...
5. Jörg sammelt ...
6. Und Peter und Uwe, sie ...

a. Briefmarken
b. Fernsehen.
c. Freunde.
d. schwimmen sehr gern.
e. Musik gern.
f. Fußball gern.

15 Hör gut zu!

Two of Tara's friends, Claudia and Michael, are trying to figure out what to do today. Listen to their conversation and write down which activities Claudia likes, which ones Michael likes, and what they finally decide to do together.

Grammatik   The present tense of verbs

The statements and questions you have been practicing all refer to the present time and have verbs that are in the present tense. In English there are three ways to talk about the present tense, for example, *I play, I am playing,* or *I do play*. In German there is only one verb form to express the present tense: **ich spiele.**

All verbs have a basic form, the form that appears in your word lists (**Wortschatz**) or in a dictionary. This form is called the infinitive. The infinitive of all verbs in German has the ending -**en** as in **spielen** or -**n**, as in **basteln**. When a verb is used in a sentence with a subject, the verb is conjugated. That means that the -**en** (or -**n**) of the infinitive is replaced with a specific ending. The ending that is used depends on the noun or pronoun that is the subject of the verb.

The following chart summarizes these different verb forms using **spielen** as a model.

Ich	spiele	
Du	spiel**st**	Tennis.
Holger (Er)	spiel**t**	
Tara (Sie)		

Wir	spiel**en**	
Ihr	spiel**t**	Tennis.
Holger und		
Tara (Sie, pl)	spiel**en**	

Almost all German verbs follow this pattern. Two verbs that you already know—besides **spielen**—are **kommen** and **machen.**

When speaking to adults who are not family members or relatives, you must use the formal form of address: **Sie. Sie** is used with the verb form ending in -**en**, the same form used with **wir** and **sie** (plural). It is always capitalized.

Spielen Sie Tennis, Herr Meyer?
Wie heißen Sie?
Woher sind Sie, Frau Schmidt?

EIN WENIG LANDESKUNDE

Germans tend to be more formal than Americans, and teenagers rarely call adults by their first names. While there are no hard and fast rules about using **du** and **Sie**, it is safer to err in the direction of being too formal. If people want you to call them **du**, they will tell you.

16 Hör gut zu!

As you listen to these conversations, decide whether the speakers are talking to someone they know well, or someone they don't know so well.

	very well	not very well
1		
2		

17 Bilder-Quiz

Using the photos as cues, take turns with a partner saying what the following people do in their free time.

Wir ...
Du ...
Sie (*you*, formal) ...

Klaus ...
Du ...
Ihr ...

Ahmet und Holger ...
Ich ...
Sie (pl) ...

Das Mädchen ...
Der Junge ...
Ihr ...

18 Frag mal deinen Lehrer! *Ask your teacher!*

Ask your teacher about his or her interests. Work with a partner and write down five questions to ask, for example, **Spielen Sie Tennis? Hören Sie gern Musik?**

19 Was machst du gern?

Look at the vocabulary on pages 45 and 49 again. Tell your partner five things you like to do and two that you do not like to do. Then your partner will do the same. Make a list of your partner's likes and dislikes and circle the items you both like and dislike.

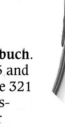

20 Für mein Notizbuch

Write down some things you like to do in your **Notizbuch**. For the names of any activities not listed on pages 45 and 49, refer to the Additional Vocabulary section on page 321 in the back of your book. These are words and expressions you can use whenever you're asked about your own interests.

21 Was macht ihr gern?

Work with two or four other classmates. Students in your group should pair off, leaving one person to be IT (**ES**). Using German, each pair should decide on one activity they both like to do. The person who is IT has to find out what that activity is by asking questions: **Spielt ihr gern Volleyball? Besucht ihr gern Freunde?** Students should answer truthfully with **Nein, wir ... nicht gern ...** or, when IT guesses correctly, **Ja, wir ... gern ...** The person who is IT reports each pair's activity to the class. Take turns being IT.

Was machst du gern?

What kinds of interests do you think German teenagers might enjoy? What sports do you play? What interests do you have? Make a list of the things you like to do in your free time. Then, read what these teenagers said about their free time activities.

Michael, *Hamburg*

„Ich mach' also am lieb-
sten in meiner Freizeit
Basketballspielen oder
ausgehen, so in Diskos
mit meinen Freunden
oder auch Fahrrad
fahren."

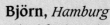

Björn, *Hamburg*

„Tja, ich sitze eigentlich
ziemlich oft vor dem
Computer. Ich seh' auch
gerne fern oder guck' mir
ein Video an. Dann fahr'
ich ganz gerne Rad und
schwimme auch manch-
mal ganz gerne."

Christina,
Bietigheim

„Ich les' gern, ich
hör' gern Musik
und ich fahr' gern
Moped."

Heide, *Berlin*

„Ich mach' dreimal in
der Woche Sport. Da
jogg' ich vier Kilometer
mit Trimm-Dich-Pfad,
dann fahr' ich auch
noch Fahrrad, danach
so eine Stunde mit
einem Freund."

Elke, *Berlin*

„Ich spiele jetzt gern
Volleyball. Im Sommer
surf' ich, und im Win-
ter geh' ich mit meinen
Eltern nach Österreich
Ski laufen."

A. 1. Work with a partner. Make a list of what each person interviewed likes to do. Organize your answers in a chart with the headings **Sport** and **andere Interessen.** After making your chart, what can you say about the personality of each person interviewed?

2. Answer the following questions with your classmates. Look back at the list of interests you made for yourself before reading. What are some similarities and differences between the free time activities teenagers in the German-speaking countries like to do, and what teenagers like to do where you live? What do you think students in German-speaking countries imagine that teenagers in the United States like to do? Where do they probably get their ideas?

B. You and your partner are exchange students in Potsdam and have been asked to come up with a plan of activities for an afternoon at a local **Jugendzentrum** (youth center). There will also be some other exchange students there, so you will need to plan activities that most everyone will enjoy. Make your plan on a large piece of paper or poster board with a lot of color (you could even cut some pictures out of magazines). Then present your activity plans to the class.

DRITTE STUFE

Saying when you do various activities; asking for an opinion and expressing yours; agreeing and disagreeing

SO SAGT MAN DAS!

Saying when you do various activities

To find out when people do things, you might ask:

Was machst du nach der Schule?
What do you do after school?

Und am Wochenende? Was machst du am Wochenende?

Was machst du im Sommer?
What do you do in the summer?

They might tell you:

Am Nachmittag mache ich Sport.
In the afternoon I play sports.

Und am Abend mache ich die Hausaufgaben und schaue Fernsehen. *In the evening I do my homework and watch television.*

Tja, am Wochenende besuche ich Freunde.

Im Sommer wandere ich gern.

What do you notice about the responses in this box? Do they all begin with the subject?[1] What do you observe about the position of the subject in these sentences? What is the position of the verb in all the sentences?[2]

WORTSCHATZ

Wann machst du das?

im Frühling   im Sommer   im Herbst   im Winter

---

1. These sentences begin with a time expression, rather than with the subject. **2.** The verb is in second position, followed by the subject.

22 Hör gut zu!

You will hear one of Holger's new classmates, Uschi, talk about when she does various activities. First, write the activities as you hear them mentioned, then match the activities with the phrases that tell when Uschi does them.

a. im Frühling **c.** im Herbst **e.** im Sommer
b. am Wochenende **d.** am Nachmittag **f.** am Abend

23 Wann ...?

Based on the page from Tara's weekly planner, answer the following questions.

1. Was macht Tara nach der Schule?
2. Wann wandert sie?
3. Wann besucht sie Steffis Familie?
4. Wann spielt sie Fußball?

24 Wann machst du das?

List five activities you like to do and when you do them.

25 Zum Schreiben

Using complete sentences, write a description of what activities you like to do and when you like to do them. Use the list you made in Activity 24.

MAI

15. Montag

16. Dienstag

17. Mittwoch 7.00 – Steffi u. Ahmet besuchen

18. Donnerstag 2.00 – Basketball

19. Freitag

20. Samstag 2.00 – Fußball mit Joachim

21. Sonntag 3.00 – wandern mit Ahmet u. Jens

Grammatik Word order: verb in second position

As you noticed on page 53, German sentences do not always begin with the subject. Often another word or expression (**nach der Schule, im Sommer**) is the first element. What happens to the verb in such cases?[1]

Wir	spielen	nach der Schule	Fußball.
Nach der Schule	spielen	wir	Fußball.
Tara und Steffi	besuchen	im Sommer	Freunde.
Im Sommer	besuchen	Tara und Steffi	Freunde.

26 Für mein Notizbuch

Exchange the sentences you wrote in Activity 25 with a partner. Check each other's sentences to make sure that the verbs are in second position and that all the verbs have the proper endings. Then trade papers back again, after you and your partner have made corrections or changes. You may want to modify some of your sentences, putting something else besides the subject at the beginning for a little variety. When you have finished, write your corrected sentences in your **Notizbuch**.

1. The verb is in second position, even when something other than the subject begins the sentence.

27 Und was machst du?

Ask your partner what he or she does at various times. Then switch roles. Use the phrases in the boxes below to help you answer your partner's questions. Be prepared to report your partner's answers to the class.

am Wochenende
am Nachmittag
am Abend
nach der Schule
im Herbst
im Sommer
im Winter
im Frühling

Hausaufgaben machen
Freunde besuchen
Fernsehen schauen
Musik hören
Karten spielen
Basketball spielen
Fußball spielen
schwimmen

SO SAGT MAN DAS!

Asking for an opinion and expressing yours

To find out what someone thinks about something, you might ask:

Wie findest du Tanzen?

Und wie findet Georg Tanzen?

Some possible responses are:

Ich finde Tanzen langweilig. *I think dancing is boring.*
Tanzen ist Spitze! *Dancing is great!*
Tanzen macht Spaß. *Dancing is fun.*
Er findet Tanzen langweilig.

Grammatik Verbs with stems ending in d, t or n

Finden and other verbs with stems ending in **d, t** or **n** do not follow the regular pattern in the **du-** and **er/sie-**forms. These verbs add **-est** to the **du-**form (**du findest**) and **-et** to the **er/sie-** and **ihr-** forms (**er/sie findet, ihr findet**). Another verb that follows this pattern is **zeichnen** (**du zeichnest, er/sie zeichnet, ihr zeichnet**). You will learn more about these verbs later.

28 Blöd oder Spitze?

Express your opinion about the following activities. You may choose expressions from the list.

1. Ich finde Briefmarkensammeln ...
2. Fernsehen ist ...
3. Musik hören ist ...
4. Basteln finde ich ...
5. Wandern finde ich ...
6. Volleyball ...
7. Freunde besuchen ...
8. Schach ...

Degrees of enthusiasm

Spitze!
super!
Klasse!
toll!
prima!
interessant!
macht Spaß!

langweilig!
blöd!
macht keinen Spaß!

29 Wie findest du …?

Ask your partner his or her opinion of three activities. Then switch roles. Be prepared to report your partner's opinions to the class.

SO SAGT MAN DAS!

Agreeing and disagreeing

If someone expresses an opinion such as **Ich finde Volleyball langweilig,**

you might agree: | Or you might disagree:

Ich auch! *or* | **Ich nicht!** *or*
Das finde ich auch. | **Das finde ich nicht.**

If someone makes a statement like **Basteln ist blöd!**

you might agree: | or disagree:

Stimmt! | **Stimmt nicht!**

Ein wenig *G*rammatik

Verbs that end in **-eln**, like the verb **basteln**, change in the **ich**-form: the **e** drops from the verb stem, and the verb becomes **ich bastle**. Can you guess what the **ich**-form of **segeln** is?[1]

30 Hör gut zu!

Listen to the conversation between Ahmet and a friend as they discuss free time activities. Do they agree or disagree? About what?

31 Ein Brief

You have just written the letter on the right to your pen pal in Germany. Unfortunately, on the way to the post office it started to rain and your letter got a little smeared. Rewrite the letter, fixing all the smeared words.

Liebe Katja

Du fragst, was wir in den USA spielen. Ja, wir Fußball und wir spielen auch Basketball. Im Winter laufen wir Ski, und im Sommer gehen wir schwimmen. ... ihr auch Fußball?

Wir machen viel Sport. Ich, zum Beispiel, fahre gern Rad. Im Sommer gehe ich wandern, und ich spiele viel Tennis. Ich finde Tennis toll! Du auch? Meine Freunde und ich — ja, wir hören Musik, und am Nachmittag spielen wir immer Volleyball.

Was macht Ihr in Deutschland?

Dein(e)...

---

1. **Ich segle.**

32 Und deine Meinung? *And your opinion?*

1. List six activities and write your opinion of each one next to it.
2. Work with a partner. Ask your partner what he or she thinks of each activity on your list. Agree or disagree with your partner's opinion. When you disagree, express your own opinion.
3. Respond to your partner's list.
4. Which activities do you and your partner agree on? Which ones don't you agree on? Make a list and be prepared to report to the class.

33 Zum Schreiben

In this chapter you have learned a lot about how Germans spend their free time. Imagine you are Katja and respond to the letter on page 56. Refer to the **Landeskunde** for ideas.

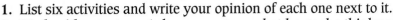

Richtig aussprechen / Richtig lesen

A. To practice the following sounds, say the words and sentences below after your teacher or after the recording.

1. The letter combination **ie:** The vowel combination **ie** sounds much like the long *e* in the English word *me*.
spielen, viel, vier / Sie und ihre sieben Brüder spielen Klavier.

2. The letter combination **ei:** The vowel combination **ei** is pronounced like the long *i* in the English words *mine* and *shine*.
schreiben, deiner, Freizeit / Heike findet Zeichnen langweilig.

3. The letter **j:** The letter **j** is pronounced like the *y* in the English word *yes*. In words borrowed from other languages, such as **Jeans**, the **j** is pronounced as it is in English.
Jens, Jürgen, Junge / Wer ist der Junge? Der Junge heißt Jens.

4. The letter **z:** The letter **z** is pronounced like the consonant combination *ts* as in the English word *hits.*
zur, zehn, zwölf / Zwei und zehn sind zwölf.

Richtig Schreiben / Diktat

B. Write down the sentences that you hear.

ZUM LESEN

Was machen wir am Wochenende?

LESETRICK

Look at the ads and articles on this page. Where would you normally find texts like these? Would you use them for a specific purpose? What would it be?

Scanning for specific information. When you are reading material like this, you are generally looking for specific information—a time, a date, or a location, for example. When that is your purpose, you do not have to read or understand every word. You simply scan your eyes over the material until you find what you are looking for.

1. Scan the articles for the following information:
   a. the day and time when you can hear a jazz concert in the **HAP-Grieshaber-Halle**
   b. the number of hot air balloon clubs in Hessen
   c. the three kinds of bands that will perform at the UNI summer festival

   Did you have to read every word of the ad in order to find that information?

2. You live in Eningen and have friends visiting for the weekend. They are interested in jazz, so you want to take them to the jazz festival. Now you will need to get more specific information.
   a. How many groups can you hear at the festival? Where are the groups from?

Immer mehr machen mit

Immer mehr Leute unterschiedlichen Alters begeistern sich fürs Ballonfahren. Bei den sechs hessischen Ballon-Clubs, die die luftige Fahrt auch für Vereinsgäste anbieten, ist ein Jahr Wartezeit für die Aufnahme in den Club die Regel. Im März dieses Jahres war Stuttgart Ziel des 22. Deutschen Freiballonfahrertages.

Eninger HOT JAZZ Festival

**Am 30. Juni
von 17–24 Uhr
in der HAP-Grieshaber-Halle**

Mit   Tante Frieda's Jazz Kränzchen, Reutlingen
All Star Groove, Stuttgart
Royal Garden Ramblers, Stuttgart
Stuttgarter Dixieland All Stars
Budapest Ragtime Orchestra, Ungarn

Hallenbewirtschaftung mit Faßbier und kleineren Speisen.

Eintrittskarten sind zu 20.– DM bei allen Zweigstellen der Kreissparkasse Reutlingen und »Sigi's Jazz House«, Im Bebenhäuser Hof, Reutlingen sowie an der Abendkasse zu 25.– DM erhältlich.

Hallenöffnung: 16.00 Uhr

Skat

Die Karten in Mittelhand: Kreuz-Bube, Pik-Bube, Herz-Bube, Karo-Bube, Kreuz-As, Herz-As, Dame, Pik-König, Dame, 9 Vorhand paßt nach ausgereiztem Null ouvert Hand. Mittelhand spielt kurzentschlossen Pik Solo Hand, doch das Spiel endet, obwohl es kaum begonnen hat, mit 60:60 Augen. Die Gewinnchancen für einen Grand Hand waren sicher größer, doch käme es hierbei auch auf den Kartensitz bei der Gegenpartei an. Schließlich reizte Vorhand bis 59, und es war nicht auszuschließen, daß Vorhand im Besitz der restlichen Pikkarten sein konnte. Vorhand führt in zwei roten Farben (4+5 K.) 24 Augen, dazu eine schwarze Lusche. Hinterhand führt in zwei schwarzen Farben (1+6 K.) 17, dazu in einer roten Farbe 18 Augen.

Potsminton

BADMINTON-TURNIER

Sonntag, 24. Juni 1990, von 11.00 bis 16.00 Uhr

Vom Freizeitsportler bis zum Aktiven bieten wir für jeden etwas. Hobby-Sportler können alles Wichtige über Federball und Badminton erfahren. Aktiven Spielern verrät unser Fachtrainer Hasso Böttcher Tricks und Kniffe oder gibt Tips für das individuelle Training.

Natürlich können Sie auch unsere Court's einfach nur mal testen.

Leihschläger liegen für Sie bereit!

Potsminton/Potsdam Sport-Center
Brandenburger Str. 73
14467 Potsdam
Telefon (003733) 458317

Potsminton

UNI
23. Juni **19.00 Uhr**

Sommerfest

- Eintritt frei - Bewirtung -

-Neue Aula-Geschwister-Scholl-Platz-

Festsaal
- Workshop Orchester der Tübinger Musiktage
- Tanzband Die Piccolos
- Vorführgruppe Elementarer Tanz
- Die hüpfenden und tanzenden Tonnen
- Modern- und Jazz-Tanzgruppe des Sportinstituts

Neue Aula Foyer
- Big Band Such Over Sky

Geschwister-Scholl-Platz
- Neckartown-Jazzband

Bar
- Karl Springer - Piano

Schach

Nr. 2743 – Dr. Siegfried Brehmer
„Schachexpress" 1948

Matt in zwei Zügen

Weiß: Kb8, De7, Tb7, Ld6, Sd3 (5)
Schwarz: Kc6, De1, Ta5, Th4, Lh2, Lh3, Sc3, Sg3, Ba7, d5, d7, e5, h6 (13)

Liebe (Lieber) ═══!
Morgen habe ich viel vor. Am Vormittag ═══.
Später ═══. Am Abend gehe ich zum Sommerfest. Dort ═══. Bevor ich ins Bett gehe, ═══.
Dein (e)

---

b. How much will the tickets cost if you buy them at the **Kreissparkasse** in Reutlingen? How much will they cost if you wait and buy them on the evening of the performance? How early can you enter the concert hall?

3. What would you and your friends probably be interested in if you wanted to attend the **UNI Sommerfest**? Can you figure out who is sponsoring this event? When will the event take place (time and date) and where? How much will it cost to get into the festival?

> **Weißt du noch?** *Remember?* You will often be able to use visual clues to figure out the meaning of a text.

4. List any visual clues on this page that help you determine the meaning of the texts.

5. If your friends would like to learn badminton better, where should they go? What telephone number should they call?

6. With a friend, make a list of places you want to go or activities you want to participate in. Use the ads on these two pages, but feel free to add activities which you particularly enjoy. Are there activities mentioned here that you would not want to do? Write those activities on a separate list.

7. Write a postcard to a friend about what you have planned for tomorrow. Use the partial sentences on the postcard as your guide, filling in the blanks with activities that you enjoy. Use words from the newspaper ads or other words you have learned.

1 You will hear several people talk about their interests and activities. Take notes as you listen, then answer the questions **Wer? Was? Wann?** for each conversation

2 **a.** Listen to the description of **der Sporti** and **die Sporti** pictured below. Write down any sports and activities that are mentioned but **not** pictured.
b. Pick one of the **Sportis** below and tell your partner everything the **Sporti** does. Your partner will tell you about the other **Sporti**.

der Sporti   die Sporti

3 Look at the drawings of **der Sporti** and **die Sporti** above and use them for clues to answer the following questions.
a. Was machst du in deiner Freizeit? Wann machst du das? Was machst du nicht?
b. Wie findest du das alles? Zum Beispiel, wie findest du Fußball, Tennis, usw.?

4 Everyone in class will write on a slip of paper the German name for an activity presented in the chapter. Put all the slips of paper into a small box, then get into two teams. Two students, one from each team, together draw a slip of paper from the box. These two "mimes" will act out the activity, and the teams will take turns guessing what they are doing. The first person to guess right wins a point for his or her team. Guesses must be in this form: **Ihr spielt Tennis!**

5 Read the following student profiles. Working with a partner, take turns choosing one of the people pictured below and telling your partner about that person's name, age and interests.

Nicole König, 14
Hamburg
   Tennis und Volleyball
   spielen, zeichnen,
   Freunde besuchen

Martin Braun, 16
Düsseldorf
   Fußball und Gitarre
   spielen, Briefmarken
   sammeln, wandern

Julia Meier, 15
Ludwigsburg
   schwimmen, Klavier
   spielen, basteln, Schach
   spielen, Musik hören

 6 Working in groups of three, interview each member of your group and write descriptions like the ones above. First, decide together which questions you need to ask. Then, while one person interviews another, the third writes down the information on a separate piece of paper, leaving out the person's name. When the whole class is finished, put the descriptions in a box and take turns drawing them and telling the class about that person. Your class-mates will guess who is being described.

 7 One of the students pictured above is visiting your school, and you have to introduce him or her at a German club meeting. Write down what you are going to say in complete sentences.

8

R O L L E N S P I E L

Get together with two of your classmates and act out the following situation.

It's Friday after school. You and two of your friends are really bored, and you are trying to find something fun to do. Discuss the activities that each of you likes, then try to find several that you can do to-gether. Make a plan that includes several different activities and dis-cuss when you want to do them. Be prepared to report your plans to the class.

KANN ICH'S WIRKLICH?

Can you ask about someone's interests, report them, and tell your own? (p. 46)

1 How would you ask a classmate about interests, using the verbs **spielen, machen, schwimmen**, and **sammeln**?

2 How would you report someone else's interests?

    a. **Susanne: tanzen, wandern, Gitarre spielen**
    b. **Jörg: Golf spielen, basteln, zeichnen**
    c. **Johannes: Schach spielen, Freunde besuchen**
    d. **Uschi: Fernsehen schauen, Musik hören, Karten spielen**

3 How would you tell some of the things you do?

Can you ask what others like to do and don't like to do, report what they say, and tell what you and your friends like and don't like to do? (p. 48)

4 a. How would you say what activities you like and don't like to do?

    b. How would you ask a classmate what he or she likes to do and report that information to someone else?

    c. How would you ask these people what they like to do and then report what they say?
       Katharina und Ute: schwimmen, Schach spielen, Musik hören

    d. How would you ask your teacher if he or she plays basketball or chess, or if he or she collects stamps?

Can you say when you do various activities? (p. 53)

5 How would you say that you

    a. watch TV after school   c. go hiking in the spring
    b. play soccer in the afternoon   d. swim in the summer

6 How would you ask a classmate what he or she thinks of

    a. tennis   b. music   c. drawing   d. hiking

Can you ask for an opinion, agree, disagree and express your own opinion? (pp. 55, 56)

7 Agree or disagree with the following statements. If you disagree, express your opinion.

    a. Schach ist langweilig.   c. Briefmarkensammeln ist interessant.
    b. Basteln macht Spaß.   d. Tennis ist super!

8 How would you express your opinion of the following activities:

    a. Fußball spielen   c. wandern
    b. Briefmarkensammeln   d. schwimmen

ERSTE STUFE

TALKING ABOUT INTERESTS

Was machst du in deiner Freizeit?
What do you do in your free time?
Machst du Sport? *Do you do sports?*
machen *to do*
spielen *to play*

Ich spiele Fußball. *I play soccer.*
Basketball *basketball*
Volleyball *volleyball*
Tennis *tennis*
Golf *golf*
Spielst du ein Instrument? *Do you play an instrument?*
Ich spiele Klavier. *I play the piano.*
Gitarre *guitar*
Karten *cards*

Schach *chess*
Hast du andere Interessen? *Do you have other interests?*

OTHER USEFUL WORDS AND PHRASES

viel *a lot, much*
nicht *not, don't*
andere *other*
Ich glaube... *I think...*
oft *often*

ZWEITE STUFE

EXPRESSING LIKES AND DISLIKES

gern (machen) *to like (to do)*
nicht gern (machen) *to not like (to do)*
nicht so gern *not to like very much*

ACTIVITIES

Briefmarken sammeln *to collect stamps*
Comics sammeln *to collect comics*

Freunde besuchen *to visit friends*
Fernsehen schauen *to watch TV*
Musik hören *to listen to music*
zeichnen *to draw*
basteln *to do crafts*
schwimmen *to swim*
tanzen *to dance*
wandern *to hike*

PRONOUNS

ich *I*
du *you*
wir *we*
ihr *you (pl)*

er *he*
sie *she*
sie *they*
Sie *you (formal)*

OTHER USEFUL WORDS AND PHRASES

so *so*
sehr *very*
Sag mal,... *Say,...*
Tja... *Hm...*
schreiben *to write*
Ich gehe schwimmen. *I go swimming.*

DRITTE STUFE

SAYING WHEN YOU DO VARIOUS ACTIVITIES

die Hausaufgaben machen *to do homework*
Wann? *When?*
nach der Schule *after school*
am Nachmittag *in the afternoon*
am Abend *in the evening*
am Wochenende *on the weekend*
im Frühling *in the spring*
im Sommer *in the summer*
im Herbst *in the fall*
im Winter *in the winter*

EXPRESSING OPINIONS

Wie findest du (Tennis)? *What do you think of (tennis)?*
Ich finde (Tennis) ... *I think (tennis) is...*
Spitze! *super!*
super! *super!*
Klasse!
prima! } *great! terrific!*
toll!
interessant *interesting*
langweilig *boring*
blöd *dumb*

(Tennis) macht Spaß. *(Tennis) is fun.*
(Tennis) macht keinen Spaß. *(Tennis) is no fun.*

AGREEING AND DISAGREEING

Ich auch. *Me too.*
Ich nicht. *I don't./Not me!*
Stimmt! *That's right! True!*
Stimmt nicht! *Not true!*
Das finde ich auch. *I think so too.*
Das finde ich nicht. *I disagree.*

KAPITEL 3

Komm mit nach Hause!

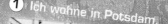
1 Ich wohne in Potsdam.

Students in German-speaking countries often go straight home after school—to eat, to do their homework, or to be with their families. What do you and your friends usually do after school? Let's find out more about teenagers in German-speaking countries — their after-school activities, their rooms, and their families.

② Das ist meine Kusine Handan.

In this chapter you will learn

- to talk about where you and others live; to offer something to eat and drink and respond to an offer; to say please, thank you, and you're welcome
- to describe a room
- to talk about family members; to describe people

And you will

- listen to a description of someone's room
- read personal profiles of students in German-speaking countries
- write a description of a real or imaginary family, based on a family tree that you will make
- find out about the homes and families of German-speaking students

③ Möchtest du ein Stück Kuchen?

Los geht's!

Jens   Tara

Holger   Mutti

Bei Jens zu Hause!

Look at the photos that accompany the story and try to guess where Jens and Holger are. What are they doing? What do you think they are talking about?

①

Du gehst zu Fuß nach Hause? Wo wohnst du denn?

In der Kopernikusstraße.

Wo ist denn die?

In Babelsberg.

Ich wohn' auch da in der Nähe. Möchtest du mit mir nach Hause kommen?

Ja, prima!

②

Hallo, Mutti! Wo bist du?

Hier oben! Ich komme gleich runter.

③

Du, Mutti, das ist Holger, ein Klassenkamerad. Er ist neu.

Guten Tag, Frau Hartmann!

Guten Tag, Holger!

④

Möchtet ihr etwas trinken? Oder etwas essen?

Was möchtest du, Holger?

Ach, ich möchte ... ich trinke eine Cola.

Und ich ein Mineralwasser. Haben wir noch Kuchen, Mutti?

Ich glaube ja.

⑤

Hier, deine Cola und dein Kuchen.

Danke!

Bitte!

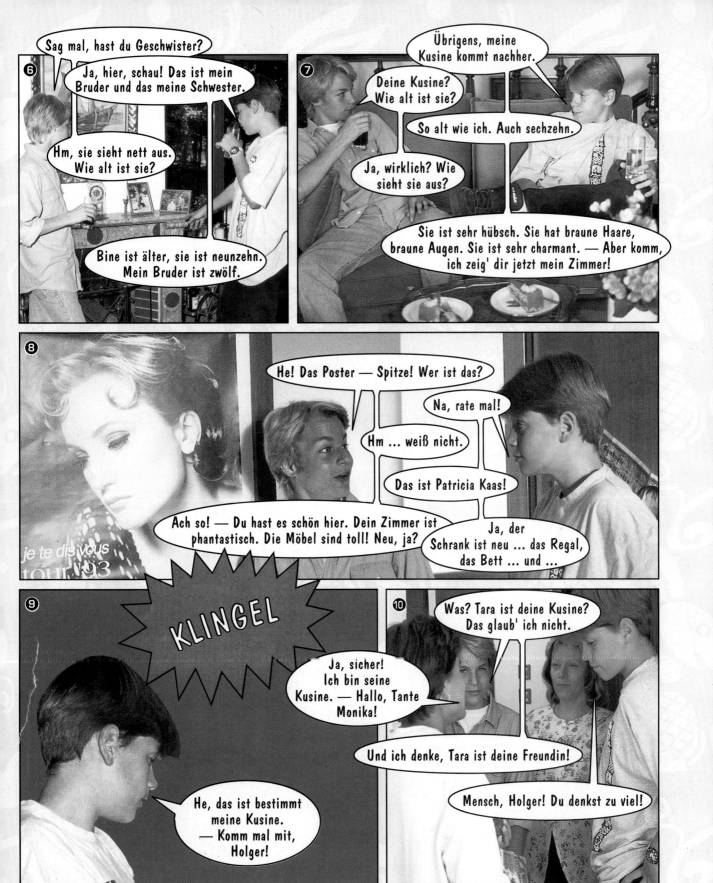

1 Was passiert hier?

Do you understand what is happening in the **Foto-Roman**? Check your comprehension by answering these questions. Don't be afraid to guess.

1. Where do Jens and Holger go together after soccer practice?
2. What do the boys do first when they get home?
3. What kinds of photos does Jens show Holger?
4. How does Holger like Jens' room?
5. Who comes to visit? Why do you think Holger is surprised?

2 Genauer lesen

Reread the conversations. Which words or phrases do the characters use to

1. introduce someone else
2. name foods or drinks
3. name family members
4. describe people
5. name or describe furniture

3 Stimmt oder stimmt nicht?

Are these statements right or wrong? Answer each one with either **stimmt** or **stimmt nicht**. If a statement is wrong, try to state it correctly.

1. Holger geht mit Jens nach Hause.
2. Frau Hartmann ist Holgers Mutter.
3. Holger trinkt eine Cola und ißt ein Stück Kuchen.
4. Jens hat zwei Geschwister: einen Bruder und eine Schwester.
5. Der Bruder ist neunzehn, und die Schwester ist zwölf.
6. Holger hat auch eine Kusine. Sie heißt Tara.

4 Was paßt zusammen?

Match each statement or question on the left with an appropriate response on the right.

1. Wo wohnst du?
2. Mutti, das ist Holger.
3. Möchtest du etwas trinken?
4. Jens, hast du Geschwister?
5. Wie sieht deine Kusine aus?
6. Dein Zimmer ist schön! Sind die Möbel neu?
7. Ich denke, Tara ist deine Freundin!

a. Der Schrank ist neu.
b. Ja, das ist meine Schwester, und das ist mein Bruder.
c. In der Kopernikusstraße.
d. Nein, sie ist meine Kusine.
e. Ich möchte eine Cola, bitte!
f. Sie ist sehr hübsch.
g. Guten Tag, Holger!

5 Nacherzählen

Put the sentences in logical order to make a brief summary of the **Foto-Roman**.

1. Zuerst fährt Holger mit Jens nach Hause.

Und dann zeigt er Holger sein Zimmer.

Frau Hartmann sagt Holger „Guten Tag".

Er zeigt Holger Fotos von der Familie.

Zuletzt kommt Tara, die Kusine von Jens.

Und Jens gibt Holger eine Cola und ein Stück Kuchen.

Talking about where you and others live; offering something to eat and drink and responding to an offer; saying please, thank you, and you're welcome

SO SAGT MAN DAS!

Talking about where you and others live

To find out where someone lives, you ask:

Wo wohnst du?

Wo wohnt der Jens?

The responses might be:

Ich wohne in Los Angeles. *or* **In Los Angeles.**

Er wohnt in Babelsberg. *or* **In Babelsberg.**

How would you ask someone where Tara lives?[1]

WORTSCHATZ

AHMET	Wo wohnst du?
MITSCHÜLER	Ich wohne ...

Michaela

in der Stadt

AHMET	Wohnt ihr **weit von hier?**
GÜNTHER	Nein, ich wohne **in der Nähe.**
ANDREA	Ja, ich wohne **weit von hier.**

Andrea

auf dem Land

Dieter

in Babelsberg, das ist ein
Vorort von Potsdam

Günther

in der Brunnenstraße

1. **Wo wohnt (die) Tara?**

6 Hör gut zu!

You will hear four students talk about where they live. Match each description
with one of the pictures below.

a.   b.   c.   d.

7 Wo wohnen die Schüler?

Ahmet wants to know where these students live. Answer his questions using the
pictures as cues.

1. Wo wohnt die Sara?
2. Wo wohnt der Georg?
3. Wo wohnen Jürgen und Simone?
4. Wo wohnt die Anja?

8 Wer wohnt wo?

Ask your partner where he or she lives, then switch roles. Describe where you live in as
much detail as you can, using the phrases you learned in the **Wortschatz** box. Be prepared
to tell the class as much as you can about where your partner lives.

SO SAGT MAN DAS!

Offering something to eat and drink and responding to an offer

Often, when friends come over, you ask what they would like to eat and drink.

You might ask: The response might be:

    Was möchtest du trinken?   **Ich möchte ein Mineralwasser trinken.**

    Was möchte Holger trinken?   **Er möchte im Moment gar nichts.**

To offer several friends something
to eat, you might ask: The response might be:

    Was möchtet ihr essen?   **Wir möchten ein Stück Kuchen, bitte.**

Can you figure out what **möchte** means?[1]

1. *would like to*

Was möchtet ihr trinken?

Eine Cola, bitte!

Ein Glas
Orangensaft.

Und was möchtet ihr essen?

Ein Stück Kuchen,
bitte!

Ich möchte Obst.

Ein Mineralwasser.

Ein Glas Apfelsaft.

Ein paar Kekse.

Danke, nichts!

9 Hör gut zu!

Ahmet and Tara come over to Jens' house. Listen
to their conversation with Jens and write down what
each one would like to eat and drink.

10 Was möchtest du?

Look at the pictures in the **Wortschatz** box above
and ask your partner what he or she would like to
eat and drink. Then switch roles.

EIN WENIG LANDESKUNDE

If someone asks for **ein
Glas Wasser, ein Glas
Mineralwasser** will be
served. Germans rarely
drink tap water, consid-
ering it to be unhealthy.
In addition, Germans
very rarely use ice
cubes in cold drinks,
even in cafés and
restaurants.

*G*rammatik   The **möchte**-forms

The **möchte**-forms express what you *would like* or *would like* to do. They are
often used with another verb, but if the meaning is obvious, the second verb can
be omitted.

> Ich möchte ein Glas Orangensaft trinken.
> Ich möchte Obst essen.
> Ich möchte Obst.

Here are the forms of **möchte**:

Ich **möchte** eine Limo.	Wir **möchten** Kekse.
Du **möchtest** Saft?	Ihr **möchtet** nichts?
Sie/Er **möchte** Kuchen.	Sie(pl) / Sie } **möchten** auch Kuchen.

11 Was möchten sie alle?

Say what everyone would like using the words and pictures as cues.

1. Wir …   2. Ihr …   3. Er …   4. Du …   5. Ich …   6. Jens und Holger …

SO SAGT MAN DAS!

Saying please, thank you, and you're welcome

To say *please*, you can simply say **bitte**. You can also add **bitte** to a request: **Ich möchte eine Limo, bitte.**

Here are several ways to say thank you:

    Danke!
    Danke sehr!
    Danke schön!

Here are several ways to say you're welcome:

    Bitte!
    Bitte sehr!
    Bitte schön!

12 Snacks für deine Freunde

Role-play the following situation with three classmates. Use as many forms of **möchte** as possible. You have invited three friends home for a snack after school. One friend will help you get the snack ready by asking the other two "guests" what they would like to eat and drink. After they answer, your helper will tell you what everyone would like. When you have finished, switch roles until everyone has been the "host" and the "helper."

Ein wenig Grammatik

Some of the names for the various snack items pictured on page 71 are preceded by either **ein** or **eine**. What do you think these words mean?[1] Now look at the words below.

    ein Junge
    ein Stück (Kuchen)
    eine Limo

Why are there different forms of **ein**?[2]

LERNTRICK

You don't always have to respond to a question with a whole sentence. Sometimes a word or phrase is enough: **Was möchtest du trinken? — Ich möchte eine Limo, bitte!** or simply **Eine Limo, bitte!**

Und dann noch …

eine Limo   eine Tasse Kaffee   eine Tasse Tee
eine Banane   eine Orange   ein Stück Melone

1. **Ein** and **eine** mean *a, an*.   2. Masculine and neuter nouns are preceded by **ein**, feminine nouns by **eine**.

Wo wohnst du?

We asked several teenagers where they live. Before you read their interviews, write where you live, using as much detail as you can. Two of these teenagers were not born in Germany. Can you guess who they are?

Dominick, *Hamburg*
„Ich heiss' Dominick Klein. Ich bin zwölf Jahre alt und wohn' in Hamburg, also Pinneberg."

Thomas, *München*
„Ich heiße Thomas Schwangart. Ich wohne in München. Ich bin an der Reichenau-Schule und komme aus Italien."

Jasmin, *München*
„Ich heiße Jasmin und bin fünfzehn. Ich geh' in die Reichenau-Schule. Und äh ... ich wohne in München, und äh ... ich komme aus der Türkei."

Johanna, *Hamburg*
„Ich heiss' Johanna. Ich bin zwölf Jahre alt und ich wohn' in Hamburg."

Ingo, *Hamburg*
„Ich wohn' hier in der Nähe, also in der Gustav-Falke-Straße. Es ist zehn Minuten von hier."

A. 1. Write the name of each person interviewed and what each person says about where he or she lives.
2. Now look at what you wrote earlier. Did any of these teenagers say where they live in the same way you did? If so, which ones? What seems to be the most natural response to the question **Wo wohnst du?** Is this also your first response?
3. Discuss these questions with your classmates: Who are the two teenagers not born in Germany? Where are they from? Did you pick the right people before you read the interviews? What influenced your choice? Considering that two out of these five teenagers were not born in Germany, what can you infer about the ethnic makeup of German society in the large cities?

B. There are many ethnic groups represented in German society: Turks, Italians, Greeks, and many Eastern Europeans, just to name a few. Italian, Greek, Chinese, Indonesian and Thai foods have become very popular with native Germans. Why do you think some of these ethnic groups might be attracted to Germany? How does this compare with the situation in the United States? Discuss these questions with your classmates and then write a brief essay answering these questions.

Describing a room

Jens zeigt Holger sein Zimmer.

HOLGER   Deine Möbel sind schön!
JENS   Ja, wirklich? Schau!

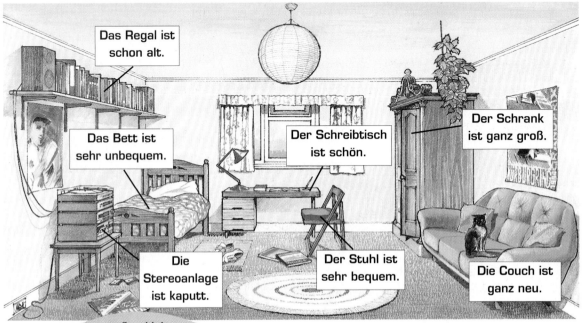

Das Regal ist schon alt.

Das Bett ist sehr unbequem.

Der Schreibtisch ist schön.

Der Schrank ist ganz groß.

Die Stereoanlage ist kaputt.

Der Stuhl ist sehr bequem.

Die Couch ist ganz neu.

groß – klein
bequem – unbequem
alt – neu
schön – häßlich
kaputt

If **bequem** means *comfortable*, what does **unbequem** mean? What do you think the word **häßlich** means? **Groß** means *large*; what do you think **klein** means? The word **neu** looks like what word in English? What is its opposite?

Schon bekannt
Ein wenig *G*rammatik

In **Kapitel 1** you learned that there are three classes of German nouns: masculine, feminine, and neuter. The definite articles **der**, **die**, and **das** tell which class the noun belongs to:

der Schrank	*masculine*
die Couch	*feminine*
das Bett	*neuter*

13 Hör gut zu!

Listen as Steffi describes her room to Ahmet, and match each piece of furniture on the left with the appropriate adjective on the right.

1. die Stereoanlage
2. der Schrank
3. das Regal
4. der Schreibtisch
5. der Stuhl
6. das Bett

a. bequem
b. schön
c. groß
d. neu
e. alt
f. klein

Describing a room

To describe your room, you might say:

Die Stereoanlage ist alt. Sie ist auch kaputt!
Das Bett ist klein aber ganz bequem. *or*
Das Bett ist klein, aber es ist ganz bequem.

A friend might ask: You might respond:
Ist der Schreibtisch neu?   **Ja, er ist neu, aber der Stuhl ist alt.**

What do you think the words **er**, **sie**, and **es** refer to?[1] What is the English equivalent?[2] Why are there three different words that mean the same thing?[3]

14 Versteckte Sätze

How many sentences can you make using the words in the boxes? Use the picture of Jens' room on page 74 for clues.

BEISPIEL   **Die Couch ist neu, aber unbequem.**

Die Couch	bequem	alt
Der Schrank	häßlich	neu
Das Bett	klein	bequem
Das Regal	ganz unbequem	unbequem
Der Schreibtisch	schon alt	schön
Die Stereoanlage	schon kaputt	häßlich
Das Zimmer	neu	groß
Der Stuhl	ganz schön	klein
	sehr groß	kaputt

ist — aber

Grammatik   Pronouns

Er, **sie**, and **es** are called pronouns. **Er** refers to a masculine noun, **sie** to a feminine noun, and **es** to a neuter noun.

masculine	**Der Schreibtisch** ist neu.	*or* **Er** ist neu.
feminine	**Die Stereoanlage** ist kaputt.	*or* **Sie** ist kaputt.
neuter	**Das Regal** ist häßlich.	*or* **Es** ist häßlich.

The pronoun **sie** is also used to refer to a plural noun.

plural	**Die Möbel** sind schön.	*or* **Sie** sind schön.

15 Im Klassenzimmer

Describe your classroom and some of the furniture in it.

1. The nouns mentioned in the preceding sentences. 2. Here, **er**, **sie** and **es** are all equivalent to *it*. 3. The nouns they refer to belong to different noun classes, i.e., masculine, feminine, and neuter..

16 Was fehlt hier?

Jens has seen Holger's new room and is talking to Steffi about it. Complete his description by filling in the correct article and pronoun.

__1__ Zimmer ist sehr groß, und __2__ ist ganz schön. __3__ Couch ist schön, und __4__ ist auch neu. __5__ Bett ist ziemlich klein, aber __6__ ist sehr bequem. __7__ Schrank ist wirklich alt, und __8__ ist sehr groß. __9__ Stereoanlage ist super! __10__ ist ganz neu. __11__ Schreibtisch ist groß, aber __12__ ist leider häßlich. Und dann noch __13__ Regal. __14__ ist auch sehr groß. __15__ Möbel sind wirklich toll. __16__ sind Klasse!

17 Wie findest du das Zimmer?

Use one of these adjectives to describe the items below to your partner. Your partner may agree or disagree. Then switch roles.

DU **Der Schreibtisch ist sehr schön.**
PARTNER **Ja, stimmt! Er ist sehr schön.** *or*
Was? Er ist ganz häßlich!

> bequem   alt   kaputt
>
> unbequem   häßlich
>
> neu
>
> klein   groß   schön

a.

b.

c.

d.

e.

f.

18 Zum Schreiben: Mein Zimmer

Draw a diagram of your room or a room you would like to have. Label the pieces of furniture. Then write a few sentences describing your room. If you need extra vocabulary, turn to page 322.

KAPITEL 3   Komm mit nach Hause!

DRITTE STUFE

Talking about family members; describing people

WORTSCHATZ

Jens und seine Familie

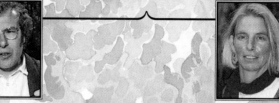

die Großmutter (Oma)
Ella

der Großvater (Opa)
Georg

meine Großeltern

meine Eltern

die Mutter
Monika

der Vater
Dieter

die Tante
Hannelore

der Onkel
Amir

Jens

meine Geschwister
die Schwester
Sabine

der Bruder
Andreas

die Kusine
Tara

der Cousin
Tawan

die Katze
Fritzi

der Hund
Harras

meine Haustiere

Und dann noch ...

Stiefmutter	*stepmother*
Stiefvater	*stepfather*
Stiefschwester	*stepsister*
Stiefbruder	*stepbrother*
Halbschwester	*half sister*
Halbbruder	*half brother*

19 Familienquiz

Answer the following questions about Jens' family.

1. Wie heißen Sabines Mutter und Vater?
2. Wie heißen die Geschwister von Jens?
3. Wer ist die Schwester von Dieter?
4. Wie heißt Dieters Vater?
5. Wer ist der Onkel von Sabines Bruder?
6. Wer ist die Kusine von Tawan?
7. Wer ist der Bruder von Taras Mutter?
8. Wie heißen die Haustiere?

20 Hör gut zu!

Make a chart like the one below, listing all of the new vocabulary from Jens' family tree. Then listen as three friends of Jens' describe their families. Every time you hear a family member mentioned put a check next to the correct vocabulary word.

After listening to the descriptions, try to answer these questions.

1. Who mentions the most family members?
2. Who does not mention the mother?
3. Who mentions an aunt but not an uncle?
4. Who mentions an uncle but not an aunt?
5. Do any of the three friends mention pets? If so, who mentions them?

	Anja	Werner	Christa
der Vater			
die Mutter			
der Bruder			

SO SAGT MAN DAS!

Talking about family members

To find out about someone's family you might ask:

Ist das deine Schwester?
Wie alt ist sie?
Und dein Bruder? Wie heißt er?
Wie alt ist er?
Und wer ist der Mann?
Und die Frau?
Wo wohnen deine Großeltern?

The responses might be:

Ja, das ist meine Schwester.
Sie ist einundzwanzig.
Mein Bruder heißt Robert.
Er ist schon dreiundzwanzig.
Das ist mein Opa.
Das ist meine Oma.
In Köln.

What is the difference between **dein** and **deine**? **Mein** and **meine**? What do the words mean? When is each one used?

21 Deine Familie und meine Familie

Steffi and Tara are looking at photos of their families. Complete their conversation by filling in the blanks with **mein/meine** or **dein/deine**.

TARA Ist das __1__ Schwester?
STEFFI Ja, das ist Angelika.
TARA Wie alt ist __2__ Schwester?
STEFFI __3__ Schwester ist zwanzig. Und das ist __4__ Bruder. Er ist einundzwanzig.
TARA Und sind das __5__ Großeltern?
STEFFI Ja, das ist __6__ Oma, und das ist __7__ Opa. Ist das __8__ Vater?
TARA Nein, das ist __9__ Onkel Dieter. Und das hier ist __10__ Tante Monika.
STEFFI Ist das __11__ Kusine?
TARA Ja, das ist __12__ Kusine, die Sabine. Und das ist __13__ Cousin, Jens.
STEFFI Na klar!

Ein wenig *Grammatik*

The words **dein** and **deine** *(your)* and **mein** and **meine** *(my)* are called *possessives*.

masculine (**der**) *neuter* (**das**)	**mein, dein**
feminine (**die**) *plural* (**die**)	**meine, deine**

These words are similar to **ein** and **eine**. Because of this similarity, **mein** and **dein** are often called **ein-words**.

To talk about the ages of various family members, you need to review **die Zahlen von 0 bis 20** and learn **die Zahlen von 21 bis 100.**

21	einundzwanzig	26	sechsundzwanzig	30	dreißig	70	siebzig
22	zweiundzwanzig	27	siebenundzwanzig	40	vierzig	80	achtzig
23	dreiundzwanzig	28	achtundzwanzig	50	fünfzig	90	neunzig
24	vierundzwanzig	29	neunundzwanzig	60	sechzig	100	hundert
25	fünfundzwanzig						

a. With your classmates, count aloud to one hundred, first by tens, then by fives, then by twos. Students take turns leading the counting.

b. Make up simple math problems with no results greater than 100. Working with a partner, ask each other the problems you each wrote down and see how fast you can solve them. Some words you may need are **und** *(plus),* **minus** *(minus),* **mal** *(times),* and **durch** *(divided by).*

22 Hör gut zu

Listen as Steffi tells Tara more about her family. First list the names of the family members in the order you hear them. Then listen a second time and write their ages beside their names.

die Kusine Anna   die Tante   der Vater
der Onkel Florian   der Großvater
die Großmutter   die Mutter   der Cousin Bernhard

23 Wer ist das? Wie alt ist er? Wie alt ist sie?

Bring some photos of family members to class, or if you like, bring in pictures from magazines and create a make-believe family. Show the photos to your partner, and he or she will ask you questions about them. Then switch roles. When you have finished, tell your classmates what you learned about one of your partner's relatives.

BEISPIEL   **Sein(e)** *(His)* ...
Ihr(e) *(Her)* ...

> ### Ein wenig *G*rammatik
>
> The words **sein** *(his)* and **ihr** *(her)* are also possessives. They take the same endings as **mein** and **dein.**
>
> *masculine* (der) } **sein, ihr**
> *neuter* (das)
>
> *feminine* (die) } **seine, ihre**
> *plurals* (die)

24 Für mein Notizbuch

Write four sentences in which you tell about two of your favorite family members or people who are close to you.

Steffi zeigt Tara ein Fotoalbum. Steffi:

Meine Mutter hat lange, rote Haare und grüne Augen. Sie spielt gern Schach.

Mein Vater hat braune Haare und blaue Augen. Er spielt sehr gut Klavier.

Und mein Bruder Ralf ist ein- undzwanzig. Er hat kurze, blonde Haare und hat eine Brille. Er schwimmt sehr gern.

Meine Großmutter Marie ist fünfundsechzig. Sie hat weiße Haare und blaue Augen. Sie hört gern Musik.

Und meine Kusine Anna ist zweiundzwanzig. Sie hat kurze, schwarze Haare und braune Augen. Sie geht oft wandern.

Mein Onkel Florian hat eine Glatze und grüne Augen. Er hat auch eine Brille. Er sam- melt gern Briefmarken.

25 Steffis Familie

Working with your partner, create a chart of the characteristics of Steffi's family. Write the names of the various family members across the top and their characteristics underneath using the categories, **Alter, Haarfarbe, Augenfarbe,** and **Interessen.**

SO SAGT MAN DAS!
Describing people

If you want to know what someone looks like, you might ask:

Wie sieht dein Bruder aus?

The response might be:

Er hat lange, blonde Haare und braune Augen.

If you are asking about more than one person, you say:

Wie sehen deine Großeltern aus?

Mein Opa hat weiße Haare und grüne Augen. Und meine Oma hat graue Haare und blaue Augen.

26 Wie sieht Steffis Familie aus?

Referring to the chart you and your partner made for Activity 25, try to answer the following questions about Steffi's family.

1. Wer hat blaue Augen?`
2. Wie alt ist Steffis Bruder? Und ihre Kusine?
3. Wie sieht Onkel Florian aus?
4. Was macht die Mutter in der Freizeit? Der Vater? Anna?
5. Wie sehen die Eltern aus?
6. Wer hat schwarze Haare?
7. Wer hat kurze Haare? Lange Haare?
8. Wie alt ist die Großmutter? Wie sieht sie aus?
9. Wer hat eine Brille?

27 Rate mal!

Pick one person in the room and think about how you might describe him or her to someone else. Your partner will ask you questions and try to guess whom you have chosen. Then switch roles.

BEISPIEL   PARTNER   **Hat diese Person blonde Haare?**

au**A** U /x/**S** S^eu**P** R /ʒ/**A** C /ts/**H** E ö

Richtig aussprechen / Richtig lesen

A. To practice the following sounds, say the words and sentences below after your teacher or after the recording.

1. The letter **o**: The long **o** is pronounced much like the long *o* in the English word *oboe,* however the lips are more rounded.

   Obst, Moped, schon / Wo wohnt deine Oma?

2. The letter **u**: The long **u** is similar to the vowel sound in the English word *do,* however the lips are more rounded.

   Stuhl, super, Kuchen / Möchtest du ein Stück Kuchen?

3. The letters **s, ß, ss**: When the letter **s** begins a word or syllable and is followed by a vowel, it is pronounced like the *z* in the English word *zebra.* In the middle or final position of a syllable, the letter s sounds similar to the *s* in the English word *post.* The letters **ß** and **ss** are also pronounced this way.

   so, sieben, Sonja / Deine Kusine sieht sehr hübsch aus.
   aus, das, es / Die Couch ist zu groß und ganz häßlich.

Richtig schreiben / Diktat

B. Write down the sentences that you hear.

ZUM LESEN

Wo wohnst du denn?

1. What do you think the classified ads are about? You know the word **wohnen**. Does knowing the meaning of **wohnen** help you understand the ads? Make a list of words built on the stem of **wohnen** (**wohn-**) and try to guess what they mean.

2. Working with a partner, match these German words with their English equivalents. Remember to look for the root words.
   1. **Wochenendheimfahrerin**
   2. **Eigentumswohnung**
   3. **Einfamilienhäuser**
   4. **Grundstück**
      a. *plot (of land)*
      b. *someone who goes home on the weekend*
      c. *condominium*
      d. *single-family homes*

3. There are two types of ads on this page: ads describing available houses and apartments, and ads placed by people looking for a place to live. Can you figure out

Auf dem Lande
Großzügiges Einfamilienhaus mit Einliegerwohnung in Remmingsheim. Allerbeste Ausstattung mit wertvollen Einbauten und offenem Kamin. Insg. 174 m² Wfl. bei 7 1/2 Zimmern, gepflegtes Grundstück mit 3,5 Ar, Garage und Autoabstellplätze, sofort beziehbar.
DM 458 000.–

2-Zi.-Eigentumswohnung
(Baujahr 1985) in Entringen, sofort beziehbar, 52 m² Wohnfläche, Einbauküche, Balkon, Keller, Stellplatz.
DM 190 000.–

which ads fit into each of these categories?

4. Which ads would be most interesting to these people:
   a. a large family wanting to buy a house
   b. a couple in Tübingen-Lustnau looking for a condominium
   c. the owner of several rental properties, looking for prospective tenants
5. Working with a partner, try to find the following information.
   a. the most expensive house or apartment
   b. the least expensive house or apartment
   c. the house or apartment with the most rooms
   d. the house or apartment with the most square meters of living space
   e. the house or apartment with the least amount of living space
   f. the places that have either a garage or a space to park a car
6. If you were looking for a place to live, which of these ads would appeal to you the most? Be prepared to tell (in English) why you would choose one place over another.
7. a. Assume that you are going to Germany for a year and need a place to live. Write an ad in German that summarizes what you need.
   b. Many Americans and Europeans swap houses for several weeks at a time, so that they can live in a different culture without having to pay enormous hotel expenses. Imagine that you are going to take part in such an **Austausch** (*exchange*). Using the format of these ads, write a classified ad for your home that you could place in a German newspaper.

ANWENDUNG

1 You are at your partner's house in the afternoon. Your partner offers you something to eat and drink, and you say what you would like using **möchte**. Then ask your partner what he or she would like. Write the conversation and act it out together.

2 Write a brief physical description of your partner on a 3x5 card. Find out his or her age and where he or she lives and include that information, as well. Everyone will put his or her description in a box. Students will take turns drawing cards and reading the information aloud while the other students take turns guessing who it is.

3 At a party last week you met someone you really like. You learned a lot about the person, but you don't know how to get in touch with him or her. Write a short paragraph describing him or her that you could pass along to your friends. Include the person's age, name, where he or she lives, his or her interests, and a physical description.

4 Listen to Tara's description of her room and indicate which of the drawings below matches the description you hear.

a.

b.

c.

5 Using the adjectives to the right, describe your room to your partner. He or she will draw a sketch based on your description. Then switch roles.

> neu   alt   häßlich   groß   kaputt
> schön   bequem   unbequem   klein

6 You would like to put a personal ad in a teen magazine.

    a. Your partner is a reporter for the magazine and will interview you. Unfortunately, no photo can be found, so you must give a complete description of yourself. Your partner will ask questions and take down the information. Then switch roles. When you are the reporter, be prepared to share with the class the information you obtained.

    b. Now write your partner's ad the way it will appear in the magazine. Your partner will write yours. Use the profiles on page 85 as models.

7 These personal profiles appeared in a magazine for teenagers.
  a. Read each profile.

Bettina Schilling	**Peter Fischer**	**Helmut Heine**
Schulstraße 27	Körtestraße 8	Königstraße 24
60594 Frankfurt a.M.	10967 Berlin	39116 Magdeburg
14 J.	15 J.	16 J.
Interessen: Musik, Klavier, Reiten, Schwimmen	Interessen: Wandern, Musik, Fußball	Interessen: Radfahren, Basteln, Comics sammeln

  b. Choose one of the profiles above and describe the person in the profile using complete sentences.
  c. Now listen to Holger's description of a girl named Sonja whom he read about in a magazine. Based on what he says, with which of the students above would Sonja have the most in common?

8 a. Bring in photos of your family or clip out photos of a family from magazines.
  b. Write a few sentences about each family member, telling his or her age, where he or she lives, some interests he or she has, and a brief physical description.
  c. Make a poster of your family tree (**Stammbaum**) using your photos. You can use Jens' family tree on page 77 as a model. Label each family member and write at least one sentence about that person below his or her picture.
  d. Show your family tree to the class. After you've told your classmates a little about your family, they will ask you more questions about various family members.

R O L L E N S P I E L

Two friends whom you have not seen for a while come to your house after school. First, offer your friends something to eat and drink, then show them your room. You have recently made some changes, so the three of you talk about your furniture. Then your conversation turns to family. Take turns describing various family members, what they look like, and what their interests are. Write out the conversations and practice them. Then role-play them in front of the class.

Can you talk about where people live? (p. 69)

1 How would you ask a classmate where he or she lives and tell him or her where you live?

2 Say where the following people live:
- **a.** Thomas (Land)
- **b.** Britte (Hegelstraße)
- **c.** Marian und Karl (Brauhausberg, Vorort von Potsdam)
- **d.** Renate (Köln)
- **e.** Sabine und Rolf (Stadt: Bismarckstr.)

Can you offer something to eat and drink (using möchte) and respond to an offer? (p. 70)

3 How would you ask a classmate what he or she would like to eat and drink? How would you ask more than one classmate? How would you tell a classmate that you would like a lemon-flavored soda?

4 If you and some of your classmates were at a friend's house, how would you help your friend by telling her or him what everyone was having for a snack?
- **a.** Anna, eine Cola
- **b.** Martin und Klaus, ein Stück Kuchen
- **c.** Nicole und Jörg, ein paar Kekse
- **d.** Ayla, Obst

Can you say please, thank you, and you're welcome? (p. 72)

5 How would you ask your friend politely for a few cookies? How would you thank him or her? How would he or she respond?

Can you describe a room? (p. 75)

6 How would you describe these pieces of furniture? Make two sentences about each one using the correct pronoun **er, sie, es,** or **sie** (pl) in the second sentence.
- **a.** der Schrank (*old, ugly, large*)
- **b.** das Bett (*small, comfortable, new*)
- **c.** die Möbel (*beautiful, new, large*)
- **d.** die Couch (*old, ugly, broken*)

Can you talk about family members? (p. 78)

7 How would you tell a classmate about five of your family members, giving their relationship to you, their names, and their ages?

Can you describe people? (p. 80)

8 How would you describe the people below?

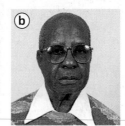

9 How would you ask a classmate what his or her brother, sister, grandfather, parents, and cousins (male and female) look like?

ERSTE STUFE

TALKING ABOUT WHERE YOU LIVE

nach Hause gehen   *to go home*
wohnen   *to live*
Wo wohnst du?   *Where do you live?*
  in der Stadt   *in the city*
  auf dem Land   *in the country*
  ein Vorort von   *a suburb of*
  weit von hier   *far from here*
  in der Nähe   *nearby*
  in der ... Straße   *on . . . Street*

THINGS TO EAT AND DRINK

möchten   *would like (to)*
essen   *to eat*
Was möchtest du essen?   *What would you like to eat?*
  ein Stück Kuchen   *a piece of cake*
  Obst   *fruit*
  ein paar Kekse   *a few cookies*
trinken   *to drink*
Was möchtest du trinken?
  What would you like to drink?
  ein Glas Apfelsaft (Orangensaft)
    a glass of apple juice (orange juice)
  eine Cola   *cola*

ein Glas (Mineral) Wasser   *a glass of (mineral) water*
Nichts, danke!   *Nothing, thank you!*
Im Moment gar nichts.   *Nothing at the moment (right now).*

SAYING PLEASE, THANK YOU, AND YOU'RE WELCOME

Bitte!   *Please!*
Danke!   *Thank you!*
Danke (sehr) (schön)!   *Thank you (very much)!*
Bitte (sehr) (schön)!   *You're (very) welcome!*

ZWEITE STUFE

DESCRIBING A ROOM

das Zimmer, -   *room*
die Möbel (pl)   *furniture*
  der Schrank, ⸚e   *cabinet*
  der Schreibtisch, -e   *desk*
  die Stereoanlage, -n   *stereo*
  die Couch, -en   *couch*
  das Bett, -en   *bed*
  das Regal, -e   *bookcase, shelf*
  der Stuhl, ⸚e   *chair*

neu   *new*
alt   *old*
klein   *small*
groß   *big*
bequem   *comfortable*
unbequem   *uncomfortable*
schön   *pretty, beautiful*
häßlich   *ugly*
kaputt   *broken*

PRONOUNS

er   *he, it*
sie   *she, it*
es   *it*
sie (pl)   *they*

OTHER USEFUL WORDS AND EXPRESSIONS

ganz   *really, quite*
aber   *but*

DRITTE STUFE

TALKING ABOUT THE FAMILY

die Familie, -n   *family*
Das ist ...   *That's...*
  die Mutter, ⸚   *mother*
  der Vater, ⸚   *father*
  die Schwester, -n   *sister*
  der Bruder, ⸚   *brother*
  die Großmutter, ⸚ (Oma)   *grandmother*
  der Großvater, ⸚ (Opa)   *grandfather*
  die Tante, -n   *aunt*
  der Onkel, -   *uncle*
  die Kusine, -n   *cousin (female)*
  der Cousin, -s   *cousin (male)*
  das Haustier, -e   *pet*
  der Hund, -e   *dog*

die Katze, -n   *cat*
der Mann, ⸚er   *man*
die Frau, -en   *woman*
Das sind ...   *These are...*
  die Eltern (pl)   *parents*
  die Geschwister (pl)   *brothers and sisters*
  die Großeltern (pl)   *grandparents*

DIE ZAHLEN VON 21 BIS 100

see page 79

DESCRIBING PEOPLE

Wie sieht er aus?   *What does he look like?*
Wie sehen sie aus?   *What do they look like?*

lange (kurze) Haare   *long (short) hair*
rote (blonde, schwarze, weiße, graue, braune) Haare   *red (blonde, black, white, gray brown) hair*
blaue (grüne, braune) Augen   *blue (green, brown) eyes*
eine Glatze haben   *to be bald*
eine Brille   *a pair of glasses*

POSSESSIVES

dein, deine   *your*
mein, meine   *my*
sein, seine   *his*
ihr, ihre   *her*

KAPITEL 4, 5, 6

Komm mit nach

Schleswig-Holstein!

CONCORDIA DOMI FORIS

Schleswig-Holstein

Einwohner: 2,6 Millionen

Fläche: 16 000 Quadratkilometer (6 177 Quadratmeilen), ungefähr so groß wie Connecticut

Landeshauptstadt: Kiel (257 000 Einwohner)

Große Städte: Lübeck, Flensburg, Neumünster

Flüsse: Elbe, Eider

Inseln: Helgoland, Sylt, Föhr, Fehmarn

Kanäle: Nord-Ostsee-Kanal

Seen: über 300

Industrien: Schiffbau, Ackerbau, Viehzucht

Beliebte Gerichte: Matjes, Krabben, Aale, Räucherspeck, Buttermilchsuppe, Rote Grütze

Foto ①: Das Holstentor in Lübeck, Geburtsstadt von Thomas Mann (1875-1955)

DÄNEMARK
Nordsee
Ostsee
Kiel
Hamburg
Wedel
POLEN
Berlin
NIEDERLANDE
BEL.
Frankfurt
TSCHECH. REPUBLIK
LUX.
FRANK-REICH
SCHWEIZ
ÖSTERREICH

HEICK & SCHMALTZ

Schleswig-Holstein

*Schleswig-Holstein is the northernmost German state, (**Land**). It is bordered on the west by the North Sea (**Nordsee**), on the east by the Baltic Sea (**Ostsee**), and on the north by Denmark (**Dänemark**). In addition to the dunes, rocky cliffs, tranquil beaches, and fishing villages along its 500-kilometer long coastline, Schleswig-Holstein also has rolling meadows, rich farmland, over 300 lakes and ponds, and beautiful cities, such as Flensburg and Lübeck.*

④ Kiel Week (**Kieler Woche**). Every year some of the best sailors in the world gather here to sail.

③ This north Frisian house with thatched roof (**Reetdach**) is typical for the island of Sylt. Thousands of Germans vacation here every year.

② The Westerhaver Lighthouse (**Leuchtturm**) is surrounded by a type of salty marshland that makes up much of Schleswig-Holstein.

Chapters 4, 5, and 6 take place in the small Holstein town of Wedel. Wedel lies directly on the Elbe, not far from Hamburg, and has a proud heritage as a **Freistadt,** an independent trading town. Among its 30,000 inhabitants are the teenagers you will meet in the next three chapters. They attend the **Johann-Rist-Gymnasium** in Wedel.

⑤ **Das Reepschläger-haus.** At one time, ropes were manufactured in this Frisian house. Today it is a tearoom **(Teestube)** and is one of Wedel's famous landmarks.

⑥ In the open-air market **(Marktplatz)** in Wedel stands a statue of Roland, symbolizing Wedel's ancient rights as a free city.

⑦ Heiko, Katja, Sonja, Julia, and Michael say hello and invite you to join them in Wedel.

4

Alles für die Schule!

① Wann habt ihr Sport?

When a new school year begins, students are often curious about their friends' classes: When do they meet? Which ones are their favorites? What school supplies do they need? There are some similarities and some differences in what students in German-speaking countries and in the U.S. experience in school. Let's find out what they are.

In this chapter you will learn

- to talk about class schedules; to use a schedule to talk about time; to sequence events
- to express likes, dislikes, and favorites; to respond to good news and bad news
- to talk about prices; to point things out

And you will

- listen to German-speaking students talk about their schedules
- read ads for school supplies and become familiar with German money
- write a report card for yourself in German
- find out what German students have to say about school

② Was kosten die Hefte?

③ Am Freitag haben wir Mathe.

dreiundneunzig   93

Los geht's!

Michael   Sonja   Katja   Heiko

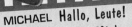

Michael kauft Schulsachen

Look at the photos that accompany the story.
What are the characters doing in each photo?
Where might the scenes be taking place?

MICHAEL Hallo, Leute!

SONJA Hallo, Michael!

MICHAEL Suchst du denn was?

KATJA Ja, wo ist der Stundenplan? Sag, wann haben wir Mathe?

MICHAEL Weiß ich nicht.

HEIKO Ah, Mathe ... haben wir nach der Pause, um 9 Uhr 45.

KATJA Danke, Heiko! Und was haben wir heute zuerst?

HEIKO Zuerst Deutsch, dann Bio, danach Mathe, dann Englisch und Sport.

SONJA Du, heute bekommen wir die Mathearbeit zurück.

MICHAEL Ich hab' bestimmt wieder eine Vier.

SONJA Meinst du?

MICHAEL Ja, leider. In Mathe hab' ich immer schlechte Noten.

SONJA Schade!

MICHAEL Na ja, du bist gut in Mathe.

SONJA Ja, ich hab' Mathe gern. Das ist mein Lieblingsfach.

SONJA Na, Michael, was machst du denn hier? — Ach, ich seh's: einen Taschenrechner!

MICHAEL Schau mal, Sonja! Der Rechner ist toll, nicht?

SONJA Ja, du hast recht.

MICHAEL Und er ist nicht teuer.

SONJA Stimmt! Nur dreiundzwanzig Mark!

SONJA	Entschuldigung! Wo sind bitte die Hefte und die Bleistifte?
VERKÄUFER	Die sind da drüben.
SONJA	Und Wörterbücher?
VERKÄUFER	Da hinten!

VERKÄUFER	Der Rechner, dreiundzwanzig Mark, bitte!
MICHAEL	Ach, wie blöd! Jetzt hab' ich nur zwanzig Mark dabei.
SONJA	Macht nichts, Michael! Ich geb' dir das Geld.
MICHAEL	Oh, das ist sehr nett, Sonja!

MICHAEL	Warte, Sonja!
SONJA	Was ist los?
MICHAEL	So ein Mist! Das ganze Zeug auf der Straße!
SONJA	Der Taschenrechner, geht er noch?
MICHAEL	Ach wo! Er ist kaputt! So ein Pech!
SONJA	So ein Glück! Die Brille ist noch ganz!

1 Was passiert hier?

Do you understand what is happening in the story? Check your comprehension by answering these questions. Don't be afraid to guess.

1. How is Sonja in math? What about Michael?
2. Where do Sonja and Michael meet again? What kinds of things are they looking for?
3. What does Michael want to buy? Why does he need it?
4. Michael has both bad luck and good luck on the way home. What happens to him?

2 Genauer lesen

a. Reread the conversations. Which words or phrases do the characters use to

1. name school subjects
2. name school supplies
3. express annoyance
4. point out something
5. express regret
6. express bad luck; good luck

b. In what three ways are numbers used in the conversations?

3 Stimmt oder stimmt nicht?

Are these statements right or wrong? Answer each one with either **stimmt** or **stimmt nicht**. If a statement is wrong, try to state it correctly.

1. Michael hat immer schlechte Noten in Mathe.
2. Katja und Heiko haben nach der Pause Deutsch.
3. Sonja hat Mathe nicht gern.
4. Der Rechner ist sehr teuer.
5. Sonja gibt Michael das Geld.
6. Die Brille ist kaputt.

4 Was paßt zusammen?

Match each statement or question on the left with an appropriate response on the right.

1. Was haben wir zuerst?
2. Und wann hast du Mathe?
3. Dieser Taschenrechner ist toll — und nicht teuer.
4. Ich habe nur 20 Mark dabei.
5. Schau mal! Der Taschenrechner ist kaputt!
6. Aber die Brille ist noch ganz.

a. Macht nichts! Ich gebe dir das Geld.
b. Also, zuerst Deutsch, dann Bio.
c. So ein Pech!
d. Das stimmt! Er kostet nur 23 Mark.
e. Nach der Pause.
f. So ein Glück!

5 Nacherzählen

Put the sentences in logical order to make a brief summary of the story.

1. Katja sucht den Stundenplan.

Danach sprechen Sonja und Michael über die Mathearbeit und Michaels Noten.

Also gibt Sonja Michael das Geld.

Später kommt Michael in einen Schreibwarenladen. Er möchte einen Taschenrechner.

Auf dem Weg nach Hause fällt Michaels ganze Zeug auf die Straße.

Aber er hat nur 20 Mark dabei.

Talking about class schedules; using a schedule to talk about time; sequencing events

WORTSCHATZ

Hier ist Heikos und Katjas Stundenplan *(class schedule):*

Ich wollt, ich wär ein Teppich. Dann könnt ich jeden Morgen liegen bleiben!

QUICK SCHUH

Stundenplan für

NAME *Katja*   KLASSE *9a*

ZEIT	MONTAG	DIENSTAG	MITTWOCH	DONNERSTAG	FREITAG	SAMSTAG
8:00- 8:45	Deutsch	Deutsch	Mathe	–	Physik	frei
8:45-9:30	Deutsch	Bio	Deutsch	Physik	Mathe	
9:30-9:45	Pause	–	–	–	–	
9:45-10:30	Religion	Mathe	Englisch	Bio	Deutsch	
10:30-11:15	Bio	Englisch	Latein	Englisch	Latein	
11:15-11:30	Pause	–	–	–	–	
11:30-12:15	Latein	Sport	Geschichte	Englisch	Kunst	
12:20-13:05	Musik	Sport	Erdkunde	Latein	–	

What do you think the word **Zeit** in the schedule means? What do the other words next to **Zeit** (**Montag**, etc.) refer to? All but four of the class subjects are cognates. Which ones do you recognize?

Kunst

Geschichte

Erdkunde

6 Heikos und Katjas Stundenplan

Look at Heiko's and Katja's class schedule and try to answer the following questions in German.

1. On what day(s) do Heiko and Katja have religion? And biology?
2. Which subjects do they have on Tuesday? On Wednesday?
3. On which day(s) do they have art? And history?
4. At what times do Heiko and Katja have math?* On which day(s)?
5. At what time(s) do they have German?

*To read times from a schedule simply read the numbers and insert **Uhr** between the hour and minutes: 10.30 reads 10 Uhr 30 (**zehn Uhr dreißig**); 8.45 reads 8 Uhr 45 (**acht Uhr fünfundvierzig**).

Look at the class schedule. How many different subjects do Heiko and Katja have, and when do they have them? How does this compare to your class schedule?

German schools are also different in that Heiko, Katja, and their classmates stay together for all their classes and, for the most part, in the same classroom. The teachers move from room to room.

What do you think the word **Pause** means, judging by the time alloted for it? Where do you think German students eat lunch? Like you and your friends, students in German-speaking countries have some activities after school: school-sponsored sports, clubs, and social activities. There are, however, fewer such activities in Germany than in the United States.

7 Zum Schreiben: Dein Stundenplan

Now make your own class schedule in German. Here are some other subjects you may need to complete your schedule. Turn to page 322 for additional vocabulary.

Und dann noch ...

Spanisch, Französisch, Chemie, Chor, Algebra, Informatik, Orchester, Werken, Sozialkunde, Technik, Hauswirtschaft

SO SAGT MAN DAS!

Talking about class schedules

If you want to discuss class schedules with your friends, you might ask:

Welche Fächer hast du?
Was hast du am Donnerstag?
Was hat die Katja am
   Donnerstag?

Julia, Bernd, welche Fächer
   habt ihr heute nach der Pause?
Und was habt ihr am Samstag?

You might get the responses:

Ich habe Mathe, Bio, Kunst ...
Deutsch, Englisch und Sport.

Sie hat Physik, Bio, Englisch und
   Latein.

Wir haben Mathe und Musik.
Wir haben frei!

The word **Fächer** used above means *subjects*. What do you think the equivalent of **welche** is?[1] Could you use **welche** in the second, third and fifth questions? The word **am** always precedes the days of the week. What do you think this word means?[2] With what other time expressions have you already used **am**?[3]

8 Welche Fächer hast du?

Using the schedule you created in Activity 7, tell your classmates which subjects you have and when you have them.

---

1. *which* 2. here: *on* 3. **am Wochenende, am Abend, am Nachmittag**

9 Hör gut zu!

Listen carefully as Michael asks his classmates when they have various classes. Match the subjects below with the days of the week in the box to the right.

a. Bio   b. Musik   c. Kunst   d. Mathe   e. Geschichte

f. Erdkunde   g. Sport   h. Deutsch

am Dienstag   am Montag
am Mittwoch   am Freitag
am Samstag   am Donnerstag

SO SAGT MAN DAS!

Using a schedule to talk about time

It's the first day of school, and you are curious about when your friends have their classes.

You might ask:

Wann hast du Erdkunde?

Was hast du um 11 Uhr 20?

Was hast du von 8 Uhr 45 bis 9 Uhr 30?

Und wann hast du Kunst?

You might get the responses:

Um 11 Uhr 20.

Erdkunde.

Ich habe Bio.

Um 10 Uhr 30, nach der Pause.

What do you think **wann** means?[1] How do you answer a question that starts with **wann**?[2] How is the answer to this question different from the answers to questions that begin with **was**? What is the English equivalent of **um**?[3]

EIN WENIG LANDESKUNDE

Do any of the times in Heiko's and Katja's schedule look unusual to you? When does their last class end? Schedules like this one, and other official schedules, like the train schedule to the right, are based on the 24-hour system of telling time. This system starts immediately after midnight (**00.01 Uhr**) and ends at midnight (**24.00 Uhr**). What time would correspond to 2 P.M.? to 3 P.M? to 8:30 P.M.? What time would you have to board the train in order to get to **Köln**? **Mannheim**?

Bochum → München

Hauptbahnhof   Hauptbahnhof

Preis pro Person in DM. Einfache Fahrt.
* Bei Benutzung von EC/IC 6, – DM Zuschlag.

Mögliche Fahrpreisermäßigungen siehe Kapitel „So günstig fahren Sie Bahn".

ab	Zug	Umsteigen	an	Verkehrstage	Fahrpreis 1. Kl. Fahrpreis 2. Kl. Bemerkungen
14.49	IC 823	Köln IC Stuttgart EC	22.11	1234567	
14.49	IC 823	Würzburg D	22.29	1234567	
14.59	S	Duisburg IC Stuttgart EC	22.11	12345--	an Werktagen nicht 24., 31. 12.
15.23	IR 2553	Kassel-Wilh. ICE	22.06	1234567	
15.49	IC 523	Köln IC Mannheim ICE	22.17	1234567	
15.49	IC 523	Köln IC Karlsruhe IR	23.40	1234567	
16.22	IC 517		23.11	12345-7	nicht 24, 12, -2. 1., 9,- 11.4.
16.49	IC 603	Mannheim ICE	23.17	------ 7	auch 12. 4., nicht 11. 4.

1. *when*   2. with a time expression   3. here: *at*

10 Hör gut zu!

Listen carefully as Klaus, a friend of Sonja's, talks about the busy schedule he has on Wednesdays. Copy the names of the following subjects onto a piece of paper, then complete his schedule by filling in the times as you hear them.

Mathe Latein
Englisch
Deutsch
Erdkunde Geschichte

11 Wann hast du Deutsch?

Working in small groups, take turns asking each other which subjects each of you has and at what times during the day. Remember, you do not need to answer in complete sentences. Sometimes just a phrase will do:

BEISPIEL   PARTNER   **Wann hast du Englisch?**
           DU   **Um 10 Uhr.**   *oder*   **Um 10.**

Grammatik   The verb **haben**, present tense

Look at the conversation below:

       SONJA   **Was hat Katja nach der Pause?**
       BEATE   **Sie hat Bio. Und was hast du?**
       SONJA   **Ich habe Deutsch.**

What do you notice about **haben** that is different from verbs like **spielen** or **wohnen**?[1] Here are the forms of the verb **haben** (*to have*) in the present tense:

Ich	**habe** Mathe.		Wir	**haben** Kunst.
Du	**hast** Deutsch.		Ihr	**habt** Geschichte.
Er/Sie	**hat** Bio.		Sie (pl) / Sie	**haben** Latein.

---

12 Was sagen die Schüler im Schulhof?

a.

Several students in the **Schulhof** are talking about their schedules. Look at these drawings carefully, and match each conversation with one of the drawings.

1. —Haben Monika und Berndt jetzt Englisch? / Nein, sie haben jetzt Musik.
2. —Wann hast du Deutsch? / Nach der Pause.
3. —Wann hat Sabine Kunst? / Um 12.
4. —Wann habt ihr Physik? / Am Dienstag.

b.

c.

d.

1. **haben** is irregular in the **du-** and **er/sie**-forms: **du hast, er/sie hat**

13 Ein Interview

a. Prepare a list of questions for your partner in order to find out exactly what his or her schedule is for the semester (which classes he or she has, the times of the classes).

b. Now interview your partner using your list of questions and, as you interview, fill out his or her schedule on another piece of paper. Then your partner will interview you. Compare schedules to see if both of you understood everything correctly.

c. Be prepared to report the information you obtained back to the class.

Deutsch	8.05
Geschichte	8.55
Latein	9.45
Sport	10.30

SO SAGT MAN DAS!

Sequencing events

You might want to know the order in which your friends have their classes on a certain day.

You might ask:

Welche Fächer hast du am Freitag?

If your friend had the schedule above he or she would answer:

Zuerst hab' ich Deutsch, dann Geschichte, danach Latein, und zuletzt hab' ich Sport.

What do the words **zuerst, dann, danach,** and **zuletzt** mean?[1]

14 Was hast du am Mittwoch?

Heiko asks Sonja which classes she has on Wednesday. Working with a partner, put these questions and answers in the appropriate order. Then, together with your partner, read the conversation out loud.

HEIKO   Sonja, was hast du zuerst am Mittwoch?

HEIKO   Und zuletzt?

SONJA   Danach hab' ich Deutsch um 10 und dann Kunst.

SONJA   Zuletzt hab' ich Chemie.

HEIKO   Was hast du danach?

HEIKO   Und dann?

SONJA   Dann hab' ich um 9 Uhr Musik.

SONJA   Zuerst habe ich Sport.

15 Was hast du zuerst? Und zuletzt?

Using the sequencing words **zuerst, dann, danach,** and **zuletzt,** tell your classmates the order in which you have your classes on Monday. You can use **dann** and **danach** several times if you have more than four classes.

16 Zum Schreiben

Write a short paragraph describing what you do on a typical Saturday, using some of the activities you learned in **Kapitel 2,** for example, **Tennis spielen, Freunde besuchen,** or **Hausaufgaben machen.** In your description, use the sequencing words you have learned (**zuerst, dann, danach,** and **zuletzt**).

1. *first, then, after that, last of all*

Expressing likes, dislikes, and favorites; responding to good news and bad news

SO SAGT MAN DAS!

Expressing likes, dislikes, and favorites

In **Kapitel 2** you learned to say which activities you like and don't like to do using **gern** and **nicht gern**. You might also want to talk about which classes you like and don't like, and which is your favorite.

Your friend might ask you:	You might respond:
Welche Fächer hast du gern?	Ich habe Kunst und Englisch gern.
Was hast du nicht so gern?	Chemie.
Und was ist dein Lieblingsfach?	Deutsch, ganz klar!

17 Hör gut zu!

Listen as Katja describes to Rainer the subjects she is taking. Write down which subjects Katja likes, dislikes, and considers her favorite subjects.

gern	nicht gern	Lieblingsfächer

Ein wenig *Grammatik*

Lieblings- is a prefix that can be used with many different nouns to indicate favorites. Can you guess what these words mean: **Lieblingsbuch, Lieblingsinstrument**, and **Lieblingsfilm**?

18 Und dein Lieblingsfach?

Find out which subjects your partner likes and dislikes, and his or her favorite subject. Create a chart like the one you filled out for Activity 17. Using the chart, report the information about your partner back to the class. Remember to use **sein** or **ihr** when you are reporting about your partner's **Lieblingsfach**.

19 Trends: Eine Umfrage

Working in small groups, conduct a survey about some of the things teenagers like best. Each member of the group asks two students at least three questions. Use topics from the box to prepare the questions. When you have finished the interviews, prepare a summary in chart form.

Lieblingsbuch   Lieblingsrockgruppe   Lieblingsauto   Lieblingssänger

Lieblingsmusik   Lieblingsfilm   Lieblingslehrer   Lieblingsfarbe

Zeugnis

für _Michael Hauser_,
geboren am _7. 6. 1978_   Klasse _8 b_

Allgemeine Beurteilung: _Muß sich in Latein u. Mathe verbessern!_

Deutsch .... _3_
   mündlich ...... _4_ schriftlich ...... _4_
Geschichte/Sozialkunde .... _2_
   Geschichte ...... _2_ Sozialkd ...... _2_
Erdkunde .... _2_
1. Fremdsprache: _Englisch_ ...... _1_
   mündlich ...... _1_ schriftlich ...... _1_
2. Fremdsprache: _Latein_ ...... _5_
   mündlich ...... _=_ schriftlich ...... _5_

Wahlpflichtfach

3. Fremdsprache: _Französisch_ _2+_
   mündlich ...... _1_ schriftlich ...... _2_

Freiwillige Unterrichtsveranstaltungen

Mathematik .... _4_
Physik .... _2_
Chemie .... _=_
Biologie .... _3_
Musik .... _1_
Bildende Kunst/
   Bildende Ku
Sport ....

EIN WENIG LANDESKUNDE

Look at Michael's report card. What grades (the numbers) did he get in **Mathe, Erdkunde, Deutsch,** and **Latein?**

He was very happy about his geography grade, not too disappointed with the grade in German, very worried about his math grade, and afraid to show his Latin grade to his parents. With this information, can you figure out how the German grading system, which is based on the numbers 1-6 rather than on letters, works? Which numbers go with which descriptions?

sehr gut (*excellent*)

ungenügend (*failing*)

befriedigend (*satisfactory*)

ausreichend (*just passing*)

gut (*good*)

mangelhaft (*unsatisfactory*)

20 Hör gut zu!

Listen as Sonja talks about the grades she received on her last report card. First write down the subjects she mentions in the order you hear them. Then listen again and fill in the **Note** (*grade*) she got for each subject. In which subjects did Sonja do well? In which subjects did she not do so well? Then answer the following questions in German.

1. In which subject did she get the best grade? And the worst?
2. In which subject did Sonja receive a "satisfactory" grade?
3. Judging by her grades, which subject do you think Sonja enjoys the most?
4. In which subject do you think Sonja needs to study more?

SO SAGT MAN DAS!

Responding to good news and bad news

You will often want to respond to your friends' good news and bad news. Katja is asking Heiko about his grades. Notice her responses to his answers.

She asks:	Heiko answers:	Katja responds:
Was hast du in Musik?	Eine Eins.	Toll! Das ist prima!
In Physik?	Eine Drei.	Nicht schlecht.
Und in Englisch?	Ich habe bloß eine Vier.	Schade! So ein Pech!
Und Mathe?	Eine Fünf.	Schade! Das ist sehr schlecht!

Heiko was probably hoping for a better grade in English. What do you think he means by **bloß eine Vier?**[1]

21 Logisch oder unlogisch?

Read what these students say about their grades. Does the response in each case make sense? If so, answer **Das ist logisch**, if not, answer **Das ist unlogisch**, and try to think of a response that is more appropriate.

1. —Ich habe eine Fünf in Latein!
   —Toll! Das ist gut!
2. —Du hast eine Vier in Mathe?
   —Ja, das ist blöd, nicht?
3. —Englisch ist mein Lieblingsfach. Ich habe eine Zwei.
   —Super! Das ist wirklich gut!
4. —In Erdkunde habe ich eine Drei.
   —Hm, nicht schlecht!
5. —Und in Deutsch habe ich eine Eins!
   —Ach wie blöd! So ein Pech!

Degrees of Enthusiasm

Spitze!
Super!
Toll!
Prima!
Das ist gut!
Nicht schlecht!

Schade!
So ein Pech!
Das ist schlecht!
So ein Mist!

22 Dein Zeugnis

a. Imagine that you are an exchange student in Wedel and have just received your report card for the semester. Design and fill out a German report card for yourself. Write all your subjects and give yourself a grade according to the German grading system.
b. With your report card in hand, have a conversation with a classmate, asking your partner which grades he or she has in various subjects, responding appropriately, and telling him or her about your classes and grades. Use the phrases above in your responses.

23 Für mein Notizbuch

Schreib ein paar Sätze über dich und deine Schule! Welche Fächer hast du? Welche Fächer hast du gern? Welche Fächer hast du nicht gern? Was ist dein Lieblingsfach? In welchen Fächern sind deine Noten gut? In welchen sind die Noten nicht so gut?

1. *only a four* (**ausreichend**)

Was sind deine Lieblingsfächer?

We asked several teenagers in German-speaking countries what school subjects they have and which ones they like and don't like. Before you read the interviews, make a list of your classes and indicate which ones are your favorites and which ones you don't like very much.

Jasmin, *München*

„Ich hab' Arbeitslehre — als Lieblingsfach, und Kunst und Mathe mag ich gar nicht; Physik mag ich auch nicht so gerne. Und sonst Sport mag ich noch und dann Englisch, das mag ich auch — das ist auch mein Lieblingsfach, weil ich sehr gern Englisch lernen will."

Dirk, *Hamburg*

„Ich bin eigentlich genau das Gegenteil von Michael, weil ich ja auch total auf Sprachen basier'. Ich hab' Englisch als Leistungskurs, Spanisch und Französisch hab' ich gehabt. Ich will ja auch mit Sprachen mal was machen, Diplomatie oder so. Mal seh'n!"

Michael, *Hamburg*

„Ich interessiere mich hauptsächlich für Mathe und Physik und Kunst, also weil ich Architekt werden will. Chemie mag ich überhaupt nicht. Also ich glaube, es ist auch wichtig. Sonst komm' ich mit den meisten Fächern zurecht."

Lugana, *Bietigheim*

„Okay, ich heiße Lugana, bin Griechin und hier geboren. Bin sechzehn Jahre alt, gehe aufs Ellental-Gymnasium, und Lieblingsfächer sind Englisch und Deutsch."

Björn, *Hamburg*

„In der Schule mag ich am liebsten Physik, Mathematik und Informatik — das ist mit Computern. Das kommt, weil ... ich bin gut in Mathe. Ich arbeite gern an Computern, und ich mag Physik ganz gerne, weil mich die Themen einfach interessieren."

A. 1. What subjects do these teenagers like and dislike? Make a grid.
2. Which of these teenagers likes the same subjects you do? What are these subjects?
3. Several of these teenagers give reasons why they like certain subjects. Work with a partner and decide what these reasons are.
4. Look at the list you made. Try to think of reasons why you like the subjects you indicated. What do your opinions have to do with your future career plans?

B. Do you think teenagers in German-speaking countries start thinking about their future careers earlier than teenagers in the United States do? What can you find in the interviews to support your answer? Discuss the topic with your classmates and then write a brief essay on this question.

DRITTE STUFE

Talking about prices; pointing things out

WORTSCHATZ

Was kosten die Schulsachen im Schul-Shop?

das
Wörterbuch — DM 14,90

die Schultasche — DM 40,00

die Kassette — DM 5,00

der
Taschenrechner — DM 16,20

das Heft — DM 1,20

der
Radiergummi — DM 0,95

der Bleistift — DM 0,70

der Kuli — DM 2,50

Notice the prices that Germans pay for school supplies. How does this compare with the prices you would pay? How many of each of these supplies do you have with you right now in the classroom?

24 Im Schul-Shop

Compare the endings of the words in the school supplies ad with the words printed under each illustration. What do you observe? List the differences and compare your list with that of a classmate. Why do you think the words are written differently?

Grammatik Noun plurals

As you discovered in Activity 24, there are many different plural endings for German nouns. There is no one rule that tells you which nouns take which endings.

Every German dictionary includes the plural ending of a noun next to the main entry, which is the singular form. In the **Vocabulary** in this book begin-

das **Wort**, ¨er *word*, 9*
das **Wörterbuch**, ¨er *dictionary*, 4
der **Wortschatz** *vocabulary*, 1
die **Wortschatzübung**, -en *vocabulary exercise, practice*, 1
wunderbar *wonderful*, 11

ning on page 340, you will see entries like those above.

Look up the following words and write sentences using the plural forms of these words:

der Stuhl, der Keks, die Kassette

* ¨er means that the plural form of **Wort** is **Wörter**.

25 Hör gut zu!

Listen to this conversation between Johanna and Daniel in the stationery store. As you listen, put the four pictures in the correct sequence.

a.

b.

c.

d.

SO SAGT MAN DAS!

Talking about prices

If you and your friend are in a store, you might ask one another about the prices of various items.

You might ask:

Was kostet der Taschenrechner?
Was kosten die Bleistifte?

Your friend might respond:

Er kostet nur 23 Mark.
Sie kosten 80 Pfennig.

After you hear the price you might comment to your friend:

Das ist (ziemlich) teuer!   *That's (quite) expensive!*
Das ist (sehr) billig!   *That's (very) cheap!*
Das ist (sehr) preiswert!   *That's a (really) good deal!*

EIN WENIG LANDESKUNDE

The unit of German currency is the **Deutsche Mark**. How is it abbreviated? How are these prices written differently than prices in the United States? One **Deutsche Mark** has one hundred **Pfennige**. **DM 1,00** reads **eine Mark**. **DM 0,80** reads **achtzig Pfennig**. **DM 2,20** reads **zwei Mark zwanzig**. How would you read **DM 1,50**? **DM 6,70**? **DM 24,00**?

Schon bekannt
Ein wenig Grammatik

In **Kapitel 3** you learned that the pronouns **er, sie, es,** and **sie** (pl) can refer to objects: **Die Couch ist neu. Sie ist bequem.** When do you use each of these pronouns?[1]

1. **er** refers to masculine nouns, **sie** to feminine nouns, **es** to neuter nouns, **sie** (pl) to plural nouns.

26 Was kostet ... ?

You are starting school and need to buy school supplies. You have DM 30,00 to spend. Make a list of the things you need to buy. Your partner is the **Verkäuferin** *(salesclerk)* at the store and will create a price list, using the items and prices in the **Wortschatz** box as cues. Ask your partner how much the items on your list cost, then figure out how much you must spend. Be sure to be polite!

SO SAGT MAN DAS!

Pointing things out

When you go to a store, you may need to ask the **Verkäuferin** where various items are located.

You might ask:

> **Entschuldigung, wo sind die Schultaschen?**
> **Und Taschenrechner? Wo finde ich sie?**
> **Und die Kulis auch?**
> **Wo sind bitte die Kassetten?**
> **Und dann noch Hefte. Wo sind die, bitte?**

The responses might be:

> **Schauen Sie!* Dort drüben!**
> **Dort!**
> **Nein, sie sind dort drüben!**
> **Kassetten sind da hinten.**
> **Die sind hier vorn.**

How would the salesperson tell you that the pencils are in the front of the store if he or she were also in the front of the store?[1]

*This is the polite form of **Schau!** that is used among friends. In a store, a salesperson would use the polite form **Schauen Sie!**

27 Im Schreibwarenladen

Heiko has asked the **Verkäuferin** where various school supplies are located and what they cost. Complete what the **Verkäuferin** says with the items pictured in the drawing. Be sure to use the correct endings for the plural (including umlauts). More than one answer may be possible.

Bitte, __1__ sind hier vorn. Sie kosten nur DM 2,75. __2__ sind dort drüben und kosten DM 21,00. Das ist sehr preiswert. Und __3__ sind hier vorn. Sie sind im Sonderangebot für nur DM 0,75. __4__ sind auch hier vorn, und __5__ sind da drüben, __6__ sind aber weit da hinten. Oh, und __7__ sind dort drüben. Sie kosten DM 2,95.

1. **Bleistifte sind hier vorn.**

108   *hundertacht*   KAPITEL 4   Alles für die Schule!

28 Eine Werbung *Advertisement*

You are the owner of a store that sells school supplies and you are writing an advertisement to be read over the radio. Make up a name for your store, then pick five school supplies and write an ad describing them.

BEISPIEL **Wir haben Taschenrechner, sie kosten nur 19 Mark 95. Sehr preiswert, nicht? Und Bleistifte nur 85 Pfennig. Super! Die ...**

29 Wir brauchen Schulsachen *We need school supplies*

a. Get together with three other classmates and take turns reading the advertisements you wrote in Activity 28. While one person reads, the others will be "listening on the radio" and will write down the various school supplies they hear mentioned and the price of each.

b. Decide with your classmates which store your group will visit. Whoever's store is chosen will play the **Verkäufer** and should set up his or her store (or draw a floorplan). The others will play the customers. The three customers will make a list of all the things they need from the store.

c. Create a conversation between the **Verkäufer** and the customers in the store. The customers ask the **Verkäufer** questions about where the school supplies on their list are located and how much they cost in order to make sure they have heard the ad on the radio correctly. Role-play your scene before the class, using props.

AUSSPRACHE

Richtig aussprechen / Richtig lesen

A. To practice the following sounds, say the words and sentences below after your teacher or after the recording.

1. The diphthongs **äu** and **eu**: The diphthongs **äu** and **eu** sound similiar to the *oy* sound in the English word *boy*.
   teuer, deutsch, Verkäufer / Der Verkäufer ist Deutscher.

2. The diphthong **au**: The diphthong **au** is pronounced much like the *ow* sound in the English word *cow*.
   Pause, schauen, bauen / Ich schaue Fernsehen nach der Pause.

3. The letters **b**, **d**, and **g**: At the end of a syllable or word, the consonants **b**, **d**, and **g** are pronounced as follows: the letter **b** sounds like the *p* in the English word *map;* the letter **d** is pronounced like the letter *t* in the English word *mat;* and the letter **g** is pronounced like the *k* sound in the English word *make.*
   Liebling, gelb, schreib / Schreib dein Lieblingsfach auf!
   Rad, Geld, blöd / Ich finde Radfahren blöd.
   Sag, Montag, Tag / Sag mal, hast du am Montag und Freitag Physik?

Richtig schreiben / Diktat

B. Write down the sentences that you hear.

Institut Rosenberg

Eine der führenden Schweizer Internatsschulen für Mädchen und Jungen seit 1889

Abitur

Deutsches Abitur im Hause
Vorbereitung für Eidgenössische Maturitätsprüfungen
Vobereitung für das Studium in England und in den USA
Maturità Italiana

Privatunterricht gewährleistet • Überwachtes Studium
Internationale Atmosphäre

Sportarten:

Tennis • Wasserski • Reiten • Skifahren • Basketball • Volleyball etc.

Auskunft: O. Gademann
Institut Rosenberg • Höhenweg 60 • CH-9000 St.Gallen
Tel. 004171-27 77 77 Fax 004171-27 98 27

LESETRICK

Understanding Compound Words German has many compound words. Often at least one part of a compound word is a cognate that you will recognize from English. Figuring out the meaning of individual words within a compound will often help you determine the meaning of the entire word.

1. Look at the following words and try to determine what they might mean by looking at the cognates within the compounds. You do not have to know the exact meaning of the compound word, but you can probably come close to figuring it out. For example, you can see that the word **Gesangunterricht** (abbreviated **Gesangunterr.** in the ad) has something to do with singing.
   a. **Keyboardschule** ═════
   b. **Deutschkurse** ═════
   c. **Privatunterricht** ═════
   d. **Volksschule** ═════
   e. **Schulverbund** ═════

2. Work with a partner. Write down the kinds of information you would be looking for if you were looking in the classified ads for a tutor in English.

3. Scan the ads for the following information:
   a. the telephone number you would call if you wanted singing lessons
   b. what the American wants to tutor
   c. the address of the **Schulverbund Passau**

4. Read the ads and answer the questions about each ad.
   a. Who might be interested in the programs offered by the **Schulverbund?**
   b. Can students eat at the schools in the **Schulverbund?** What tells you this information? Why would they need to?
   c. What new branch of the **Donau-Gymnasium** has been operating since September 1993?
   d. How much does the German course for foreigners cost? How much does a trial class period cost? How long is the course?

   e. In what country is the **Institut Rosenberg** located? Is it a girls' school? What might it prepare you for?

5. Write some notes that you could use if you wanted to obtain more information from the school that offers German classes to foreigners. You might want to ask, for example, when and where the class meets.

6. With a partner write a short ad to offer tutoring in whatever you do best. It may be an academic class or a skills-oriented class. Use the classified ads on this page as your model.

7. You are going to be an exchange student in Germany. Which one of these schools would you like to attend. Why? Discuss this with a partner.

ANWENDUNG

1 Working in small groups, use the ad on page 106 for clues to make up price tags in German for various school supplies in the classroom. Put the tags on the appropriate objects and arrange them as in a store window or as in a store. Now take turns role-playing customer and salesclerk, asking how much things cost and where they are located.

2 What do the items below tell you about the student, Claudia Müller? Use them to answer the questions that follow.

ZEIT	MONTAG	DIENSTAG	MITTWOCH	DONNERSTAG	FREITAG	SAMSTAG
7⁵⁰ - 8³⁵ Uhr	Geschichte	Deutsch	Mathe	Deutsch	Latein	frei
8⁴⁵ - 9³⁰ Uhr	Sport	Französisch	Latein	Biologie	Physik	
9⁴⁵ - 10³⁰ Uhr	Mathe	Erdkunde	Deutsch	Mathe	Mathe	
10⁴⁰ - 11²⁵ Uhr	Latein	Kunst	Geschichte	Englisch	Deutsch	
11⁴⁰ - 12²⁵ Uhr	Bio	Kunst	Sport	Sport	Englisch	
12³⁰ - 13¹⁵ Uhr	Englisch	Physik	Chemie		Chemie	

2+

BIOLOGIE
Klassenarbeiten

STADTBUS
SCHÜLERAUSWEIS

NAME ___Claudia Müller___

GEBURTSDATUM ___7.1.1980___

GÜLTIG VON ___15.9.94___ BIS ___30.6.95___

Claudia Müller
UNTERSCHRIFT DES SCHÜLERS

Luise-Schmitt-Gymnasium

ZEUGNIS

für _Claudia Müller_ geb am _7.1.1980_

Schuljahr 19 _94_, _95_   Klasse _9 B_   _1_ Halbjahr

LEISTUNGEN
Pflichtunterricht

Geschichte.... _gut_	Deutsch............ _gut_
Mathe.......... _sehr gut_	Latein............. _befriedigend_
Sport............. _befriedigend_	Französisch... _sehr gut_
Biologie......... _gut_	Physik............. _gut_
Erdkunde....... _gut_	Kunst............. _sehr gut_
Englisch......... _sehr gut_	Chemie......... _ausreichend_

1. Wie heißt Claudias Schule?
2. Wie kommt Claudia zur Schule?
3. Sind Claudias Noten gut?
4. Welche Note hat sie in Bio?
5. Wann hat sie Mathe?

3 Look at the items in the preceding activity again.
Use the information to write five German sentences about Claudia.

KAPITEL 4   Alles für die Schule!

4 Create an activity calendar for yourself in German for the coming Saturday. Include all the things you would like to do and the times you expect to do them. Then, working with a partner, imagine that you ran into him or her after school and are talking about your plans for the weekend. Use the sequencing words **zuerst, dann, danach,** and **zuletzt.** Try to find a time when you are both free and make plans to do something together.

5 Look at the two drawings below. What items can you name in the drawing on the left? What items are missing in the drawing on the right?

BEISPIEL **Die Bleistifte fehlen**. *oder* **Das Heft fehlt**.

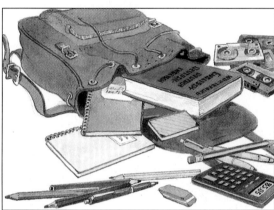 

6 Write a letter to your pen pal and tell him or her about school. Write about which classes you have and when, which classes you like or do not like, and which are your favorites. Then write something about how you are doing in various subjects so far.

7 On the first day of school your German teacher is telling you what school supplies you will need. Write them as you hear them mentioned.

8

R O L L E N S P I E L

With your school supply list from Activity 7 in hand, you go to the school supply store where you run into two friends. Develop a conversation with your two friends and role-play it in front of the class. Make sure to include

a. which classes you have and when
b. which classes you like, dislike and your favorite class
c. grades in some of your classes (make sure your friends respond appropriately)

After your conversation, ask the salesperson where various school supplies are located and what they cost.

KANN ICH'S WIRKLICH?

Can you talk about schedules using haben? (p. 98)

1 How would you say the following in German:

- a. Ulrike has German on Wednesday and Friday.
- b. Monika and Klaus have history on Tuesday and Thursday.
- c. Richard has no classes on Saturday.

2 How would you ask a friend what classes he or she has on Monday? How might he or she respond? How would you ask two friends? How might they respond if they both have the same schedule?

Can you use a schedule to talk about time? (p. 99)

3 Say when these people have these classes.

a. Martin	8.30	Mathe
b. Claudia und Ingrid	9.45	Latein
c. Heiko	10.20	Musik
d. Michaela und Manfred	3.00	Kunst

4 How would you tell someone what time you have your German class, using the expression **von** ... **bis** ...?

Can you sequence events using zuerst, dann, danach, and zuletzt? (p. 101)

Can you express likes, dislikes, and favorites? (p. 102)

5 How would you tell a classmate the sequence of your classes on Thursday?

6 How would you say which subjects you like, dislike, and which is your favorite? How would you ask your friend for the same information?

Can you respond to good news and bad news? (p. 104)

7 How would you respond if Ahmet, an exchange student at your school, told you:

- a. Ich habe eine Eins in Bio.
- b. Ich habe eine Vier in Latein.
- c. Ich habe eine Zwei in Englisch.

Can you talk about prices? (p. 107)

8 How would you ask a salesperson how much these items cost: calculators, notebooks, erasers, pencils, pens, school bag, dictionaries, and cassettes?

9 How would you tell your friend what each of the following items costs? How might he or she comment on the prices?

- a. Wörterbuch DM 18,00
- b. Kuli DM 3,20
- c. Schultasche DM 24,00

Can you point things out? (p. 108)

10 Write a conversation in which your friend asks you where several things are located in a store. You point them out and give a general location. Then tell him or her how much they cost.

ERSTE STUFE

TALKING ABOUT CLASS SCHEDULES

die Schule, -n* *school*
haben *to have*
er/sie hat *he/she has*
die Klasse, -n *grade level*
der Stundenplan, ¨e *class schedule*
die Zeit *time*
das Fach, ¨er *(class) subject*
Welche Fächer hast du? *What (which) subjects do you have?*
Ich habe Deutsch ... *I have German...*
  Bio (Biologie) *biology*

Englisch *English*
Erdkunde *geography*
Geschichte *history*
Kunst *art*
Latein *Latin*
Mathe (Mathematik) *math*
Religion *religion*
Sport *physical education*

USING A SCHEDULE TO TALK ABOUT TIME

Wann? *when?*
um 8 Uhr *at 8 o'clock*
von 8 Uhr bis 8 Uhr 45 *from 8 until 8:45*

nach der Pause *after the break*
  am Montag *on Monday*
  Dienstag *Tuesday*
  Mittwoch *Wednesday*
  Donnerstag *Thursday*
  Freitag *Friday*
  Samstag *Saturday*
  Sonntag *Sunday*
Wir haben frei. *We are off (out of school).*

SEQUENCING EVENTS

zuerst *first*
dann *then*
danach *after that*
zuletzt *last of all*

ZWEITE STUFE

EXPRESSING LIKES, DISLIKES, AND FAVORITES

gern haben *to like*
nicht gern haben *to dislike*
Lieblings- *favorite*

GRADES

die Note, -n *grade*

eine Eins (Zwei, Drei, Vier, Fünf, Sechs) *grades: a 1 (2, 3, 4, 5, 6)*

RESPONDING TO GOOD NEWS AND BAD NEWS

gut *good*
schlecht *bad*
Schade! *Too bad!*

So ein Pech! *Bad luck!*
So ein Mist! *That stinks!/What a mess!*
So ein Glück! *What luck!*

OTHER WORDS AND PHRASES

Ganz klar! *Of Course!*
bloß *only*

DRITTE STUFE

SCHOOL SUPPLIES

Das ist/Das sind . . . *That is/Those are*
die Schulsachen (pl) *school supplies*
das Buch, ¨er *book*
der Kuli, -s *ballpoint pen*
das Wörterbuch, ¨er *dictionary*
die Schultasche, -n *schoolbag*
der Taschenrechner, - *pocket calculator*
der Radiergummi, -s *eraser*
der Bleistift, -e *pencil*
das Heft, -e *notebook*

die Kassette, -n *cassette*

TALKING ABOUT PRICES

kosten *to cost*
Was kostet ... ? *How much does . . cost?*
Das ist preiswert. *That's a bargain.*
  billig *cheap*
  teuer *expensive*
das Geld *money*
DM = Deutsche Mark *German mark (German monetary unit)*
die Mark, - *mark*

der Pfennig, - *(smallest unit of German currency; 1/100 of a mark)*

POINTING THINGS OUT

Schauen Sie! *Look!*
Schau! *Look!*
dort *there*
dort drüben *over there*
da vorn *up there in the front*
da hinten *there in the back*

OTHER WORDS AND EXPRESSIONS

ziemlich *rather*
nur *only*

*Plural forms will be indicated in this way from now on.

Klamotten kaufen

① Ich finde das T-Shirt echt stark.

Teenagers in German-speaking countries usually dress casually, often wearing jeans and T-shirts. They enjoy shopping and talking about clothes and like to follow trends. What kinds of clothes do you and your friends wear? Do you think that clothing styles in the German-speaking countries are similar to those in the United States? Let's find out what teenagers in those countries like to buy.

In this chapter you will learn

- to express wishes when shopping
- to comment on and describe clothes; to give compliments and respond to them
- to talk about trying on clothes

And you will

- listen to people talk about clothes
- read ads for clothing stores
- write a clothing ad for a newspaper
- find out what teenagers in German-speaking countries like to wear to parties

② Ich brauche ein T-Shirt in Rot.

③ Was ziehst du zu Sonjas Fete an?

Los geht's!

Was ziehst du an?

Look at the photos that accompany the story. Who are the people pictured? Where are they at the beginning of the story and where do they go? Based on this information, what do you think they are talking about?

Michael

Katja

Julia

❶

Was ziehst du denn zu Sonjas Fete an? Rock, Pulli?

Ach was! Ich zieh' meinen Jogging-Anzug an.

Und ich meine Shorts. Ich brauche aber etwas, eine Bluse oder ein T-Shirt. Das ist zu alt und gefällt mir nicht.

Und ich brauche ein Stirnband für meine Haare. Komm, gehen wir zum Sport-Kerner!

❷

Schau, der Michael!

Hallo, ihr beiden!

Was hast du denn da in der Tüte?

Na, wie gefällt euch mein T-Shirt?

Mensch, scheußlich!

Wirklich? — Also, ich finde es stark!

❸

Haben Sie einen Wunsch?

Ich suche eine Bluse.

Blusen haben wir in allen Größen und allen Farben. — Hier haben wir etwas für Sie: Toll, nicht?

Haben Sie auch Blusen in Blau?

Natürlich! Hier, in Blau. Größe 40. Paßt bestimmt.

1 Was passiert hier?

Do you understand what is happening in the **Foto-Roman**? Check your comprehension by answering these questions. Don't be afraid to guess.

1. What does the word **Fete** mean? Who is having one?
2. What do Katja and Julia still need to do before the **Fete**?
3. What does Michael think about his purchase? What do Julia and Katja think of it?
4. Does Katja like the first thing she tries on? What does she say?
5. What does Katja finally buy? Why does she hesitate at first?
6. What do you think about her purchase?

2 Genauer lesen

Reread the conversations. Which words or phrases do the characters use to

1. name articles of clothing
2. describe or comment on clothing
3. name colors
4. tell a price

3 Stimmt oder stimmt nicht?

Are these statements right or wrong? Answer each one with either **stimmt** or **stimmt nicht**. If a statement is wrong, try to state it correctly.

1. Julia hat eine Fete.
2. Katja hat Shorts, aber sie braucht eine Bluse.
3. Michael findet sein T-Shirt stark.
4. Katja sucht einen Pulli.
5. Katja möchte die Bluse in Blau haben.
6. Blau ist Katjas Lieblingsfarbe.

4 Was paßt zusammen?

Match each statement or question on the left with an appropriate response on the right.

1. Was ziehst du zu Sonjas Fete an?
2. Wie gefällt euch mein T-Shirt?
3. Haben Sie einen Wunsch?
4. Wir haben Blusen in allen Farben.
5. Das T-Shirt kostet 42 Mark 90.
6. Das ist eine gute Farbe für dich.

a. Mensch, scheußlich!
b. Weiß ist meine Lieblingsfarbe.
c. Gut! Ich möchte eine Bluse in Blau.
d. Ja, ich suche eine Bluse.
e. Meinen Jogging-Anzug.
f. Das ist teuer!

5 Welches Wort paßt?

Based on the **Foto-Roman,** rewrite the following narrative by supplying the missing words.

Katja __1__ eine Bluse für Sonjas Fete und geht mit Julia zum Sport-Kerner. Dort sehen die zwei __2__ den Michael. Er zeigt ihnen sein neues T-Shirt. Katja __3__ das T-Shirt scheußlich, aber Michael findet es __4__. Im Sport-Kerner möchte Katja eine Bluse in __5__ sehen, und sie probiert eine Bluse an. Die Bluse gefällt ihr aber nicht. Die T-Shirts sind aber __6__ sportlich und fesch. Julia findet das T-Shirt mit dem Texas-Motiv ganz toll. Katja __7__ das weiße T-Shirt an, denn Weiß ist Katjas __8__. Sie möchte es nehmen, aber es ist __9__. Am Ende kauft Katja das T-Shirt doch.

Blau	Lieblingsfarbe	probiert		stark
findet	sehr	sucht	teuer	Mädchen

Expressing wishes when shopping

WORTSCHATZ

der Rock das Hemd die Stiefel

das Kleid die Hose der Gürtel

die Bluse
die Jacke
die Jeans
die Socke
die Shorts
das T-Shirt
der Pulli (Pullover)
der Jogging-Anzug

die Turnschuhe

FÜR DAMEN

Hosen, Leinenstruktur	75.-
Damenhafte Röcke in Leinenoptik	55.-
T-Shirts, bedruckt, mit Perlen und Pailletten	38.-
Coloured Jeans mit Gürtel	60.-
Bedruckte Blusen mit modischen Details	55.-
T-Shirts mit Applikationen	35.-
<u>YOUNG COLLECTIONS</u> Strickkleider in verschiedenen Formen und Farben	28.-

FÜR HERREN

Jacken	85.-
Blouson oder Polo-Shirts, 1/2 Ärmel	50.-
Uni-Socken, Superstretch, 5 Paar	19.-
Seiden-Hemden, sandwashed bedruckt, 1/2 Ärmel	45.-
Streifen-Polo-Shirts, 1/2 Ärmel	48.-
Gymnastik-Shorts	30.-

Many clothing items in this ad are cognates. Which ones do you recognize?
Which items are for women, which for men? Which words are used to describe shirts
and T-shirts? What do they mean?

6 Hör gut zu!

A certain **Modegeschäft** (*clothing store*) has been doing a lot of advertising lately. As you
listen to one of their radio ads, first write down the items in the order you hear them mentioned. Then figure out which items are for men, and which for women. What does this
store have for "**die ganze Familie**"?

To the right is an **Umrechnungstabelle** (*conversion table*) for determining how to convert marks to dollars and vice versa. How many dollars will you receive for one mark? How many marks would you receive for one dollar? The table always has a date, because the exchange rate varies from day to day. When was this table printed? Looking at the clothing ad and using the **Umrechnungstabelle**, compare the prices for clothing in Germany with what you pay in the United States. In general, in which country do you think clothes are more expensive? What types of clothes would you expect to be more expensive in Germany than in the United States?

Umrechnungstabelle
USA

Stand: Febr. '93

DM	Dollar	Dollar	DM
1,–	–,59	–,10	–,17
2,–	1,18	–,50	–,85
3,–	1,76	1,—	1,70
4,–	2,35	2,50	4,25
5,–	2,94	5,—	8,50
10,–	5,88	10,—	17,—
20,–	11,76	20,—	34,—
25,–	14,71	30,—	51,—
30,–	17,65	40,—	68,—
40,–	23,53	50,—	85,—
50,–	29,41	60,—	102,—
75,–	44,12	70,—	119,—
100,–	58,82	80,—	136,—
200,–	117,65	90,—	153,—
250,–	147,06	100,—	170,—
300,–	176,47	200,—	340,—
500,–	294,12	300,—	510,—
750,–	441,18	400,—	680,—
1.000,–	588,24	500,—	850,—
2.000,–	1.176,47	1.000,—	1.700,—

1 Dollar (USD) = 100 Cents

Die errechneten Beträge sind nur Annäherungswerte, da die Kurse für An- und Verkauf von Schecks, Noten und Münzen verschieden sind und Schwankungen unterliegen. – Alle Angaben ohne Gewähr.

COMMERZBANK
Die Bank an Ihrer Seite

7 Wie sind die Preise?

Using the **Umrechnungstabelle** for clues, create a price list for the following items listed in the **Wortschatz** but not in the ad: **Gürtel**, **Jogging-Anzug**, **Turnschuhe**, **Pulli**, and **Stiefel**. Your partner will ask you how much these items cost, and you will answer, using your price list and the ad on page 121. Then switch roles. Be polite!

8 Was gibt es im Modegeschäft?

You want to buy something new to wear to your friend's party, but you can't decide what to buy. You have DM 200 to spend. Using the ad on page 121 and your price list, put together three different outfits that would be within your budget. With which outfit would you have the most money left over?

SO SAGT MAN DAS!

Expressing wishes when shopping

You have already used the **möchte**-forms to say what you would like to eat and drink. You can use these same forms when you go shopping for other things, such as clothes.

The salesclerk might ask:

Bitte? *or*
Was möchten Sie?
or
Was bekommen Sie?
or
Haben Sie einen Wunsch?

You can respond:

Ich möchte eine Jacke, bitte!
Ich brauche ein T-Shirt.
I need a T-shirt.
Einen Pulli in Grau, bitte!
A sweater in gray, please!
Ich suche eine Bluse.
I'm looking for a blouse.

What is the subject of the sentence in each of the salesclerk's questions? Look at the sentence **Einen Pulli in Grau, bitte!** Is there a subject or verb? What do you think is intended?

Grammatik   Definite and indefinite articles, accusative case

Look at the following sentences:

Der Pulli kostet 30 Mark.   Möchten Sie **den Pulli**?
Ein Pulli kostet 30 Mark.   Möchten Sie **einen Pulli**?

What is the difference between the noun phrases **der Pulli/ein Pulli** on the left and the noun phrases **den Pulli/einen Pulli** on the right?

The noun phrases (**der Pulli/ein Pulli**) on the left are the *subjects* (nominative case) of the sentences. The noun phrases **den Pulli/einen Pulli** on the right are *direct objects* (accusative case) of the sentences. Only articles for masculine nouns change when they are used as direct objects. The articles for feminine, neuter, and plural nouns stay the same:

Das T-Shirt kostet 10 Mark.	Möchten Sie **das T-Shirt**?	Ja, ich möchte **das T-Shirt**.
Die Jacke ist schön.	Möchten Sie **die Jacke**?	Ich nehme **die Jacke**.
Die Turnschuhe kosten 40 Mark.	Möchten Sie **die Turnschuhe**?	Ja, ich möchte **die Turnschuhe**.

9 Hör gut zu!

Listen carefully to these students commenting on different clothes, and decide whether the item of clothing in each exchange is the subject or direct object of the sentences.

10 Julia geht einkaufen

Read this conversation between Julia and the salesclerk at **Sport-Kerner**. Look carefully at the conversation and determine what the subject and/or direct object is in each sentence. Then answer the questions that follow.

VERKÄUFERIN   Guten Tag! Haben Sie einen Wunsch?
JULIA   Ich suche einen Rock in Blau. Was kostet der Rock hier?
VERKÄUFERIN   Er kostet nur 60 Mark.
JULIA   Und haben Sie vielleicht auch eine Bluse in Weiß?
VERKÄUFERIN   Ja, die Bluse hier kostet 45 Mark. Wir haben auch das weiße T-Shirt hier im Sonderangebot. Nur 20 Mark. Paßt auch schön zu Röcken.
JULIA   Das T-Shirt ist schön, aber ich brauche ein T-Shirt in Schwarz. Also ich nehme nur den Rock und die Bluse. Danke!

1. What is Julia looking for?
2. Why doesn't she want the T-Shirt?
3. How much is her final purchase?

| Ich | brauche möchte | Pulli
Rock
Jeans
Hemd
T-Shirt
Stiefel
Gürtel | Turn-schuhe
Bluse
Kleid
Hose
Socken
Jacke |

11 Was brauchst du?

a. Tell some of your classmates what clothes you need, using the indefinite article when appropriate.

b. Now point to various articles of clothing that your classmates are wearing and say that you would like to have them, using the definite article.

12 Rollenspiel im Kaufhaus

You are in a department store that has many items on sale (**im Sonderangebot**). Make a list of the clothes you would like to buy. Your partner will play the salesperson and ask you what you want and tell you where everything is. In the boxes to the right are some words and phrases you might need.

dort
da drüben
hier vorn
da hinten

der/ein
den/einen
die/eine
das/ein

13 Haben Sie das auch in ...?

You didn't find the colors you like at the last store. Ask the salesperson at the new store below if he or she has the items you want in certain colors. Also ask about prices. Then switch roles.

EIN WENIG LANDESKUNDE

The store hours listed below are typical for stores in Germany. What are the hours for the different days of the week? Is this different from stores where you live? What time do stores close on Saturday? When do they reopen? The first Saturday of each month, referred to as **langer Samstag**, the large stores stay open longer, usually until 6 p.m.

WORTSCHATZ

Farben! Haben Sie das auch ...?

in Blau in Grün in Weiß in Hellblau in Rot

in Dunkelblau in Braun in Gelb in Grau in Schwarz

14 Zum Schreiben: Alles ist im Sonderangebot!

Design your own newspaper ad based on four items in the ad on page 121 or cut out pictures from a magazine. Remember, everything is on sale at your store. Be sure to mention prices and colors in stock. Be prepared to share your ads with the class.

Commenting on and describing clothes; giving compliments
and responding to them

SO SAGT MAN DAS!

Commenting on and describing clothes

If you want to know what someone thinks about a particular item
of clothing, you might ask:

Wie findest du das Hemd?

You might get positive comments, such as:

Ich finde es fesch.
Es sieht schick aus!
Es paßt prima.
Es gefällt mir.

Or you might get negative comments, such as:

Ich finde es furchtbar.
Es sieht blöd aus.
Es paßt nicht.
Es gefällt mir nicht.

If the person you ask isn't sure, he or she might say:

Ich weiß nicht. *or*
Ich bin nicht sicher.

15 Hör gut zu!

Several students are in a store looking at clothes
and talking about what they like and don't like.
Determine whether the person speaking likes
the item of clothing or not.

Ein wenig *Grammatik*

Look at these sentences:

Wie findest du den Rock?
Er gefällt mir.
Und die T-Shirts?
Sie gefallen mir auch.

What are the subjects in the two
responses?[1] When using the verb
gefallen to say you like something,
you need to know only two forms:
gefällt and **gefallen**.

Er/sie/es gefällt mir. *I like it.*
Sie (pl) gefallen mir. *I like
them.*

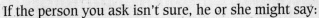

1.   2.

3.   4.   5.

1. er (der Rock), sie (die T-Shirts)

16 Wie findest du das?

Look at the items pictured in Activity 15 and ask your partner if he or she likes each item. Then switch roles.

WORTSCHATZ

Nichts paßt!

Das Kleid ist zu lang.

Der Pulli ist viel zu weit.

Die Jacke ist zu groß.

Die Hose ist zu kurz.

Das Hemd ist zu eng.

Die Schuhe sind ein bißchen zu klein.

HERRENGRÖSSEN

	USA	BRD
Hemden	13	36
	15	38
	16	40
	17	42
Pullover	S	36-38
	M	39
	L	40-41
	XL	42-44
Anzüge	34	44
	36	46
	40	50
	44	54
	46	56
Schuhe	7, 7½	40
	8	41
	8½	42
	9, 9½	43
	10, 10½	44
	11, 11½	44
	12, 12½	45

DAMENGRÖSSEN

	USA	BRD
Blusen, Pullover	8	36
	10	38
	12	40
	14	42
Kleider, Mäntel	8	38
	10	40
	12	42
	14	44
Schuhe	5	36
	6	37
	7	38
	8	39
	9	40
	10	41

EIN WENIG LANDESKUNDE

German sizes are different from American sizes. However, clothes manufactured in the United States and imported to Germany carry U.S. sizes. For example, jeans are often measured in inches, and T-shirts have the designations **S**, **M**, **L**, **XL**, and **XXL**. Look at the size charts on the right. What size would you take if you were buying German clothes or shoes in Germany?

17 Was ist los?

You and a friend are spending the afternoon **in der Innenstadt** (*downtown*). You encounter the people pictured below and discuss their clothing. Take turns describing the clothing pictured to each other.

SO SAGT MAN DAS!

Giving compliments and responding to them

On numerous occasions you'll want to be able to compliment your friends on their clothes.

You could say:
Die Jacke sieht lässig aus! *or*
Die Jacke gefällt mir!

The other person might respond:
Ehrlich? *or*
Wirklich? *or*
Meinst du?
Nicht zu lang (kurz, groß)?

You could answer:
Ehrlich!
Wirklich!
Ja, bestimmt!
Nein, überhaupt nicht!

18 Was meinst du?

a. Find five pictures of clothing items in your favorite magazine. Write at least two sentences to describe each item and one sentence to express your opinion about each picture.

fesch schick blöd furchtbar
Spitze scheußlich prima
toll stark lässig

b. Show your partner the pictures you cut out and ask what he or she thinks of your clothing choices. If your partner compliments you on your choices, respond appropriately.

Grammatik   Direct object pronouns

In **Kapitel 3** you learned that the pronouns **er**, **sie**, **es**, and **sie** (pl) can refer to both people and objects. Look at the following sentences:

Der Pulli ist sehr preiswert.	Ich finde **den Pulli** toll.
Ja, **er** ist nicht teuer.	Ich finde **ihn** auch toll.

What are the pronouns in these sentences? What do you think **er** and **ihn** refer to? **Er**, the pronoun on the left, is the *subject* (nominative case) of the sentence and refers to **der Pulli**. The pronoun **ihn** on the right is the *direct object* (accusative case) of the sentence and refers to **den Pulli**. Only the masculine pronoun changes when it is used as a direct object. The feminine **sie**, neuter **es**, and plural pronoun **sie** stay the same:

Die Bluse (sie) ist hübsch.	Ich finde **sie** scheußlich.
Das Hemd (es) kostet 40 Mark.	Ich finde **es** teuer.
Die Stiefel (sie) sind echt toll!	Aber ich möchte **sie** in Schwarz.

19 Hör gut zu!

Listen to this conversation between two students who are talking about clothes they want to buy. The first time you hear the conversation, figure out whether the pronouns they mention are subjects or direct objects. Then listen again and match the article of clothing with the words used to describe it.

BEISPIEL   —Ich finde die blaue Bluse sehr
schön. Und du?
—Ja, ich finde sie hübsch.

	Subject	Direct object
0		X
1		
2		

hellgrün   schick
schwarz
preiswert
teuer   toll
stark   schön
hübsch

die Bluse da vorn   der Rock   die blaue Bluse

das T-Shirt   die Turnschuhe

der Jogging-Anzug   der Pulli   die Bluse

20 Welcher Satz paßt?

Katja and Sonja are in a store trying on clothes. Choose the appropriate responses to complete their conversation. Then read the conversation aloud with your partner.

> Ich finde ihn toll, aber er ist viel zu lang für dich.

> Hm, ich finde sie schön, aber sie paßt nicht.

> Bist du sicher? Sie sind sehr teuer.

> Ja, es sieht super aus!

SONJA Wie findest du die Bluse in Rot?

KATJA ══════.

SONJA Meinst du? Wie findest du den Rock hier in Schwarz?

KATJA ══════.

SONJA Ehrlich? So ein Mist! Vielleicht kaufe ich das T-Shirt in Blau.

SONJA ══════.

KATJA Dann kaufe ich das T-Shirt und die Schuhe.

SONJA ══════.

KATJA Ich weiß, aber sie gefallen mir sehr.

21 Wie findest du ...?

Find out what your partner thinks about the clothes that Georg and Beate are wearing to Sonja's party. One of you comments on Georg's clothing, and the other on Beate's. When you have finished, switch roles.

Georg   Beate

22 Zum Schreiben

With your partner, write a conversation that could go with the picture below. Practice your conversation and be prepared to share it with the class.

Welche Klamotten sind „in"?

What do you think German students usually like to wear when they go to a party? We asked many students, and here is what some of them said. Listen first, then read the text.

LANDESKUNDE

Sandra,
Stuttgart

„Also, wenn ich zu einer Party gehe, dann ziehe ich am liebsten Jeans an und vielleicht einen Body ... und einen weißen Pulli darüber; meistens dann etwas in Blau oder einen weißen Pulli, jetzt, wie grad' eben, denn meine Lieblingsfarben sind doch Blau und Weiß."

Melina,
Bietigheim

„Am liebsten mag ich Jeans, vor allem helle, oder ja so lockere Blusen, kurze halt, und jetzt vor allem T-Shirts, einfarbige; und sie sollen halt schön lang sein und ein bißchen locker. Und ja, meine Lieblingsfarben sind Blau, Apricot oder Rot, Lila auch noch."

Alexandra,
Bietigheim

„Ja, ich zieh' am liebsten Jeans an, und Lieblings-farben sind dann so Blau oder Pastellfarben, und auf Partys oder so eigentlich immer in Jeans und mal etwas Schöneres oben, in Diskos dann auch, und ab und zu hab' ich mal gern einen Rock."

Iwan,
Bietigheim

„Also, wenn ich auf eine Party gehe, zieh' ich am liebsten ein T-Shirt an und eine kurze Hose. Am lieb-sten trag' ich Schwarz, so einfach, weil es halt schön aussieht und weil es be-quem ist."

A. 1. What items of clothing are mentioned most by these students? Make a list of the cloth-ing each student prefers and list the colors he or she seems to like best.

2. Which of these students would you like to meet and why? Do you and the student you selected have similar tastes in clothes? Explain. What do you generally wear and what are your favorite colors? What do you usually wear to a party?

B. What is your overall impression of the way these German teenagers dress? Compare it with the typical dress for teenagers in the United States. Do you think students in the United States are more or less formal than students in Germany? Why do you think so? Write a brief essay explaining your answer.

Talking about trying on clothes

23 Hör gut zu!

Jürgen goes to a clothing store to find something to wear to Sonja's party. You will hear four short pieces of his conversation with the salesman. On a separate sheet of paper, put the photos in order according to their conversation.

a.

b.

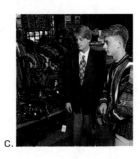
c.

d.

SO SAGT MAN DAS!

Talking about trying on clothes

When you go shopping for clothes, you will want to try them on.

You might say to the salesperson:

Ich probiere das T-Shirt an.   *or*   **Ich ziehe das T-Shirt an.**

If you decide to buy it: If not:

Ich nehme es. *or*   **Ich nehme es nicht.** *or*
Ich kaufe es.   **Ich kaufe es nicht.**

Grammatik   Separable-prefix verbs

The verbs **anziehen** (*to put on, wear*), **anprobieren** (*to try on*), and **aussehen** (*to look, appear*), belong to a group of verbs that have a separable prefix. The prefix is at the beginning of the verb: *an*ziehen, *an*probieren, *aus*sehen. In the present tense, the prefix is separated from the verb and is at the end of the clause or sentence.

anziehen
Was **ziehe** ich **an**?
Ich **ziehe** Shorts **an**.
Ich **ziehe** Shorts und ein T-Shirt **an**.
Ich **ziehe** heute Shorts und ein T-Shirt **an**.
Ich **ziehe** heute zu Sonjas Fete Shorts und ein T-Shirt **an**.
Ja, zu Sonjas Fete **ziehe** ich ganz bestimmt Shorts und ein T-Shirt **an**!

24 Sätze bauen

Build as many sentences as you can.
Be sure to use the correct articles.

A number of German verbs have prefixes but not all of them are separable (for example, **gefallen** and **bekommen**). You can usually recognize separable prefixes if they are words that can also stand alone (such as **mit, auf,** and **aus**) and if they carry the main stress of the compound verb. Compare **ánziehen** and **bekómmen**.

Ich	zieht … an	Hemd
Er	ziehe … an	gut
Bluse	sieht … aus	blöd
Schuhe	sehen … aus	scheußlich
Sie	probiert … an	Pulli
Jogging-Anzug	probiere … an	Jacke
Jeans		Jeans
Gürtel		

Ein wenig *Grammatik*

The verbs **nehmen** (*to take*) and **aussehen** (*to appear, look*) are called stem-changing verbs. In these verbs, the stem vowel changes in the **du**- and **er/sie**-forms. These verbs do not follow the regular patterns of verbs like **spielen**.

Du **nimmst** den Rock.   Du **siehst** gut **aus**!
Er **nimmt** die Jacke.   Sie **sieht** gut **aus**!

You will learn more about these verbs later.

25 Was ziehen sie zu Sonjas Fete an?

a. Look at the pictures of clothing below and ask your partner what Julia, Katja, Michael, and Heiko will wear to Sonja's party. Your partner's responses will be based on the illustrations. Switch roles and vary your responses.

b. You and your partner have been invited to Sonja's party. Ask your partner what he or she would wear based on the pictures of clothing. Then switch roles.

26 Was nimmst du?

You have picked out five items of clothing that you like. Your partner asks you which items you will try on and which ones you would like to buy. Answer, then switch roles.

27 Für mein Notizbuch

For your **Notizbuch** entry, write a paragraph describing what you and your friends usually wear to a party. Describe the kinds of clothes you like and some that you do not like. Describe some of the latest fashions for teens and write what you think about them.

28 Im Fernsehen

You work for an ad agency. Get together with two other classmates and write a TV commercial that will convince your audience to shop at a certain clothing store. Be sure to mention prices, colors, and how well the clothes fit and look.

Richtig aussprechen / Richtig lesen

A. To practice the following sounds, say the words and sentences below after your teacher or after the recording.

1. The letter **i:** When the letter **i** is followed by two consonants, it sounds like the short *i* in the English word *pit*.
   schick, bestimmt, bißchen / Ich finde das Kleid schick. Ehrlich.

2. The letters **ä** and **e:** The letters **ä** and **e** are pronounced as short vowels when followed by two consonants. They sound similar to the short *e* in the English word *net*.
   lässig, hell, gefällt / Das fesche Hemd gefällt mir.

3. The letter **a:** The letter **a** is roughly equivalent to the *a* sound in the English word *father*.
   haben, lang, Jacke / Wir haben Jacken in allen Farben.

4. The letter combinations **sch, st,** and **sp:** The consonant combination **sch** is pronounced like the *sh* in the English word *ship*. When the letter **s** is followed by **p** or **t** at the beginning of a syllable, it is also pronounced in this way.
   schwarz, Turnschuh, Stiefel / Die schwarzen Stiefel sind Spitze!

Richtig schreiben / Diktat

B. Write down the sentences that you hear.

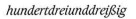

ZUM LESEN

Kleider machen Leute!

1. Look at a clothing ad from a magazine written in English and make a list of some of the words and expressions that you find in the ad.

2. When you look in a newspaper or magazine for some good buys in clothing, what are some words or phrases that tell you that you would be getting a bargain? Write down some of these English words and phrases.

3. Scan these two pages and write any German words or phrases you find that correspond to the words and phrases you listed in Activities 1 and 2 above. Group the words you find in categories (prices, colors, etc.) and list as many words in each category as you can.

4. Look at the prices of the clothing being advertised. Judging from the photos, are these prices reasonable? Are there prices you could afford? Do you think they are the original prices in all

Ohne Shirts und Shorts geht im Sommer nichts. K + L Ruppert hat für Sie die schönsten ausgesucht. Sagenhafte Vielfalt und sommerleichte Qualitäten. Zu Preisen, die Ihnen passen werden!

Alex, 16 Jahre
„Ich trage Schwarz. Ich ändere das nie. Andere Sachen habe ich nicht. Ich glaube, mit Mode kann man etwas erklären, ohne zu reden."

Sandra, 16 Jahre
„Zu meinem braunen Kleid trage ich schwarze Strümpfe und schwarze Schuhe mit Klumpabsatz. Ich ziehe mir auch Sachen an, wenn sie nicht 'in' sind. Es gibt wichtigeres als Mode."

Manu, 16 Jahre
„Meine Jeans und die Lederjacke sind Markenprodukte, keine billigen Kopien. Ich finde das wichtig."

KRIEGBAUM AKTUELL

Stark Reduziert!

(3) 19.90

(2) 12.90

2) **Kapuzen-T-Shirts**
100% reine Baumwolle, in vielen
Farben sortiert, Größe M-XXL **12.90**

3) **Kapuzen-T-Shirts**
100% reine Baumwolle, top Farben,
bedruckt **19.90**

Volker, 16 Jahre

„Das sind meine Sachen: Jeans,
Sportschuhe, Kapuzen-Shirt. Ich
trage sie, weil sie mir gefallen.
Mode interessiert mich nicht."

29.-

29.-

cases? What phrase gives you the information to answer that question?

5. Not all the texts on these pages are ads. What other type of text can you identify? What type of magazine would you expect texts like these to come from?

6. What is the age of the students who are describing their clothing? What generalizations can you make about the clothing of these students? Find words in the text that support your answer.

7. In the ad to the left, what kind of guarantee does **K&L Ruppert** offer for its merchandise?

8. What does Volker wear? Where could he buy a shirt like the one he says he likes to wear? How much would it cost? Do you know why it has that name?

9. What does Alex mean when he says „**Ich glaube, mit Mode kann man etwas erklären, ohne zu reden.**"? (**ohne zu reden**-*without speaking*) Work with a partner and come up with some examples that illustrate this statement.

10. How does Manu differ from Sandra and Volker?

11. You are planning a trip to Germany. Your hosts will meet you at the airport, but they have never seen you. Write them a postcard with a short description of what you look like and what you will be wearing (**Ich trage ...**).

12. Your club at school is planning a garage sale. Write an ad for the school or local newspaper in which you describe the kinds of clothing you will sell.

1 You have been hired to write for a German fashion magazine on trends among teens today. Interview your partner about his or her taste in clothes. When you have finished, switch roles and then interview one other person. Find out what clothes they like to wear, what they wear to a party, their favorite color, and their favorite article of clothing. Take notes and write an article in German based on your interviews.

2 Look at the two display windows for **Mode-Welt.** With a partner compare the two windows and take turns telling each other which items are missing (**fehlen**) from the second window.

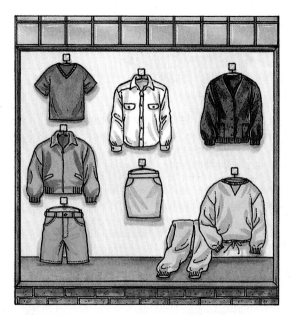

3 What questions would the salesperson and customer have to ask in order to get the responses in this conversation?

VERKÄUFERIN   ═══?
     KUNDIN   Ich brauche eine Bluse in Weiß. ═══?
VERKÄUFERIN   Sie kostet DM 43,00.
     KUNDIN   ═══?
VERKÄUFERIN   Ja, die haben wir auch in Gelb.
     KUNDIN   Und ═══?
VERKÄUFERIN   Ich finde die Bluse sehr schick. Die hat nicht jeder.
     KUNDIN   Ich probiere sie mal an. ═══?
VERKÄUFERIN   Sie paßt prima!
     KUNDIN   ═══?
VERKÄUFERIN   Nein, die Bluse ist überhaupt nicht zu eng. ═══?
     KUNDIN   Ja, ich nehme sie. Danke!

4 You are in a store looking for some new clothes and your partner, a pushy salesperson, tries to convince you to try on and get clothes that are the wrong color and don't fit. You try them on, and he or she tells you how good they look and how well they fit. You're not so sure. Express your uncertainty and hesitancy. Will you succumb to the pressure in the end and buy the clothes? Develop a conversation based on this scenario and practice it with your partner.

5 You will hear some conversations in a clothing store. In each case the customer has decided not to buy the item. Determine the reason. Is it the price, the color, or the fit?

	Preis	Farbe	paßt nicht
1			
2			

DAS WEISSE HEMD

Ein weißes Hemd ist das, was Modekenner einen „all time classic" nennen: schick, aber trotzdem leger—ein Basisstück für jede Garderobe. In dieser Saison ist das weiße Hemd das Lieblingskind der Designer, die sich in ihren Variationen gegenseitig übertreffen. Asymmetrisch, geknotet oder aus Leinen, lang oder kurz—zu Jeans, Shorts oder Röcken: alles geht.

6 Read the fashion review to the right then answer these questions.
   1. What clothing item is the fashion editor talking about?
   2. Is he or she enthusiastic or skeptical about the item?
   3. What does he or she say about the clothing being reviewed?

7 Find a photo of someone wearing an interesting outfit, and write a review of the clothes he or she is wearing. Share your review with the class.

8

ROLLENSPIEL

You and two friends are at home trying to find something to wear to a party.

a. One of you is trying on clothes, but you can't find anything that fits or is the right color. Your friends comment on the clothes you try on.

b. Unsuccessful, in the end you all decide to go to the store. Look at the display windows in Activity 2 on page 136 again. Choose one window on which to base your conversation. This time one of you is the salesperson. The other two will be the customers. Ask for items in specific colors. The salesperson will tell you what's available. Will you try the clothes on? How do they look? Will you buy them? Role-play your scene in front of the class using props.

Can you express wishes when shopping? (p. 122)

1 How would a salesperson in a clothing store ask what you would like?

2 How would you answer, saying that you were looking for the following? (Be sure to practice using the articles correctly, and watch out for direct objects.)

a. a sweater   c. pants in red   e. a jacket in light gray
b. boots in black   d. a shirt in brown   f. a dress in blue

Can you comment on and describe clothing? (p. 125)

3 How would you ask a friend what he or she thinks of these clothes:

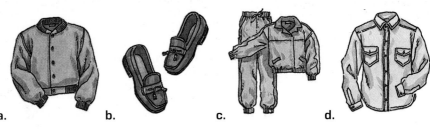

a.   b.   c.   d.

4 How might your friend respond positively? Negatively? With uncertainty?

5 How would you disagree with the following statements by saying the opposite? Use the correct pronoun.

a. The jacket is too short.   e. I think the belt is terrible.
b. The shoes are too tight.   f. I like the tennis shoes.
c. The jogging suit is too small.   g. I think the dress is too long.
d. The shirt fits just right.   h. The skirt looks stylish.

Can you compliment someone's clothing and respond to compliments? (p. 127)

6 How would you compliment Katja, using the cues below?

a. blouse   b. sweater   c. T-shirt   d. skirt

7 a. How might Katja respond to your compliments?
b. What would you say next?

8 How would you tell a friend what the following people are wearing to Sonja's party? (Remember to use **anziehen**!)

a. Julia   b. Katja   c. Heiko

Jeans   Bluse   T-Shirt
Shorts   Turnschuhe
Jogging-Anzug   Gürtel

Can you talk about trying on clothes? (p. 131)

9 How would you tell the salesperson that you would like to try on a shirt in red, pants in white, a sweater in yellow, and a jacket in brown?

10 How would you tell your friend that you will get the shirt, the sweater, and the jacket? (Use **nehmen** or **kaufen**.)

ERSTE STUFE

EXPRESSING WISHES WHEN SHOPPING

Bitte?   *Yes? Can I help you?*
Was bekommen Sie?
 What would you like?
Haben Sie einen Wunsch?
 May I help you?
Ich möchte ...   *I would like...*
Ich brauche ...   *I need...*
Ich suche ...   *I'm looking for...*
Einen Pulli in Grau, bitte.
 A sweater in gray, please.
Haben sie das auch in Rot?
 Do you also have that in red?
die Farbe, -n   *color*
 in Rot   *in red*

in Blau   *in blue*
in Grün   *in green*
in Gelb   *in yellow*
in Braun   *in brown*
in Grau   *in gray*
in Schwarz   *in black*
in Weiß   *in white*
in Dunkelblau   *in dark blue*
in Hellblau   *in light blue*
die Klamotten (pl)   *casual term for clothes*
die Bluse, -n   *blouse*
der Rock, ¨e   *skirt*
das Kleid, -er   *dress*
das Hemd, -en   *shirt*
die Jeans, -   *jeans*
der Gürtel, -   *belt*

die Hose, -n   *pants*
die Jacke, -n   *jacket*
der Pulli, -s (Pullover,-)   *sweater*
der Jogging-Anzug, ¨e
 jogging suit
das T-Shirt, -s   *T-shirt*
der Turnschuh, -e   *sneaker, athletic shoe*
der Stiefel, -   *boot*
die Socke, -n   *sock*
die Shorts, -   *shorts*

MASCULINE ARTICLES ACCUSATIVE CASE

den   *the*
einen   *a, an*

ZWEITE STUFE

COMMENTING ON AND DESCRIBING CLOTHES

Er/Sie/Es gefällt mir.   *I like it.*
Sie gefallen mir.   *I like them.*
Der Rock sieht ... aus.   *The skirt looks....*
 hübsch   *pretty*
 lässig   *casual*
 schick   *chic, smart*
 fesch   *stylish, smart*
 scheußlich   *hideous*
 furchtbar   *terrible, awful*
Der Rock paßt prima!   *The skirt fits great!*

Ich finde den Pulli echt stark!   *I think the sweater is really awesome!*
Ich bin nicht sicher.   *I'm not sure.*
Ich weiß nicht.   *I don't know.*
die Größe, -n   *the size*
zu   *too*
viel zu   *much too*
ein bißchen   *a little*
weit   *wide*
eng   *tight*
lang   *long*
kurz   *short*

GIVING AND RESPONDING TO COMPLIMENTS

Meinst du?   *Do you think so?*
ehrlich   *honestly*
wirklich   *really*
überhaupt nicht   *not at all*
bestimmt   *definitely*
Nicht zu lang?   *Not too long?*

MASCULINE PRONOUN: ACCUSATIVE CASE

ihn   *it; him*

DRITTE STUFE

TALKING ABOUT TRYING ON CLOTHES

aussehen (sep)*   *to look (like), appear*
 er/sie sieht aus**   *he/she looks*
anprobieren (sep)   *to try on*

anziehen (sep)   *to put on, wear*
nehmen   *to take*
 er/sie nimmt   *he/she takes*
kaufen   *to buy*

*Verbs with separable prefixes will be indicated with (sep) **For verbs with stem-vowel changes, the third person singular form will be listed to show you the vowel change that occurs.

6

Pläne machen

① Wir wollen ins Café gehen, ein Eis essen.

After school and on the weekend, when you have finished your homework, there are a lot of things you can do. You can go to a movie, go shopping, or just hang out with your friends at your favorite café. If you were in Wedel and wanted to make plans, there are a number of things you would need to be able to say in German.

In this chapter you will learn

- to start a conversation; to tell time and talk about when you do things
- to make plans
- to order food and beverages; to talk about how something tastes; to pay the check

And you will

- listen to students making plans and ordering food and beverages
- read a story, a letter, a menu, and authentic German advertisements
- write about what you and your friends do and write an invitation
- find out how German students spend their free time

③ Wie spät ist es?

② Was bekommen Sie?

Los geht's!

Wollen wir ins Café gehen?

Look at the photos that accompany the story. Where are the scenes taking place? What are the people doing? What do you think will happen in the story?

 Heiko   **Julia**

 Katja Michael

① Hallo, Heiko! Wie geht's denn so?

Hm ... So lala.

② Was machst du jetzt so hier? Wohin gehst du?

Zu Katja. Wir machen zuerst Hausaufgaben, und dann wollen wir ins Café Freizeit, ein Eis essen. Willst du mitkommen?

Gern! Wann wollt ihr gehen?

③ Wie spät ist es jetzt?

Viertel nach drei.

Ja, so um halb fünf?

④ Okay!

Bis dann, tschüs!

Tschüs!

⑤ Guten Tag! Was bekommt ihr?

Ich bekomme einen Eisbecher. Fruchteis.

Ich möchte einen Cappuccino, bitte.

Hm ... Ich will im Moment gar nichts. Ich esse später etwas.

Und ich esse jetzt eine Pizza. Nummer eins, bitte.

IMBISS-KARTE
Café Freizeit
Für den kleinen Hunger und Durst

KLEINE SPEISEN

NUDELSUPPE MIT BROT	DM 4,50
KÄSEBROT	5,20
WURSTBROT	5,10
WIENER MIT SENF — 2 PAAR	5,80
PIZZA (15 cm)	
Nr. 1 mit Tomaten und Käse	6,00
Nr. 2 mit Wurst und Käse	6,50
Nr. 3 mit Wurst, Käse und Pilzen	8,50

EIS

	KUGEL DM	1,10
FRUCHTEIS	KUGEL	1,30
SAHNEEIS		6,80
EISBECHER		

1 Was passiert hier?

Do you understand what is happening in the **Foto-Roman**? Check your comprehension by answering these questions. Don't be afraid to guess.

1. What plans have Julia and Katja made for the afternoon?
2. What is Heiko going to do?
3. Where do the three friends meet Michael?
4. Why does Michael apologize to Katja? How does Katja react?

2 Genauer lesen

Reread the conversations. Which words or phrases do the characters use to

1. ask how someone is doing
2. talk about time
3. name foods and drinks
4. tell a waiter they want to pay
5. apologize

3 Was paßt zusammen?

Match each statement or question on the left with an appropriate response on the right.

1. Wie geht's denn?
2. Wohin gehst du?
3. Wie spät ist es jetzt?
4. Wer bekommt den Cappuccino?
5. Ich möchte zahlen.

a. Er ist für mich.
b. So lala.
c. Das macht zusammen vierzehn Mark zehn.
d. Viertel nach drei.
e. Zu Katja.

4 Was fehlt hier?

Based on the **Foto-Roman** that you've just read, complete each of the sentences below with an appropriate item from the list.

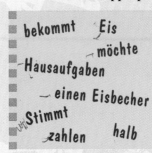

bekommt Eis
        möchte
Hausaufgaben
      einen Eisbecher
Stimmt
    zahlen halb

Katja und Julia machen zuerst die __1__. Dann wollen sie in ein Café gehen, ein __2__ essen. Sie wollen so um __3__ fünf gehen. Im Café fragt der Kellner: „Was __4__ ihr?" Katja __5__ einen Cappuccino. Julia sagt: „Ich bekomme __6__, Fruchteis." Michael will gehen. Er sagt: „Ich möchte __7__, bitte." Der Kellner sagt: „Vierzehn Mark zehn." Und Michael antwortet: „Fünfzehn Mark. __8__ schon."

Café am Markt		
Nudelsuppe	DM	4,50
Käsebrot		5,20
Wurstbrot		5,60
Wiener mit Senf		5,80
Pizza		8,00
Apfelkuchen		2,00
Eis		1,10
Mineralwasser		3,50
Kaffee		4,20
Cola		3,00

5 Und du?

Look at the menu from the **Café am Markt**. Which items are foods, and which are beverages? If you were with your friends at the **Café am Markt**, what would you order? Make a list, including the prices.

Starting a conversation; telling time and talking about when you do things

SO SAGT MAN DAS!
Starting a conversation

If you want to find out how someone is doing, you ask:

Wie geht's? *or* **Wie geht's denn?**

The person might respond in one of these ways, depending on how he or she is doing.

Sehr gut! Prima!	Danke, gut! Gut!	Danke, es geht. So lala. Nicht schlecht.	Nicht so gut. Schlecht.	Sehr schlecht. Miserabel!

Sven	Silke	Nadja	Kemal	Jörg

6 Hör gut zu!

You will hear several students respond to the question **Wie geht's?** As you listen, look at the faces in the box above and determine who is speaking.

7 Hallo! Wie geht's?

Greet several students around you and ask them how they are doing.

8 Was hast du um ... ?

Get together with your partner, greet him or her, and ask how he or she is doing. Then take turns asking each other what classes you have at the times shown below.

BEISPIEL   DU   **Was hast du um ... ?**

a.

b.

c.

d.

Die Uhrzeit You already know how to express time when referring to schedules: **um acht Uhr dreißig, um acht Uhr fünfundvierzig.** Now you will learn a more informal way of telling time.

neun Uhr

zehn vor zehn

zehn nach neun

vor

nach

Viertel vor zehn

Viertel nach neun

zwanzig vor zehn

zwanzig nach neun

halb zehn

SO SAGT MAN DAS!

Telling time and talking about when you do things

You might ask your friend:

Wann gehst du ins Café?
Und um wieviel Uhr gehst du schwimmen?
Wie spät ist es?
Wieviel Uhr ist es? ⎫

The responses might be:

Um halb fünf.

Um Viertel nach drei.

Es ist Viertel vor zwei.

What specific information does each question ask for?

---

9 Wieviel Uhr ist es, bitte?

Using the clocks in the **WORTSCHATZ** box, take turns asking and telling your partner what time it is.

10 Was fehlt hier?

Katja is trying to find Heiko. His mom explains where he will be this afternoon. Complete what she says by filling in the blanks according to the times given. Use the words and phrases in the box to the right.

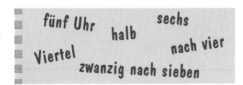

fünf Uhr   halb   sechs
Viertel   nach vier
zwanzig nach sieben

Um ═══ drei (2.30) geht er ins Einkaufszentrum. Dann hat er um Viertel ═══ (4.15) Fußballtraining. Danach geht er mit Michael um ═══ (5.00) ins Schwimmbad. Um ═══ vor ═══ (5.45) gehen die zwei Jungen ins Café Freizeit. Und dann kommt Heiko um ═══ (7.20) nach Hause.

11 Wie spät ist es?

You are making plans to meet friends. Ask your partner what time it is. Take turns.

1.

2.

3.

4.

5.

6.

12 Wann macht Ulrike alles?

Work with a partner to reorder these statements into a chronological description of how Ulrike spends a typical Monday.

1. Jeden Montag um acht Uhr gehe ich zur Schule.

Und am Abend schaue ich Fernsehen.

Dann um halb elf, direkt nach der Pause, habe ich Bio.

Um Viertel nach neun habe ich Mathe.

Um drei Uhr oder um halb vier esse ich Kuchen oder vielleicht etwas Obst.

Und jeden Montag um vier Uhr gehe ich schwimmen.

Danach mache ich so um fünf Hausaufgaben.

Nach der Schule gehe ich nach Hause.

13 Hör gut zu!

Match what these students say with the illustrations below.

14 Wann? Wer? Was?

Schau die Zeichnungen an!

1. Make a list of the times and corresponding activities shown in Activity 13.
2. Choosing your own activities, write six sentences stating what you do at the times shown above.

15 Um wieviel Uhr …?

Ask your partner at what time he or she does various activities or has certain classes.

SPRACHTIP

Denn, mal, halt, and **doch** are words that you've seen a lot throughout this book. None of these words has a direct translation, but they are often used in everyday conversations to give emphasis to a question, command, or statement. For example, **Wie sieht er denn aus? Sag mal, wann gehst du? Das hat halt nicht jeder.** and **Wir gehen doch um vier.** Using these words in your conversations will help your German sound more natural.

ZWEITE STUFE

Making plans

Wohin gehen? Was machen? Lies, was Katja und Julia planen! Julia sagt: „Katja und ich, wir wollen ..."

in ein Café gehen,
ein Eis essen

ins Schwimmbad gehen,
baden gehen

ins Kino gehen,
einen Film sehen

in eine Disko gehen,
tanzen und Musik hören

in die Stadt gehen,
Klamotten kaufen

ins Rockkonzert gehen,
Musik hören

16 Hör gut zu!

You will hear two students talk about their plans for the weekend. List all of the places they want to go in the order you hear them mentioned.

17 Was wollen wir machen?

Wir wollen ...

ins Schwimmbad
ins Kino
in ein Café
in die Stadt
in eine Disko
ins Rockkonzert

gehen und ...

tanzen
Klamotten kaufen
Musik hören
schwimmen
einen Film sehen
ein Eis essen

18 Für mein Notizbuch

In your **Notizbuch** write some of the places you go and some of the things you do after school and on weekends. Look on page 321 for additional words you might want to use.

SO SAGT MAN DAS!

Making plans

You have been using the **möchte**-forms (*would like to*) to express your intentions:
Er möchte Musik hören. You can also use **wollen** (*to want to*).

Talking to someone: Talking about yourself:
Heiko, was willst du machen?   **Ich will in ein Café gehen.**

Talking about someone:
Wohin will Birte gehen?   **Sie will ins Schwimmbad gehen.**

Grammatik   The verb **wollen**

Wollen means *to want* or *to want* to do. The forms of this verb—and of other
modal verbs — are different from those of regular verbs. Here are the forms:

Ich **will** ein Eis essen.	Wir **wollen** Tennis spielen
Du **willst** Musik hören.	Ihr **wollt** ins Kino gehen.
Er/Sie **will** tanzen gehen.	Sie (pl) / Sie **wollen** in eine Disko gehen.

What do you notice about the **ich** and **er/sie** forms?[1] Like the **möchte**-forms you
learned in **Kapitel 3**, **wollen** is also a modal auxiliary verb. It is often used with
another verb, although the second verb can be omitted if the meaning is obvious:

Ich will ins Schwimmbad gehen.
Ich will ins Schwimmbad.

Note the position of the verb **wollen** and the
second verb, the infinitive.

---

19 Was willst du machen?

Julia and her friend Sonja are talking about
their plans for the day. Complete their
conversation with the correct forms of **wollen**.

JULIA   Was __1__ du heute machen?
SONJA   Ich __2__ nach Hamburg fahren.
        Die Katja __3__ mitkommen.
JULIA   Und Michael? __4__ er auch mitkommen?
SONJA   Ich glaube, ja. Katja, Heiko und Michael
        __5__ alle mitkommen.
JULIA   Um wieviel Uhr __6__ ihr fahren?
SONJA   So um drei. Wir __7__ um sieben
        wieder zu Hause sein.

Fischmarkt in Hamburg

---

1. Though the pronouns are different, the verb forms are alike.

20 Sätze bauen

Wie viele Sätze kannst du bauen?

BEISPIEL **Katja will um vier Uhr ins Kino gehen.** *oder*
Um vier Uhr will Katja ins Kino gehen.

ich Katja du wir ihr die Jungen	wollen willst will wollt	am Nachmittag nach der Schule um vier Uhr von 3 bis 5 Uhr am Abend	in ein Café gehen ins Kino gehen tanzen gehen in die Stadt gehen ins Konzert gehen Musik hören

21 Heikos Pläne für nächste Woche

1. Look at Heiko's plans for next week. Take turns saying what Heiko plans to do each day.

   BEISPIEL **Am Dienstag will er ins Kino gehen.**

2. Take turns asking each other when Heiko plans to do each of his activities.

22 Deine Pläne für nächste Woche

1. Write your own plans for the coming week on a calendar page. For each day write what you want to do and at what time you plan to do it.

2. Your partner will ask you about your plans. Tell him or her what you want to do and at what time. Then switch roles. Be prepared to share your partner's plans with the class.

26 Montag	Fußball 16³⁰ Schach mit Sven 19⁰⁰ Arbeitsgruppe Umwelt 20³⁰
27 Dienstag	Kino 14⁴⁵
28 Mittwoch	?
29 Donnerstag	schwimmen mit Michael 17⁴⁵
30 Freitag	16⁰⁰ – 18⁰⁰ zu Hause helfen
31 Samstag	18⁰⁰ Klavierstunde Disko 19³⁰
1 Sonntag	13³⁵ segeln radfahren

Monika could say of Katja:

Katja will am Freitag in die Stadt gehen. *or*
Am Freitag will Katja in die Stadt gehen.

You saw this type of word order before in **Kapitel 2**, when you learned about German word order:

Wir spielen um 2 Uhr Fußball.
Um 2 Uhr spielen wir Fußball.

What is the position of the conjugated verbs in the above sentences[1]?

1. The conjugated verb is in second position.

23 Monikas Pläne fürs Wochenende

Read the letter that Monika has written to Katja,
then answer the questions that follow.

Liebe Katja,

Es freut mich, daß Du am Donnerstag kommst.
Hier sind meine Pläne fürs Wochenende: Am
Freitag will ich mit Dir in die Stadt gehen —
zuerst ein paar Klamotten kaufen (ich brauche
Tennisschuhe!), dann etwas essen, danach ins
Kino gehen.

Samstag ist immer mein Sporttag. Am
Vormittag können wir radfahren, baden gehen
(wir haben ein prima Schwimmbad!), und später
am Abend will Vati für uns ein Grillfest
machen. Neun Klassenkameraden kommen!
Was willst Du am Sonntag machen? Willst Du
wieder in die Stadt fahren? In ein Museum
gehen? In ein Café gehen? Oder willst Du
faulenzen?
Mach's gut und bis bald.

Deine Monika

1. Why is Monika writing to Katja? How do you know?
2. When will Katja visit Monika?
3. How long will she stay? How do you know?

24 Monikas Pläne

List Monika's plans for Friday and Saturday and her suggestions for Sunday. Include all
the words that indicate the sequence of the plans.

Am Freitag: **in die Stadt gehen**
Zuerst ...
Dann ...

25 Ihr macht Pläne

You and two of your friends are discussing your plans for the weekend. All of you are very
busy, but you want to get together. Decide on several things you could do and places you
could go together, then create a conversation discussing your plans.

Was machst du in deiner Freizeit?

What do you think students in Germany like to do when they have time to spend with their friends? We have asked a number of students from different places this question, but before you read their responses, write down what you think they will say. Then read these interviews and compare your ideas with what they say.

Sandra
Stuttgart

„Also, meine Freizeit verbringe ich am liebsten mit ein paar Freundinnen oder Freunden. Dann gehen wir abends in die Stadt Eis essen, oder wir setzen uns einfach in ein Café rein und reden. Aber am liebsten gehen wir halt tanzen."

Annika
Hamburg

„Ich bin bei den Pfadfindern; da fährt man halt am Wochenende auf Fahrt, und ja, mit denen mach' ich auch hauptsächlich ziemlich viel, auch mal außerhalb, ins Kino gehen und so — und sonst spiel' ich noch Klavier."

Marga
Bietigheim

„Während der Woche verabrede ich mich an sich nicht so oft, weil ich da ziemlich viel mit der Schule zu tun hab', Hausaufgaben und so. Aber sonst am Wochenende geh' ich eben abends weg ins Kino oder in die Disko. Und sonst tanz' ich und einmal in der Woche spiele ich Flöte."

Karsten
Hamburg

„Also, ich mach' als erstes natürlich Hausaufgaben und dann irgend etwas mit Sport, oder ich geh' in die Stadt einkaufen, oder meistens treff' ich mich mit meinen Freunden."

A. 1. Working with a partner, write beside each student's name where he or she likes to go and what he or she likes to do.

2. Compare the lists you have prepared for the four German students. Which activities do they have in common?

3. Discuss with your classmates which activities you and your friends like to do that are similar to those done by the students in Germany. Which are different?

B. Look at the list you made before you read the interviews. Does what you wrote match what the students say? If it is different, how? Where do your ideas about German students come from? How do you think students in Germany might describe a "typical" American student? Where might they get their ideas? Write a brief essay discussing these questions.

Ordering food and beverages; talking about how something tastes; paying the check

26 Im Café Freizeit

Read the menu of **Café Freizeit**, then list what you would order for yourself. Add up the cost of your snack. With a partner, compare your order and the amount each of you would spend.

IMBISS-KARTE

Café Freizeit

Für den kleinen Hunger und Durst

KLEINE SPEISEN

NUDELSUPPE MIT BROT	DM 4,50
KÄSEBROT	5,20
WURSTBROT	5,10
WIENER MIT SENF — 2 PAAR	5,80
PIZZA (15 CM)	
Nr. 1 mit Tomaten und Käse	6,00
Nr. 2 mit Wurst und Käse	6,50
Nr. 3 mit Wurst, Käse und Pilzen	8,50

EIS

FRUCHTEIS KUGEL	DM 1,10
SAHNEEIS KUGEL	1,30
EISBECHER	6,80

GETRÄNKE

1 TASSE KAFFEE		DM 4,30
1 KÄNNCHEN KAFFEE		7,60
1 TASSE CAPPUCCINO		5,20
1 GLAS TEE MIT ZITRONE		3,20

ALKOHOLFREIE GETRÄNKE

MINERALWASSER	0,5 l	DM	3,50
LIMONADE, FANTA	0,5 l		3,60
APFELSAFT	0,2 l		2,50
COLA	0,2 l		3,00

KUCHEN

APFELKUCHEN	STÜCK	DM	2,80
KÄSEKUCHEN	STÜCK		3,00

---

27 Hör gut zu!

You will hear four students saying what they want to eat and drink. Listen and decide what each one is ordering.

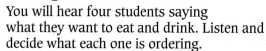

SO SAGT MAN DAS!

Ordering food and beverages

Here are some expressions you can use when you order something in a café or restaurant.

The waiter asks for your order:
- **Was bekommen Sie?**
- **Ja, bitte?**
- **Was essen Sie?**
- **Was möchten Sie?**
- **Was trinken Sie?**

You order:
- **Ich möchte ein Wurstbrot.**
- **Ich möchte ein Stück Kuchen, bitte.**
- **Einen Eisbecher, bitte!**
- **Ich trinke einen Apfelsaft.**
- **Ich bekomme einen Kaffee.**

You might ask your friend:
- **Was nimmst du?**
- **Was ißt du?**

Your friend might respond:
- **Ich nehme ein Käsebrot.**
- **Ich esse ein Eis.**

HEIKO: Was nimmst du?
MICHAEL: Ich nehme…

eine Nudelsuppe

ein Wurstbrot

ein Käsebrot

eine Pizza

ein Eis/
einen Eisbecher

ein Stück
Apfelkuchen

eine Tasse Kaffee

ein Glas Tee

28 Du hast Hunger!

Imagine that you are in **Café Freizeit**. You are very hungry and order a lot of food. Your partner plays the waiter, writing down everything you order, then tells the class what you have ordered. Switch roles.

BEISPIEL **Was bekommen Sie?**
DU **Ich esse … dann… und danach …**

Schon bekannt
Ein wenig *Grammatik*

Remember from **Kapitel 5**:
Ich möchte einen Pullover.

Now look at this sentence:
Ich möchte einen Eisbecher.

Name the nouns in these two sentences. What similarities do they have?[1]

Grammatik Stem-changing verbs

Remember the verb **nehmen** that you used in **Kapitel 5**? **Nehmen** has a change in the stem vowel of the **du**- and **er/sie** forms: **du nimmst, er/sie nimmt.** Another verb in this group is **essen** (*to eat*). Here are the forms of **essen**:

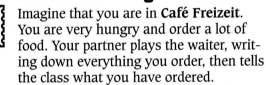

Ich	**esse** ein Eis.	Wir	**essen** Pizza.
Du	**ißt** eine Nudelsuppe?	Ihr	**eßt** Apfelkuchen.
Sie/Er	**ißt** ein Wurstbrot.	Sie *(pl)* / Sie	**essen** Obst.

29 Was wollen alle essen?

Du hast großen Hunger! Schau auf die Speisekarte von Café Freizeit auf Seite 154.

a. Was ißt du?
b. Was ißt dein Partner? Frag ihn!

LERNTRICK

Listening for gender cues. It is important to listen not only for meaning, but also for other cues that may be helpful. If someone asks: **Nimmst du einen Apfelsaft?** the **einen** tells you that **Apfelsaft** is a masculine noun. You can have your response ready immediately:

Ja, einen Apfelsaft, bitte. *or*
Ja, bitte! Der Apfelsaft ist wirklich gut.

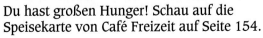
1. Both are masculine and in the accusative case.

SO SAGT MAN DAS!

Talking about how something tastes

If you want to ask how
something tastes, you ask:

Some possible responses are:

Wie schmeckt's?

- **Gut! Prima! Sagenhaft!**
- **Die Pizza schmeckt lecker!** (*tasty, delicious*)
- **Die Pizza schmeckt nicht.**

Schmeckt's?

- **Ja, gut!**
- **Nein, nicht so gut.**
- **Nicht besonders.** *Not especially.*

30 Wie schmeckt's?

1. Your partner was really hungry and ordered a lot to eat. Everything looks great! Ask him or her how the different dishes taste. (React to the foods ordered in Activity 29.)
2. The food doesn't taste very good. Ask your partner about different dishes that she or he has ordered. Then switch roles.

SO SAGT MAN DAS!

Paying the check

Calling the waiter's attention	**Hallo!**
Asking for the check	**Hallo! Ich will/möchte zahlen.**
Totaling up the check	**Das macht (zusammen)...**
Telling the waiter to keep the change	**Stimmt schon!**

31 Hör gut zu!

After Heiko and his friends eat, the waiter brings them the check. Listen as he adds up the bill, then write down each individual price you hear, the total, and what they round it off to as a tip.

Café Freizeit

geöffnet: Mo-Sa 10-10 Uhr
Sonntag: Ruhetag

6,—
5,60
3,50
3,00
———
18,10

32 Du willst zahlen

You have finished your meal. Tell the waiter you want to pay. Before you pay the check, the waiter mentions every item you ordered and adds up the total. Role-play this situation with a partner, using the orders below and the menu on page 154. Be polite!

1. Nudelsuppe mit Brot, Mineralwasser
2. Tasse Cappuccino, Käsekuchen, Sahneeis
3. Wurstbrot, Cola, Tee mit Zitrone

33 Kommst du mit?

Get together with two other classmates and role-play the following situations.

1. Your German pen pal is visiting you while you are in Wedel. Treat him or her to dinner at **Café Freizeit**. Talk about what both of you want to eat and drink. Order for the two of you. A waiter will take the order.
2. The waiter brings the order but can't remember who ordered what. Help him out.
3. While you are eating, you comment to each other about how the food tastes.
4. Your friend wants to order something else. Call the waiter over and tell him what else you want.
5. It is time to pay. Call the waiter and ask for the check. The waiter will name everything you ordered and add up the bill. You pay and leave a tip.

aUSSPRACHE

Richtig aussprechen/richtig lesen

A. To practice these sounds pronounce after your teacher or after the recording the words and sentences in bold.

1. The letter combination **ch**: The consonant combination **ch** can be pronounced two different ways. When preceded by the vowels **i** and **e**, it sounds similar to the *h* in the English word *huge*. When preceded by the vowels **a**, **o** or **u**, it is produced farther back in the throat.
   ich, Pech, dich / So ein Pech! Ich habe es nicht.
   ach, doch, Buch / Was macht Heiko am Wochenende? Spielt er Schach?

2. The letter **r**: The German **r** sound does not exist in English. To produce this sound, put the tip of your tongue behind your lower front teeth. Then tip your head back and pretend that you are gargling.
   rund, recht, Freizeit / Rolf, Rudi, und Rita gehen ins Café Freizeit.

3. The letter combination **er**: At the end of a word the letter combination **er** sounds almost like a vowel. It is similar to the *u* in the English word *but*.
   super, Lehrer, Bruder / Wo ist meine Schwester?

Richtig schreiben / Diktat

B. Write down the sentences that you hear.

ZUM LESEN

Wohin in Hamburg?

*P*eople who live in Wedel often go into Hamburg for a day of entertainment.

1. What are the two main types of ads on these pages?

2. a. Use context clues to guess the meaning of these German words. Match each word with its English equivalent.

   1) lädt   a) enjoy
   2) genießen   b) meeting
   3) Treffpunkt   place
   4) Bratkartoffel- c) a dish of
      gerichte   ice cream
   5) Eisbecher   d) invites
                      e) fried potato
                         dishes

b. What kinds of foods are advertised here? Which restaurant ad interests you the most?

c. Where can you eat Mexican food? On what day?

d. Where can you get a "great Eisbecher"? Where is this place located?

3. a. Where can you hear music? What kinds of music can you hear?

b. What are the names of the discos? How long is the **Liberty** open?

c. When (day and time) can you see Bonnie Tyler? Peter Gabriel? Will Lynyrd Skynyrd fans get to hear them on 13.4? If not, why not?

4. What is the social purpose of the **Milchbar**? What word supports your opinion?

5. Remembering the word you learned for "juice," find the word that means "juicy."

6. Assume you and your family are in Wedel. You want to go to Hamburg for two or three days.

a. To which places would you more likely go with your parents?

b. To which places would you more likely go with your friends?

c. Write a postcard to a friend telling of your plans for your weekend in Hamburg. Be sure to use sequencing words appropriately.

ANWENDUNG

1 Express the times shown in as many different ways as you can.

2 In each of the following reports an activity is mentioned. If the activity mentioned is shown in the photos below, match the activity with the appropriate photo.

3 Look at the photos. Your partner will ask you what you want to do. Choose three activities from above and tell your partner which ones you want to do and at what time you want to do them. Then switch roles.

4 You have a week off from school. What will you do? Jot down some plans in your calendar. Write down what you plan to do, when, and with whom. You need to study, too, so plan some time for that.

 5 Just after you've made your plans, a friend calls to find out what you are doing during your week off and suggests doing something together. Decide what you want to do and when you want to do it. Consult your calendar.

 6 Write in German a conversation you might have had when you last ate a meal or a snack in a restaurant. Include ordering your food, some comments on how it tasted, and paying for it.

Hausaufgaben machen   Eis essen

ins Einkaufszentrum gehen   lesen

Tennis spielen

in ein Museum gehen

schwimmen   ins Kino gehen

7

R O L L E N S P I E L

Du bist mit einem Freund in Hamburg. Ihr habt Hunger und möchtet etwas essen.

You are in a hurry for the Peter Gabriel concert, so you decide to put dinner off until later and just grab a snack at an **Imbiß-stand**. You also don't want to spend very much money—each of you is limited to 10 marks.

a. Create a conversation in which you discuss the possibilities that are available, decide what each of you wants, and figure out how much it will cost.

b. One partner can then play the role of vendor, and you can order the food and drink that each of you decided upon. After you receive your food, pay for it.

Verkauf am Fenster

Sensationell

1/2 Hähnchen 3,20

	3,00
Käsebrot	2,90
Wurstbrot	6,60
La Flute m. Schinken & Ananas	
Gr. Fladenbrot (Giros/Kochschinken/	8,40
Schinken/Spießbraten)	9,50
Giros mit Krautsalat	gr. 4,00
Currywurst, kl. 3,70	1,90
Rostbratwurst	1,90
Bockwurst	2,70
Schokoladeneis	2,70
Vanilleeis	2,80
Fruchteis	

	Becher 0,3	1,50	0,4	1,90
Cola	0,3	1,80	0,4	2,20
Milchshake	0,3	1,80	0,4	2,40
Apfelsaft	0,3	1,80	0,4	2,40
Orangensaft				1,95
Mineralwasser				
Fanta	0,3	1,30	0,4	1,80

KANN ICH'S WIRKLICH?

Can you start a conversation? (p. 145)

1 How would you greet a friend and ask how he or she is doing. If someone asks how you are doing, what could you say?

Can you tell time? (p. 146)

2 How would you ask what time it is? Say the times shown below, using expressions you learned in this chapter.

1. 1.00 **2.** 11.30 **3.** 9.50 **4.** 2.15 **5.** 7.55

Can you talk about when you do things? (p. 146)

3 **a.** Using the time expressions above, say when you and your friends intend to

a. go to the movies
b. go to a café
c. go to the swimming pool

4 How would you ask a friend when he intends to do the activities in Activity 3?

Can you make plans using wollen? (p. 150)

5 Say you intend to go to the following places and tell what you plan to do there. Establish a sequence: *first..., then...*

a. café
b. swimming pool
c. movies
d. department store
e. disco

6 How would you say that the following people want to go to a concert?

1. Michael
2. Silke
3. ihr
4. wir
5. Peter und Monika

Can you order food and beverages? (p. 154)

7 You are with some friends in a café. Order the following things for yourself.

a. (noodle) soup
b. a glass of tea with lemon
c. a cheese sandwich

8 Say that these people are going to eat the foods listed. Then say what you are going to eat (using **ich**). How would you ask your best friend what he or she is going to eat (using **du**)?

a. Michael - Käsekuchen
b. Holger und Julia - Apfelkuchen
c. Monika - Käsebrot
d. Ahmet und ich - Wiener mit Senf
e. Ich ...
f. Und du? Was ...?

Can you talk about how something tastes? (p. 156)

9 How would you ask a friend if his or her food tastes good? How might he or she respond?

Can you pay the check? (p. 156)

10 Ask the waiter for the check, then tell him to keep the change.

ERSTE STUFE

STARTING A CONVERSATION

Wie geht's (denn)? *How are you?*
Sehr gut! *Very well!*
Prima! *Great!*
Gut! *Good/Well!*
Es geht. *Okay.*
So lala. *So-so.*

Schlecht. *Bad(ly).*
Miserabel. *Miserable.*

TELLING TIME

Wie spät ist es? *What time is it?*
Wieviel Uhr ist es? *What time is it?*
Um wieviel Uhr ...? *At what time...?*

Viertel nach *a quarter after*
halb (eins, zwei, usw.) *half past (twelve, one, etc.)*
Viertel vor ... *a quarter to ...*
(zehn) vor ... *(ten) till ...*
um (ein) Uhr ... *at (one) o'clock*

ZWEITE STUFE

MAKING PLANS

Wohin? *Where (to)?*
in ein Café/ins Café *to a café*
ein Eis essen *to eat ice cream*
in die Stadt gehen *to go downtown*

ins Schwimmbad gehen *to go to the (swimming) pool*
baden gehen *to go swimming*
ins Kino gehen *to go to the movies*
einen Film sehen *to see a movie*

in eine Disko gehen *to go to a disco*
tanzen gehen *to go dancing*
ins Konzert gehen *to go to a concert*
wollen *to want (to)*
er/sie will *he/she wants (to)*

DRITTE STUFE

ORDERING FOOD AND BEVERAGES

Was bekommen Sie? *What will you have?*
Ich bekomme ... *I'll have...*
eine Tasse Kaffee *a cup of coffee*
ein Glas Tee *a (glass) cup of tea*
mit Zitrone *with lemon*
eine Limo(nade) *a lemon-flavored soda*
eine Nudelsuppe *noodle soup*
mit Brot *with bread*
ein Käsebrot *cheese sandwich*
einen Eisbecher *a dish of ice cream*

ein Wurstbrot *sandwich with cold cuts*
eine Pizza *pizza*
Apfelkuchen *apple cake*
ein Eis *ice cream*
essen *to eat*
er/sie ißt *he/she eats*

TALKING ABOUT HOW FOOD TASTES

Wie schmeckt's *How does it taste?*
Schmeckt's? *Does it taste good?*
Sagenhaft! *Great!*

Lecker! *Tasty! Delicious!*
Nicht besonders. *Not really.*

PAYING THE CHECK

Hallo! Ich möchte/will zahlen! *The check please!*
Das macht (zusammen) ... *That comes to....*
Stimmt (schon)! *Keep the change.*

OTHER WORDS AND PHRASES

Paß auf! *Watch out!*
nun *now*

Komm mit nach

München!

München

Landeshauptstadt von Bayern

Einwohner: 1,3 Millionen

Fluß: München liegt an der Isar

Berühmte Gebäude: Frauenkirche, Rathaus, Maximilianeum, Theatinerkirche

Museen: Alte und Neue Pinakothek, Deutsches Museum, Glyptothek

Industrien: Elektrotechnik und Elektronik, Automobilindustrie, Brauereien, Verlage, Filmindustrie

Bedeutende Münchner: Josef von Fraunhofer (1787-1826, Physiker); Moritz von Schwind (1804-1871, Maler); Karl Valentin (1882-1948, Komiker); Annette Kolb (1870-1967, Schriftstellerin)

Typische Gerichte: Schweinshaxe, Leberkäs, Weißwürste

Foto ① **Ein Blick über die Dächer von München**

DÄNEMARK
Nordsee
Ostsee
NIEDERLANDE
POLEN
★ Berlin
BEL.
Frankfurt
TSCHECH. REPUBLIK
LUX.
B A Y E R N
FRANK-REICH
München
SCHWEIZ
ÖSTERREICH

München

Munich is the capital of the state of Bavaria. Famous for its museums, theaters, and sports facilities (the city hosted the 1972 Olympic Games), Munich is also a center for automobile, computer, and aerospace industries.

2 Two men in **Lederhosen,** the traditional folk costume of **Oberbayern** *(Upper Bavaria).* The man on the right is also wearing a hat with a **Gamsbart** made from the hair of the chamois, an antelope-like animal living in the Alps.

3 A busy street in the center of **München** with a view of the twin towers of the **Frauenkirche.** In the foreground people enjoy a meal in a typical open-air café.

4 A maypole with figures showing scenes from everyday life. At the bottom you see the blue and white coat of arms of Bavaria and the **Münchner Kindl** symbolizing Munich.

5 A view of the **Marienplatz** showing the **Mariensäule**, with the Old Town Hall in the background. This is part of the **Fußgängerzone** (pedestrian zone).

6 The **Viktualienmarkt** in the center of **München** offers a wide variety of fruits and vegetables. Many **Münchner** come here for their daily shopping.

*Chapters 7, 8, and 9 take place in Munich. The students in these chapters attend different schools. Flori goes to the **Einstein-Gymnasium**, Markus and Claudia attend the **Theodolinden-Gymnasium**, and Mara goes to the **Rudolf-Diesel Realschule**.*

7 Mara, Flori, Markus, and Claudia welcome you to Munich

7

Zu Hause helfen

① Wir gehen in den Englischen Garten. Kommst du mit?

What is a typical Saturday like for teens in German-speaking countries? They get together with friends, make plans according to the weather, and help around the house. What do you do on Saturday? Do you see your friends? Do you also help with chores? If so, what do you do? What do you think German teens might do to help at home?

In this chapter you will learn

- to extend and respond to an invitation; to express obligations
- to talk about how often you have to do things; to ask for and to offer help and tell someone what to do
- to talk about the weather

And you will

- listen to German weather reports
- read weather forecasts from a German newspaper
- make a list of the chores you have to do
- find out how teenagers in the German-speaking countries help around the house

② Du kannst für mich den Rasen mähen.

③ Ich muß Staub saugen.

Los geht's!

 ## Was mußt du machen?

Look at the photos that accompany the story.
Who are the people pictured? What are they doing?
Where are they? What do you think they are talking about?
What do you suppose will happen in the story?

 Claudia

 Flori

 Markus

 Mara

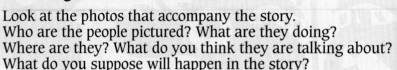

Claudia, hallo!

Wohin geht's?

In den Englischen Garten. Komm doch mit!

Das geht nicht. Ich muß zu Hause helfen.

Was mußt du denn tun, Claudia?

Schade, daß du nicht mitkommen kannst! Es ist heute so schönes Wetter zum Radeln.

Ich muß mein Zimmer aufräumen, den Müll sortieren, das ...

Ein Moment! Ich hab' eine Idee. Fahren wir alle zu Claudia und helfen ihr.

Prima Idee! — Ja, dann ist sie schnell fertig und kann mitkommen!

Das ist lieb von euch.

BEI CLAUDIA

Markus, du und der Flori, ihr könnt den Müll sortieren. Die Flaschen kommen hier rein, die Dosen kommen da rein.

Und die Zeitungen?

Die Zeitungen kommen in den Korb da.

1 Was passiert hier?

Do you understand what is happening in the **Foto-Roman**? Check your comprehension by answering these questions. Don't be afraid to guess.

1. Where do Claudia's three friends (Mara, Markus, and Flori) invite Claudia to go?
2. Does Claudia go along? Why or why not?
3. What does Flori suggest?
4. What are some things the friends do at Claudia's house?
5. Is the weather good enough for an outing in the park? What about tomorrow's weather?
6. At the end of the story, there is still a problem. What is it?

2 Genauer lesen

Reread the conversations. Which words or phrases do the characters use to

1. invite someone   2. express obligation   3. name chores   4. describe the weather

3 Was ist richtig?

Choose the best answer to complete each of the following statements.

1. Claudia muß ======.
   a. in den Englischen Garten gehen   b. zu Hause helfen   c. radeln

2. Claudias Freunde wollen helfen. Das findet Claudia ======.
   a. furchtbar   b. nicht schlecht   c. lieb

3. Mara will ======.
   a. die Katze füttern   b. den Müll sortieren   c. Claudias Klamotten nicht aufräumen

4. Die Katze ist ======.
   a. schon im Haus   b. nicht zu Hause   c. im Englischen Garten

4 Was paßt zusammen?

Match each statement or question on the left with an appropriate response on the right.

1. Wohin geht's?   a. Das geht nicht.
2. Komm doch mit!   b. Gut! Mach' ich!
3. Was mußt du tun?   c. In den Englischen Garten.
4. Du kannst den Müll sortieren.   d. Ich muß zu Hause helfen.
5. Was sagt der Wetterbericht?   e. Ja. Wir müssen sie suchen.
6. Ist die Katze wieder weg?   f. Morgen regnet es.

5 Nacherzählen

Put the sentences in a logical order to make a brief summary of the **Foto-Roman**.

1. Mara, Markus und Flori wollen in den Englischen Garten gehen.

Dann wollen sie gehen, aber Micky ist weg.

Sie müssen zuerst die Katze suchen.

Sie müssen den Müll sortieren, das Zimmer aufräumen, Staub saugen und die Katze füttern.

Aber Claudia kommt nicht mit, denn sie muß zu Hause helfen.

Claudias Freunde wollen helfen.

Extending and responding to an invitation; expressing obligations

Was mußt du zu Hause tun? — Ich muß ...

mein Zimmer
aufräumen

das Bett machen

meine Klamotten
aufräumen

die Katze füttern

den Tisch decken

den Tisch abräumen

das Geschirr spülen

die Blumen gießen

den Müll sortieren

den Rasen mähen

Staub saugen

die Fenster putzen

6 Was muß Claudia tun?

Claudia needs to make a list of all the things she has to do around the house. Help her out by completing each of the items on the left with the appropriate verb from the box.

1. das Zimmer
2. das Bett
3. den Rasen
4. die Katze
5. den Tisch
6. das Geschirr
7. den Müll
8. die Blumen

spülen   aufräumen
füttern
machen   mähen
gießen
decken   sortieren

7 Hör gut zu!

Jürgen has a few chores to do before he and Peter can go to the movies. Listen to their conversation and put the illustrations below in the correct order.

a.

b.

c.

d.

e.

SO SAGT MAN DAS!

Extending and responding to an invitation

In **Kapitel 6** you learned to make plans. How would you invite someone to come along with you?

You might ask:
  Willst du in den Englischen Garten? *or*
  Wir wollen in den Englischen Garten. Komm doch mit! *or*
  Möchtest du mitkommen?

Your friend might accept: Or decline:
  Ja, gern! *or*   **Das geht nicht.** *or*
  Toll! Ich komme gern mit.   **Ich kann leider nicht.**

8 Hör gut zu!

Listen to the conversations and decide if the person being invited is accepting or declining the invitation. What is each person being invited to do?

SO SAGT MAN DAS!

Expressing obligations

If you decline an invitation, you might want to explain your prior obligations.

You might say:
  Ich habe keine Zeit. Ich muß zu Hause helfen.

Your friend might ask: You might respond:
  Was mußt du denn tun?   **Ich muß den Rasen mähen.**

What do you think the phrase **keine Zeit** means?[1]

1. *no time*

9 Kommst du mit?

Think of several places you would like to go and invite a classmate to come along. He or she will accept or decline and give a reason. Here are some suggestions to help you.

ins Kino gehen   in ein Konzert gehen
Tennis spielen   ein Eis essen
in die Disko gehen   schwimmen gehen

10 Was ist los?

What would you tell this little boy to do instead of what he is doing? (Use **Du mußt ...**)

a.   b.   c.   d.   e.

11 Ich muß zu Hause ...

Make a list in German of the things you do around the house, then take turns asking your classmates what they do and telling them what chores you do.

Grammatik   The verb **müssen**

The verb **müssen** expresses obligation and means that you *have to* or *must* do something. Here are the forms of **müssen**:

Ich **muß** zu Hause helfen.   Wir **müssen** das Bett machen.
Du **mußt** das Geschirr spülen.   Ihr **müßt** den Tisch decken.
Er/Sie **muß** den Rasen mähen.   Sie(pl)/ Sie **müssen** auch helfen.

Müssen is usually used with a second verb (an infinitive), although the second verb can be omitted if the meaning is obvious.

12 Was müssen alle tun?

Thomas has his friends over to help with spring-cleaning. Complete his sentences as he explains what everyone must do.

1. Zuerst muß ich ...   2. Mara und ich, wir ...   3. Du ...   4. Und die Nikki ...

13 Was mußt du machen?

Using the list you made in Activity 11, you and your partner will take turns asking each other which chores you do around the house. As you talk, make a list of what your partner does. Compare lists to make sure you both understood everything correctly.

14 Und meine Familie

What are some of the things that your other family members have to do around the house? Share the information with your classmates.

15 Ich lade dich ein

a. First make a list of things you would like to do this afternoon and when you plan to do them.

b. Then invite your partner to do some of the activities on your list. Your partner will accept or decline and give a reason. Switch roles and let your partner invite you. Make a list of the things you agreed to do together and share your plans with the class.

16 Ein Brief

a. Read Markus' letter to his friend Roland and answer the questions that follow.

1. Wer kommt am Wochenende nach München?
2. Was wollen Markus und Flori am Freitag machen?
3. Was muß Markus am Samstag machen?
4. Gefällt es Markus, daß er zu Hause helfen muß? Woher weißt du das?

b. If Markus were coming to visit you this weekend, what would the two of you do? Write him a letter inviting him to do whatever you have planned. Be sure to tell him any chores you have to do this weekend that might get in the way of your plans.

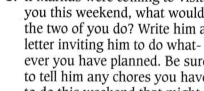

4. März 1994

Lieber Roland!

Mensch, das freut mich, daß Du am Wochenende hier in München bist!
Flori und ich wollen am Freitag ins Konzert. Die „Jungen Katzen" spielen! Toll, nicht! Willst Du auch mitkommen?
Am Samstag muß ich wie immer zu Hause helfen. Wie blöd! Ich muß den Rasen mähen, mein Zimmer aufräumen, die Blumen gießen und auch Staub saugen. Ach, das ist zu viel, nicht? Mußt Du auch zu Hause so viel tun?
Na ja, macht nichts. Am Sonntag hab' ich frei. Du, Flori und ich machen alles, was wir wollen.

Bis dann!
Dein Markus

Was tust du für die Umwelt?

In both the old and new states, Germans today are very aware of the need to protect the environment. Young people all over Germany are involved in projects that range from recycling to cleaning up rivers and forests. We asked several students what they do for the environment, and here is what they told us.

LANDESKUNDE

Marga, *Bietigheim*
„Also bei uns zu Hause wird jeder Müll sortiert, eben in Plastik, Aluminium, Papier und so weiter. Das halten wir also ziemlich streng ein. Ja, und wenn schönes Wetter ist und es sich vermeiden läßt, mit dem Auto zu fahren, nehme ich lieber das Fahrrad."

Fabian, *Hamburg*
„Wir tun für die Umwelt, daß wir einmal Müll vermeiden, daß wir unser Altpapier wegbringen, Glas sammeln und möglichst auch Glas, was wiederverwertet werden kann, kaufen, also sprich Mehrwegflaschen, und daß wir halt möglichst wenig Putzmittel oder so sparsam brauchen."

Elke, *Berlin*
„Ich habe mit meinen Eltern angefangen, Flaschen zu sortieren und regelmäßig zum Container zu bringen. Der Müll wird meistens auch separat sortiert und dann, ja, einzeln weggebracht. Jetzt zähl' ich dazu, daß man mit dem Bus zur Schule fährt und nicht mit dem Auto."

A. 1. Write the names of the students interviewed, and beside each name, write what that student does for the environment. What things do they have in common?
2. Think about what you have learned about Germany. Do you think the environmental concerns of the Germans are the same as those of Americans? Why or why not?

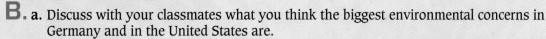

3. Compare what you and your friends do for the environment with what these German students do. Is there anything you do that was not mentioned in these interviews?

B. a. Discuss with your classmates what you think the biggest environmental concerns in Germany and in the United States are.
b. Write in German your answer to the question **Was tust du für die Umwelt?**

Talking about how often you have to do things; asking for and offering help and telling someone what to do

SO SAGT MAN DAS!

Talking about how often you have to do things

You might want to ask a friend how often he or she has to do certain things, such as chores.

You might ask:

Wie oft mußt du Staub saugen?

Und wie oft mußt du den Tisch decken?

Und wie oft mußt du den Rasen mähen?

Your friend might respond:

Einmal in der Woche.

Jeden Tag.

Ungefähr zweimal im Monat.

Look at the words **einmal** and **zweimal**. What words do you recognize within each of these words?[1] What do you think the phrases **einmal in der Woche** and **zweimal im Monat** mean?[2] How would you say "three times a week"?[3] "Four times a month"?[4] What does the expression **jeden Tag** mean?[5] (*Hint: Look at the chore the speaker above does **jeden Tag**. How often would you do that task?*)

WORTSCHATZ

Wie oft ... ?
einmal, zweimal, dreimal
... in der Woche
... im Monat
immer   *always*
oft   *often*
manchmal   *sometimes*
nie   *never*

17 Sätze bauen

Wie viele Sätze kannst du bauen? Wann und wie oft machst du das alles?

Im Herbst	spiele	(ein)mal in der Woche	Karten
Im Frühling	spüle	(zwei)mal im Monat	Gitarre
Im Winter	putze	nie	Klavier
Im Sommer	gehe	oft	Geschirr
Am Montag	decke	manchmal	die Fenster
Am Wochen-ende	räume ... auf	immer	ins Konzert
Nach der Schule			den Tisch
Am Nachmittag			Fußball
Am Abend			Basketball
			in eine Disko
			mein Zimmer

ich

1. **ein(s), zwei** 2. *once a week, twice a month* 3. **dreimal in der Woche** 4. **viermal im Monat** 5. *every day*

18 Hör gut zu!

Listen as Markus describes when and how often he does things. First make a calendar page for one week and then fill in a possible schedule for his activities.

S P R A C H T I P

Often, other elements besides the subject are placed at the beginning of a sentence to give them special emphasis. For example, if someone asks you: **Kannst du heute Volleyball spielen?**, you might respond: **Nein, heute muß ich zu Hause helfen, aber morgen kann ich sicher spielen.** The time expressions are placed first, because time is the most important issue in this conversation. By putting something other than the subject in first position, you not only add variety to your conversations but express yourself more exactly.

SO SAGT MAN DAS!

Asking for and offering help and telling someone what to do

If your friend has a lot to do, you might offer to help. Then he or she could explain what to do.

You might ask:
> **Was kann ich für dich tun?** *or*
> **Kann ich etwas für dich tun?**

Your friend might answer:
> **Ja, du kannst den Müll sortieren.** *or*
> **Willst du für mich Staub saugen?**

You agree:
> **Gut! Mach' ich!**

What are the English equivalents of the phrases **für dich** and **für mich**?[1]

Ein wenig *Grammatik*

The words **kann** and **kannst** are forms of the verb **können**, a modal auxiliary verb. **Kann** is a cognate. What does it mean?[2] Here are the forms of **können**:

ich	**kann**	wir	**können**
du	**kannst**	ihr	**könnt**
er/sie	**kann**	sie (pl) Sie	**können**

19 Du kannst für mich ...

Several people are offering to help their friends around the house. Create exchanges for the pictures below.

BEISPIEL

Können wir etwas für dich tun? Ja, ihr könnt den Rasen mähen. Danke!

1. *for me/for you*; 2. *can*

20 Peter macht ein Geschäft

Katrin and her brother, Peter, are at home trying to get their chores done for the weekend. Read the conversation and answer the questions below.

KATRIN   Ach, ich hab' heute viel zu tun. He, du Peter! Kannst du etwas für mich tun?
PETER   Vielleicht.
KATRIN   Kannst du die Blumen gießen?
PETER   Ja, gern. Was kann ich noch für dich tun?
KATRIN   Müll sortieren?
PETER   Okay, aber das kostet fünf Mark. Danke!

Ayla und Mario kommen vorbei.

MARIO   Na, Katrin und Peter, was macht ihr? Können wir etwas für euch tun?
PETER   Sicher! Ihr könnt für uns die Blumen gießen und dann den Müll sortieren. Geht das?
MARIO   Klar. Wir helfen gern!

1. What does Katrin ask her brother Peter to do?
2. What kind of a deal does Peter make with Katrin?
3. How does Peter manage to get out of his end of the bargain?
4. Compare the following sentences from the conversations above: **Was kann ich noch für dich tun?** and **Können wir etwas für euch tun?** To whom do the pronouns **dich** and **euch** refer in the conversations?
5. Now compare these sentences: **Kannst du etwas für mich tun?** and **Du kannst für uns die Blumen gießen.** To whom do the pronouns **mich** and **uns** refer?
6. Which of these pronouns are used for talking to others? Which ones are used to talk about yourself?
7. What is the English equivalent for each of these pronouns?

Grammatik   The accusative pronouns

In **Kapitel 5** you learned the accusative forms of the third person pronouns **er, sie, es,** and **sie** (pl). They are **ihn, sie, es,** and **sie.** The first and second person pronouns have these forms:

	nominative	*accusative*		*nominative*	*accusative*
first	ich	mich	*second*	du	dich
person	wir	uns	*person*	ihr	euch

The accusative forms are used as direct objects, as in **Ich besuche dich morgen,** or as objects of prepositions, such as **für,** as in **Du kannst für mich den Müll sortieren.** To ask for whom someone is doing something, use **für wen: Für wen machst du das?**

21 Was kann ich für dich kaufen?

Mara is going to the **Schreibwarenladen** to buy a few things for herself. Before she leaves she asks some friends if she can buy anything for them. Create an exchange for each picture, telling what Mara would ask, and how the person or people pictured would respond.

BEISPIEL   MARA   **Kann ich etwas für dich kaufen?**
               MARKUS   **Ja, bitte. Du kannst für mich einen Bleistift kaufen.**

1.   2.   3.   4.

22 Zu Hause helfen

Two of your friends are coming over to help you with your chores so that you can go swimming together. Before they arrive, make a list of six chores you have to do today. Then, with your partners, develop a conversation in which your friends offer to help and you discuss together who will do each of the chores. Be creative!

23 Arbeit suchen

You want to earn extra money doing odd jobs, so you need to place an ad in several public places. Include in your ad the following information: which chores you do, how often you can work, how much you charge, on which days of the week you are available, and how you can be reached.

Und dann noch . . .

der Vogel   die Maus

das Meer-
schweinchen   der Fisch

das Kaninchen   der Hamster

24 Für mein Notizbuch

Schreib, was du zu Hause alles machen mußt! Wann und wie oft machst du das? Was machst du gern? Was machst du nicht gern? Hast du ein Haustier? Wie heißt es? Wer füttert das Tier?

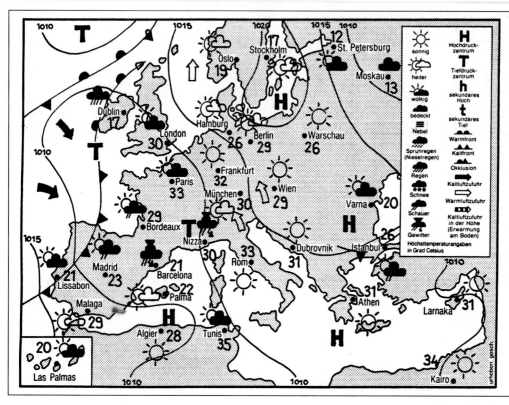

Deutscher Wetterdienst Vorhersagekarte für 9. Juni 1993 12 Uhr (UTC)

Lage: Am Rande einer Hochdruckzone über Osteuropa gelangt auch weiterhin Warmluft nach Deutschland.

Vorhersage: Am Mittwoch sonnig und trocken, dabei Temperaturanstieg auf 28 bis 32, im Nordosten auf Werte um 26 Grad. Nachts vielfach klar, Tiefstwerte um 16 Grad. Schwacher, tagsüber auflebender Wind aus unterschiedlichen Richtungen.

Aussichten: Am Donnerstag sonnig, im Tagesverlauf im Süden und Westen einzelne Gewitter, sehr warm. Am Freitag von Westen her aufkommende Bewölkung und nachfolgend Schauer und Gewitter, etwas kühler:

25 Was sagt der Wetterbericht?

Answer the following questions about the weather map shown above.

1. What area of the world is this weather map for?
2. What kinds of information can you get from the map?
3. Look at the table of symbols and the words that go with them. Can you figure out what each word means?
4. Which cities are the coldest? What do you think the reason for this is?
5. Name three cities where you might need an umbrella.
6. Name three cities where you might do outdoor activities.
7. List the words in the weather forecast that describe the weather for Thursday and Friday.

Das Wetter

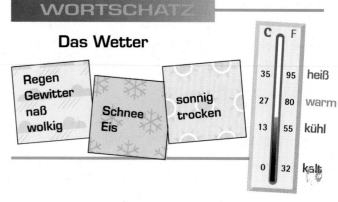

Regen
Gewitter
naß
wolkig

Schnee
Eis

sonnig
trocken

C	F	
35	95	heiß
27	80	warm
13	55	kühl
0	32	kalt

SO SAGT MAN DAS!

Talking about the weather

For some plans you make with your friends, you might first need to know about the weather.

You could ask:

Wie ist das Wetter heute?

Or you might want to ask about tomorrow:

Wie ist das Wetter morgen?

Or you might want to ask for specific information:

Regnet es heute?
Schneit es heute abend?
Wieviel Grad haben wir heute?

Some possible responses are:

Heute regnet es.
Wolkig und kühl.

Sonnig, aber kalt.

Ich glaube schon.
Nein, es schneit nicht.
Ungefähr 10 Grad.

What do you think the word **Grad** means?[1] Look at the response for a clue. When you tell someone the temperature, you might not know exactly what it is, so you say **ungefähr** ... What do you think **ungefähr** means?[2]

Ein wenig Grammatik

What do you notice about the verb that is used to ask and tell about the weather for tomorrow? The present tense is often used when referring to the near future. The meaning is made clear with words such as **morgen**. How would you invite a German friend to go to the movies tomorrow?[3]

26 Hör gut zu!

Listen to the weather reports from German radio. For each report determine which activity fits best with the weather described.

a.

b.

c.

d.

27 Wie ist das Wetter bei euch?

With your partner, discuss the weather where you live. Include the following topics in your discussion. For additional words, see page 323.

1. Wie ist das Wetter heute?
2. Wieviel Grad haben wir heute?
3. Und was sagt der Wetterbericht für morgen?
4. Wie ist das Wetter im Januar? Und im Juli?
5. Und im April? Und im Oktober?

1. *degree* 2. *approximately* 3. **Ich gehe morgen ins Kino. Kommst du mit?**

EIN WENIG LANDESKUNDE

Weather in the German-speaking countries is extremely variable, depending on the latitude and seasons. These countries usually get a lot of rainfall. Summers are often rainy, and winters can be cold, especially in the Alps. As in other European countries, German-speaking countries use the Celsius system of measuring temperature, rather than the Fahrenheit system. Look at the thermometer. If it were 35°C would you need a jacket? If the temperature fell below 0°C would you expect rain or snow? What is a comfortable room temperature in Celsius? Look at the weather map on p. 182. If you were in Moscow, what kinds of clothes would you be wearing? In Athens?

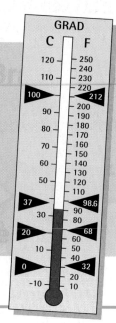

WORTSCHATZ

Wie ist das Wetter im …?

Januar	März	Mai	Juli	September	November
Februar	April	Juni	August	Oktober	Dezember

28 Gespräche

Put the following sentences in the correct order to form conversations based on the pictures below.

1. BRITTE   Hallo, Gupse! Gehen wir morgen schwimmen?

1. HANNES   Tag, Jörg! Ich geh' ins Kino. Kommst du mit?

Toll! Also, bis morgen!

Ja, klar. Aber was sagt der Wetterbericht?

Gut! Dann gehen wir schwimmen.

Morgen ist es sonnig und warm.

Gern! Du kannst für mich die Blumen gießen.

Nein, ich kann nicht. Ich muß den Rasen mähen.

Gut! Mach' ich! Aber schau mal, Hannes! Es regnet jetzt!

Ach, dann gehen wir doch ins Kino!

Brauchst du Hilfe, Jörg?

29 Ein Wetterbericht für ...

Using the weather map on page 182, choose a city and write a weather report for that city. Describe what the weather is like there.

30 Pläne machen

With a partner, pretend that you are meeting tomorrow in the city that you chose for Activity 29. You would like to invite your friend to do something special that is appropriate for the expected weather. Create a conversation in which you invite your partner to do something. He or she will ask about the weather, and you say what you know about it. Your partner can either accept or decline the invitation. Then switch roles and create another conversation, using your partner's city.

au**A** U /x/ S S e u P R ǝ A C /ts/ H E ö

Richtig aussprechen / Richtig lesen

A. To practice the following sounds, say the words and sentences below after your teacher or after the recording.

1. **The letter o:** In **Kapitel 3** you learned how to pronounce the letter **o** as a long vowel, as in **Oma**. However, when the letter **o** is followed by two or more consonants, it is pronounced as a short vowel, like the *o* in the English word *cot*.
   wolkig, Sonne, Woche / Im Oktober ist es sonnig und trocken.

2. **The letter u:** In **Kapitel 3** you learned how to pronounce the letter **u** as a long vowel, as in **super**. However, when the letter **u** is followed by two or more consonants, it is pronounced as a short vowel, like the *u* in the English word *put*.
   uns, muß, putzen / Mutti, ich muß die Fenster putzen.

3. **The letter l:** The letter **l** is pronounced like the *l* in the English word *million*. It is much more tense than the *l* sound in the English word *bill*.
   Müll, kühl, April / Der Lehrer kann im Juli mit dem Müll helfen.

4. **The consonant combination th:** The combination **th** within the same syllable is pronounced the same as the letter **t** in German.
   Theater, Mathe, Theatinerkirche / Wie komme ich zur Theatinerkirche und zum Theater?

5. **The letter combination pf:** The consonant combination **pf** sounds similar to the *pf* combination in English, as in the word *cupful*. However, in German this letter combination often occurs at the beginning of a word and is pronounced as one sound.
   Pfennig, Pfund, Kopfsalat / Zwei Pfund Pflaumen kosten neunundneunzig Pfennig.

Richtig schreiben/Diktat

B. Write down the words and sentences that you hear.

Wem hilfst du?

LESETRICK

Finding relationships between ideas. Subordinating conjunctions (words such as *if, when, because,* or *although* in English) indicate the relationship of the idea in the dependent clause to the idea in the main clause. For example, they may indicate when or under what conditions (**wenn**), a reason (**weil**), a concession (**obwohl**), or introduce an opinion or fact (**daß**). Knowing the meaning of a conjunction can help you guess the meaning of a sentence, even if you do not understand each word.

Weißt du noch? Using visual clues, such as illustrations or photos, will give you advance information about a text before you try to read it.

1. Before you try to read these three interviews, look at the title and at the photos. What do you expect the articles to be about?
2. What do these three texts have in common? What kind of texts do you think they are?
3. You probably figured out that these articles have to do with young people helping others. Working in groups of three or four students, write as many German phrases as you can that have to do with offering to help people.
4. Read the interview questions. Even though you may not know all the words in each question, you can probably figure out what is being asked. With a partner, write what you think is being asked in each question.

WEM HILFST DU?

Helfen Jugendliche ihren Eltern und Freunden? Verdienen sie dabei Taschengeld?

Oder bieten sie Hilfe freiwillig an? JUMA - Reporter Bernd hat sich umgehört.

Hallo Heiko!

Wem hilfst du? Ich helfe meiner Mutter.

Und wobei hilfst du? Ab und zu bei der Hausarbeit. Zum Beispiel helfe ich meiner Mutter beim Staubsaugen oder beim Wäscheaufhängen. Mein Zimmer räume ich allerdings seltener auf. Dazu habe ich meistens keine Lust. Und das Auto wäscht mein Vater lieber selbst. Dann wird es sauberer als bei mir.

Bekommst du etwas für deine Hilfe? Nein. Aber wenn ich längere Zeit nichts mache, schimpfen meine Eltern. Natürlich haben sie damit recht, wenn ich faul bin.

Gibt es Menschen oder besondere Organisationen, denen du gerne helfen würdest? Ich weiß jetzt nichts Spezielles. Aber ich weiß, wem ich nicht gerne helfen würde: aufdringlichen Freunden.

Warum hilfst du anderen Menschen? Ich finde wichtig, daß man anderen eine Last abnimmt. Außerdem ist Mithilfe eine nette Geste, über die sich wahrscheinlich jeder freut.

Hallo Tina!

Wem hilfst Du? Meiner Familie, meinen Freunden und meinen Bekannten.

Und wobei hilfst Du? Ich passe auf Kinder auf oder helfe meiner Schwester bei den Hausaufgaben. Im Haushalt mache ich eigentlich alles: Spülen, Bügeln oder Putzen.

Bekommst Du etwas für Deine Hilfe? Ich helfe freiwillig, obwohl ich meiner Schwester die Hausaufgaben nicht so gerne erkläre. Meinen Eltern und Bekannten biete ich auch schon mal Hilfe an.

Gibt es Menschen oder besondere Organisationen, denen Du gerne helfen würdest? Ja. Ich möchte gerne einmal in einem Kinderhort mitarbeiten. Das ist bestimmt anstrengend, aber interessant.

Warum hilfst du anderen Menschen? Wichtig für mich ist es, Pflichten zu erfüllen. Anderen zu helfen, ist eine Pflicht.

Hallo Sven

Wem hilfst du? Ich helfe meistens meinen Freunden.

Und wobei hilfst du? Eigentlich bei allem, was mit Schule zu tun hat. Meistens aber bei Hausaufgaben und Prüfungsvorbereitungen. Nachhilfestunden in Biologie oder Chemie gebe ich ziemlich regelmäßig, weil ich in diesen Fächern ganz gut bin.

Bekommst du etwas für Deine Hilfe? Ja, manchmal. Ich bessere mein Taschengeld mit Nachhilfe auf.

Gibt es Menschen oder besondere Organisationen, denen du gerne helfen würdest? Allen netten Leuten helfe ich gerne.

Warum hilfst du anderen Menschen? Es ist schön, wenn sie sich über Mithilfe freuen.

5. Scan the articles and list any subordinating conjunctions that you find. Using the information in the **Lesetrick,** determine what you expect each of the clauses introduced by these conjunctions to contain: a condition, a reason, a concession, an opinion, or a statement of fact. Write your guess beside the corresponding conjunction.

6. Read each clause that begins with a subordinating conjunction. Can you determine what the clause means? Now read the entire sentence. What does each sentence mean?

7. Now read the articles for the following information:
   a. Whom do these young people help? What are some of the things they do to help?
   b. When do Heiko's parents complain? Does Heiko think they have a right to complain? How do you know? What does Heiko say about "taking a burden from others"?
   c. What does Tina not like to do? Where does she want to work someday? What does she say is a "duty"?
   d. Why does Sven tutor other students in biology and chemistry? Whom does he like to help?

8. If you had been asked these questions by *Juma,* how would you have answered them?

9. Imagine that you will spend the next year as an exchange student with a German family. Write a letter to your host family and include an explanation of some of the chores you regularly do at home. Offer to do them for your German family while you are there.

ANWENDUNG

1 You will hear five students invite their friends to do something. Sometimes their friends accept, and sometimes they decline and give a reason. Listen to the exchanges and write the information you hear. Compare your notes with those of a classmate. The chart to the right will help you organize your information.

invitation	accept/decline	reason
BEISPIEL schwimmen gehen	kommt nicht	muß Zimmer aufräumen

2 Below is a page from Flori's calendar for the month of **März**. Take turns asking and telling your partner when and how often Flori does the activities. Now make your own calendar page. Fill in all the activities you do in a typical month. Describe to your partner the things you wrote on your calendar, and he or she will try to find out when and how often you do them. Then switch roles.

März

Mo	Di	Mi	Do	Fr	Sa	So
	1 Staub saugen	2	3	4 Müll sortieren	5 Fenster putzen 4:00 Fußball spielen	6
7 9:30 mit Michael ins Konzert	8 Staub saugen	9 3:30 Klavier= unterricht 7:00 Volleyball	10	11 9:00 Disko	12 Rasen mähen 4:00 Fußball spielen	13
14 8:30 Kino mit Sabine	15 Staub saugen	16 3:30 Klavier= unterricht	17	18 Müll sortieren	19 Fenster putzen 4:00 Fußball spielen	20
21 4:00 Schwimmen	22 Staub saugen	23 3:30 Klavier= unterricht	24	25 9:00 Disko	26 Rasen mähen 4:00 Fußball spielen	27
28	29 Staub saugen	30 3:30 Klavier= unterricht	31			

3 Ask your partner when and how often he or she does the activities shown in the photos below. Does he or she enjoy each activity? Then your partner will ask you the same questions.

a.

b.

c.

d.

f.

4 Look at the weather map for Western Europe and answer the following questions in German.

1. Which cities are expecting rain?
2. In which cities could you probably go swimming?
3. Which city is expected to have the lowest temperature?
4. Which city will be the warmest?
5. What kinds of activities might you plan in **Berlin** for Monday, April 7?
6. Where might you go skiing?
7. Claudia is planning to drive to the **Zugspitze,** and then to have a picnic in the **Englischer Garten.** What would she say if she wanted to invite you? Would you accept or decline the invitation?

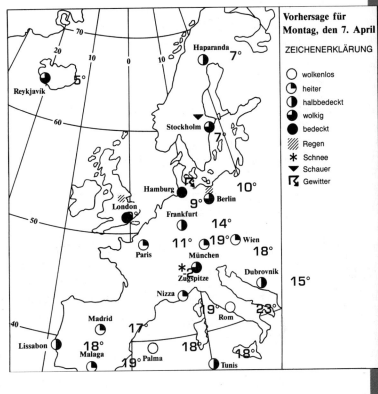

Vorhersage für Montag, den 7. April

ZEICHENERKLÄRUNG

○ wolkenlos
◐ heiter
◑ halbbedeckt
◕ wolkig
● bedeckt
▨ Regen
✳ Schnee
▼ Schauer
⚡ Gewitter

5 You and your friends are weather forecasters for the local TV station. Working in small groups, take turns reporting the local weather to your class every day for a week. Your report should include the forecast for the following day. Create a weather chart to use with your reports. On Friday, of course, you will want to sum up the week's weather. Always begin your **Wetterbericht** with: **Guten Tag, liebe Zuschauer!**

6

ROLLENSPIEL

It's raining today, so you are at home doing your chores. Your friends show up and offer to help. As you and your friends work around the house, you decide to invite your friends to go somewhere tomorrow. Great crashes of thunder turn your conversation to the weather for tomorrow. What will you do? Create a conversation with two other classmates. Be prepared to act it out in front of the class with props that will convey the idea of doing chores around the house.

KANN ICH'S WIRKLICH?

Can you extend and respond to an invitation? (p. 174)

1 How would you invite a friend to go

    a. to a movie   **b.** to a café   **c.** shopping   **d.** swimming

2 Accept or decline the following invitations. If you decline, give a reason why you can't go.

    a. Wir gehen jetzt in eine Disko. Komm doch mit!
    b. Ich muß in die Stadt gehen. Möchtest du mitkommen?
    c. Wir spielen jetzt Tennis. Kannst du mitkommen?

Can you express obligation using müssen? (p. 174)

3 Say that the people below have to do the things indicated.

    Bernd   Leyla   Pedro und Felipe   Karin

Can you talk about how often you have to do things? (p. 178)

4 How would you ask a classmate how often he or she has to

    a. wash the windows   **c.** clear the table
    b. vacuum   **d.** do the dishes

5 How would you tell a classmate how often you have to do each of the things above?

6 How would you ask a classmate if you could help him or her? How would you ask two classmates?

Can you offer help and tell someone what to do using expressions with für? (p. 179)

7 Using **können**, explain to each of these people what they can do to help you:

    a. Sara: das Geschirr spülen
    b. Silke und Peter: das Zimmer aufräumen
    c. Markus: das Bett machen
    d. Claudia und Daniel: den Tisch decken

8 How might a friend respond if he or she agreed to do some chores for you?

Can you talk about the weather? (p. 183)

9 How would you tell a classmate what the weather is like today? How would you tell him or her the weather forecast for tomorrow?

10 How would you tell someone new to your area what the weather is like in

    a. January   **c.** June   **e.** December
    b. March   **d.** October

ERSTE STUFE

EXTENDING AND RESPONDING TO INVITATIONS

mitkommen (sep)   *to come along*
Komm doch mit!   *Why don't you come along!*
Ich kann leider nicht.   *Sorry, I can't.*
Das geht nicht.   *That won't work.*

EXPRESSING OBLIGATION

tun   *to do*
helfen   *to help*

zu Hause helfen   *to help at home*
müssen   *to have to*
ich muß ...   *I have to...*
  mein Zimmer aufräumen (sep)   *clean up my room*
  Staub saugen   *vacuum*
  den Müll sortieren   *sort the trash*
  den Rasen mähen   *mow the lawn*
  die Katze füttern   *feed the cat*
  den Tisch decken   *set the table*
  den Tisch abräumen (sep)   *clear the table*

das Geschirr spülen   *wash the dishes*
die Blumen gießen   *water the flowers*
das Bett machen   *make the bed*
meine Klamotten aufräumen   *pick up my clothes*
die Fenster putzen   *clean the windows*
Ich habe keine Zeit.   *I don't have time.*

ZWEITE STUFE

SAYING HOW OFTEN YOU HAVE TO DO THINGS

Wie oft?   *How often?*
nie   *never*
manchmal   *sometimes*
immer   *always*
einmal, zweimal, dreimal ...   *once, twice, three times...*
  in der Woche   *a week*
  im Monat   *a month*

jeden Tag   *every day*

ASKING FOR AND OFFERING HELP AND TELLING SOMEONE WHAT TO DO

können   *can, to be able to*
Was kann ich für dich tun?   *What can I do for you?*
Kann ich etwas für dich tun?   *Can I do something for you?*
Du kannst ...   *You can...*

Gut! Mach' ich!   *Okay! I'll do that!*
für   *for*
Für wen?   *For whom?*
mich   *me*
dich   *you*
uns   *us*
euch   *you* (pl)

OTHER USEFUL WORDS AND EXPRESSIONS

ungefähr   *about, approximately*

DRITTE STUFE

TALKING ABOUT THE WEATHER

Was sagt der Wetterbericht?   *What does the weather report say?*
Wie ist das Wetter?   *How's the weather?*
Es ist...   *It is...*
  heiß   *hot*
  warm   *warm*
  kühl   *cool*
  kalt   *cold*
  trocken   *dry*
  naß   *wet*
  sonnig   *sunny*

wolkig   *cloudy*
der Schnee   *snow*
Es schneit.   *It's snowing.*
der Regen   *rain*
Es regnet.   *It's raining.*
das Eis   *ice*
das Gewitter   *thunder-storm*
Die Sonne scheint.   *The sun is shining.*
heute   *today*
morgen   *tomorrow*
heute abend   *this evening*
Wieviel Grad haben wir?   *What's the temperature?*
der Grad   *degree(s)*

zwei Grad   *two degrees*
der Monat, -e   *month*
der Januar   *January*
  im Januar   *in January*
  Februar   *February*
  März   *March*
  April   *April*
  Mai   *May*
  Juni   *June*
  Juli   *July*
  August   *August*
  September   *September*
  Oktober   *October*
  November   *November*
  Dezember   *December*

Einkaufen gehen

1 Ein Kilo Tomaten, bitte.

② Ich hab' ein paar Blumen gekauft.

One way that teenagers in German-speaking countries help out is by shopping for groceries. Do you sometimes go grocery shopping for your family? If you are in a German-speaking country and want to go shopping for groceries, there are a number of expressions that you need to know.

In this chapter you will learn

- to ask what you should do; to tell someone what to do
- to talk about quantities; to say that you want something else
- to give reasons; to say where you were and what you bought

And you will

- listen to customers ordering groceries in different stores
- read food ads and recipes
- write a shopping list
- find out how people in German-speaking countries do their shopping

Hasen Futter ...mh!!

③ Möchten Sie noch etwas?

Knackige Kirschen

Los geht's!

Flori   Omi

Alles für die Oma!

Look at the photos that accompany the story.
Who are the people pictured? What are they doing?
Where are they? What do you think they are talking about?
What do you suppose will happen in the story?

❶

FLORI	Hallo, Omi!
OMI	Hallo, Flori!
FLORI	Hm, Omi, was kochst du denn? Es riecht so gut! Kaiserschmarren? Super!
OMI	Den ißt du doch so gern!
FLORI	Und wie!

❷

FLORI	Hm, Omi, der Kaiserschmarren war gut! Wie immer!
OMI	Wirklich? Nicht zu süß?
FLORI	Nein, überhaupt nicht. Er war gerade richtig!
OMI	Na, das freut mich!

FLORI	Und was soll ich heute für dich einkaufen?
OMI	Hier ist der Einkaufszettel.
FLORI	Wo soll ich denn die Tomaten kaufen?
OMI	Die kannst du im Supermarkt kaufen. Dort sind sie nicht so teuer.
FLORI	Und das Brot? Kann ich es auch gleich da kaufen?
OMI	Hol das Brot lieber beim Bäcker! Dort ist es immer frisch und schmeckt besser.

❸

OMI Hier sind hundert Mark. Verlier das Geld nicht!
FLORI Keine Sorge, Omi! Ich pass' schon auf!

FLORI Hm ... ein Pfund Hackfleisch, bitte!
VERKÄUFERIN Hast du noch einen Wunsch, bitte?
FLORI Dann noch hundert Gramm Aufschnitt.
VERKÄUFERIN Sonst noch einen Wunsch?
FLORI Nein, danke! Das ist alles.

VERKÄUFERIN Bitte schön?
FLORI So ein Brot, bitte!
VERKÄUFERIN Sonst noch etwas?
FLORI Jetzt bekomme ich noch zwei Semmeln.
VERKÄUFERIN Macht fünf Mark und achtzig, bitte!
FLORI Einen Moment! Dann noch bitte so eine Brezenstange für mich!
VERKÄUFERIN Alles, dann? Sechs Mark vierzig dann, bitte!

FLORI So, Omi, hier bin ich wieder. Hier sind noch ein paar Blumen für dich!
OMI Das ist aber nett!
FLORI So, jetzt packen wir erst mal aus! Die Eier, die Butter ... Tja, wo ist denn das Portemonnaie?
OMI Wo warst du denn zuletzt?
FLORI Einen Moment, Omi, ich bin gleich wieder da! Tschau!

1 Was passiert hier?

Do you understand what is happening in the story? Check your comprehension by answering these questions. Don't be afraid to guess.

1. What does Flori do when he first arrives at his grandmother's house?
2. What does Flori offer to do for his grandmother?
3. Why does she give him money? What else does she give him for his errand?
4. What types of stores does Flori go to?
5. Why do you think Flori rushes out of his grandmother's house at the end of the story?

2 Genauer lesen

Reread the conversations. Which words or phrases do the characters use to

1. express satisfaction or praise
2. refer to different kinds of stores
3. name foods
4. express quantities in weight
5. ask if someone wants more

3 Wo war Flori?

Flori went to several different stores when he was shopping for his grandmother. In which of the places listed might he have made these statements?

1. Ein Pfund Hackfleisch, bitte!
2. Jetzt bekomme ich noch zwei Semmeln.
3. Ein Kilo Tomaten, bitte!
4. Ich möchte bitte ein paar Rosen.

a. beim Bäcker
b. beim Metzger
c. im Blumengeschäft
d. im Supermarkt

4 Was paßt zusammen?

You can use the word **denn** (*since, for, because*) to show the relationship between two sentences that express an action and the reason for that action: **Hol das Brot beim Bäcker, denn dort ist es immer frisch**! Connect the following pairs of sentences in this way to logically explain some of the actions in the story.

1. Es riecht sehr gut bei Omi
2. Flori kauft Tomaten im Supermarkt
3. Flori kauft Brot beim Bäcker
4. Omi gibt Flori einen Einkaufszettel
5. Flori geht schnell weg

a. er geht für sie einkaufen.
b. dort ist es immer frisch.
c. dort sind sie nicht so teuer.
d. er kann das Portemonnaie nicht finden.
e. sie kocht Kaiserschmarren.

5 Nacherzählen

Put the sentences in logical order to make a brief summary of the story.

1. Zuerst kocht die Großmutter Kaiserschmarren für den Flori.

Die Tomaten kauft er im Supermarkt, das Brot beim Bäcker und das Hackfleisch beim Metzger.

Dann gibt sie Flori auch das Geld.

Dann fragt Flori die Großmutter, was er für sie einkaufen soll.

Zuletzt kauft er auch Blumen für die Großmutter.

Sie gibt Flori den Einkaufszettel.

Nach dem Einkaufen kommt Flori wieder zurück.

Aber er kann das Portemonnaie nicht finden und geht es suchen.

Asking what you should do; telling someone what to do

Einkaufen gehen

Look at the ads below. What type of store is represented by each ad? What other things could you buy at each store?

Beim Bäcker Motz

Semmel
Stück -,30

Brot
1 kg 3,40

Brezeln
Stück -,55

Torte
Stück 2,40

BEIM METZGER SEIBT

Hackfleisch
1 kg
5,98

Hähnchen
7,95

Aufschnitt
100 g 1,19

Bratwurst
100 g 1,29

Im Obst-
und Gemüseladen
Frisch

Tomaten
1 kg 4,80

Kartoffeln
1 kg 1,98

Äpfel
1 kg 3,20

Salat
St. -,99

Trauben
1 kg 4,98

IM SUPERMARKT KRAUS

Kleefeld
H
fettarme
Milch
1,5 %
1 Liter

Milch
l 2,20

Eier
10 St.
2,20

IDEE
KAFFEE

Kaffee
1 Pfd.
7,49

Süßrahm-
Butter
Deutsche Markenbutter

Butter
250 g
2,20

Fisch   100 g 1,69

WARBURGER
ZUCKER
FEIN

Zucker
1 kg 4,20

Käse
100 g
1,39

Goldstaub
Mehl
TYPE 405

Mehl
500 g
Beutel
2,80

LEBENSMITTEL • GANZ PREISWERT!

Although there are many large, modern supermarkets in Germany, many people still chop in small specialty stores or at the open-air markets in the center of town. Many Germans shop frequently, buying just what they need for one or two days. Refrigerators are generally much smaller than in the United States, and people prefer to buy things fresh.

6 Hör gut zu!

Flori and Claudia are at a café discussing their plans for the day. They decide to do their shopping together. Make lists of the things they are going to buy at each of the following kinds of stores.

im Supermarkt   beim Bäcker
beim Metzger   im Obst- und Gemüseladen

Milch   Kuchen   Wurst
Hackfleisch   Aufschnitt
Brot   Äpfel
Fisch   Bratwurst
Butter   Semmeln   Brezeln

7 Was möchtest du kaufen?

Look again at the ads on page 197 and decide what you would like to buy at each store. Make an **Einkaufszettel** using the stores listed in Activity 6 as heads, then add up the prices. How do the prices compare with what you would spend at home?

8 Was möchte dein Partner?

Working with your grocery list from Activity 7, ask your partner what items he or she would like to buy. Take notes. Then switch roles. Be prepared to report to the class what your partner said.

BEISPIEL   DU   **Beim Bäcker möchte er/sie …**

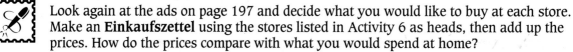

SO SAGT MAN DAS!

Asking what you should do

If you were going to help a friend or relative run errands, you would first ask what you should do: The responses might be:

Was soll ich für dich tun?   **Du kannst für mich einkaufen gehen.**
Wo soll ich das Brot kaufen?   **Beim Bäcker.**
**Soll ich das Fleisch im
     Supermarkt holen?**   **Nein, du holst das besser beim
          Metzger.**

**Und die Tomaten? Wo soll ich
     sie kaufen?**   **Im Gemüseladen, bitte.**

What do you think the word **soll** means? In the sentences with **soll** and **kannst** what happens to the word order? Where is the main verb?

9 Sätze bauen!

Wie viele Fragen kannst du bauen? (Be sure to match the food items with the correct store.)

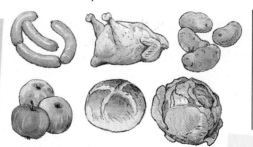
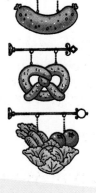

Sollen
Sollt
Sollst
Soll

ich
wir
er
ihr
du
Flori und
Claudia

holen?
kaufen?

10 Wo soll ich ... kaufen?

You are an exchange student living in Germany. Your host mother has asked you to go shopping for her and has given you the grocery list. Using the list to the right, take turns with your partner asking and answering where you should buy the various items.

Wurst
Käse
Brot
Äpfel
Semmeln
Salat
Mineralwasser
Zucker
Aufschnitt

SO SAGT MAN DAS!

Telling someone what to do

You have learned one way to tell someone what he or she can do to help you using **können**. Here are some other ways to express the same thing:

Someone might ask: The response might be:
  Was soll ich für dich tun?   **Geh bitte einkaufen!** *or*
                                           Tomaten und Milch holen, bitte!

What would be the English equivalent of the first response?[1] Look at the second response. Why do you think only a phrase is used here?[2]

---

1. *Go shopping, please.* 2. The command form **geh** is understood.

Look at the following sentences:

> **Kauf** Brot und Käse für die Oma!
> **Komm** doch mit!
> **Nimm** das Geld mit!

The above sentences are commands. These command-forms are used to tell one person you know well what to do. The verb is formed by using the **du**-form of the verb without the -**st** ending. How do these sentences compare to commands in English?

11 Hör gut zu!

Flori's grandmother is preparing lunch on Saturday for him and his friends, Markus and Mara. She needs help and tells everyone what to do. Listen and decide what each person is supposed to do. Under each of their names (Markus, Mara, Flori) list their tasks.

12 Alles ist in Unordnung!

Frank has been really busy with school and has neglected his household chores for quite a while. Look at the illustration below and take turns with your classmates saying what you think Frank's parents would tell him to do in order to get things cleaned up.

13 Eine Fete

You are having a party and two friends are helping you get ready. You've already gone shopping but have forgotten some of the things you need. Get together with two other classmates and, using your lists from Activity 7, each of you chooses six things you still need to buy. First you are the host, and your partners will ask what they can do to help. Tell each person to buy three items and where to buy them. Then switch roles so that each person plays the host once.

Was machst du für andere Leute?

How do you think students in German-speaking countries help others? We asked several students whom they help and in what ways they help them. Before you read, try to guess what they might say.

LANDESKUNDE

Silvana, *Berlin*

„Zweimal in der Woche gebe ich Nachhilfe, und hab' ich einen kleinen Schüler. Der ist in der dritten Klasse, und dem geb' ich Nachhilfe in Rechtschreibung und Lesen und Mathematik."

Brigitte, *Bietigheim*

„Also, ich hab' mit Kindern zu tun. Ich hab' mal Kinderkirche sonntags, und da beschäftigt man sich mit kleinen Kindern und spielt mit denen, und das mach' ich aber unregelmäßig. Also ich habe das schon lange Zeit nicht mehr gemacht."

Sandra, *Stuttgart*

„Bei uns in der Nachbarschaft gibt's grad' ältere Leute. Und unter uns wohnt eine Frau, die ... für die mach' ich manchmal kleine Einkäufe oder geh' einfach nur hin und rede mit ihr, damit sie halt nicht grad' so allein ist, und besuch' sie einfach oder bring' ihr halt mal was rüber, wenn wir zum Beispiel Obst aus dem Garten haben."

Iwan, *Bietigheim*

„Also meistens da helf' ich zum Beispiel meinem Bruder irgendwie, wenn er irgendwelche Probleme in der Schule hat. Und wenn ich bei meiner Oma bin, dann helf' ich auch meiner Oma."

A. 1. Write each student's name. Then write whom each student helps.
2. The people whom the students help fall into two groups. What are they? With a partner, make a chart for these two groups and list the ways in which the students help each one.
3. Now make a list of the people you help and how you help them. Ask your partner what he or she does to help others: **Was machst du für andere Leute?** Then switch roles.

B. With your classmates, discuss some of the ways you help other people. Do you do any of the same things the German students do? What is your impression: Do people help others more in Germany than in the United States? What are your reasons for deciding one way or the other? When you have finished your discussion, write a brief essay explaining your answers.

Talking about quantities; saying that you want something else

WORTSCHATZ

Und wieviel?

wiegen ungefähr
1 Kilo (kg)
= 1000 Gramm (g)
= (*2.2 lb.*)

wiegen ungefähr
1/2 (ein halbes) Kilo
= 500 Gramm
= 1 (deutsches)
  Pfund (Pfd.)

wiegt ungefähr
100 Gramm

1 Liter (l) ist
ein bißchen mehr
als *1 quart*
= (*1.057 quarts*)

2 Pfund = 1 Kilo = 1000 Gramm

Das amerikanische
Pfund hat nur 453 g.

Das deutsche
Pfund hat 500 g.

SO SAGT MAN DAS!

Talking about quantities

When shopping for groceries in Germany, you will need to know how much
to ask for using weights. For example, at the butcher's the salesperson might
ask you:

You might respond:

ask you:	You might respond:
Was bekommen Sie?	**Aufschnitt und Hackfleisch, bitte.**
Wieviel Hackfleisch?	**500 Gramm Hackfleisch.**
Und wieviel Aufschnitt?	**100 Gramm, bitte!**

14 Hör gut zu!

You are standing in line at the **Gemüseladen** and overhear other customers asking the
salesperson for specific amounts of certain items. First, listen to the conversations and
write down what the customers are asking for. Then listen again and decide how much of
each item they want.

Look back at the ads on page 197 and find the abbreviations that are used to describe quantities. What do they stand for? How many different units of measurement are listed? How does this compare with measures in the United States? In German-speaking countries, the metric system is used for weights and measures. At the open-air markets, and in many specialty stores, such as the bakery and the butcher shop, you will have to ask the salesperson for certain foods rather than serve yourself. You will need to be able to tell the vendor how much of each item you would like.

15 Was bekommen Sie?

You are in a store using the shopping list on the right. Your partner, the salesperson, asks what you need, and you respond using at least four items from the list and the quantities indicated. Then switch roles.

VERKÄUFER **Was ...?**
DU **Ich brauche ...**
VERKÄUFER **Wieviel?**
DU **...**

1 kg Tomaten
250 g Kaffee
250 g Butter
1 ℓ Milch
100 g Käse
200 g Aufschnitt
500 g Hackfleisch

SO SAGT MAN DAS!

Saying that you want something else

In **Kapitel 5** you learned how to tell a salesperson what you would like. You will also need to know how to tell him or her if you need something else.

The salesperson might ask:

Sonst noch etwas?
or
Was bekommen Sie noch?
or
Haben Sie noch einen Wunsch?

You might respond:

Ja, ich brauche noch ein Kilo Kartoffeln.
Ich bekomme noch sechs Semmeln.
Nein, danke. *or*
Danke, das ist alles.

In several of the questions and answers, the word **noch** appears. Can you guess what it means?

16 Hör gut zu!

Listen to these conversations in various food stores and determine whether the response in each case is logical or not.

	logisch	unlogisch
1		
2		

17 Noch einen Wunsch?

You are trying out new recipes tonight, and you still need to buy several things. Make shopping lists for the two recipes below. Then get together with two other classmates. One will play the salesperson at the supermarket, and the other will be another customer shopping for the second recipe. The salesperson will ask the customers what and how much they need and if they need something else.

Salami-Riesenpizza

Pizzateig (32 cm ⌀) für 2 Personen mit 4-6 Eßlöffeln Tomatenstückchen belegen. 125 g Pizzakäse in Streifen schneiden, gitterförmig darüber legen.

10-12 Scheiben Salami und 6-8 blättrig geschnittene Champignons auf der Pizza verteilen.

Mit 1/2 Teelöffel Pizzagewürz bestreuen und bei 250 Grad 14 Minuten im Ofen backen.

Pikanter Quark

Zutaten:

250 g Quark
• etwa 4 Eßlöffel Sahne
• etwa 4 Eßlöffel Milch
• 1 Knoblauchzehe
• 1 Teelöffel Kümmel
• Salz

Insgesamt etwa 2370 Joule/565 Kalorien

18 Das Angebot der Woche

Pick a specific kind of food store and make your own ad. Either cut pictures from a newspaper or draw your own pictures. You may want to refer to page 197 for a model. Below are some additional grocery items you may want to include. Remember to include prices per unit (**Kilo**, **Gramm**, **Pfund**, or **Liter**).

Und dann noch . . .

Bananen	**Joghurt**
Erdnußbutter *peanut butter*	**Ananas** *pineapple*
Marmelade *jam, jelly*	**Birnen** *pears*
Erdbeeren *strawberries*	**Melonen**
Apfelstrudel	**Müsli**

LERNTRICK

When you are learning a lot of new words, group them together in meaningful categories: group baked goods under **die Bäckerei**, meat items under **die Metzgerei**, etc. Putting the words in context will help you recall them more easily.

19 Für mein Notizbuch

Schreib in dein Notizbuch, wo du gern einkaufst! Was kaufst du? Was kaufst du gern? Was ist dein Lieblingsgericht (*favorite dish*)? Welches Essen schmeckt dir und welches Essen schmeckt dir nicht?

Giving reasons; saying where you were and what you bought

Die elegante Fassade fällt auf, weil sie frei von jeglichen Preisplakaten ist.

„Für mich gibt's zum Braten nichts Besseres, denn Butaris und der feine Buttergeschmack sind einfach unschlagbar."

Butaris® BUTTERSCHMALZ
Zum Braten, Backen, Kochen und Fritieren soft 250 g

Milch veredelt den Geschmack und ist gut für Ihr Wohlbefinden, denn Milch bringt erst die Wirkung des Koffeins in Einklang!

20 Warum?

Look at the ads above and answer the following questions.

1. Using the reading strategies you have learned so far, try to get the gist of each ad. What is each ad promoting? What reason does each ad give to persuade you to buy the product or to shop at a particular store?
2. Identify the words **weil** and **denn**. What do they mean? How do you know?
3. In the **SPAR Supermarkt** ad, what is the position of the verb in a clause that starts with **weil**? How does this compare with clauses starting with **denn**?

SO SAGT MAN DAS!

Giving reasons

In **Kapitel 7** you learned how to make an excuse and express obligation using **müssen: Claudia kommt nicht mit. Sie muß zu Hause helfen.** You can also do this with expressions beginning with **weil** or **denn**.

A friend might ask you:
   **Kannst du für mich
      einkaufen gehen?**

You might respond giving a reason:

   **Es geht nicht, denn ich
      mache die Hausaufgaben.** *or*
   **Ich kann jetzt nicht (gehen), weil
      ich die Hausaufgaben mache.**

---

21 Hör gut zu!

Mara is having a party on the weekend. Listen to the messages left on her answering machine and take down the following information: the name of the person who called, if that person is coming to the party, and if not, the reason why not.

wer	ja oder nein?	warum (nicht)?
BEISPIEL Markus	nein	geht ins Kino

Ein wenig Grammatik

Denn and **weil** are called *conjunctions*. Using them will help your German sound more natural. Both words begin clauses that give reasons for something (for example, why you can or can't do something). Clauses beginning with **denn** have the regular word order pattern, that is, the conjugated verb is in second position. However, in clauses that begin with **weil**, the conjugated verb is in final position.

22 Pläne fürs Wochenende

Using the cues in the left hand column or other activities, tell your classmates the things you can do this weekend. Then identify the activities you cannot do and give a reason from the right hand column using **weil**. Pay attention to word order!

BEISPIEL   DU   **Am Wochenende kann ich ins Kino gehen.
Am Wochenende kann ich nicht ins Konzert gehen,
weil ich keine Zeit habe.**

Am Wochenende

Was?
Baseball spielen
ins Kino gehen
tanzen gehen
Klamotten kaufen
wandern
ins Café gehen
Freunde besuchen
Volleyball spielen
Pizza essen
?

weil

Warum?
ich habe keine Zeit
ich habe kein Geld
ich muß zu Hause helfen
ich mähe den Rasen
ich putze die Fenster
ich lerne für die
   (Mathe)prüfung
ich mache Hausaufgaben
die Großeltern besuchen uns
?

23 Bist du damit einverstanden? *Do you agree?*

Look at the following statements. Agree or disagree and give a reason why. First write your answers, then discuss your opinions with your classmates.

BEISPIEL   **Ich bin damit einverstanden, weil/denn ...**
           Ich bin nicht damit einverstanden, weil/denn ...

1. Jugendliche sollen das ganze Jahr in die Schule gehen.
2. Jugendliche sollen nicht Auto fahren, bevor sie 18 sind.
3. Wir sollen mehr Geld für die Umwelt (*environment*) ausgeben.
4. Jugendliche müssen vor 10 Uhr abends zu Hause sein.

SO SAGT MAN DAS!

Saying where you were and what you bought

If a friend wants to find out where you were or what you bought, he or she might ask:

You might respond:

Wo warst du heute morgen?

**Zuerst war ich
beim Bäcker und dann beim Metzger.
Danach war ich im Supermarkt und
zuletzt war ich im Kaufhaus.**

**Und was hast du beim
Bäcker gekauft?**

Ich habe Brot gekauft.

Wo warst du gestern?

Ich war zu Hause.

What do the phrases **ich war** and **du warst** mean? What are their English equivalents? What other words or expressions in these sentences indicate the past?

WORTSCHATZ

gestern *yesterday*
vorgestern *day before yesterday*
gestern abend *yesterday evening*

heute morgen *this morning*
heute nachmittag *this afternoon*
letztes Wochenende *last weekend*

Grammatik   The past tense of **sein**

War and **warst** are past tense forms of the verb **sein** (*to be*) and are used to talk about the past. Look at the following sentences.

Ich **war** heute beim Metzger.
Du **warst** gestern im Supermarkt.
Er/Sie **war** am Montag beim Bäcker.

Wir **waren** gestern zu Hause.
Ihr **wart** im Kino.
Sie (pl)/Sie **waren** letzte Woche
in der Stadt.

What are the English equivalents of these sentences?

24 Hör gut zu!

Listen to the following exchanges as Claudia talks with her friends. For each conversation, decide if the person Claudia is talking to has already done the activity mentioned or plans to do it in the future.

	already done	plans to do
1		
2		

25 Wo waren Flori und Mara heute?

Look at the pages out of Mara's and Flori's lists of things to do. Your partner will ask you where Flori was during the day. Use his schedule to answer your partner's questions. Then switch roles and ask your partner about Mara's day. Remember to use **zuerst**, **dann**, **danach**, and **zuletzt** to organize your answers.

Mara
10:00 Supermarkt für Mutti
12:00 mit Markus im Café essen
13:00 ins Einkaufszentrum gehen, Klamotten kaufen
14:30 Zimmer aufräumen

Flori
9:30 Brot und Äpfel für die Omi kaufen
13:00 zu Hause Mittagessen
13:30 Omis Fenster putzen
15:00 Kaufhaus, Fußball kaufen

26 Wer hat was gemacht?

Claudia has been trying to make plans with her friends, but she has had a hard time getting hold of anyone. Match each exchange with one of the illustrations below.

a. b. c. d.

1. CLAUDIA Sag mal, Petra, wo warst du denn heute morgen?

   PETRA Ich war in der Stadt. Zuerst war ich beim Bäcker, dann im Obstladen. Heute abend essen meine Tante und mein Onkel bei uns.

2. CLAUDIA Und wo war denn die Michaela? Weißt du das? Sie war auch nicht zu Hause.

   PETRA Na, sie war im Eiscafé mit Gabi und Susanne. Die drei essen immer nur Joghurteis! Ingo hat sie später in der Disko gesehen.

3. CLAUDIA Tag, Oma! Wo warst du denn heute morgen? Ich bin vorbeigekommen, und du warst nicht da.

   OMA Die Tante Dorle war da, und wir haben im Café am Markt zu Mittag gegessen. Ach, Kind, das Essen war köstlich!

4. CLAUDIA Hallo, ihr zwei! Wo wart ihr am Samstag abend?

   HEIKE Robert und ich, wir waren im Kino — im neuen Cinedom. Mensch, das war echt toll! Wir haben den Film *Cape Fear* gesehen. Unheimlich spannend!

27 Einkaufsbummel

Your partner just got back from shopping **am langen Samstag**. Your partner will decide on three items that he or she bought at each of the stores pictured. Ask your partner what he or she bought at each store. Switch roles, and be prepared to tell the class about your **Einkaufsbummel**.

AUSSPRACHE

Richtig aussprechen / Richtig lesen

A. To practice or review the following sounds, say the words and sentences below after your teacher or after the recording.

1. The letters **ü** and **ö**: In **Kapitel 1** you learned how to pronounce the letters **ü** and **ö** as long vowels, as in **Tschüs** and **Hör**. However, when the letters **ü** and **ö** are followed by two or more consonants, they are pronounced as short vowels.
   müssen, Stück, Würste / Wir müssen fünf Stück Kuchen holen.
   können, köstlich, Wörterbuch / Könnt ihr für mich ein Wörterbuch kaufen?

2. The letter combinations **ei** and **ie**: The letter combination **ei** is pronounced like the *i* in the English word *mine*. The combination **ie** is pronounced like the *e* in the English word *me*.
   Bäckerei, Eier, Fleisch / Kauf das Fleisch in der Metzgerei!
   wieder, wieviel, lieber / Wieviel bekommen Sie? Vier Stück?

3. The letter **z**: In **Kapitel 2** you learned that the letter **z** is always pronounced like the *ts* sound in the English word *hits,* although in German, this sound often occurs at the beginning of a word.
   Zeit, zahlen, ziehen / Ich habe keine Zeit, in den Zoo zu gehen.

Richtig schreiben / Diktat

B. Write down the sentences that you hear.

Richtig essen!

LESETRICK

Combine the strategies that you have learned As you learn to read German, keep in mind that you will use many different reading strategies at the same time. You will combine them in different ways, depending on the type of text you are trying to read. You will probably go through several steps every time you read new material: you may start by looking at visual clues, then skim to get the gist, scan for specific information, and finally read the text for comprehension.

1. Before you read these ads, think about what foods you like to eat. Which of the food items you eat on a regular basis are really good for you?
2. Compare your weekly diet to a partner's and try to figure out together what percentage of your diet is carbohydrate, fat, and protein.
3. Look at the illustrations in the ads, then try to figure out the meaning of the boldfaced titles and subtitles. Judging from what you learned from these two sources, what do you think these ads are about?
   a. snack foods
   b. healthful foods
   c. ways to make sandwiches
4. You have figured out the general topic of these articles. Now skim the ads to get the gist. What information are these ads trying to get across to you?

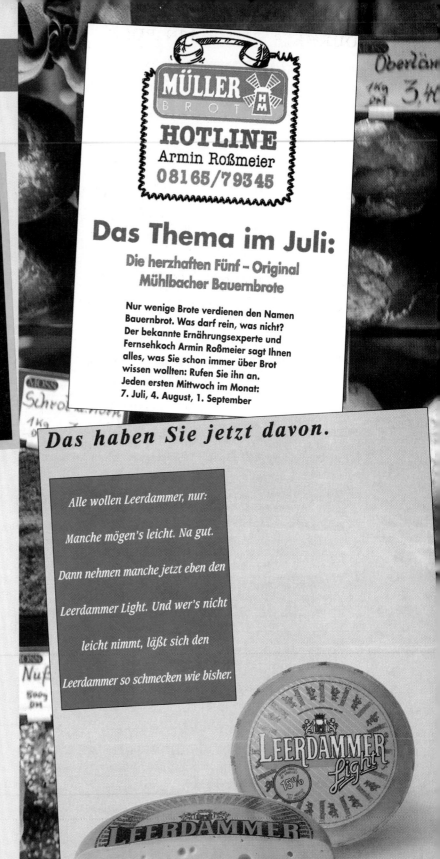

MÜLLER BROT
HM

HOTLINE
Armin Roßmeier
08165/79345

Das Thema im Juli:
Die herzhaften Fünf – Original Mühlbacher Bauernbrote

Nur wenige Brote verdienen den Namen Bauernbrot. Was darf rein, was nicht? Der bekannte Ernährungsexperte und Fernsehkoch Armin Roßmeier sagt Ihnen alles, was Sie schon immer über Brot wissen wollten: Rufen Sie ihn an. Jeden ersten Mittwoch im Monat: 7. Juli, 4. August, 1. September

Das haben Sie jetzt davon.

Alle wollen Leerdammer, nur:

Manche mögen's leicht. Na gut.

Dann nehmen manche jetzt eben den

Leerdammer Light. Und wer's nicht

leicht nimmt, läßt sich den

Leerdammer so schmecken wie bisher.

LEERDAMMER Light
15%

LEERDAMMER

5. Based on your knowledge of German, match these compound words with the most logical English equivalent.

> **Weißt du noch?** Remember that knowing the meaning of root words can help you guess the meaning of many compound words.

1. Mahlzeit
2. Fernsehkoch
3. alltäglich
4. Ernährungs-experte
5. Vollkornbrot
6. der Weich-käse

a. daily
b. soft cheese
c. whole-grain bread
d. television chef
e. meal
f. nutrition expert

6. Read the ad for **Vollkornbrot**. Which word in the ad means "well-being"? According to the ad, in order to have 100% physical well-being, what is the percentage of carbohydrates you should eat on the average in a week? What is the percentage of fat? And what is the percentage of protein?

7. According to the ad, what is the most important meal of the day?

8. What is the name of the person who has the hotline? When can you call him? What kind of information would he give you?

9. Scan the articles for the following information.
   a. Who can enjoy **Almenrausch** soft cheese?
   b. What kind of **Leerdammer** do some people want to eat?
   c. What company advertises itself as a whole-grain specialist?

10. You are an exchange student in Germany. You and your friends are opening up a student-run snack stand at school, and you plan to have plenty of healthful snacks. Write an article for the school newspaper describing the foods you will offer at your stand.

1 Flori's mother would like him to go shopping for her. Listen as she tells him what to get, and make a shopping list for Flori. Be sure to include the amounts she needs.

 2 You and a friend are about to go grocery shopping. You have only 25 marks and want to get the most for your money. **Kaufmarkt** always has great daily specials. Look at the ads on the right and tell your partner eight things you want to buy and how much of each you are buying. Your partner will make a list and add up the cost for you. When finished, switch roles.

Fleisch

Schweine-Kotelett
zart   1kg **6,48**

Schweinebraten
ohne Knochen,
mit Kruste   1kg **4,98**

Schweine-Schulter
wie gewachsen   1kg **2,98**

Schweine-Halsgrat
saftig   1kg **7,48**

Schweine-Brustspitzen
frisch   1kg **5,98**

Hals-Steaks
vom Schwein   1kg **9,98**

Sur-Hax'n
mild gesalzen   1kg **3,98**

Holzfällersteak
gewürzt   1kg **5,98**

Konditorei

Erdbeerkuchen
mit frischen
Früchten   Stück **2,45**

Gemischter
Obstkuchen
auf zartem
Wiener Biskuit   Stück **2,25**

Himbeerkuchen
mit Mandeln nach
Hausfrauenart   Stück **1,95**

Bamberger
Butterhörnchen
mit reiner Butter
gebacken   Stück **,90**

Schwäbischer
Käsekuchen
mit bestem Konditorquark
und mit Sahne verfeinert
                     Stück **1,95**

Fleisch

Schweinswürstel
frisch   100g **1,09**

Wollwurst   100g **,98**
Kalbsbratwürstl
gebrüht   100g **1,19**

Kalbsbrust   1kg **9,98**

Kalbsrücken
(Lende ohne
Knochen)   1kg **32,90**

Frische
Putenschnitzel
                     1kg **9,98**

Neuseeland
Hirschkalb-Steak
frisch,
Spitzenqualität 1kg **29,98**

Lammsteak
gefr.   1kg **11,98**

 3 Could you convince someone to buy a specific product? Bring in pictures of several food or clothing items from a magazine, or use props, and create a commercial to convince your classmates to buy one or more of the products. Use statements with **denn** and **weil** to persuade them. Then present your commercial to the class. Here are some phrases that might be helpful:

Obst + Gemüse aus aller Welt

 TÄGLICH FRISCH

250 g Erdbeeren
aus Spanien, Kl.I
                    Schale **,99**

1 kg Bananen
reich an Vitaminen
und Aufbaustoffen **1,39**

1 kg blaue Trauben
„Barlinka", aus
Spanien, Kl.I   **4,98**

1 kg Granny-Smith-Äpfel
aus Chile, Kl.I   **1,98**

10 Grapefruits
aus der Türkei   Beutel **1,98**

500 g Spargel
aus Griechenland,
16 mm, Kl.I   Bund **3,88**

Blumenkohl Kl.II
frisch aus Italien **1,98**

500 g grüner Paprika
Kl.II
aus Spanien   Beutel **1,98**

Frische Radieschen
aus der Pfalz,
Kl.I   Großbund **,98**

Frische Gurken
aus Holland, Kl.I
                    Stück **,88**

ist gesund (healthy)   *hat wenig Kalorien (few calories)*   *ist schön*

paßt prima   *ist sehr preiswert*

sieht phantastisch aus   *schmeckt besonders gut*   *ist gar nicht teuer*

4 You and two of your friends work with a local charity organization that helps people who have a hard time doing things around the house. Your team has been assigned three different people to help today. As leader of the team, it is your job to go over each list with each volunteer and tell that person what to do. When you have finished, switch roles, so that each person on the team is the leader once.

Frau Meyer:
Fenster putzen
Müll sortieren
½ Pfd. Kaffee kaufen
Staub saugen
5 Semmeln kaufen
375 g Wurst kaufen

Herr Schmidt:
Wohnzimmer aufräumen
500 g Aufschnitt kaufen
250 g Butter kaufen
Müll sortieren
400 g Hackfleisch
holen
Blumen gießen

Frau Heppner:
Blumen gießen
1 Kilo Kartoffeln kaufen
Staub saugen
Fisch holen
Rasen mähen
1 Pfd. Tomaten kaufen

5 A relative sent you 100 marks for your birthday. Write a letter thanking him or her for the money and describing what you bought with it.

Liebe(r) ▬▬ !

Herzlichen Dank für das
Geburtstagsgeschenk. Ich habe …

Dein(e) …

6

ROLLENSPIEL

Get together with a classmate and role-play the following scenes.

a. You and a friend are preparing lunch. Read the recipe for **Obstsalat** and tell your friend what you need, where to get it, and how much you need based on the recipe. Your friend will make a shopping list.

b. With your list in hand, go to the store to get what you need. Your partner plays the salesperson and will ask what you need, how much, and if you need anything else.

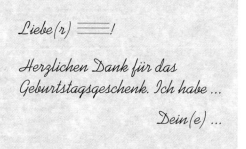

OBSTSALAT

1 Apfel, 2 Bananen, 1 Birne,
1 Kiwi, 150 g Trauben (blau),
1 Orange, 2 EL Zitronensaft,
3 EL Honig, 2 EL Rosinen,
2 EL Walnußkerne, gehackt

Zubereitung: 20 Minuten

185 Kalorien

Can you ask someone what you should do using sollen? (p. 198)

1 How would you ask someone what you should do for him or her? How might he or she answer using the following items?

a. bread: at the baker's   c. milk: at the supermarket

b. ground meat: at the butcher's   d. apples: at the produce store

Can you tell someone what to do using a du-command? (p. 199)

2 How would you tell someone where to buy the food items above?

3 How would you tell a friend to

a. mow the lawn   c. clean the room

b. buy 500 grams of tomatoes   d. get 6 apples

Can you ask for specific quantities? (p. 202)

4 How would you tell a salesperson you need the following things?

a. 500 Gramm Hackfleisch   d. 1 Pfd. Tomaten

b. Brot   e. 2 Kilo Kartoffeln

c. 1 Liter Milch

Can you say that you want something else? (p. 203)

5 How would a salesperson ask you if you wanted something else? How would you respond using the following items?

a. 10 Semmeln   b. 100 Gramm Aufschnitt   c. 200 Gramm Käse

Can you give reasons using denn and weil? (p. 206)

6 How would you say that you can't do each of the following and give a reason why not?

a. go to a movie   b. go shopping   c. go to a café

Can you say where you were (using sein) and what you bought? (p. 207)

7 How would you ask someone where he or she was yesterday? How would you ask two friends? Can you say where you were using the following cues?

a. at the baker's in the morning   c. at the butcher's yesterday morning

b. at the supermarket yesterday   d. at home this afternoon

8 How would you ask your friend what he or she bought? How would you say that you bought the following items?

a. bread   c. a sweater   e. pants

b. a shirt   d. cheese

ERSTE STUFE

ASKING WHAT YOU SHOULD DO; TELLING SOMEONE WHAT TO DO

sollen   *should, to be supposed to*
einkaufen gehen   *to go shopping*
einkaufen (sep)   *to shop*
holen   *to get, fetch*
der Laden, ¨   *store*
die Lebensmittel (pl)   *groceries*
die Bäckerei, -en   *bakery*
 beim Bäcker   *at the baker's*
das Brot, -e   *bread*
die Semmel, -n*   *roll*
die Brezel, -n   *pretzel*
die Torte, -n   *layer cake*

die Metzgerei, -en   *butcher shop*
 beim Metzger   *at the butcher's*
das Fleisch   *meat*
das Hackfleisch   *ground meat (mixture of beef and pork)*
die Wurst, ¨e   *sausage*
der Aufschnitt   *cold cuts*
das Hähnchen,-   *chicken*
der Obst- und Gemüseladen, ¨   *fresh produce store*
 im Obst- und Gemüseladen   *at the produce store*
 das Obst   *fruit*
 die Traube, -n   *grape*
 der Apfel, ¨   *apple*
 das Gemüse   *vegetables*
 die Kartoffel, -n   *potato*

die Tomate, -n   *tomato*
der Salat, -e   *lettuce*
der Supermarkt, ¨e   *supermarket*
 im Supermarkt   *at the supermarket*
die Milch   *milk*
die Butter   *butter*
der Käse   *cheese*
das Ei, -er   *egg*
der Kaffee   *coffee*
der Zucker   *sugar*
das Mehl   *flour*
der Fisch, -e   *fish*

OTHER USEFUL WORDS

besser   *better*
frisch   *fresh*

ZWEITE STUFE

TALKING ABOUT QUANTITIES

Wieviel?   *How much?*
wiegen   *to weigh*
das Pfund   *pound*
das Gramm   *gram*
das Kilo   *kilogram*

der Liter   *liter*
ein bißchen mehr   *a little more*

SAYING YOU WANT SOMETHING ELSE

Sonst noch etwas?   *Anything else?*

Haben Sie noch einen Wunsch?   *Would you like anything else?*
Ich brauche noch ...   *I also need...*
Das ist alles.   *That's all.*

DRITTE STUFE

GIVING REASONS

denn   *because, for*
weil   *because*

SAYING WHERE YOU WERE AND WHAT YOU BOUGHT

war   *was (see p. 207)*
Wo warst du?   *Where were you?*
Ich war beim Bäcker.   *I was at the baker's.*

Was hast du gekauft?   *What did you buy?*
Ich habe Brot gekauft.   *I bought bread.*

TIME EXPRESSIONS

heute morgen   *this morning*
heute nachmittag   *this afternoon*
gestern   *yesterday*
gestern abend   *yesterday evening*

vorgestern   *day before yesterday*
letztes Wochenende   *last weekend*
letzte Woche   *last week*

*In northern Germany these are called **Brötchen**, and in Baden-Württemberg and in other areas in southern Germany they are called **Wecken**.

9
Amerikaner
in München

① Entschuldigung! Wissen Sie,
wo das alte Rathaus ist?

216

It's not always easy to find your way around in a new city, and you might have to ask for directions. In this chapter you will meet some American students who are visiting Munich. How do they find their way around? What do they think of Munich? What would you like to do if you were visiting Munich?

In this chapter you will learn

- to talk about where something is located
- to ask for and give directions
- to talk about what there is to eat and drink; to say you do or don't want more; to express opinions

And you will

- listen to people ask for and give directions
- read about Munich and locate places on a map of Munich
- write a postcard giving directions
- find out about famous places in Munich

② Noch einen Saft?

③ Und dort an der Ampel geht ihr nach links.

Hausgemachter 5,50
Fleischspieß
Semmel oder Breze 0,70

Prähist. Staatssammlung
Eintritt
Sonderausstellung
DM 3
Aufbewahren und
Verlangen vorze
Fronhofer, Re

Prähist. Staatssammlung
Eintritt
Sonderausstellung
DM 3,00
Aufbewahren und auf
Verlangen vorzeigen
Fronhofer, Regensburg

Los geht's!

München besuchen

Amerikaner **Markus** **Mara**

Look at the photos that accompany the story.
Who are the people pictured? What are they doing?
Where are they? What do you think they are talking about?
What do you suppose will happen in the story?

① "Die Säfte hier sind doch wirklich Spitze!"

"Ja, und vor allem gesund!"

② "Entschuldigung!"

"Ja?"

"Wie kommen wir zum Marienplatz?"

"Ganz einfach! Da geht ihr geradeaus bis zur Ampel und dann nach rechts."

③ "Das stimmt doch gar nicht! An der Ampel nach links!"

"Klar, nach links! Da kommt ihr direkt zum Marienplatz."

"Ah, vielen Dank!"

"Bitte, gern geschehen."

④ "Ihr seid Amerikaner, nicht?"

"Ja, wir sind aus Wisconsin."

"Wirklich? Was macht ihr hier?"

"Ja ... wir wohnen in Rosenheim, und heute besuchen wir München."

SPÄTER

1 Was passiert hier?

Do you understand what is happening in the **Foto-Roman**? Check your comprehension by answering these questions. Don't be afraid to guess.

1. Where are Mara and Markus at the beginning of the story? What are they doing?
2. Who approaches Mara and Markus? What kind of information do these people need?
3. What does Markus recommend to eat? Why do you think he recommends this?
4. What do Markus and Mara decide to do at the end of the story?

2 Genauer lesen

Reread the conversations. Which words or phrases do the characters use to

1. start conversations or get someone's attention
2. end conversations
3. name foods and drinks
4. ask for and give directions
5. ask if someone would like more of something

3 Stimmt oder stimmt nicht?

Are these statements right or wrong? Answer each one with either **stimmt** or **stimmt nicht**. If a statement is incorrect, try to state it correctly.

1. Zuerst trinken Markus und Mara Kaffee.
2. Der Amerikaner möchte zum Marienplatz gehen.
3. Mara und Markus besuchen Amerika.
4. Dann wollen der Amerikaner und seine Freunde etwas essen, denn sie haben Hunger.
5. Aber Markus ißt Leberkäs nicht gern.
6. Leberkäs ist eine bayrische Spezialität.
7. Dann wollen Markus und Mara den Amerikanern die Stadt München zeigen.

4 Was paßt zusammen?

Match each statement or question on the left with an appropriate response on the right.

1. Wie kommen wir zum Marienplatz?
2. Vielen Dank!
3. Was macht ihr hier?
4. Was eßt ihr hier?
5. Ißt du noch eine Bratwurst?
6. Schmeckt's?

a. Wir besuchen die Stadt München.
b. Gern geschehen!
c. Ihr müßt an der Ampel nach links.
d. Ja, wirklich gut!
e. Hier gibt's Leberkäs und Weißwurst.
f. Nein, danke! Ich habe genug.

5 Nacherzählen

Put the sentences in a logical order to make a brief summary of the **Foto-Roman**.

1. Am Saftstand trinken Mara und Markus einen Saft.

Dann probiert er den Leberkäs.

Später wollen der Junge und seine Freunde wissen, was Mara und Markus essen.

Er wohnt in Rosenheim und besucht heute München.

Danach zeigen Mara und Markus den Amerikanern München.

Ein Junge kommt vorbei und möchte wissen, wie er zum Marienplatz kommt.

Talking about where something is located

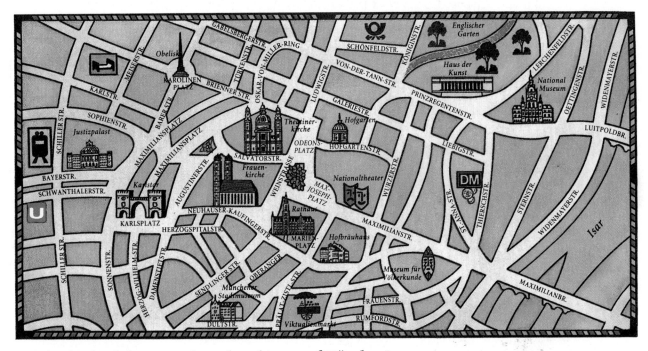

What kinds of places are pictured on this map of **München**? What do you think a **Kirche** is? And the **Rathaus**? How many museums can you find? And parks? Judging by the types of buildings on this map, what part of the city do you think this is?

EIN WENIG LANDESKUNDE

Many cities in Germany were originally built around the **Markt-platz**, with the **Rathaus** and the main **Kirche**, nearby. A wall surrounded the city and offered protection to the inhabitants. In a number of cities, parts of the original city wall are still standing around the **Innenstadt** (*downtown*). In many cities the main streets are closed to traffic and are designated as a **Fußgängerzone** (*pedestrian zone*).

WORTSCHATZ

In der Innenstadt   Wo ist ... ?

das
Hotel

die
Kirche

das
Rathaus

der
Marktplatz

die
Bank

die
Post

das
Museum

der
Bahnhof

das
Theater

der
Garten

die
U-Bahn-
station

SO SAGT MAN DAS!

Talking about where something is located

If you are in a new city, you might need to ask where things are located.

You might ask a passer-by:

> **Verzeihung! Wissen Sie, wo das Rathaus ist?**
>
> **Und wo ist das Karlstor?**
>
> **Entschuldigung! Weißt du, wo der Bahnhof ist?**
>
> **Und wo ist hier ein Café?**

You might get the responses:

> **In der Innenstadt am Marienplatz.**
>
> **In der Neuhauser Straße.**
>
> **Es tut mir leid. Das weiß ich nicht.**
>
> **Keine Ahnung! Ich bin nicht von hier.**

What is the position of the second verb in questions that begin with **wissen** and **weißt**? Which expression might you use to ask someone older than yourself? To ask a person your own age? Which responses were probably made by someone who does not live in Munich?

---

6 Hör gut zu!

At the tourist information center in **München** you overhear a conversation between an American tourist and someone who doesn't know the city very well. Using the map on page 221, decide whether the information the tourist is given for each of the places listed below is correct or incorrect.

1. ein Hotel
2. die Post
3. eine Bank
4. eine U-Bahnstation
5. das Stadtmuseum
6. der Englische Garten
7. die Frauenkirche

Grammatik   The verb wissen

The verb **wissen** means *to know* (a fact, information, etc.). Here are the forms:

> Ich **weiß** nicht, wo es ist.   Wir **wissen**, wo die Kirche ist.
>
> Du **weißt** es, ja?   Ihr **wißt** das auch.
>
> Er/Sie **weiß**, wo es ist.   Sie (pl) / Sie **wissen** es nicht.

Look at the sentences below.

> Wo ist das Museum?   Ich weiß nicht.
>
> Weißt du, wo das Museum **ist**?   Ich weiß nicht, wo das Museum **ist**.

What is the position of the verbs in the clauses introduced by **wo**? Used in this way, **wo** introduces a dependent clause. The verb is in final position.

---

7 Wer weiß, wo es ist?

Mara und ihre Familie fahren heute in die Innenstadt. Sie möchten sich viel ansehen, und sie müssen auch viel einkaufen *(to shop)*. Wissen sie, wo alles ist? Ergänze Maras Aussagen mit der richtigen Form von **wissen**!

BEISPIEL   **Mutti weiß, wo das Theater ist.**

1. **Ich** …   2. **Vater und ich** …   3. **Ali** …   4. **Du** …   5. **Ihr** …   6. **Leyla und Jasmin** …

8 Amerikaner treffen Engländer in München

A group of American students is lost in **München**. Several students in the group ask passers-by how to get to various places. However, they have mistakenly asked a group of British tourists, who themselves are lost. Create possible exchanges using the correct form of **wissen**. Watch out for the position of the second verb.

9 Entschuldigung! Wissen Sie, wo …?

You are in **München** and have lost your travel guide. You need to ask where certain landmarks are located. Using the map on page 221, choose five places you would like to see. Make a list. Get together with two other classmates, one of whom will be a passer-by about 50 years old, the other a person your own age. Ask them where the places of interest on your list are located. Then switch roles.

10 Wie sieht deine Stadt aus?

A German exchange student coming to your school needs to know how to get around in your town. With your partner sketch a map of your neighborhood or downtown area. Make a list of important places. What would the student enjoy seeing? Where could he or she buy food and clothing? Label all the streets and important places on your map and share it with the class. Turn to page 323 for additional vocabulary.

Was ißt du gern?

We asked some people in the German-speaking countries to tell us about what kinds of foods they like to eat. Before you read what they said, make a list of some of the things you would consider "German specialties."

LANDESKUNDE

Schweineschnitzel

Kaiserschmarren

Würstchen

Melina,
Bietigheim

„Ich esse am liebsten so Eis, vor allem Erdbeereis oder so, mit Früchten drin. Und so … von Gerichten mag ich ja Schnitzel oder Linseneintopf. Ja, trinken mag ich eigentlich so mehr Cola oder so Apfelsaft."

Rosi,
Berlin

„Ach, ich esse auch gern Süß-speisen, also Kaiserschmarren als österreichisches [Gericht] oder Eierkuchen — ja, also eigentlich alles mögliche!"

Uli,
München

„Dafür lieb' ich Würstchen, jeglicher Art, besonders die Berliner Currywürstchen, die es hier in München leider nicht so oft gibt. Ja und das ist so das, was ich gern esse."

Here are a few other German specialties

Scholle, Hamburg

Maultaschen, Baden-Württemberg

A. 1. Write the people's names and list the German specialties each likes to eat. Are there any foods mentioned that are not German specialties?

2. Look at the list you made before reading and discuss the following questions with your classmates. Did your guesses differ from what the people said? If so, how? Where did you get your ideas about German specialties? What do you think people in German-speaking countries would name as American specialties? Where do you think they get their ideas?

B. Write a letter in German to one of the people interviewed telling her about the local spe-cialties you like to eat. The person may not know what they are, so it might be a good idea to describe the foods in as much detail as you can.

11 Den Weg zeigen

Below is a map of Mittersendling, a neighborhood in Munich. Start at the **U-Bahnstation** and follow the directions given in the **Wortschatz** box. Where do you end up when you follow these directions?

WORTSCHATZ

Gehen Sie ...

nach rechts

bis zum Krüner Platz

dann geradeaus

bis zur Ampel, dann nach rechts

dann die erste (zweite, dritte) Straße nach rechts

die nächste Straße nach links

bis zur Herrschinger Str.

und wieder nach rechts.

dann geradeaus. Da ist ...

12 Hör gut zu!

An American exchange student is trying to find the produce store, shopping center, and the bakery in Mittersendling. He is standing in front of the butcher's asking a passer-by for directions. Listen to their conversation several times and determine whether the directions given will take him where he wants to go or not. If not, where do they lead him?

13 Du gehst nach links, dann nach ...

Zeig den Weg zu den folgenden Orten (*places*) in Mittersendling! Fang beim Hotel an! Tausche die Rolle mit deinen Klassenkameraden aus!

a. vom Hotel bis zur Post
b. von der Post bis zum Supermarkt
c. von der Bank bis zum Hotel

SO SAGT MAN DAS!

Asking for and giving directions

To find out where things are located, you will want to be able to ask for directions.

You might ask a passer-by:

Verzeihung! Wie komme ich zum Hotel am Bahnhof?

Und wie kommt man* zur Bäckerei? Entschuldigung! Wie kommen wir zum Einkaufszentrum?

Und wie kommen wir zur U-Bahnstation?

The responses might be:

Gehen Sie geradeaus bis zur Alpseestraße, dann nach links! Die nächste Straße nach rechts.

Fahren Sie geradeaus bis zur Ampel, dann nach links!

Sie fahren hier nach rechts, dann die zweite Straße wieder nach rechts.

What do you think the words **zum** and **zur** mean?[1] Why is there a difference and what does it depend on?[2] In two of the responses, the verb is in first position. Can you figure out why?

1. *to the* 2. It depends on the noun that follows: masculine/neuter nouns > **zu dem (zum)**; feminine nouns > **zu der (zur)**.

***man** means *one*, *you* (in general), *people*; it is used with the **er/sie**-form of the verb: **man geht, man fährt.**

14 Wie kommt man dahin?

You are at the post office in Mittersendling and have several things to do today. You still have to buy rolls, exchange money, buy a T-shirt, and then meet your friends at the youth center. Choose two things to do and ask your partner how to get from place to place, using the map on page 225. Then switch roles.

zum Einkaufszentrum	zur Bank
zur Bäckerei	zum Jugendclub

Ein wenig Grammatik

In the **So sagt man das!** box on page 226 both **gehen** and **fahren** are used. How is **fahren** different in meaning from **gehen**? **Fahren** is used whenever someone is using a vehicle to go somewhere, such as **ein Auto, ein Bus,** or **ein Fahrrad**. **Fahren** has a stem-vowel change in the **du-** and **er/sie-**forms: **Du fährst mit dem Bus, und sie fährt mit dem Auto.** However, with **du-**commands, the umlaut is not used: **Fahr jetzt nach Hause!**

Grammatik   The formal commands with Sie

In **Kapitel 8** you learned how to use commands with people you know well: **Kauf ein Kilo Kartoffeln, bitte!** In this chapter you have seen how you would give a command to a person whom you do not know well and who is older than yourself. Look at the following sentences:

Fahren Sie nach links!   **Gehen Sie geradeaus!**

What do you notice about the word order in formal commands.[1] How would you give a command to someone your own age using **fahren** and **gehen**?[2] To two strangers older than yourself?[3]

15 Hör gut zu!

a. At the information counter at the main train station in Munich, a friend of yours is asking how to get to the **Viktualienmarkt**. Listen to the directions given several times and jot down some notes as you listen.

b. Check your notes with the map on page 221. Did you understand the directions correctly?

c. Now use your notes to explain in your own words to another friend how he or she can get to the **Viktualienmarkt**.

16 Wie kommt man zum Jugendclub?

Dein Freund kommt am Samstag mit der U-Bahn und möchte dich im Jugendclub treffen (*to meet*). Schau auf den Stadtplan auf Seite 225 und schreib die Postkarte fertig! Beschreib den Weg von der U-Bahnstation bis zum Jugendclub!

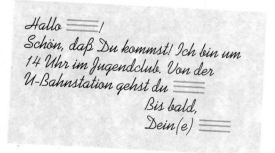

Hallo ═══!
Schön, daß Du kommst! Ich bin um 14 Uhr im Jugendclub. Von der U-Bahnstation gehst du ═══
Bis bald,
Dein(e) ═══

1. The verb is in first position and is always followed by **Sie**. 2. **Fahr/Geh ... !** 3. **Fahren/Gehen Sie ... !**

17 Wohin?

Your friend wants you to see some famous places in Munich and has left behind a set of directions from the **Bahnhof** to somewhere in Munich. However, he forgot to tell you what you will see. Read his directions and use the map of Munich (page 221) to find out where they lead. Match the destination with one of the photos.

a.

b.

c.

Also, du kommst aus dem Bahnhof, gehst über die Straße und dann in Richtung Karlsplatz. Du gehst durchs Karlstor, und hier kommst du in die Neuhauser und Kaufingerstraße. Die führen zum Marienplatz. Am Marienplatz mußt du links in die Weinstraße einbiegen. Geh jetzt immer geradeaus, bis du zum Odeonsplatz kommst. Auf der linken Seite ist ein großes Gebäude. Da bin ich!

18 Also, fahren Sie ...

Role-play the following situation with two classmates. One of you will be a German student at the **Rathaus** where several people ask you for directions. Another will be an American high school teacher sightseeing in Munich by car, and the third classmate will be a young student from Los Angeles on a bike. Each tourist will think of two places he or she wants to see in downtown **München** and will ask you for directions. Use the map on page 221 to help them. Then switch roles.

BEISPIEL   **Wie komme ich ...?**

zum Hofbräuhaus   zum Haus der Kunst
zum Münchner Stadtmuseum
zum Karlstor   zum Hofgarten
zum Nationalmuseum
zum Bahnhof   zum Englischen Garten
zur Theatinerkirche
zum Nationaltheater   zur Frauenkirche

19 Für mein Notizbuch

Ein deutscher Austauschschüler möchte dich besuchen. Beschreib in deinem Notizbuch den Weg von deiner Schule bis zu deinem Haus! Fährst du mit dem Bus oder vielleicht mit der U-Bahn? Das kannst du auch beschreiben.

BEISPIEL   **Du gehst ...   oder**
            Du fährst mit dem Bus/der U-Bahn
            Nummer ... bis ..., dann ...

DRITTE STUFE

Talking about what there is to eat and drink; saying you do or don't want more; expressing opinions

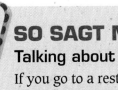

SO SAGT MAN DAS!

Talking about what there is to eat and drink

If you go to a restaurant for the first time, you might ask your friend or a waiter what there is to eat or drink.

You might ask:

Was gibt es hier zu essen?

Und zu trinken?

The response might be:

Es gibt Leberkäs, Vollkornsemmeln, Weißwurst ...

Cola, Apfelsaft und auch Mineralwasser.

What do you think the expressions **Was gibt es?** and **Es gibt ...** mean?

Ein wenig *Grammatik*

The phrase **es gibt** (*there is, there are*) is a fixed expression that stays the same despite the number of objects referred to. In the example **Gibt es hier in der Nähe einen Supermarkt?** is **Supermarkt** in the nominative or accusative case? How can you tell? What can you say about noun phrases following **es gibt?**[1]

EIN WENIG LANDESKUNDE

Leberkäs is a Bavarian specialty of ground beef or pork liver, pork, and spices. Most people eat it with a **Semmel** or **Brezel** and sweet mustard. How would you tell a German friend about specialties available in your area?

20 Was gibt es hier zu essen und zu trinken?

Du kannst dich nicht entscheiden (*to decide*), was du in der **Imbißstube am Rathaus** bestellen möchtest. Frag deinen Partner, was es zu essen und zu trinken gibt! Sag deinem Partner, was du möchtest! Tauscht dann die Rollen aus!

1. Noun phrases that follow **es gibt** are always in the accusative case.

Saying you do or don't want more

In **Kapitel 8** you learned how to ask if someone wants something else when shopping. When eating at a café or at your friend's house, you may also be asked what else you would like.

The host or your friend might ask:

Möchtest du noch etwas?

Möchtest du noch einen Saft?

Noch eine Semmel?

You might respond:

Ja, bitte, ich nehme noch eine Brezel. *or*
Nein, danke! Ich habe keinen Hunger mehr. *or*
Nein, danke! Ich habe genug. *or*
Danke, nichts mehr für mich.
Ja, bitte. Noch einen Saft. *or*
Nein, danke, keinen Saft mehr.
Ja, gern!

What do you think the phrases **noch einen Saft** and **keinen Saft mehr** mean?[1]
What subject and verb might be understood in the question **Noch eine Semmel?**[2]

21 Hör gut zu!

Markus is having a **Grillfest**. His friends have just finished eating, and he asks them if they want more. Listen to the conversations and decide what each person had to eat or drink. Then listen again and determine whether each person wanted more or not.

	Mara	Silvia	Thomas	Flori	Claudia	Frank
zu essen						
zu trinken						
noch mehr?						

22 Logisch oder unlogisch?

Sind die folgenden Aussagen logisch oder unlogisch? Wenn sie unlogisch sind, ändere die Aussagen, damit sie logisch sind!

1. Ja, bitte, ich möchte noch einen Leberkäs. Ich habe keinen Hunger.
2. Nein, danke! Nichts mehr für mich. Ich möchte noch eine Weißwurst.
3. Ja, ich habe Hunger. Ich möchte noch eine Semmel.
4. Ja, bitte, ich trinke noch einen Saft. Ich habe Apfelsaft gern.
5. Ich habe noch Hunger. Ich nehme noch ein Käsebrot.
6. Ja, bitte, noch eine Tasse Tee. Ich trinke Tee nicht gern.

Schon bekannt
Ein wenig *Grammatik*

In **Kapitel 5** you learned about the indefinite article **ein** (*a, an*). If the noun is a subject, **ein** is used with masculine and neuter nouns, and **eine** with feminine nouns. When the noun following **ein** is used as a direct object, the masculine form is **einen**. The possessive pronouns **mein, dein, sein,** and **ihr** also have these same endings.

When **noch** precedes the indefinite article **ein**, it has the meaning of *another*.

1. *another juice, no more juice* 2. **Möchtest du**

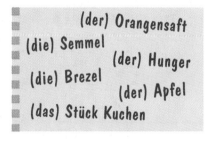

> (der)
> **Blumenkohl**
> *(cauliflower)*
>
> (der) **Rosenkohl**
> *(Brussel sprouts)*
>
> (die) **Zwiebel** *(onion)*
>
> (die) **Milch** (der) **Spinat**
> *(spinach)*
>
> (der) **Haferbrei**
> *(oatmeal)*
>
> (die) **Leber**
> *(liver)*
>
> (die) **Wurst**

23 Was ißt oder trinkst du überhaupt nicht?

Are there some things that you refuse to eat or drink? Take turns asking and telling your classmates about these things, using **kein** in your answers. For example, **Ich trinke keine Limo.** Use the box for ideas or turn to page 321 for additional words.

24 Noch etwas?

Nach der Schule sind einige Freunde bei Mara zu Hause und essen etwas. Ergänze das Gespräch mit den Wörtern im Kasten und der richtigen Form von **kein** und **noch ein!**

MARA Wer möchte noch was trinken oder essen? Du, Flori, möchtest du __1__?
FLORI Ja, gern, Äpfel esse ich sehr gern.
MARA Und mehr Orangensaft?
FLORI Nein, danke. __2__ mehr.
MARA Und du Claudia, du hast nur ein Stück Kuchen gegessen. Möchtest du noch etwas?
CLAUDIA Ja, __3__ bitte und auch ein Mineralwasser.
MARA Und Markus? Willst du auch noch eine Semmel?
MARKUS Nein, __4__ mehr. Danke! Ich habe __5__.
MARA Und du, Rolf? Hast du noch Hunger?
ROLF Ja, ein bißchen. Ich hab' nur eine Brezel gegessen. Ich möchte __6__. Brezeln esse ich immer gern!
CLAUDIA Das weiß ich!

> (der) **Orangensaft**
> (die) **Semmel**
> (der) **Hunger**
> (die) **Brezel**
> (der) **Apfel**
> (das) **Stück Kuchen**

25 Möchtest du noch ein …?

Du hast jetzt ein Grillfest. Es gibt noch viel zu essen und zu trinken. Frag deinen Partner, ob er noch etwas haben möchte! Dein Partner sagt ja (mit **noch ein**) oder nein (mit **kein … mehr**). Dann tauscht ihr die Rollen aus!

LERNTRICK

Take note of words that are similar and follow the same grammatical patterns. For example, **ein** and **kein** look and sound alike and have the same endings before nouns. Can you think of other words you have learned that look and sound like **ein** and **kein**?[3]

---

1. *not, not any,* or *no* 2. **Kein** has the same endings as **ein**. 3. **mein, dein,** and **sein**.

26 Ein Leserbrief

Lies diesen Brief an die Zeitschrift **Jugend** und beantworte die Fragen!

a.
1. Woher kommt Eva?
2. Wann ist sie geboren?
3. Welches Hobby hat Eva?
4. Wie finden die Eltern Evas Hobby?
5. Was hofft Eva? (**hoffen** *to hope*)

b. Find the two sentences in which the word **daß** is used. What is Eva trying to express in these sentences? What is the English equivalent of **daß**? What is the position of the verb in the clauses that begin with **daß**?

Hobby

Ich heiße Eva Hörster und bin am 17.10.74 in München geboren. Ich laufe mit den Rollschuhen auf der Straße oder auf der Rollschuhbahn. Meine Eltern finden es gut, daß ich Sport treibe. Sie begleiten mich immer zum Training und Langlauf. Ich hoffe, daß Rollschuhlaufen eine olympische Sportart wird. Das Foto ist nach meinem ersten Pokalsieg aufgenommen worden.

Viele Grüße,
Eva Hörster, München

SO SAGT MAN DAS!

Expressing opinions

In **Kapitel 2** you learned to express opinions such as: **Ich finde Tennis super!** You can also use a **daß**-clause to elaborate on your opinions.

Your friend might ask:

Wie findest du München?

You might respond:

Super! Ich finde es toll, daß es hier so viele Parks und Museen gibt. Und ich glaube, daß die Leute sehr freundlich sind. Aber ich finde es schlecht, daß das Essen so teuer ist.

What are the different phrases that begin the sentences expressing opinions? What is the subject in each **daß**-clause? What opinion is being expressed in each sentence?

Grammatik   The conjunction daß

Look again at the responses in the **So sagt man das!** box. Name the verbs in the **daß**-clauses.[1] What is the position of these verbs?[2] The conjunction **daß** often begins clauses that express opinions: **Ich finde, daß .... Ich glaube, daß ....** In clauses that begin with **daß**, the conjugated verb is at the end of the clause.

München **ist** sehr schön.

Ich glaube, daß München [ ] sehr schön **ist**.

What other conjunction do you know that affects the word order in the same way?[3]

---

1. **gibt, sind, ist** 2. at the end of the clause 3. **weil**

27 Hör gut zu!

You're listening to a radio talk show as several teenagers call in to give their opinion on different topics. Listen to the four call-ins and for each one write the name and the age of the person calling and the general topic on which he or she is expressing an opinion.

28 Was sagst du dazu?

Sag deinen Klassenkameraden, was du glaubst!

BEISPIEL   **Die Münchner sind sehr freundlich.**
         DU   **Ich glaube, daß die Münchner sehr freundlich sind.** *oder*
                 Ich glaube nicht, daß die Münchner sehr freundlich sind.

1. Kinokarten sind zu teuer.
2. Politik ist interessant.
3. Hausaufgaben machen Spaß.
4. Fernsehen macht klug *(smart)*.
5. Schüler sind faul *(lazy)*.
6. Pizzaessen ist gesund *(healthy)*.

29 Wie findest du ...?

Write down at least two opinions about three of the topics on the right. Then, work with your partner and ask each other about some of the topics.

BEISPIEL   DU   **Wie findest du ...**
           PARTNER   **Ich glaube, daß ...**

> Rollschuhlaufen   der Präsident*
> Deutsch   Englisch   Sport
> Auto fahren   Fernsehsendungen

AUSSPRACHE

Richtig aussprechen / Richtig lesen

A. To practice the following sounds, say the words and sentences below after your teacher or after the recording.

1. The long vowels **ü** and **ö**: In **Kapitel 1** you learned how to pronounce the letters **ü** and **ö** as long vowels.

   führen, für, spülen / Kannst für mich das Geschirr spülen?
   blöd, hören, Österreich / Ich höre gern Rock, aber Disko finde ich blöd.

2. The letters **s, ss,** and **ß**: At the beginning of a syllable the letter **s** is pronounced much like the *z* in the English word *zebra.* However, if it is followed by the letters **t** or **p**, it sounds like the *sh* combination in the English word *shine.* In the middle or at the end of a syllable, the letter **s** is pronounced the same as the *s* in the English word *post;* the letters **ß** and **ss** are always pronounced this way as well.
   Senf, super, Semmel / Sonja will eine Wurst mit Senf und eine Semmel.
   Straße, Innenstadt, Spaß / Wo ist die Spatzenstraße? In der Innenstadt?
   Wurst, besser, Imbiß / Die Wurst ist besser in der Imbißstube hier rechts.

Richtig schreiben / Diktat

B. Write down the sentences that you hear.

***Der Präsident** belongs to a small group of nouns (called *weak nouns*) that add **-n** or **-en** in the accusative case: **Ich kenne den Präsidenten.** Some other nouns in this group are: **der Name (den Namen), der Junge (den Jungen),** and **der Herr (den Herrn).**

Ein Bummel durch München

LESETRICK

Reading for a purpose
When you read for information, it is a good idea to decide beforehand what kind of information you want. If you simply want an overview, a general reading will suffice. If you need specific information, a close reading will be required.

1. These articles are from a book called **Merian live! München**. What kind of book do you think it is?
   a. a history book
   b. a book about parks and gardens
   c. a travel guide

2. When you read a travel guide, you generally have one of two specific purposes: to gather general information about what is going on, or to find specific information about an event — cost, time, date, etc. In which case would you skim to get the gist, and in which case would you scan for specific information?

3. How is information in a travel guide organized? Group the places listed below under one of these three general headings: **Essen und Trinken, Einkaufen, Sehenswertes.**

Sportmode, Deutsches Museum, Cafés, Restaurants, Geschenkwaren, Alte Pinakothek, Peterskirche, Stehimbisse, Kaufhäuser, Englischer Garten, Konditoreien, Fotogeschäfte

	Durchschnittstemperaturen in °C		Sonnenstunden	Regentage
	Tag	Nacht	pro Tag	
Januar	1,4	-5,6	1,8	11
Februar	3,4	-5,1	2,9	10
März	8,7	-1,5	3,9	9
April	13,5	2,8	5,4	10
Mai	18,0	6,6	6,0	12
Juni	21,3	10,0	7,5	14
Juli	23,2	12,1	7,8	13
August	22,7	11,4	6,7	12
September	19,6	8,4	6,0	10
Oktober	13,3	3,7	4,5	9
November	6,6	0,1	1,9	9
Dezember	2,3	-3,8	1,2	10

Quelle: Deutscher Wetterdienst, Offenbach

Lebensmittel

Dallmayr
In den heiligen Hallen der Gaumenfreuden wird sogar der Kauf einer banalen Kiwi zum gastronomischen Ereignis. Münchens ältestes Feinkosthaus ist nicht zuletzt seines aromatischen Kaffees wegen weit über die Grenzen der Stadt hinaus bekannt geworden.
2 Dienerstr. 14/15
U-/S-Bahn: Marienplatz

Januar
Fasching
Die »närrische Saison« beginnt in München mit dem 7. Januar und endet in der Nacht zwischen Faschingsdienstag und Aschermittwoch. In diesen Wochen quillt das städtische Veranstaltungsprogramm über von Faschingsbällen aller Art – exklusiven und volkstümlichen, intimen und massenhaften.

Als gesellschaftliche Höhepunkte der Faschingssaison gelten der Chrysanthemenball, Magnolienball, Madameball, Filmball und Presseball. Die phantasievollsten oder auch aufwendigsten Kostüme und Dekorationen sind beim Karneval in Rio im Bayerischen Hof, bei den Festen der Damischen Ritter, den Weißen Festen und der Vorstadthochzeit zu sehen.

Seiner Tradition nach findet der Münchner Fasching im Saal statt, nicht auf der Straße wie etwa der Rheinische Karneval. Nur während der drei letzten Faschingstage – von Sonntag bis Dienstag – tummelt sich das närrische Volk auch im Freien, vor allem in der Fußgängerzone, am Marienplatz und auf dem Viktualienmarkt, wo am Faschingsdienstag ab 6 Uhr in der Früh die Marktfrauen tanzen.

Englischer Garten
Münchens vielgeliebte »grüne Lunge« – etwa 5 km lang, bis zu 1 km breit und mit einer Gesamtausdehnung von nahezu 4 km². Entstanden ist der Englische Garten aus einer Anregung des unter Kurfürst Karl Theodor amtierenden Ministers Benjamin Thompson (später Graf Rumford), einen Volkspark in der Art der englischen Landschaftsgärten in den Isarauen anzulegen. 1789 begannen die Arbeiten am Park, die ab 1804 vom Gartenarchitekten Ludwig von Sckell geleitet wurden. Am auffälligsten unter den Bauten im Park sind der Chinesische Turm (1790), nach der Zerstörung im Krieg 1952 originalgetreu wiederaufgebaut, der Monopteros, ein klassizistischer Rundtempel nach einem Entwurf Leo von Klenzes im Auftrag Ludwigs I. (1837/38), das Japanische Teehaus, das Mitsuo Nomura 1972 anläßlich der Olympischen Spiele in München als Geschenk Japans an die Olympia-Stadt erbaut hat. Hinzu kommt der künstlich angelegte Kleinhesseloher See mit drei kleinen Inseln, einem Bootsverleih und dem Seehaus (Restaurant und Biergarten).

Zugänge zum Park gibt es am Haus der Kunst, an der Veterinärstraße (Nähe Universität), Gunezrhainerstraße (Nähe Münchner Freiheit), am Seehaus (Ausfahrt Mittlerer Ring) sowie an der Tivolistraße (Nähe Max-Joseph-Brücke). (→ Spaziergänge)

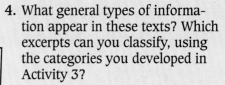

Olympiapark

Auf dem ehemaligen Oberwiesenfeld wurde für die XX. Olympischen Spiele 1972 von der Architektengemeinschaft Günter Behnisch und Partner dieser Park entworfen.

Der 52 m hohe Olympiaberg wurde auf zusammengetragenen Ruinentrümmern des Zweiten Weltkrieges angelegt und mit voralpiner Vegetation begrünt.

Als weitere Sportstätten gibt es das Eissportstadion, die Schwimmhalle (»Europas schönstes Garten-Hallenbad«) und das Radstadion. Die Olympiahalle selbst dient auch Kongressen, Ausstellungen und Konzerten.

Kaufhäuser

Ludwig Beck

Eine Münchner Institution. Auf vier Stockwerken gibt es vom Lodenmantel bis zum Gaultier-Jäckchen vor allem Mode zu kaufen; man findet aber auch den passenden Schmuck dazu, Tisch- und Bettwäsche, originelles Küchenzubehör, eine riesige Jazz-Auswahl auf CD – sowie Münchens nettester Verkäufer! Für das leibliche Wohl empfehlen sich drei Restaurants, darunter eine Sushi-Bar.
Marienplatz 11
U-/S-Bahn: Marienplatz

Medizinische Versorgung

Bitte wenden Sie sich an den Hotelportier.

Auskunft dienstbereiter Apotheken:
Tel. 59 44 75

Große Apotheken im Zentrum:
Internationale Ludwigs-Apotheke
Neuhauser Str. 8
Von Mendel'sche Apotheke
(große Abteilung für homöopathische Medikamente)
40 Leopoldstr. 58

Peterskirche, St. Peter

Erste und lange Zeit einzige Pfarrkirche der Stadt, deren erster Bau (erste Hälfte 11. Jh.) älter als die Stadt selbst ist. In der Folgezeit erlebte das Gotteshaus zahlreiche Erweiterungen und Modernisierungen in den Stilen der Gotik, der Renaissance und des Barock. Die Bombenzerstörungen der Jahre 1944/45 waren so schwer, daß man die Kirche beinahe gänzlich gesprengt hätte.

Der **Turm »Alter Peter«** ist – neben den Türmen der Frauenkirche – das Wahrzeichen der Stadt geblieben. 302 hölzerne Stufen führen an den vier Glocken vorbei zur Aussichtsgalerie.

DER BESONDERE TIP

Isar-Floßfahrt Floßfahrten auf der Isar zwischen Wolfratshausen und München sind eine bei Alt und Jung sehr beliebte »Gaudi«. Die Fahrt selbst dauert etwa sieben Stunden; eine Mittagspause wird an Land eingelegt. Zu einer Floßfahrt kann man sich freilich nicht spontan entschließen: Die meisten Termine sind (von Firmen, Vereinen, Freundeskreisen) schon lange im voraus gebucht. Einzelpassagiere wenden sich an das Amtliche Bayerische Reisebüro (ABR), das sich ein Kontingent für »Individualisten« zu sichern pflegt.

Feuchtfröhliche Gaudi ohnegleichen: Isarfloßfahrten

4. What general types of information appear in these texts? Which excerpts can you classify, using the categories you developed in Activity 3?

5. What are the names of some places to go shopping for fine foods? For fashionable clothes?

6. Where would you go in these situations?
   a. It's the middle of January and you want to go dancing.
   b. You want to go for a long relaxing walk.
   c. You have a sore throat and you need throat lozenges.
   d. You have been invited to someone's home and you want to buy a special coffee for them.

7. If you had a whole day free and wanted to do something out of the ordinary, what special tip does the guidebook give? Could you do it on the spur of the moment, or do you have to plan ahead? How do you know?

8. Read the excerpts **Peterskirche, St. Peter** and **Olympiapark** and see if you can answer these questions. How old is the **Peterskirche**? What would you see if you climbed the steps of the **Alter Peter**? When was the **Olympiapark** built? How high is the mountain in the **Olympiapark**, and what is it made out of?

9. You are going to be in Munich for a day in June. Plan what you would do. How will the weather chart help you in making your plans? What can you do in June that you could not have done in January? What could you have done in January that you cannot do in June?

1 Listen to some American students tell their friends back in Rosenheim about their day in **München** with Mara and Markus. Make a list of where they were and what they bought.

 2 You work at the information desk in the train station, and several people need your help. Take turns with your partner asking for and giving the requested information. Use the cues below to formulate your questions. Different people want to know:

where a bank is

where the post office is

where a restaurant is

if there is a hotel here

if there's a subway station here

where to buy flowers

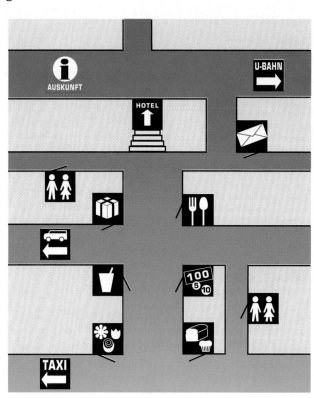

3 Lies die Postkarte rechts und beantworte die folgenden Fragen!

a. Wie findet Jörg die Stadt München? Was sagt er?

b. Warum ißt er soviel Leberkäs und so viele Weißwürste?

c. Was besichtigt (besichtigen: *to sightsee*) Jörg in München?

Hallo Bärbel!
Einen kurzen Gruß aus
München, wo ich kaum was
anderes als Leberkäs und
Weißwurst esse, weil sie hier
sagenhaft gut sind. Ich mache
aber auch hier einen echten
Kulturtrip mit Frauenkirche,
Rathaus usw. Ich finde, daß
München eine unheimlich starke
Stadt ist, weil es hier eine gute
Szene gibt, viele junge Leute,
viel zu tun.
Mehr wenn wir uns wieder-
sehen. Bis dann, Alles Gute   Jörg

Bärbel Hörster
Eichenwegstr. 35
48161 Münster

4 In this chapter you have learned a lot about Munich. Write a postcard either to your parents or to a friend giving your opinions about the city or write a postcard about some other place you have visited. Use the postcard on page 236 as a model for your salutation and closing.

5 You have learned your way around Mittersendling but your visiting American friend has not. Your friend will tell you three things he or she needs to do or buy. Tell your friend where he or she needs to go (bakery, butcher shop, etc.) and how to get there. Decide together on a starting point and use the map on page 225. Then switch roles.

DU **Ich brauche ...** *oder* **Ich muß ... kaufen.**
PARTNER **Also, du mußt zum/zur ... gehen?**
Geh ...!

6

R O L L E N S P I E L

Get together with two other classmates and role-play the following scene.

Design a menu for an **Imbißstube** and write it on a piece of paper or poster board. Then, with three other classmates, develop a conversation at the snack stand that is based on the following situation.

a. You are discussing with your friends what's available at the stand. Then each of you orders something. Ask what it costs and pay the person behind the counter. Be polite!

b. As you enjoy the food, discuss how the food tastes and if someone wants more or not. If so, order more. Discuss with your friends some of your opinions about the city of Munich, which you are visiting today.

Can you talk about where something is located? (p.222)

1 How would you ask an older passerby where the following places are using **wissen**? How would you ask someone who is your own age? How would you answer?

  a. Frauenkirche (... Straße)
  b. Rathaus (Marienplatz)
  c. Museum (Maximilianstraße)

Can you ask for and give directions? (p. 226)

2 How would you ask for directions from the **X**-mark to the following places?

  a. zum Bahnhof
  b. zum Theater
  c. zum Marktplatz
  d. zur Bank

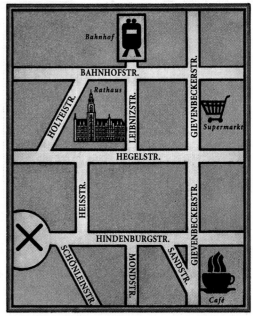

3 How would you tell an older person to get to the following places using the command forms? Someone your own age? Use the **X**-mark as the starting point.

By vehicle:	On foot:
a. to the train station	a. to the supermarket
b. to the town hall	b. to the café

Can you talk about what there is to eat and drink? (p. 229)

4 How would you ask what there is to eat? And to drink? How would you tell someone what there is to eat or drink, using the items below?

  a. **Leberkäs**   c. apple juice   e. salad
  b. whole wheat rolls d. tea   f. grilled chicken

Can you ask or tell someone that you do or don't want more? (p. 230)

5 How would you ask someone if he or she wants more? How would you tell someone that you want more of the items below or that you don't want more, using **noch ein** and **kein ... mehr**?

  a. piece of cake   c. mineral water
  b. roll   d. ice-cream

Can you express opinions using daß-clauses? (p. 232)

6 a. How would you give your opinion about the following statement. How would you agree with it? And disagree?

  Autofahren ist gefährlich.

  b. State your opinions about school in general. Write at least two sentences using **daß**-clauses.

ERSTE STUFE

IN DER INNENSTADT

die Stadt, -̈e   *city*
das Rathaus, -̈er   *city hall*
der Marktplatz, -̈e   *market square*
die Post   *post office*
der Bahnhof, -̈e   *railroad station*
die Bank, -en   *bank*

die Kirche, -n   *church*
das Hotel, -s   *hotel*
der Garten, -̈   *garden*
das Museum, die Museen   *museum*
das Theater, -   *theater*
die U-Bahnstation, -en   *subway station*

TALKING ABOUT WHERE SOMETHING IS LOCATED

die Straße, -n   *street*
am ... platz   *on ... Square*
wissen   *to know (a fact, information, etc.)*
Entschuldigung!
Verzeihung! } *Excuse me!*
Es tut mir leid.   *I'm sorry.*
Keine Ahnung!   *I have no idea!*

ZWEITE STUFE

ASKING FOR AND GIVING DIRECTIONS

Wie komme ich zum (zur) ...   *How do I get to ...*
nach links   *to the left*
nach rechts   *to the right*
geradeaus   *straight ahead*
bis zur Ampel   *until you get to the traffic light*

bis zur ... Straße   *until you get to ... Street*
bis zum ... Platz   *until you get to ... Square*
die nächste Straße   *the next street*
die erste (zweite, dritte, vierte) Straße   *the first (second, third, fourth) street*

wieder   *again*
fahren   *to go somewhere, ride, drive (using a vehicle)*
er/sie fährt   *he/she drives is driving/is going*
Vielen Dank!   *Thank you very much!*
Gern geschehen!   *My pleasure!*

DRITTE STUFE

TALKING ABOUT WHAT THERE IS TO EAT AND DRINK

die Imbißstube, -n   *snack bar*
der Leberkäs   *Bavarian specialty* See p. 229.
   mit Senf   *with mustard*
die Weißwurst, -̈e   *Southern German sausage specialty* See p. 229.
die Vollkornsemmel, -n   *whole grain roll*
das Gyros   *gyros*

SAYING YOU DO OR DON'T WANT MORE

Ich möchte noch ein(e)(en) ...   *I'd like another ...*
Ich möchte kein(e)(en) ... mehr.   *I don't want another .../anymore*
noch ein(e) (en)   *more, another one*
genug   *enough*
kein   *no, none, not any*
kein (en)... mehr   *no more ...*
Nichts mehr, danke!   *No more, nothing else, ... thanks!*

EXPRESSING OPINIONS

daß   *that*
Ich finde, daß ...   *I think that...*
Ich finde es gut/schlecht, daß ...   *I think it's good/ bad that...*
die Leute (pl)   *people*

OTHER WORDS AND PHRASES

probieren   *to try*
mal   (short for **einmal**) *once*

KAPITEL 10, 11, 12

Komm mit nach

Baden-Württemberg!

Baden-Württemberg

Einwohner: 9 300 000

Fläche: 36 000 Quadratkilometer (13 896 Quadratmeilen), etwa halb so groß wie Südkarolina

Landeshauptstadt: Stuttgart (570 000 Einwohner)

Große Städte: Mannheim, Karlsruhe, Freiburg, Heilbronn, Heidelberg, Pforzheim

Flüsse: Donau, Rhein, Neckar, Jagst, Kocher

Seen: Bodensee

Berge: Feldberg (1493 Meter hoch), Belchen (1414 Meter hoch)

Industrien: Maschinenbau, Automobilindustrie, Elektrotechnik, Chemie, Feinmechanik, Optik

Beliebte Gerichte: Spätzle, Schwarzwälder Kirschtorte, Maultaschen, Schinken

Foto ①: **Das Alte Schloß in Meersburg am Bodensee**

Baden-Württemberg

*The southwestern German state of Baden-Württemberg is known both for its charming landscapes and for its high-tech industries. The **Schwarzwald** (Black Forest) with its traditional farmhouses is one of Germany's most popular tourist regions. The area around Stuttgart, the state capital, is home to major automobile and electronics firms, as well as hundreds of highly specialized small companies producing textiles, watches, and optical iinstruments.*

③ A typical village in the Black Forest

② The **Hexenloch Mühle** in St. Märgen in the Black Forest.

④ The picturesque town of Besigheim on the river Enz

⑤ The City Hall **(Rathaus)** in Bietigheim, built in 1507

*The remaining chapters (10, 11, and 12) are set in Bietigheim-Bissingen, a town near Stuttgart. This historic town on the River Enz still has many old half-timbered houses. Among its inhabitants are the teenagers in these three chapters, who attend the **Ellental Gymnasium**.*

⑥ A typical house facade along the witches' walk **(Hexenwegle)** in Bietigheim

⑦ Martin, Andreas, Thomas, Sabine, Sandra, and Nicole invite you to join them in Bietigheim.

10
Kino und Konzerte

1 Ich mag am liebsten klassische Musik.

Teenagers in German-speaking countries like to do things together. Sometimes they go to movies and concerts. Groups of students often go to someone's house and watch a video or just sit around and talk. Does this sound like you and your friends? Do you go out together—or stay at home and watch videos, listen to music, and talk? When you get together with your friends, there are a lot of things you'll want to be able to talk about.

In this unit you will learn

- to express likes and dislikes;
  to express familiarity
- to express preferences and favorites
- to talk about what you did in your free time

And you will

- listen to a popular German song
- read reviews of films, music, and books
- write about your favorite music group,
  singer, or movie star
- find out what kind of movies, music, and books students in German-speaking countries enjoy

Sommer-Programm im August

Dienstags 22.⁰⁰ ➤➤➤ KINO

Monty Python:
2 Folgen Flying Circus
+ Die wunderbare Welt
der Schwerkraft
3.8. Beatles Night
Yellow Submarine + Help
10.8. Die Kleinen Stolche
17.8. Das siebte Zeichen
24.8. Cyrano de Bergerac
31.8. Zeit des Erwachens

③ Hast du „Monty Python" gesehen?

② Actionfilme sehe ich furchtbar gern.

Los geht's!

Wie verbringt ihr eure Freizeit?

Look at the above title and the photos that accompany these interviews. What are the people in the photos doing? What clues in the photos help you determine what the students might be talking about?

THOMAS

Wir sind eine Clique, drei Jungen und drei Mädchen, und — na ja — wir machen viel zusammen, besonders Sport. Wir joggen zusammen, wir fahren Rad, einmal im Monat gehen wir kegeln. Aber sonst hat jeder auch seine eigenen Interessen. Ich zum Beispiel gehe oft in Konzerte. Rockkonzerte höre ich am liebsten.

SANDRA

Ab und zu gehe ich auch in ein Rockkonzert. Aber die Karten sind so furchtbar teuer und, ehrlich gesagt, höre ich lieber Country. Die Clique kommt manchmal zu mir, und jeder bringt eine Kassette oder eine CD. Wir hören dann Musik und spielen Karten oder Brettspiele.

MARTIN

Ich muß sagen, ich mag Rock
überhaupt nicht. Ich mag auch
die meisten Country Sänger nicht.
Ich mag am liebsten klassische
Musik, Brahms, Ravel und so.
Ich gehe sehr gern ins Konzert
und auch in die Oper.

BEI JUGENDKARTEN IST
AUF VERLANGEN EIN GÜLTIGER
SCHÜLERAUSWEIS O.Ä.
VORZUZEIGEN

KINO
DELTA-CENTER

EINHEITSPREIS AUF ALLEN PLÄTZEN 10.-

**MONTAG
KINOTAG**
DER TAG, AN DEM ES PROZENT GIBT.
* **JEDEN
DONNERSTAG**
DER BESONDERE FILM

JUGEND BIS 14 J.
EINHEITSPREIS AUF ALLEN PLÄTZEN
NUR NACHMITTA
BEI JUGENDFRE
FIL

FREI AB 12

Komm, wir gehn ins **KINO**

NICOLE

Was ich am liebsten mache? Ganz
einfach! Ich geh' am liebsten ins
Kino. Fantasyfilme und Komödien
sind meine Lieblingsfilme. Was ich
nicht mag? Ich hasse Actionfilme.
Die sind meistens so brutal. Mein
Lieblingsfilm ist und bleibt *Kevin
— Allein zu Haus,* und meine
Lieblingsschauspieler sind Joe
Pesci und Whoopi Goldberg.

SABINE

Ja, unsere Clique ist toll. Es
stimmt, wir sind viel unterwegs,
sehen viel. Wir kommen aber
oft zusammen und diskutieren
über Filme, Musik, Stars und so.
Ich selbst bin auch gern zu
Hause. Ich lese furchtbar gern.
Ich habe viele Bücher.

1 Was passiert hier?

Do you understand what the students are talking about in the interviews? Check your comprehension by answering the following questions. Don't be afraid to guess.

1. What is the main idea of each of the five interviews?
2. What is each student's main interest or interests?
3. Which of the students mention something they don't like? What do they mention?

2 Mix und Match: Interessen

Match each students name with his or her interests or with the interests and activities of that student's **Clique**.

1. Thomas   **a.** klassische Musik hören und in Konzerte und in die Oper gehen
2. Sandra   **b.** joggen, radfahren, kegeln
3. Martin   **c.** über Filme, Musik, Stars usw. diskutieren, Bücher lesen
4. Nicole   **d.** Musik hören, Karten und Brettspiele spielen
5. Sabine   **e.** ins Kino gehen, besonders Fantasyfilme und Komödien sehen

3 Erzähl weiter!

Which of the students might have made each of these statements in his or her interview?

1. Heute abend, zum Beispiel, gehe ich ins Beethovenkonzert. Martin
2. Mein Lieblingsbuch ist *Die unendliche Geschichte*. Sabine
3. Und ich habe alle Filme mit Steve Martin gesehen. nicole
4. Meine Freunde hören auch gern Country. Sandra
5. Ach ja! Wir segeln auch gern. Thomas

4 Genauer lesen

Reread the interviews. Which words or phrases do the students use to

1. name sports
2. name different kinds of music
3. name other free time activities
4. name different kinds of films
5. express likes and dislikes
6. say that something is their favorite

Frühkonzert in einer Halle auf dem Hamburger Fischmarkt

5 Und du?

Now write your own interview. First choose the interview that most closely describes the free time activities you like to do. Then rewrite the interview, replacing any information with your own particular interests.

Expressing likes and dislikes; expressing familiarity

WORTSCHATZ

SANDRA   Wie verbringst du deine Freizeit?

MARTIN   Ich gehe gern mit Freunden ins Kino und sehe ...

Actionfilme
Der Terminator 2

Horrorfilme
Dracula

Krimis
Eine Frage der Ehre

Abenteuerfilme
Indiana Jones–und der letzte Kreuzzug

Liebesfilme
Entscheidung aus Liebe

Kriegsfilme
Das Boot

Komödien
Kevin - Allein in New York

Westerns
Zwölf Uhr mittags

Science-fiction-Filme
Star Trek 6 - Das unbekannte Land

6 Welche Filme erkennst du? *Which films do you recognize?*

Welche Filme auf Seite 249 erkennst du? Wie heißen sie auf deutsch? Was bedeuten Wörter wie, zum Beispiel, Horrorfilme oder Krimis? Wie heißen diese Filmarten auf englisch?

SO SAGT MAN DAS!
Expressing likes and dislikes

You have learned several ways of expressing likes and dislikes, using **gern** and **nicht gern** with various verbs, and using the verb **gefallen**. Another way to express what you like or don't like is with the present tense of the verb **mögen**.

You might ask:

> **Was für Musik magst du?**
> **Und Filme?**
> **Magst du auch Abenteuerfilme?**
>
> **Magst du Kevin Costner?**

The responses might be:

> **Ich mag Rock und auch Jazz.**
> **Horrorfilme mag ich sehr gern.**
> **Ja, furchtbar gern!** *or*
> **Nein, überhaupt nicht.**
> **Ja, ich mag ihn besonders gern.**

What do you think the phrase **Was für ...** means?[1]

7 Hör gut zu!

Listen to the following interviews about the kinds of movies these German teenagers enjoy seeing. For each interview, write the name of the person being interviewed. Then, beside each name, write the kinds of movies the person likes and does not like.

8 Und was magst du?

You can use **mögen** to talk about anything you like or do not like. Ask your classmates how much they like or don't like some forms of entertainment and some of the entertainers listed in the box.

WORTSCHATZ

You can use these expressions to talk about how much you like or don't like someone or something.

furchtbar gern
besonders gern
sehr gern
gern

nicht gern
gar nicht gern
überhaupt nicht gern

Westerns   Jazz   Horrorfilme

Madonna   Andy Garcia   Krimis

Eddie Murphy   Klaviermusik

---

*G*rammatik   The verb **mögen**

The verb **mögen** (*to like, care for*) has the following forms.

Ich **mag** Filme gern.	Wir **mögen** Horrorfilme.
Du **magst** auch Jazz, nicht?	Ihr **mögt** aber Krimis, nicht?
Er/Sie **mag** Krimis nicht.	Sie/Sie(pl) **mögen** Westerns.

---

1. *what kind of...*

Alba 252 25 45 Central	3/5/7/9 Ab 12 Jahren E/d/f **LITTLE MAN TATE —** 4. Woche **Das Wunderkind Tate** Jodie Foster Bewegendes Regiedebut mit D. Wiest, Harry Connick jr. erobert im Sturm die Herzen der Presse und des Publikums . . .
Capitol 2 251 37 00 beim Central	2.45/4.45/6/45/8/45 Fr/Sa 22.45 E/d/f **THE ADDAMS FAMILY** Ab 12 J. **Verrückt sein ist relativ** . . . um das Unglück abzuwenden, muß der Clan schon seine ganze morbide Raffinesse ausspielen.
Radium 251 18 07 Mühlengasse 7	3/5/7/9 7.Woche Letzte Tage Tun/d/f **DAS VERLORENE HALSBAND DER TAUBE** **— VON DER LIEBE UND DEN LIEBENDEN** Nacer Khemirs traumhaft schöner Märchenfilm über die Liebe Ab 9 Jahren

Judging by the excerpt of movie listings from Germany to the left, from which country do you think most foreign films come? Think about how movies are rated in the U.S. Then scan the movie listing and see if you can find the rating system used in Germany. *(Hint: Look for something that has to do with age.)* How is it different from the one in the U.S.? How much does admission for one person cost in Germany? As you discovered, American movies are very popular in German-speaking countries. Most movies are dubbed into German; however, larger cities usually have at least one movie theater that shows foreign movies with the original sound track.

9 Eine Umfrage

a. Ask your partner what kinds of movies he or she likes and does not like. Then ask what kinds of movies he or she especially likes. Switch roles.

b. Working with your classmates, conduct a survey about the most popular kinds of movies (**Abenteuerfilme, Krimis usw.**). Take turns going to the front of the room and asking someone **Was für Filme mag (Susan) besonders gern?** Write the answers you get in an ongoing chart on the chalkboard. When everyone has been asked, discuss together which types of movies are most popular.

BEISPIEL   **(Cathy) mag ... besonders gern.**

WORTSCHATZ

Rock and Roll	Jazz
Heavy Metal	Disko
klassische Musik	Oper
Country	

Herbert Grönemeyer

DEUTSCHE Bestseller
Ermittelt von Media-Control

SINGLES

1 (1) 8. Wo.	**What's up** 4 Non Blondes	
2 (2) 7. Wo.	**Life** Haddaway	
3 (6) 3. Wo.	**Living on my own** Freddie Mercury	
4 (5) 5. Wo.	**Runaway Train** Soul Asylum	
5 (7) 2. Wo.	**Keep on dancing!** D.J. Bobo	
6 (4) 11. Wo.	**Somebody dance . . .** D.J. Bobo	
7 (3) 17. Wo.	**Mr. Vain** Culture Beat	
8 (8) 13. Wo.	**Falling in Love . . .** UB 40	
9 (9) 5. Wo.	**Happy Nation** Ace of Base	
10 (10) 11. Wo.	**Two Princes** Spin Doctors	

Looking at the pop chart from *Bravo* magazine, what can you say about popular music among teenagers in Germany? Where does most of it come from? There are many well-known German singers, such as Herbert Grönemeyer, Marius Müller-Westernhagen and Ina Deter.

10 Ein Interview

a. Create a list of questions to ask your partner about his or her taste in music. Be sure to obtain the following information: name, age, what kind of music the person likes or dislikes, how much he or she likes or dislikes the music mentioned; if he or she goes to concerts, when, and how often. Take notes using a chart like the one below. Then switch roles.

wer?	wie alt?	was für Musik?	gern/ nicht gern?	Konzerte?	wie oft/ wann?

b. Schreib einen Bericht über deinen Partner! Verwende dabei die Information aus dem Interview oben (*above*)!

SO SAGT MAN DAS!
Expressing familiarity

You may want to find out if your friend is familiar with the films, songs, and groups that you like. You might ask:

Kennst du den Film *Das Rußlandhaus?*

Your friend might respond positively:
Ja, sicher! *or*
Ja, klar!

Or negatively:
Nein, den Film kenne ich nicht *or*
Nein, überhaupt nicht.

11 Hör gut zu!

Listen to some students talking about movies and music with their friends. For each exchange decide whether the person they are speaking to is or is not familiar with the groups, songs or films mentioned.

12 Kennst du die neuste Gruppe aus Amerika?

List three lesser known films, songs, or groups that you like (for example, local musicians). Ask your partner if he or she is familiar with them. If not, he or she will ask questions to find out what kind of movie/music you are talking about. Describe it to your partner. Then switch roles.

Schon bekannt
Ein wenig *Grammatik*

In **Kapitel 7** you learned the verb **wissen** (*to know a fact, information*). The verb **kennen** means *to know* as in *to be acquainted or familiar with* someone or something:

Ja, ich kenne Udo Lindenberg. Kennst du das Lied „Sonderzug nach Pankow"?

The forms of **kennen** are regular in the present tense.

Expressing preferences and favorites

SO SAGT MAN DAS!

Expressing preferences and favorites

When discussing music groups and movies, your friend might ask you about your preferences and favorites.

He or she might ask:

Siehst du gern Horrorfilme?

Siehst du lieber Abenteuerfilme oder Science-fiction-Filme?

Und du, Gabi? Was siehst du am liebsten?

What is the idea expressed by **gern**, **lieber**, and **am liebsten?**[1] What other way can you express that something is your favorite?[2]

You might respond:

Ja, aber Krimis sehe ich lieber. Und am liebsten sehe ich Western.

Lieber Science-fiction-Filme. Aber am liebsten sehe ich Liebesfilme.

Am liebsten sehe ich Komödien.

Ein wenig Grammatik

The words **lieber** and **am liebsten** express preferences and favorites. They are used with **haben** and other verbs in the same way **gern** is used.

Ich sehe gern Actionfilme, aber ich sehe Komödien lieber. Am liebsten sehe ich Krimis.

13 Hör gut zu!

a. Listen to two students tell you what they like and don't like, what they prefer, and what they like most of all. Make a chart like the one below and fill in the information.

	likes	doesn't like	prefers	likes most of all
Marianne				
Stefan				

b. Using the chart you've just completed, take turns with your classmates reporting back in your own words the information from Marianne's and Stefan's interviews.

Ein wenig Grammatik

In **Kapitel 5** you learned that the verb **aussehen** *(to look, appear)* is irregular in the **du-** and **er/sie-** forms. The verb **sehen** *(to see)*, of course, follows this same pattern:

Siehst du gern Horrorfilme?
Er sieht Abenteuerfilme am liebsten.

How would you answer the question **Siehst du gern Horrorfilme?**

1. *like; prefer; like best of all* 2. **Lieblings-**

14 Was wollen wir tun?

Du willst heute abend mit deinem Partner etwas tun. Du wählst etwas von der linken Seite aus, dein Partner von der rechten. Er sagt dir, was er lieber tun möchte. Dann tauscht die Rollen aus!

DU **Wir können ...**
PARTNER **Ich möchte lieber ...**

15 Und was hast du lieber oder am liebsten?

Stell Fragen an einen Klassenkameraden! Dann beantworte die Fragen selbst *(yourself)*! Verwende die Wörter im Kasten *(in the box)* unten mit verschiedenen *(different)* Verben!

Frag deinen Partner:

a. Was hast du oder was machst du gern?
b. Was hast du oder was machst du nicht gern? Was hast du oder was machst du lieber?
c. Was hast du oder was machst du am liebsten?

Western   Country and Western   Kuchen   Pizza   Heavy Metal   Basketball
Rock'nRoll   Fußball   Kaffee   Tennis   Klavier   Cola
Oper   Horrorfilme   schwimmen   Mathe   Karten   Schach
Technik   Gitarre   kegeln   Apfelsaft   sammeln   angeln   Jazz

16 Und du? Wie steht's mit dir?

a. Create a chart in German similar to the one you used in Activity 13 and fill in the following information about yourself: the music you like, prefer, or like the best, and the music you do not like at all. Then get together with your partner and ask him or her questions in order to find out the same information. Take notes using your chart. Then switch roles. Use the chart to help you organize your answers.

b. You must introduce your partner at the next German club meeting, where the topic of the afternoon is music. Use the notes you took on your partner's preferences and favorites in music and write a paragraph introducing him or her and describing his or her interests in music.

17 Das Kinoprogramm

Look at the ads below and answer the questions that follow.

Mittwoch, 7. 7.
20.00 Uhr
Olympia Bissingen

Der mit dem Wolf tanzt
mit Kevin Costner,
Mary McDonell
Regie: Kevin Costner

Donnerstag, 8. 7.
20.00 Uhr
Delta Bietigheim

Mittwoch, 19. 5.
20.00 Uhr
Olympia Bissingen

The Wall
mit Bob Geldof,
Pink Floyd
Regie: Alan Parker

Donnerstag, 20. 5.
20.00 Uhr
Delta Bietigheim

☎ **55 75 40**

| 16.00 | MY GIRL — Meine erste Liebe | 20. Wo./ab 6 J. |

| 18.00 / 20.15 | VATER DER BRAUT | mit Steve Martin | 7. Wo./ab 6 J. |

| 22.30 | DER GEFALLEN, DIE UHR & DER SEHR GROSSE FISCH | 5. Wo./ab 16 J. |
mit Bnh Hoskins, Jeff Goldblum
„Eine sehr schöne Komödie"   tz 100%

"Peppige Dialoge, feinsinniger Humor und jede Menge skurriler Typen." Cinema

MEIN VETTER WINNIE
Eine Gerichtskomödie v. Jonathan Lynn
mit Oscar-Preisträger Joe Pesci
Schwanthalerstr. 3
Tel. 55 57 54 - ab 6 J.
14.45, 17.30, 20.15, Fr./Sa. a. 23.00

Der Boss der Familie ist der mit der großen Schnauze

Ein Hund namens Beethoven
14.00/16.00/18.00/20.00   Fr./Sa. auch 22.00

DO 27.05.	21.30	Filmkritikers Liebling
FR 28.05.		
SA 29.05.		
SO 30.05.		
MO 31.05.		
DI 1.06.		
MI 2.06.	USA 1991	

Thelma & Louise
von Ridley Scott, mit
Geena Davis, Susan Sarandon
und Harvey Keitel

„DIE LUSTIGSTE KOMÖDIE AUS DEUTSCHLAND SEIT ÜBER 10 JAHREN"
Hollywood Reporter
13. Wo.

GOTZ GEORGE • UWE OCHSENKNECHT
▼ SCHTONK!
DER FILM ZUM BUCH VOM FÜHRER
RIO-PALAST
Rosenheimer Platz, Tel. 48 69 79
18.15, 20.30, Di./Mi. auch 16.00

NEUES REX
Agricolastraße 16, Tel. 56 25 00
Täglich 20.30 Uhr

1. What kind of ads are these?
2. Which films do you recognize? Using the pictures and cognates as cues, try to guess what the English titles are for all the different movies listed.
3. What specific kinds of information can you find in these ads?
4. At what times on Friday can you see the movie *Ein Hund namens Beethoven*?
5. What telephone number do you need to call to find out what day *Vater der Braut* is showing? Figure out how long *Vater der Braut* has been showing.
6. Is the movie *Schtonk* showing in more than one movie theater? If so, what are the addresses of the theaters?
7. Look at the listing for *Der mit dem Wolf tanzt*. What does **Regie** mean?
8. How would you describe these movies using the movie categories you learned on page 249 (for example, **Horrorfilme**)?

LERNTRICK

In the expression **am liebsten**, the part of the word that expresses the superlative (= most of all) is the suffix **-sten**. Watching for this suffix will frequently help you understand the meaning of new words. In the ad for **Schtonk** you see the phrase: **die lustigste Komödie. Lustig** means *funny*. What is the ad saying about the film **Schtonk?** What kind of film are you talking about if you say **der traurigste Film?** der **brutalste Film**? You will learn more about the superlative forms later.

18 Wie findest du …?

From the films listed on page 255, choose three that you've already seen or three other movies. Write them on a piece of paper and give it to your partner. He or she will do the same. Now ask your partner his or her opinion of the movies on the list. Then switch roles. Use **weil**-clauses and the adjectives below to express why you do or don't like the movie.

BEISPIEL PARTNER **Wie findest du den Film** *Vater der Braut*?
              DU **Den Film mag ich gar nicht, weil er zu doof ist.**

WORTSCHATZ

Gut!

phantasievoll
lustig
spannend
sensationell

Schlecht!

grausam
zu brutal
zu schmalzig (*corny, mushy*)
dumm
zu traurig
doof (*stupid*)

Don't forget these words that you already know:

Spitze toll langweilig interessant blöd prima

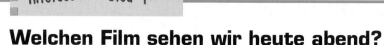

Komödien sind lustig.

Horrorfilme sind grausam, aber Krimis sind spannend.

Liebesfilme können traurig oder oft sehr schmalzig sein.

19 Welchen Film sehen wir heute abend?

You and your partner are using the movie listings on page 255 to select a movie to see tonight. Discuss the types of movies each of you prefers, then make a suggestion and see if your partner agrees. Once you agree on a movie, decide on a time. Share your plans with your classmates.

20 Rate mal!

a. Write a paragraph describing your favorite film or rock star using the new vocabulary and phrases you've learned in this chapter. Refer to your favorite star as **mein Lieblingsstar** or **mein(e) Lieblingssänger(in)**. Here are some questions you will want to answer in your paragraph.

   1. Woher kommt er/sie?
   2. Wie sieht er/sie aus?
   3. Was für Filme macht er/sie? (Was für Lieder singt er/sie?)
   4. Was ist sein/ihr neuster Film? (Was ist sein/ihr neustes Lied?)

b. Now read your description to the class. Your classmates will take turns asking questions and guessing who the mystery person is.

Welche kulturellen Veranstaltungen besuchst du?

LANDESKUNDE

We asked several teenagers in the German-speaking countries what cultural events they usually go to for entertainment. What do you think they might have said? Before you read the interviews, make a list of the types of cultural events that you think German-speaking teenagers might find interesting.

Silvana, *Berlin*

„Also, kulturelle Veranstaltungen ... geh' ich manchmal ins Ballett mit meiner Mutter, also uns interessiert das Ballett: *Schwanensee* war ich schon, *Nußknacker* von Tschaikowsky, und ab und zu gehen wir mit der Schule ins Museum oder zu irgendwelchen Ausstellungen, aber eigentlich nicht so oft."

Silke, *Hamburg*

„Ich geh' auch gern ins Theater, ich kuck' mir auch mal Shakespeare an oder so und auch mal so witzige Theaterstücke, und ich geh' auch sehr gern ins Museum. Und es gab da hier vor kurzem die Picasso-Ausstellung, und die war auch ganz gut."

Tim, *Berlin*

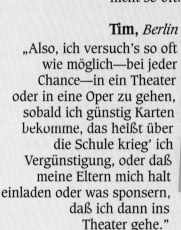

„Also, ich versuch's so oft wie möglich—bei jeder Chance—in ein Theater oder in eine Oper zu gehen, sobald ich günstig Karten bekomme, das heißt über die Schule krieg' ich Vergünstigung, oder daß meine Eltern mich halt einladen oder was sponsern, daß ich dann ins Theater gehe."

Rosi, *Berlin*

„Ich geh' nicht oft zu kulturellen Veranstaltungen, weil ... meine Eltern wollen mich da immer mitnehmen, aber ich hab' dann andere Sachen vor, dann bin ich verabredet und hab' keine Lust. Aber meine Eltern sind schon dafür, daß ich dahin gehen würde."

A. 1. What events do these teenagers like to attend? Make a list of the events each one attends.

2. With your partner, write answers for the following questions. Are all of these teenagers interested in cultural events? If not, what reasons are given for not going to the events? What does the person say? Now look at Tim's interview. What do you think might keep Tim from attending a play or an opera?

3. Compare the list you made before reading the text with what the teenagers actually said. Do teenagers in the German-speaking countries like the same types of cultural events as teenagers where you live? What are some of the differences? Do you think teenagers in the German-speaking countries are more or less interested in cultural events than teenagers where you live? Why do you think this is so? Discuss these answers with your classmates and then write a brief essay in German about the topic.

B. What would you say if you were interviewed about the kinds of cultural events you like? Write your answer in German giving reasons for why you do or don't like particular events.

Talking about what you did in your free time

Hanns-Martin-Schleyer-Halle

Sonntag, 1. März
Peter Maffay

Montag, 2. März
Joe Cocker

Sonntag, 8. März
Musikantenstadl

Samstag, 14. März
Udo Jürgens

Sonntag, 15. März
**Placido Domingo und
Julia Migenes**

Samstag, 28. März
Schöller Oldie Night

Vor und nach der Vorstellung!

Der Treff • für Leute von heute!

WÜRTTEMBERGER-STUBEN
- Dieter Franke -

70174 Stuttgart 10, Schloßstraße 33 (bei der Liederhalle) ☎ 0711/29 03 14
Täglich von 11-24 Uhr geöffnet. | **Küche bis 24 Uhr.**
Sonn - u. feiertags geschlossen.

VIDEO-HITS FILM-VERLEIH

ERMITTELT VON VIPP VIDEO

1. Kevin— Allein zu Haus
(Fox Video)

2. Der Feind in meinem Bett
(Fox Video)

3. Arielle, die Meerjungfrau
(Walt Disney)

4. Pappa ante Portas
(Warner)

5. Flatliners
(RCA/Columbia)

6. Highlander 2
(Highlight)

7. Das Rußlandhaus
(Cannon/VMP)

8. Ghost
(CIC)

9. Aus Mangel an Beweisen
(Warner)

10. Deadly Revenge
(Warner)

Belletristik

1. Antonia Byatt:
Besessen
Insel, 48 Mark (Vorwoche: 1)

2. Rosamunde Pilcher:
Die Muschelsucher
Wunderlich, 42 Mark (3)

3. Donna Tartt:
Die geheime Geschichte
Goldmann, 44 Mark (-)

4. John Grisham:
Die Akte
Hoffmann und Campe, 44 Mark (6)

5. Gabriel García Márquez
Zwölf Geschichten aus der Fremde
Kiepenheuer & Witsch, 36 Mark (8)

6. Eva Heller: Der Mann, der's wert ist
Droemer, 38 Mark (2)

7. Mel Gilden:
Heißkalte Liebe
vgs, 25 Mark (-)

8. Barbara Wood
Das Paradies
Krüger, 49,80 Mark (7)

9. Noah Gordon:
Der Schamane
Droemer, 44 Mark (9)

10. Harry Mulisch:
Die Entdeckung des Himmels
Hanser, 49,80 Mark (-)

Quelle: R. Stuart GmbH

Sachbuch

1. Michael Baigent/Richard Leigh: Verschlußsache Jesus
Droemer, 39,80 Mark (Vorwoche: 2)

2. Carmen Thomas:
Ein besonderer Saft
vgs, 24,80 Mark (1)

3. Günther Ogger:
Nieten in Nadelstreifen
Droemer, 38 Mark (3)

4. Peter Kelder:
Die Fünf „Tibeter"
Integral, 19 Mark (6)

5. Helmut Schmidt:
Handeln für Deutschland
Rowohlt, 34 Mark (4)

6. Al Gore:
Wege zum Gleichgewicht
S. Fischer, 39,80 (7)

7. Robert Eisenman/
Michael Wise:
Jesus und die Urchristen
C. Bertelsmann, 39,80 Mark (5)

8. Paul Kennedy:
In Vorbereitung auf das 21. Jahrhundert
S. Fischer, 48 Mark (9)

9. Dale Carnegie:
Sorge dich nicht
- lebe!
Scherz, 42 Mark (8)

10. Rut Brandt:
Freundesland
Hoffman und Campe, 35 Mark (-)

Quelle: R. Stuart GmbH

21 Was machen die Jugendlichen in ihrer Freizeit?

Sieh dir die Anzeigen *(ads)* zur Freizeitplanung an!

1. Was für Anzeigen siehst du hier?
2. Welche Bücher, Filme oder Stars kennst du schon? Mach eine Liste!
3. Lies die Buchtitel auf den Bestsellerlisten! Was bedeuten „Sachbuch" und „Belletristik"?
4. Wenn du Konzerte magst, welche Anzeige interessiert dich? Wann ist das Konzert von Udo Jürgens? Wo ist es?
5. Welche Videohits kennst du schon? Was kannst du im allgemeinen *(in general)* über den deutschen Videomarkt sagen?

JOACHIM Was liest du?
UTE Oh, ich lese viel, zum
Beispiel ...

Sachbücher

Romane
   Krimis
   Gruselromane
   Liebesromane
   Fantasyromane
   Science-fiction-
     Romane
Hobbybücher

Zeitungen

JOACHIM Und worüber sprichst du
mit deinen Freunden?
UTE Wir sprechen oft über ...
Politik, Mode, die Umwelt

Zeitschriften

22 Was liest du?

Beantworte die folgenden Fragen mit deinen
Klassenkameraden!

1. Liest du gern? Wenn nicht, warum nicht?
2. Was liest du am liebsten?
3. Was ist dein Lieblingsbuch? Was für ein
   Buch ist das?
4. Worüber sprichst du mit deinen Freunden?

Ein wenig Grammatik

The phrase **sprechen über** means *to
talk about* or *discuss.* When you use
a sentence with **sprechen über,** the
noun phrase following the preposition **über** is in the accusative case:

Wir sprechen über den Film
Mein Vetter Vinny.

When you want to find out what
topic people are talking about, you
use **worüber** to begin your sentence:

Worüber sprecht ihr?

Grammatik Stem changing verbs

You have learned some verbs that have stem-vowel
changes, such as **nehmen** and **essen.** Here are two
more: **lesen** *(to read)* and **sprechen** *(to speak).*

Ich	**lese** gern Romane.		Ich	**spreche** gern über Politik.
Du	**liest** oft Sachbücher.		Du	**sprichst** über Mode.
Er/Sie	**liest** gern Krimis.		Er/Sie	**spricht** Deutsch.
Wir	**lesen** Gruselromane.		Wir	**sprechen** über die Umwelt.
Ihr	**lest** Liebesromane.		Ihr	**sprecht** über Politik.
Sie (pl) / Sie	**lesen** Zeitschriften.		Sie (pl) / Sie	**sprechen** Spanish?

Where does the stem-vowel change occur?[1] What are the changes in each verb?[2]

1. **du-** and **er/sie**-forms 2. **lesen:** e>ie; **sprechen:** e>i

23 Was fehlt hier?

Complete the following interview of Nicole and her friends by choosing the correct word from the choices given.

REPORTER   Was für Bücher __1__ du am liebsten? (lese, sprecht, liest)

NICOLE   Tja, normalerweise __2__ ich Fantasybücher oder Krimis. (lesen, lest, lese)

REPORTER   __3__ du auch die Zeitung? (liest, sprechen, lesen)

NICOLE   Na klar! Aber Zeitschriften __4__ ich lieber. (lese, sprecht, spricht)

REPORTER   Und worüber __5__ du mit deinen Freunden? (spreche, lesen, sprichst)

NICOLE   Hm ... normalerweise __6__ wir über Klamotten oder über einen Film aber manchmal auch halt über Politik oder die Umwelt. (sprechen, lesen, spreche)

REPORTER   Und ihr zwei, was __7__ ihr am liebsten? (sprechen, lest, lesen)

MONIKA   Ganz einfach! Wir beide haben Gruselromane furchtbar gern. Wir __8__ sie immer! (sprechen, liest, lesen)

24 In einer Buchhandlung

You are the salesperson in a bookstore and your partner is a customer. Using the clues below, ask questions to find out what type of book to recommend. Make your recommendation, then switch roles.

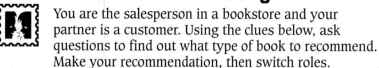

Was für Bücher ...?   Was für Interessen ...?

Worüber sprechen Sie ...?   Lieblingsbuch?

25 Was machst du heute abend?

Diskutiere mit deinem Partner, was du heute machen willst! Was macht dein Partner? Wenn du Ideen brauchst, verwende die vier Anzeigen auf Seite 258.

SO SAGT MAN DAS!

Talking about what you did in your free time

To find out what someone did last weekend you ask:

Was hast du am Wochenende gemacht?

The response might be:

Am Samstag war ich im Herbert Grönemeyer Konzert. Und ich war am Sonntag zu Hause. Am Nachmittag habe ich gelesen, und am Abend habe ich mit Thomas und Martin das Video „Der mit dem Wolf tanzt" gesehen. Danach haben wir über den Film gesprochen.

26 Hör gut zu!

Schüler erzählen, was sie letztes Wochenende gemacht haben. Sind die Antworten zu jedem Gespräch logisch oder unlogisch?

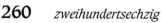

27 Sätze bauen

Was hast du letztes Wochenende gemacht? Wie viele Sätze kannst du bauen?

Ich war ...

im Konzert
im Kino
zu Hause
bei meinen
Freunden

und ich/wir habe(n) ...

den Film ...
die Gruppe ...
das Buch ...
das Video ...
über (die
Hausaufgaben)

gemacht
gesprochen
gesehen
gelesen

28 Hat es Spaß gemacht? *Was it fun?*

Was hast du am Wochenende gemacht? Mach eine Liste! Dann frag deinen Partner, was er gemacht hat! Danach tauscht ihr die Rollen aus!

29 Für mein Notizbuch

Beschreib in deinem Notizbuch dein Lieblingswochenende! Wo warst du? Was hast du alles gemacht? Was hast du gesehen, gelesen oder gekauft?

AUSSPRACHE

Richtig aussprechen / Richtig lesen

A. To review the following sounds, say the sentences below after your teacher or after the recording.

1. The long and short **o**: The long **o** sounds similar to the long *o* in the English word *toe*. When the letter **o** is followed by two or more consonants (except when followed directly by **h**), it is pronounced as a short vowel, as in the English word *top*.
   Wo wohnt die Monika? In der Bodenstraße?
   Mein Onkel Otto kommt oft in der Woche zu Besuch.

2. The long and short **u**: The long **u** is pronounced much like the vowel sound in the English word *do*. However, when the letter **u** is followed by two or more consonants, it is pronounced as a short vowel like the *u* in the English word *put*.
   Ich find' die Musik super. Du auch, Uwe?
   Ulrike mag die Gruppe „Untergrund" furchtbar gern. Und ihr?

3. The letter combination **ch**: When the consonant combination **ch** follows the vowels **e, i, ä, ö,** and **ü**, it is pronounced like the *h* in the English word *huge*. Following the vowels **a, o,** and **u**, it is pronounced further back in the throat.
   So ein Pech! Ich möchte gern mit Michaela ins Kino, aber ich kann nicht.
   Jochen geht doch lieber nach Hause und liest ein Buch und macht Hausaufgaben.

Richtig schreiben / Diktat

B. Write down the sentences that you hear.

Was sagen die Kritiker?

LESETRICK

Watch for false cognates Remember to look for cognates as individual words as well as in compound words to help you determine meanings. Occasionally, you will encounter false cognates (words that look alike in both languages but have totally different meanings). Context clues can sometimes help you recognize false cognates. (A good example of a false cognate is the English word *gift*. You will find the same word in German (**Gift**), but you would hardly want to give it to someone you care about: it means *poison!*)

1. Write the English equivalents for the following cognates:
   a. **exklusiv**
   b. **militärisch**
   c. **desillusioniert**
   d. **Radio-Meteorologe**
   e. **zynisch**
2. You already know a couple of false cognates. Try to determine (from the choices given) what the false cognates in the following sentences might mean.
   a. Wenn du wissen möchtest, welche Themen in Deutschland **aktuell** sind, mußt du eine deutsche Zeitung lesen.
      1. *actual* 2. *out of date*
      3. *current*
   b. Wer einmal diesen Krimi zu lesen begonnen hat, kann **die Lektüre** nicht unterbrechen, weil das Buch so spannend ist.
      1. *lecture* 2. *lesson* 3. *reading*
3. a. With a partner, write down all the cognates you can find in

Groundhog Day
(UND TÄGLICH GRÜSST DAS MURMELTIER)

Phil ist ein Ekel. Doch eines Tages wird der zynische und oberflächliche Radio-Metereologe verzaubert; Die Zeit steht still. Wieder und wieder muß er den von ihm so gehaßten GROUNDHOG DAY, ein Frühlingsfest, in den skurrilsten und wahnwitzigsten Situationen erleben, bis aus ihm endlich ein liebenswerter Mensch geworden ist.

GROUNDHOG DAY von Harold Ramis, mit Bill Murray, Andie MacDowell, Chris Elliott, Stephen Tobolowski u.a.
Englische Originalfassung   103 Min.

MTV NEWS

• Chris Isaak (»Blue Hotel« und »Wicked Game«) hat sich die Arbeit zu seinem neuen Video leicht gemacht. Er engagierte den Kameramann von Regisseur Bertolucci und überließ ihm die ganze Arbeit.

• Bruce Springsteen macht seinen europäischen Fans ein ganz großes Kompliment: Sie unterstützen ihn mehr als die amerikanischen!

JOHN GRISHAM
DIE FIRMA
Wer in der Firma arbeitet, kann sie nie wieder verlassen...
Der Weltbestseller
ROMAN

NEU

John Grisham • Die Firma

Etwas ist faul an der exklusiven Kanzlei, bei der Mitch McDeere arbeitet. Der hochbegabte junge Anwalt wird auf Schritt und Tritt beschattet, er ist umgeben von tödlichen Gefahren. Als er dann noch vom FBI unter Druck gesetzt wird, erweist sich der Traumjob endgültig als Alptraum ...

Roman. 544 Seiten.
Gebunden mit Schutzumschlag.

Nr. 02001 6
Club-Preis **34.⁹⁰**

K-PUR TAGESTIP

The Romeos

Nicht aus dem New Yorker Italo-Distrikt, sondern aus Bremen und Oldenburg kommen die Mitglieder der Band. Weniger banal die Musik der Jungs. Bei einer großen Plattenfirma unter Vertrag gelten sie als vielleicht eines der größten Talente der deutschen Popszene.

29.4. Marquee, 21:00 Uhr

JURASSIC PARK™

Spielbergs spektakulärster Film seit Jahren. Gen-Ingenieure haben für einen Freizeitpark Dinosaurier zum Leben erweckt. Eines Tages wird aus dem Spiel mit der Vorzeit blutiger Ernst...

Mit: Sam Neill, Laura Dern, Richard Attenborough
Regie: Stephen Spielberg
Verleih: UIP

FREITAG, 9. JULI 1993

DER MIT DEM WOLF TANZT

USA 1990, 180 Minuten, CinemaScope, Dolby-Stereo;
Ein Film von Kevin Costner.
Mit Kevin Costner, Mary MacDowell und anderen.

---

*V*om Bürgerkrieg und militärischem Drill desillusioniert , läßt sich Lieutenant John J. Dunbar, ein Offizier der Nordstaaten im äußersten Westen, am Rand der Zivilisation, im Sioux-Gebiet nieder. In einem abgelegenen Blockhaus bezieht er Stellung und knüpft behutsamen Kontakt mit den Indianern, deren Kultur er langsam zu begreifen und zu schätzen lernt. Er nimmt ihre Sitten und Gebräuche an, und sie beginnen, ihn als einer der ihren zu akzeptieren. Sie geben ihm den Namen „der mit dem Wolf tanzt". Doch die scheinbare Idylle findet ein jähes Ende, als eine Einheit der US-Kavallerie anrückt, die den verschollen geglaubten Dunbar aufspüren soll.

these selections. Include those cognates that are in compound words, even if part of the compound is not a cognate.

b. List any false cognates that you find. Were you able to figure out the meaning? If so, how?

4. What do these reading selections have in common? Where do you think you might find them?

5. How many of the selections mention something or someone you are familiar with? How does being familiar with the topics help you read the selections?

6. Read the articles and see if you can figure out
   a. what Chris Isaak did to ease the difficulties in making his new video
   b. where Bruce Springsteen thinks he has more fans: in Europe or in America
   c. the name of the group regarded as one of the most talented on the German pop scene

7. In groups of two to four, read the articles about the movies and the book, then answer these questions. Be prepared to share your findings with the class.
   a. What do you think **Original-fassung** means at the end of the article on *Groundhog Day*? What is the German word for groundhog?
   b. What do you think the word **Bürgerkrieg** means in the article on *Der mit dem Wolf tanzt*?
   c. What do you think **Traumjob** means in the article on *Die Firma*? Knowing the story, what do you think then that **Alptraum** means?

8. Your German pen pal wants to know what movies or books you have seen or read recently and would recommend. Write a two or three sentence response in German, recommending one movie or book that you like.

1 You will hear two students talk about how they spend their free time. Make a chart like the one here and fill in the information for each student as you listen.

Name	wohin?	was?	wann?	wie oft?
1				
2				

 2 Now interview two classmates, asking them where they go and what they do in their free time, and when and how often they do these things. Continue the above chart, filling in the appropriate information for your classmates. Then switch roles.

3 **a.** Choose a film or concert that you have recently seen and design a movie or concert poster for it in German.

b. Using your movie or concert poster, tell the class what kind of concert or film it is, when you saw it, and why you liked it or didn't like it.

4 Read the transcript of the song to the right and answer the following questions about it.

1. What is the person doing in the song?

2. What time of day is it?

3. What types of films is the singer watching in the first stanza? Make a list of all the film stars you recognize in this stanza.

4. What type of movie is the singer watching in the last two stanzas? How do you know?

5. How does the singer's attitude change from the beginning of the song to the end? What phrases let you know? How do you think she feels at the end?

„Kino" 99 Luftballons -

Jeden Abend um die gleiche Zeit
vor der Kasse für den Film bereit
Sternenglanz aus Hollywood
Bogart mit Trenchcoat und Hut
Alles klar!
Möchte seh'n 'nen Film mit Marylin,
oder lieber mit James Dean
Ich warte auf das Happy End
Arm in Arm mit Cary Grant
Alles klar!

Um Mitternacht sitz' ich im Kino,
Um Mitternacht läuft das Spätprogramm
Um Mitternacht sitz' ich im Kino,

Ich seh' mir alles an
In der Reihe eins bis zehn
kann man leichenblasse Leute seh'n
Hinter mir im Hochparkett
findet man die Monster nett
Alles klar!

Durch die Nacht der langen Messer geistern Zombies, Menschenfresser
Im Kino ist der Teufel los
Ich hab's gewußt, was mach' ich bloß?
Nichts ist klar!

Um Mitternacht sitz' ich im Kino, usw.
Um Mitternacht sitz' ich im Kino,
Ich seh' mir alles an.

5 Working in pairs, write the lyrics to a song expressing your feelings about "the movies" on about a specific movie you have seen.

6 Write down the nine different kinds of films you learned on page 249, each on a separate slip of paper, and put them into a container. The class will divide up into two teams. Partners from each team will take turns drawing a movie type and acting that movie type out in front of the class. The two teams will take turns guessing what kind of movie it is.

a.

b.

7 Look at the illustrations on the right, and write a story to go along with them. Your **Bildergeschichte** (*picture story*) should include something about each picture.

c.

d.

8

R O L L E N S P I E L

Get together with two or three other classmates and create an original scene for one of the following situations. Role-play your scene in front of the class.

a. You are in front of a movie theater and want to see a film. Talk about the different movies and say which ones you like, dislike, and strongly dislike, and which one(s) you have already seen. Then decide together which movie you will see.

b. You and your friends are at the video store to rent (**ausleihen**) a movie. Talk about what kinds of movies each of you likes and decide on a movie everyone will enjoy. Don't forget to mention any movies you have already seen.

KANN ICH'S WIRKLICH?

Can you express likes and dislikes using mögen? (p. 250)

1 How would you ask a friend what type of movie he or she likes? How might he or she respond?

2 How would you say that
   a. Thomas likes horror films a lot
   b. Julia really doesn't like rock music at all
   c. Sabine and Nicole like fantasy films
   d. We don't care for romance movies

Can you express familiarity using kennen? (p. 252)

3 How would a friend ask if you are familiar with
   a. the movie *Rocky 4*
   b. the singer Ina Deter
   c. the group R.E.M.
   d. the film star Clint Eastwood

4 How would you respond to each of your friend's questions?

Can you express preferences and favorites? (p. 253)

5 How would you tell a friend what type of movies you like to see, what type of movies you prefer, and what type of movies you like best of all?

6 How would you say that
   a. Martin likes adventure movies, but prefers movies about romance.
   b. Sandra likes horror films best of all
   c. Sabine doesn't like to read magazines and prefers to read newspapers

Can you talk about what you did in your free time? (p. 260)

7 How would you ask a friend what he or she did on the weekend? How would your friend respond if he or she
   a. saw the movie *Jurassic Park* on Saturday evening
   b. read a newspaper on Sunday
   c. saw the movie *Sister Act* on video on Friday evening
   d. read the book *Hunt for Red October* on Saturday
   e. was at the Billy Joel concert on Friday evening
   f. bought clothes and talked about fashion with his or her friends

8 Write a short paragraph describing what you saw, read, or talked about with your friends last weekend.

ERSTE STUFE

EXPRESSING LIKES AND DISLIKES

verbringen   *to spend (time)*
mögen   *to like, care for*
Was für Filme magst du gern?
   What kind of movies do you like?
der Film, -e   *movie*
   der Abenteuerfilm, -e   *adventure movie*
   der Actionfilm, -e   *action movie*
   der Horrorfilm, -e   *horror movie*
   die Komödie, -n   *comedy*
   der Kriegsfilm, -e   *war movie*

der Krimi, -s   *detective movie, crime drama*
der Liebesfilm, -e   *romance*
der Science-fiction-Film, -   *science fiction movie*
der Western, -   *western (movie)*
Was für Musik hörst du gern?
   What kind of music do you like?
klassische Musik   *classical music*
die Oper, -n   *opera*

EXPRESSING FAMILIARITY

kennen   *to know, be familiar or acquainted with*

der Schauspieler, -   *actor*
die Schauspielerin, -nen   *actress*
der Sänger, -   *singer (male)*
die Sängerin, -nen   *singer (female)*
die Gruppe, -n   *group*

DEGREES OF LIKING AND DISLIKING

besonders gern   *especially like*
furchtbar gern   *like a lot*
gar nicht gern   *not like at all*
überhaupt nicht gern   *strongly dislike*

ZWEITE STUFE

EXPRESSING PREFERENCES AND FAVORITIES

lieber (mögen)   *prefer*
am liebsten (mögen)   *like most of all*
sehen   *to see*
   er/sie sieht   *he/she sees*

phantasievoll   *imaginative*
spannend   *exciting, thrilling*
sensationell   *sensational*
lustig   *funny*
zu   *too*
   grausam   *cruel*

dumm   *dumb, stupid*
brutal   *brutal, violent*
schmalzig   *corny, mushy*
traurig   *sad*
doof   *dumb*

DRITTE STUFE

TALKING ABOUT WHAT YOU DID IN YOUR FREE TIME

Was hast du am Wochenende gemacht?   *What did you do on the weekend?*
lesen   *to read*
   er/sie liest   *he/she reads*
Was hast du gelesen?   *What did you read?*

der Roman, -c   *novel*
der Gruselroman, -e   *horror novel*
der Liebesroman -e   *love story*
das Sachbuch, ¨-er   *nonfiction book*
die Zeitung, -en   *newspaper*
die Zeitschrift, -en   *magazine*
das Hobbybuch, ¨-er   *hobby book*
sprechen über   *to talk about*

er/sie spricht über ...   *he/she talks about ...*
Worüber habt ihr gesprochen?
   What did you (pl) talk about?
die Politik   *politics*
die Mode   *fashion*
die Umwelt   *environment*
   Was hast du gesehen?   *What did you see?*
das Video, -s   *video (cassette)*

11
Der Geburtstag

1 Was schenkst du deiner Kusine
zu Weihnachten?

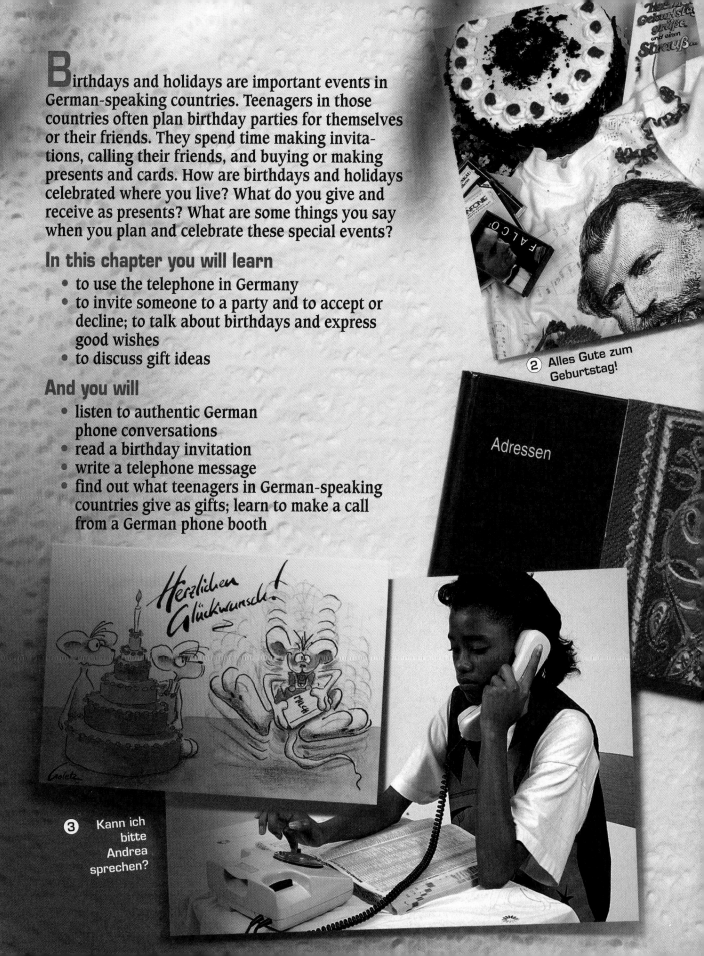

Birthdays and holidays are important events in German-speaking countries. Teenagers in those countries often plan birthday parties for themselves or their friends. They spend time making invitations, calling their friends, and buying or making presents and cards. How are birthdays and holidays celebrated where you live? What do you give and receive as presents? What are some things you say when you plan and celebrate these special events?

In this chapter you will learn

- to use the telephone in Germany
- to invite someone to a party and to accept or decline; to talk about birthdays and express good wishes
- to discuss gift ideas

And you will

- listen to authentic German phone conversations
- read a birthday invitation
- write a telephone message
- find out what teenagers in German-speaking countries give as gifts; learn to make a call from a German phone booth

② Alles Gute zum Geburtstag!

Adressen

Herzlichen Glückwunsch!

③ Kann ich bitte Andrea sprechen?

Los geht's!

Sabine   Nicole

Geschenke aussuchen

Look at the photos that accompany the story.
What are the girls doing in each picture? Where are they?
What do you think they are talking about?

 Kroll.

Guten Tag, Frau Kroll! Hier ist die Nicole. Ist die Sabine da?

Nein, Sabine ist mit ihrem Vater weg. Kann ich ihr etwas sagen?

Ja, hm ... sagen Sie ihr bitte, daß der Martin am Samstag Geburtstag hat! Und ich möchte für ihn eine Fete organisieren.

Na, prima! Ich sag es Sabine. Tschüs!

Wiederhören, Frau Kroll!

② Was schenkst du dem Martin?

Kein Problem! Ich kaufe ihm eine Kassette.

Aber er hat doch schon so viele Kassetten.

Na und?

Warum kaufst du ihm keine CD?

Er hat doch keinen CD-Player.

270 *zweihundertsiebzig*   KAPITEL 11   Der Geburtstag

Was soll ich ihm bloß schenken? Was meinst du? Du kennst ihn besser. Eine Idee?

Kauf ihm doch ein Buch! Er liest auch gerne.

Bücher sind so teuer.

③

Dann schenk ihm halt ein T-Shirt mit einem Komponisten drauf. Das mag er bestimmt auch.

Eine prima Idee!

Schau mal, Nicole! Die Karte ist lustig, nicht?

Wahnsinn! Und lies mal den Vers!

Die schenk' ich dem Martin!

④

ZU HAUSE BEI NICOLE

Übrigens, weißt du, wann der Thomas Geburtstag hat?

⑤

Irgendwann im Sommer. Ich glaube, im August.

An welchem Tag?

Warum fragst du? Willst du ...

Nein, nein. Seinen Geburtstag feiern wir nie.

Im August haben wir immer Ferien.

Zeig her!

Schau hier: am elften August!

⑥

Hier steht „Martin am achtzehnten". Er hat also nicht diesen Samstag Geburtstag!

Was? Das kann doch nicht wahr sein! Was soll ich jetzt machen? Die kommen alle diesen Samstag!

1 Was passiert hier?

Do you understand what is happening in the **Foto-Roman**? Check your comprehension by answering these questions. Don't be afraid to guess.

1. Why does Nicole call Sabine?
2. What do they discuss when they get together later?
3. What suggestions does Nicole make to Sabine? Which one does Sabine like the best?
4. What does Sabine discover when she looks up Thomas's birthday? What is Nicole's predicament?

2 Genauer lesen

Reread the conversations. Which words or phrases do the characters use to

1. begin and end a phone conversation
2. name gift ideas
3. ask for advice and opinions
4. say when someone's birthday is
5. express disbelief

3 Was ist richtig?

Complete each statement with the best possible answer based on the **Foto-Roman**.

1. Nicole ruft Sabine an. Sie will ihr sagen, ▆▆▆.
   a. daß sie eine Kassette gekauft hat
   b. daß sie für Martin eine Party geben will
   c. daß sie mit Martin ausgeht

2. Nicole kauft dem Martin keine CD, ▆▆▆.
   a. weil er so viele Kassetten hat
   b. weil er keinen CD-Player hat
   c. weil er gern liest

3. Sabine schenkt Martin auch ▆▆▆ zum Geburtstag.
   a. eine CD   b. ein Buch   c. eine Karte

4. Nicole und Sabine feiern nie den Geburtstag von Thomas, ▆▆▆.
   a. weil sie Martin eine Karte schenken möchten
   b. weil alle im August Ferien haben
   c. weil Martin am 18. Geburtstag hat

5. Am Ende weiß Nicole nicht, was sie tun soll, ▆▆▆.
   a. denn Martin hat am 18. Geburtstag, nicht diesen Samstag
   b. denn Thomas gibt Martin ein Buch
   c. denn sie hat Ferien

4 Nacherzählen

Put the sentences in logical order to make a brief summary of the **Foto-Roman**.

1. Nicole ruft Sabine an. Sie möchte über Martins Geburtstag sprechen.

Aber Sabine weiß nicht genau, was sie Martin kaufen soll.

Sabine findet, daß das T-Shirt die beste Idee ist.

Aber die Sabine ist nicht zu Hause.

Nicole will Martin eine Kassette kaufen.

Am Ende sieht Sabine in ihrem Adreßbuch, daß Martin am 18. Geburtstag hat.

Dann hat Nicole eine Idee: vielleicht ein Buch oder ein T-Shirt.

Später sprechen die zwei Mädchen über Martins Geschenk.

Danach findet Sabine eine tolle Geburtstagskarte für Martin.

5 Und du?

Was möchtest du zum Geburtstag? Mach eine Liste! Dann frag deinen Partner, was er zum Geburtstag haben möchte!

Using the telephone in Germany

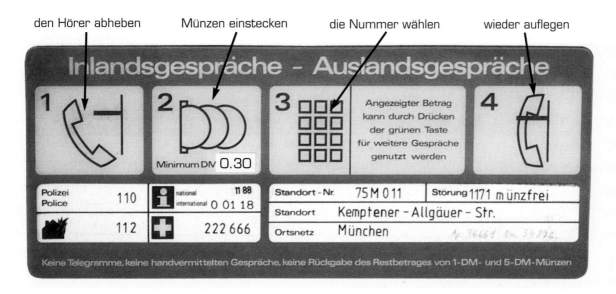

den Hörer abheben   Münzen einstecken   die Nummer wählen   wieder auflegen

Inlandsgespräche – Auslandsgespräche

1   **2**   Minimum DM 0.30   **3**   Angezeigter Betrag kann durch Drücken der grünen Taste für weitere Gespräche genutzt werden   **4**

Polizei Police	110	ℹ️ national **11 88** international 0 01 18	
🔥	112	✚ 222 666	

Standort - Nr.	75 M 0 11	Störung 1171 münzfrei	
Standort	Kemptener – Allgäuer – Str.		
Ortsnetz	München		

Keine Telegramme, keine handvermittelten Gespräche, keine Rückgabe des Restbetrages von 1-DM- und 5-DM-Münzen

6   In der Telefonzelle

Answer the following questions based on the information given above.

1. What kind of information is this? Where would you expect to find it?
2. What is the minimum amount of money you need to make a local call?
3. What number could you call to find out someone else's number in Germany?
4. Where on the directions can you find information about what services the public phone does not provide?
5. Which emergency numbers are provided?
6. How would you tell a German exchange student (in German) how to use a phone booth in the United States? Use the four steps pictured above.

Telefonieren ist nicht schwer!

telefonieren/anrufen

den Hörer abheben
die Münzen einstecken
die Telefonnummer wählen
den Hörer auflegen
besetzt (*busy*)

der Hörer

der Apparat/
das Telefon

die Telefonzelle

SO SAGT MAN DAS!

Using the telephone in Germany

Here are some phrases you will need to know in order to talk on the phone in German:

The person who answers says his or her name:	**Kroll.** *or* **Hier Kroll.**
The person calling says who he or she is:	**Hier ist die Nicole.**
The person calling asks to speak to someone:	**Ich möchte bitte Sabine sprechen.** *or* **Kann ich bitte Sabine sprechen?**
The person who answered says:	**Einen Moment, bitte.**
After the person comes to the phone, he or she might say:	**Tag! Hier ist die Sabine.**
The conversation may end with:	**Wiederhören!** *or* **Auf Wiederhören!** *or* **Tschüs!**

How are these phrases different from the ones you use when talking on the phone?

7 Hör gut zu!

Listen to four telephone conversations and match each one with an appropriate illustration.

a.

c.

b.

d.

8 Tag! Hier ist …

Get together with a classmate and practice "calling" a friend on the telephone. Your partner will be the parent of the friend you are calling. Use the expressions you have learned so far. Then practice saying good-bye. When you are finished, switch roles.

9 Willst du einen Film sehen?

"Call" your partner on the phone and ask if he or she wants to go to a movie tonight. Discuss what you want to see and what kinds of movies you like. Use the cues in the boxes below for help.

person answering

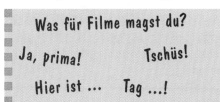

Was für Filme magst du?

Ja, prima!   Tschüs!

Hier ist ...   Tag ...!

person calling

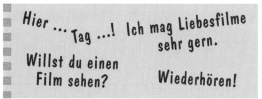

Hier ... Tag ...! Ich mag Liebesfilme sehr gern.

Willst du einen Film sehen?

Wiederhören!

10 Ich möchte bitte ... sprechen

You worked in the office at the youth center today, and a lot of people called in and left messages for their friends. Work with a partner to create the telephone conversations you would have as you attempt to pass along the messages to the appropriate people. Take turns playing the role of the office worker.

1. Call Stefan (who is not at home; you reach his mother) and let him know that Petra wants to play tennis tomorrow at 4 P.M.
2. Call Ulrike and remind her that the biology class on Tuesday is at 9 A.M instead of (**anstatt**) at 10 A.M.
3. Call Holger and tell him that soccer practice is at 3 P.M. on Tuesday.
4. Monika is not home yet, but you need to let her know that Ulla called and wants to go shopping with her on Saturday morning at 9 A.M.

Gesprächs-Notiz

Gesprächs-Notiz	Uhrzeit
	7 | 8 | 9 | 10 | 11 | 12
	Tag
mit	19
	13 | 14 | 15 | 16 | 17 | 18

◯ Straße

Ort

Vorwahl   Ruf

Betreff:

Unterschrift:

◯

11 Gesprächs-Notiz

Answer the following questions.

1. What do you think the page on the left is used for? Which words are the clues for your answer?
2. Where would you record the date and time?
3. Where would you record the information about the person who called? What specific information is asked for in this section?
4. Where would you write the message?
5. Where would you sign the page if you took the call?

12 Hör gut zu!

At your host family's home in Germany, someone calls while one of the family members is out. Make a German phone message page like the one pictured above. Then take down all the information asked for on the **Gesprächs-Notiz**. For the actual message, just write down a few notes. What phrase did the person answering the phone use at the beginning of the conversation? What is its English equivalent?

13 Zum Schreiben

Using your notes from Activity 12, rewrite the message in neat sentences so that it can be easily understood by the person receiving it. Then switch papers with a partner and check whether your partner wrote his or her message correctly.

14 Ruf mal an!

Decide on a free time activity that you would like to do with your partner. Call your partner and invite him or her to come along. Then switch roles. Here are a few possibilities:

Ich habe am Samstag eine Party. Kannst du kommen?
Ich möchte heute in die Stadt fahren. Kommst du mit?

Inviting someone to a party and accepting or declining; talking about birthdays and expressing good wishes

15 Eine Einladung

Schau die Einladung an und beantworte die folgenden Fragen!

1. Wer schickt die Einladung?
2. Für wen ist die Fete? Warum?
3. Wann ist die Fete? An welchem Tag? Um wieviel Uhr?
4. Wo ist die Fete?
5. Welche Nummer kannst du anrufen, um Information zu bekommen?
6. Was mußt du tun, um zu sagen, ob (*whether*) du kommen kannst?

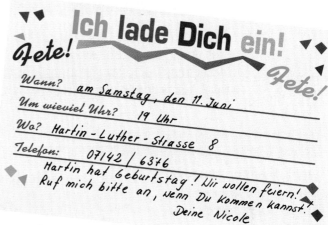

Ich lade Dich ein!

Fete! *Fete!*

Wann? am Samstag, den 11. Juni
Um wieviel Uhr? 19 Uhr
Wo? Martin-Luther-Strasse 8
Telefon: 07142 / 6376
Martin hat Geburtstag! Wir wollen feiern!
Ruf mich bitte an, wenn Du kommen kannst.
Deine Nicole

SO SAGT MAN DAS!

Inviting someone to a party and accepting or declining

You invite a friend:

Ich habe am Samstag eine Party.
Ich lade dich ein.
Kannst du kommen?

Your friend might respond:

Ja, gern! *or*
Aber sicher! *or*
Natürlich! *or*
Leider kann ich nicht.

Which response would you use if you already had a previous engagement?[1]

16 Zum Schreiben

Schreib eine Einladung! Was für eine Fete ist das? An welchem Tag ist die Fete? Um wieviel Uhr beginnt sie? Wo ist sie? Wenn man nicht kommen kann, soll man anrufen?

17 Ich möchte dich einladen!

You are having a party and want to invite several of your friends. "Call" two other classmates and invite each of them to the party. They will ask you for information about the party and then tell you whether they can come. If not, they should give you a reason. You should respond appropriately. End your conversation, then switch roles so that each person takes a turn extending the invitations.

---

1. **Leider kann ich nicht.**

SO SAGT MAN DAS!

Talking about birthdays and expressing good wishes

If you want to find out when a friend has his or her birthday,

you ask:

Wann hast du Geburtstag?

Your friend might respond:

Ich habe am 28. Oktober* Geburtstag. *or*
Am 28. Oktober.

There are a number of things you can say to express good wishes:

Alles Gute zum Geburtstag!
Herzlichen Glückwunsch zum Geburtstag!

*Read as: **am achtundzwanzigsten Oktober.**

WORTSCHATZ

am 1. = am ersten (Juli)
am 2. = am zweiten
am 3. = am dritten
am 4. = am vierten
am 5. = am fünften
am 6. = am sechsten
am 7. = am siebten
am 8. = am achten
am 9. = am neunten
am 10. = am zehnten
am 11. = am elften
     usw.
am 20. = am zwanzigsten
am 21. = am einundzwanzigsten
     usw.

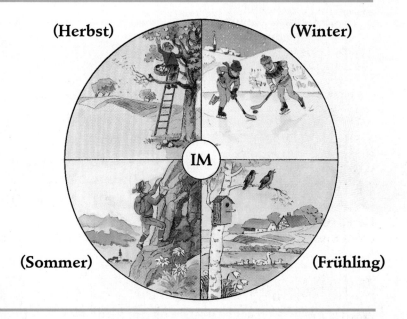

(Herbst)   (Winter)

IM

(Sommer)   (Frühling)

18 Geburtstagskette

One person in the class begins the chain by asking another: **Wann hast du Geburtstag?**
That person answers and asks someone else. Continue until everyone has been asked.

19 Hör gut zu!

Das Schuljahr ist bald zu Ende. Anja will wissen, wer im Sommer Geburtstag hat. Sie fragt ihre Klassenkameraden und schreibt dann die Geburtstage in ihr Adreßbuch. Schreib, wann Anjas Freunde Geburtstag haben!

   1. Bernd   2. Maja   3. Benjamin   4. Katrin   5. Mario

20 Für mein Notizbuch

Schreib, wann du Geburtstag hast! Welches Geschenk hast du am liebsten? Schreib auch, wann deine Eltern, deine Geschwister und deine Freunde Geburtstag haben!

EIN WENIG LANDESKUNDE

Birthdays are important occasions in German-speaking countries and are usually celebrated with family and friends. In some areas of Germany (primarily in the strongly Catholic areas) and in Austria, the **Namenstag**, or Saint's Day, is also celebrated. Children in these areas are named after certain saints, such as **Johannes, Josef**, and **Maria**. There is a saint's day for each day of the year. Anyone named for a saint also celebrates on the day that honors that saint. The **Namenstag** celebration is similar to a birthday celebration, with a party, gifts, and flowers for the honoree.

Namenstag im Juli

- 10. Erich/Erika
- 13. Margarete
- 15. Heinrich
- 24. Christine
- 25. Jakob
- 26. Anne Marie
- 29. Martha

Gratulieren Sie mit Blumen!

WORTSCHATZ

Feiertage

Weihnachten:
Fröhliche Weihnachten!

Chanukka:
Frohes Chanukka-Fest!

Ostern:
Frohe Ostern!

Vatertag:
Alles Gute zum Vatertag!

Muttertag:
Alles Gute zum Muttertag!

21 Hör gut zu!

You will hear four conversations about four different holidays. Match each conversation to the most appropriate card.

22 Eine Geburtstagskarte

Design a German birthday card or a card for another special occasion to send to a friend or family member. Below are some common German good luck symbols.

Schornsteinfeger

Glücksschwein

Glücksklee

Hufeisen

Marienkäfer

Was schenkst du zum Geburtstag?

We asked several teenagers what they usually give as birthday presents. Before you read the interviews, write what you give your friends and relatives for their birthdays.

Melanie, *Hamburg*

„Ich geh' mit Freunden essen oder lade sie zu mir ein. Und dann sitzen wir zusammen und unterhalten uns nett oder ähnliches, ... ansonsten gar nichts weiter. Bei Familienmitgliedern ist es ähnlich, da feiern wir auch in der Familie. Und schenken tu' ich dann meiner Schwester zum Beispiel, die hört ziemlich gerne Musik, und der schenk' ich dann Kassetten oder CDs oder ähnliches. Und ansonsten eben schenk' ich Bücher oder eben andere Kleinigkeiten, für die sich die Freunde oder Familienmitglieder interessieren."

Eva, *Berlin*

„Eigentlich hass' ich Geburtstage, weil ich nie weiß, was ich schenken soll. Es ist irgendwie immer dasselbe, Bücher oder Kassetten oder CDs. Und naja, dann sucht man sich immer was aus. Meistens verschenkt man Gutscheine, weil ... da kann man nichts falsch machen."

Rosi, *Berlin*

„Also wenn ich auf Geburtstage gehe von Freunden oder Freundinnen, die ich gut kenne, dann geb' ich auch mal mehr Geld aus. Dann kriegen sie schon persönliche Geschenke, wo sie sich auch darüber freuen. Und wenn ich auf Geburtstage gehe von Leuten, die ich nicht so gut kenne, dann nehme ich nur Kleinigkeiten mit. Aber ich nehm' eigentlich immer was mit, wenn ich auf Geburtstage gehe."

Jutta, *Hamburg*

„Ich hab' einen kleinen Bruder, und er ist elf, und der spielt unheimlich gern mit Lego,™ und dem schenk' ich dann was zum Spielen oder eine Musikkassette. Und wenn ich bei Freunden eingeladen bin, meistens was Selbstgemachtes, ein bemaltes T-Shirt, ja auch eine Musikkassette, ein Buch oder ein gemaltes Bild."

A. 1. Make a list of the gifts these teenagers give as birthday presents and to whom they give them. What do you think **Gutscheine** might be? *Hint: they are available for many different things, such as cassettes, CDs, and books.*
2. Rosi has two categories of people she buys gifts for. What are they? What are some of the differences in the types of gifts she buys for each one?
3. Why does Eva not care much for birthdays? Do you agree or disagree with her?
4. Of the four people interviewed, who do you think puts the most thought and time into giving just the right gift? What statements support your answer?

B. Use the list you made earlier to write an answer to the questions **Was schenkst du zum Geburtstag, und wem schenkst du das?** Share your answers with your classmates and decide which of the interviews above most closely resembles your own. Are there any differences in the things teenagers give as gifts in the German-speaking countries and in the United States? If so, what are they and why do you think this is so? If not, why not?

23 Im Geschenkladen

Here is an excerpt from an article in the teen magazine *Juma.* Look at the photo and read the caption. Then answer the questions that follow.

1. Using the photo as a cue, what do you think a **Geschenkladen** is? What do you think the topic of this article is?
2. Reread the caption. Do you think Martina is finding a lot of things she could buy? Why or why not?
3. What gift does Martina decide to buy for her friend? Do you think she buys anything else? If so, what?
4. Was für Geschenke schenkst du Verwandten (*relatives*) und Freunden? Wo kaufst du gewöhnlich Geschenke? Zehn Mark sind ungefähr sechs Dollar. Was kannst du für sechs Dollar kaufen?

Martina, 14, will ihrer Freundin etwas zum Namenstag schenken. Im Geschenkladen sucht sie lange nach einer Kleinigkeit. Die meisten Sachen kosten mehr als 10 Mark. Martina entscheidet sich für eine Kerze. Dann geht sie in ein Süßwarengeschäft.

WORTSCHA...

Geschenkideen

Bärbel: Was schenkst du Jutta zum Geburtstag?
Berndt: Ich weiß noch nicht. Vielleicht ...

eine Armbanduhr

Pralinen

einen Blumenstrauß

einen Kalender

ein Poster

eine CD

Parfüm

Schmuck

Was schenkst du zu verschiedenen Feiertagen, z. B. zu Muttertag?

SO SAGT MAN DAS!

Discussing gift ideas

When talking about birthdays and holidays with friends. you'll also want to be able to discuss gift ideas.

You might ask your friend:

Schenkst du deinem Vater einen Kalender zum Geburtstag?

Und was schenkst du deiner Mutter zum Muttertag?

Kauf ihr doch ein Buch!

Wem schenkst du den Blumenstrauß?

Your friend might respond:

Nein, ich schenke ihm wahrscheinlich eine CD, weil er doch Musik so gern hört.

Ich weiß noch nicht. Hast du eine Idee?

Prima Idee! Das mach' ich!

Der Nicole schenke ich den Strauß.

Can you find the subject and the verb in each of these sentences? What is the item being given (the direct object) in the first question?[1] Who is the person receiving the gift (the indirect object)?[2] In the first response, you see the word **ihm**. To whom does it refer?[3] To whom does the word **ihr** refer in the sentence **Kauf ihr doch ein Buch!**? [4]

24 Was soll man schenken?

Mechtild Kaldenkirchen and Gothild Thomas of Essen offer a unique information service. Read the article on the right, then answer these questions.

1. Wie heißt der Informationsservice von Mechtild und Gothild? Was für Information können sie uns geben? Gib ein oder zwei Beispiele!
2. Was muß man machen, um die Information zu bekommen?
3. Wie sagt man den letzten Satz auf Englisch?

25 Hör gut zu!

You call **Interkulturelle Beratung und Information** to find out the proper gifts for families you'll visit on your trip to France, Italy, Spain and Austria. On a separate piece of paper, write the gift(s) they advise you to give in each country: **Frankreich, Italien, Spanien,** and **Österreich.**

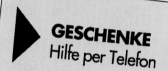

GESCHENKE
Hilfe per Telefon

Was bringt man als Gast einer Familie in Frankreich mit – Blumen, Pralinen oder Getränke? Wer viel reist, hat solche Probleme öfter. Helfen kann ein Bürgertelefon in Essen. Mechtild Kaldenkirchen und Gothild Thomas leiten die „Interkulturelle Beratung und Information": Sie informieren Anrufer aber nicht nur über Gastgeschenke im Ausland. Man kann nämlich auch erfahren, wie man sich im Ausland richtig benimmt. Denn eines ist ja allgemein bekannt: andere Länder, andere Sitten.

1. **einen Kalender** 2. **deinem Vater** 3. **ihm = Vater** 4. **ihr = Mutter**

Grammatik   Introduction to the dative case

You have learned that the subject of a sentence is in the nominative case and that the direct object is in the accusative case. A third case, the dative case, is used for indirect objects, which express the idea of "to someone" or "for someone." Look at the following sentences:

Robert, was schenkst du
  deinem Opa?   Ich schenke **ihm** einen
Und was schenkst du   Taschenrechner.
  deiner Oma?   Ich schenke **ihr** ein Buch.

How would you say each of the above sentences in English?[1] Look at the photos for cues. You have already seen several examples of the dative case with definite articles after prepositions: **mit dem Bus, mit der U-Bahn.** Definite articles may also be used with proper names in the dative case:

Was kaufst du **dem Martin?**   Ich kaufe **ihm** ein T-Shirt.
Gibst du **der Sandra** das Geld?   Ja, ich gebe **ihr** morgen das Geld.

To ask the question "To whom ...?" or "For whom ...?" you use the dative form „**wem** ...?"

    Wem schenkst du die Blumen?   *To whom are you giving the flowers?*

Dative Case

masculine	
neuter	**dem, ihm, deinem, meinem**
feminine	**der, ihr, deiner, meiner**

    What pattern do you notice in the formation of the dative case? Make a chart of the definite articles, pronouns for *he* and *she*, and the posessive **mein** for all the cases you have learned so far. What patterns do you notice?

26 Hör gut zu!

You're visiting Germany during the holiday season and would like to send something to your friends and family members. You ask your German friend for gift ideas. Your friend makes suggestions for specific family members and friends. Write down which gift he suggests for each person.

1. *Robert, what are you giving your grandfather? I'm giving him a calculator. And what are you giving your grandmother? I'm giving her a book.*

27 Sätze bauen

Put the following sentence elements in the correct order to say what you and others are planning to give as presents at an upcoming party.

1. kaufe
eine Bluse
Ich
meiner Oma

2. eine CD
Peter
schenken
Wir

3. meinem Onkel
Ich
Pralinen
schenke

4. Und ich
ihm
schenke
auch ein Buch

5. Sie
dem Opa
kauft
einen Kalender

6. schenken
ein Buch über Musik
Wir
meiner Mutter

Grammatik

Notice the word order when you use the dative case. The indirect object (dative case) comes before the direct object (accusative case):

Ich schenke meiner Mutter ein Buch.
Ich schenke ihr ein Buch.

28 Was schenkst du ...?

Take turns with your classmates asking and telling who is getting which gift. Practice replacing the noun phrases with the appropriate pronoun in the response. Use the drawings below as cues.

BEISPIEL   DU **Was schenkst du deinem Bruder?**
    MITSCHÜLER **Ich schenke ihm einen Kuli.**

dein Bruder

dein Vater

deine Kusine

deine Oma

deine Lehrerin

dein Onkel

deine Schwester

29 Memory-Spiel

Wem schenkst du ein Buch?

BEISPIEL   DU **Ich schenke meiner Mutter ein Buch.**

    MITSCHÜLER **Ich schenke meiner Mutter und meinem Freund ein Buch.**

30 Eine Geschenkliste

Make a list of what you would like to buy for three of your friends or family members for their birthdays. Give your partner a list with just the names of the people receiving gifts. Your partner will ask you what you plan to give them. Respond according to your list. Then switch roles. Jot down your partner's answers, then compare lists to see if you understood everything.

LERNTRICK

When you use indirect objects in your conversations, they must be in the dative case. It helps to remember that the dative forms for masculine and neuter articles and pronouns always end in **-m: dem, ihm, meinem, deinem.** The dative forms for feminine articles and pronouns always end with **-r: der, ihr, meiner, deiner.**

31 Deine Europareise

a. You're going to Europe! Decide which three countries you would like to visit. On a card write down the countries you choose, the souvenir you would buy from each, and the name of the person to whom you would like to give each souvenir.

Italien

Schuhe   ein Halstuch

Deutschland

einen Pulli   eine Kerze

Schweiz (in der Schweiz)

Pralinen   eine
              Armbanduhr

Spanien

einen   Kastagnetten
Fächer

Österreich

ein Sachbuch   eine CD
über   von Mozart
Musik

b. Get together with two other classmates. Tell your partners what you will buy in each country. Your partners will take turns asking whom the souvenirs are for: **Wem schenkst du ein Buch?** Share this information with your partners. Then switch roles.

32 Ein Brief aus Europa

Schreib einem Freund oder deiner Familie einen Brief über deine Europareise! Schreib, wo du warst, was du gekauft hast und wem du die Andenken (*souvenirs*) schenkst! Benutze deine Information von Übung 31!

AUSSPRACHE

Richtig aussprechen

A. To review the following sounds, say the sentences below after your teacher or after the recording.

1. The letters **r** and **er**: The letter **r** is pronounced by placing the tip of the tongue behind your lower front teeth and then tipping the head back and pretending to gargle. The combination **er** at the end of a syllable or word is pronounced like the *a* in the English word *sofa*.
Ich schenke meinem Bruder Rolf und seiner Frau ein Radio.
Und ich schenke meiner Mutter Bücher und einen Kalender.

2. The letter **a**: The letter **a** is pronounced much like the *a* sound in the word *father*.
Kaufst du dem Vater Schokolade zum Vatertag?

3. The diphthongs **eu**, **äu**, and **au**: The vowel combinations **eu** and **äu** sound similiar to the *oy* sound in the English word *toy*. The diphthong **au** is pronounced like the *ow* sound in the English word *how*.
Heute war der Verkäufer am Telefon ganz unfreundlich.
Ich kaufe der Claudia einen Blumenstrauß.

Richtig schreiben / Diktat

B. Write down the sentences that you hear.

Was gibt's heute noch für 10 Mark?

Im Supermarkt läuft Ben durch die Regalreihen und vergleicht Preise. Viele Dinge nimmt er zuerst aus dem Regal und stellt sie wieder zurück, nachdem er den Preis gelesen hat. Er kauft Orangensaft und Cola.

ch möchte etwas Sinnvolles kaufen. Etwas, das ich auch brauchen kann." Stefan lebt in der kleinen Stadt Schwalmtal nahe der niederländischen Grenze. Dort gibt es nicht viele Läden. Darum entscheidet er sich für ein kleines Schreibwarengeschäft am Marktplatz. Dort kauft er einen Zeichenblock, zwei Buntstifte, einen Anspitzer, ein Radiergummi und eine Geburtstagskarte. Die Geburtstagskarte ist das teuerste Teil seines Einkaufs: 3,50 Mark. Insgesamt hat er 10,04 Mark ausgegeben. Vier Pfennig zuviel! „Es ist fast unmöglich, für genau 10 Mark einzukaufen."

Stefan ist mit seinem Einkauf zufrieden. „Nur die Geburtstagskarte fand ich ganz schön teuer. Aber insgesamt konnte ich doch einige nützliche Dinge kaufen. Einen dicken Filzschreiber für 2,80 Mark fand ich übertrieben teuer. Den habe ich nicht gekauft."

Stefan bekommt 50 Mark Taschengeld im Monat. Den Betrag findet er „in Ordnung", obwohl das Geld selten reicht. In den Ferien verdient Stefan etwas dazu. „Dann räume ich in einem Lebensmittelgeschäft Ware in Regale ein." Von seinem Taschengeld kauft Stefan Süßigkeiten, Musik-CDs, kleine Geschenke wie Notizbücher oder Stifte und Pflanzen. Schulsachen muß er nicht kaufen. „Die bezahlen meine Eltern." Sein größter Wunsch: „Wenn ich viel Geld hätte, würde ich nach Australien oder Amerika auswandern. Und wenn ich Geld zu verschenken hätte, würden es Tierschutz- und Umweltorganisationen bekommen."

1. You are invited to a party and need to bring a gift. What can you buy for $5.00?
2. A foreign exchange student is also invited to the party. Where would you suggest that person should go to buy a gift for $5.00? What would you suggest might be a good gift for the foreign exchange student to buy?
3. Look at the title, the pictures, and the captions. Without actually reading the texts, what would you say is the type of reading selection on these pages? Are they ads, postcards, poems, or articles?
4. Judging by the title, what kind of information do you expect to find in these selections?
5. Read the article about Stefan through without

Stefans Freund Ben wohnt in der Kleinstadt Brüggen. Er entscheidet sich für den Einkauf in einem Supermarkt. „Wenn man nur 10 Mark zur Verfügung hat, bekommt man in einem Supermarkt wahrscheinlich die meisten Dinge. Außerdem gibt es in Supermärkten viele nützliche Sachen, die man für das tägliche Leben braucht." Im Supermarkt geht Ben durch die Regalreihen und vergleicht Preise. Die Auswahl fällt ihm schwer. Manche Dinge stellt er wieder ins Regal zurück. Ben bekommt für 10,10 Mark eine Zahnbürste, eine Flasche Orangensaft, eine Dose Cola, einen Sport-Drink und einen Lippenpflege-Stift. Der Lippenpflege-Stift ist teuer. Er kostet 2,69 Mark. Ben glaubt, daß er gut eingekauft hat. „Ich habe mehr bekommen, als ich dachte. Einen Riesen-Unterschied gab es allerdings bei den Preisen für Getränkedosen. Das Marken-Getränk aus der Werbung kostete 1,99 Mark. Die Dose Cola war dagegen spottbillig: nur 49 Pfennig. Ben bekommt pro Woche 8 Mark Taschengeld. Ihm reicht der Betrag. „Ich kann sogar ein bißchen Geld sparen, denn Schulsachen oder Kleidung muß ich nicht bezahlen. Diese Dinge kaufen meine Eltern." Von seinem Taschengeld kauft Ben ab und zu eine Compact Disc für sich oder ein kleines Geschenk, zum Beispiel ein Taschenbuch für seine Freunde. Was würde Ben mit viel Geld machen? „Ich würde sofort eine Taucherausrüstung kaufen. Tauchen ist mein Hobby. Und wenn ich Geld verschenken könnte, dann würde ich es zum Schutz der Weltmeere und zum Schutz der Umwelt einsetzen."

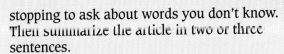

Stefan wird im Schreibwarengeschäft von der Verkäuferin beraten. Sie zeigt ihm verschiedene Dinge und nennt ihm die Preise. Stefan braucht einige Zelt, bis er möglichst viele Sachen für zehn Mark gekauft hat.

stopping to ask about words you don't know. Then summarize the article in two or three sentences.

6. Read the article about Ben through without stopping to ask about words you don't know. Then summarize the article in two or three sentences. In both articles, notice how much you can understand without knowing every word!

7. Read the article about Stefan again and try to answer these questions.
   a. What kind of store did Stefan shop in? What did he buy? What was his total bill?
   b. How much is Stefan's allowance per month? What does he buy with that money? What do his parents buy for him?
   c. What would Stefan do if he had a lot of money?

8. Read the article about Ben again and try to answer these questions.
   a. Where does Ben think he can find the largest selection of useful items for 10 marks? How does he define "useful"?
   b. What do Ben's parents buy for him? For what does he use his own money?
   c. If Ben had a lot of money, what would he buy? To what cause would he give?

9. You are planning a trip to a German-speaking country in the summer and are going to stay with a family. Write a short note asking them what small items you might bring them.

1 Listen to Helene and Volker's conversation about what they are buying their friends as birthday presents. Write down who's giving what to whom as a present.

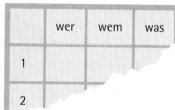

	wer	wem	was
1			
2			

2 Drei Schüler sprechen darüber, was sie am liebsten zum Geburtstag bekommen möchten und warum.

a. Read the interviews and decide what each of the three teenagers would like to have and why. Write down the information.

Ingo, 17

„Du fragst, was ich am liebsten zum Geburtstag haben möchte? — Ganz einfach! Du weißt doch, daß ich gern lese. Du kannst mir also ein Buch kaufen, vielleicht etwas über gefährdete Tiere in Afrika, oder — ich hab' da noch eine Idee. Du kannst mir zum Geburtstag ein Karl-May-Buch schenken, denn seine Bücher sind wieder ganz populär. Und ich lese Karl May furchtbar gern."

Margot, 16

„Ja, am liebsten möchte ich irgend etwas, was mit Musik zu tun hat. Eine prima Kassette, Mathias Reim vielleicht, oder eine CD. Du weißt, ich höre auch klassische Musik gern. Und unter den Klassikern gibt es eine wirklich große Auswahl, zum Beispiel etwas von ... nein, ich hab's: die schönsten Arien aus den populärsten Opern. Das ist etwas für mich!"

Clarissa, 16

„Du kannst mir eine große Freude machen und mir eine Karte zum nächsten Rockkonzert schenken. Die „Toten Hosen" kommen nächsten Monat hierher, und die möchte ich unbedingt hören. Natürlich sind die Karten furchtbar teuer, ich weiß. Aber du kannst dich vielleicht mit zwei andern Leuten zusammentun, und ihr könnt mir gemeinsam eine Karte kaufen. Dann ist es für jeden nicht so teuer."

b. Now let your partner interview you to find out what you would like to have and why. Based on your answers, he or she will write an interview similar to the ones above. Then switch roles and interview your partner.

3 Gabriele and Philipp are making plans for Bernhard's birthday. What do they plan to do first? First look at the pictures and decide what Gabriele and Philipp are doing in each one. Then listen to their conversation and put the following drawings in the correct order.

a.

b.

c.

d.

4 a. Get together with two or three classmates and plan an end-of-school party. Decide where and when it will take place.

b. Within your group, tell each other the things you'll need for the party. Use the words in the box for ideas. Create a list of at least six things you need, then each of you volunteer to take care of certain things on the list.

> Getränke CDs Kassetten
> Tassen Kuchen oder Kekse
> Obst- und Gemüseteller
> Chips 'n Dip Ballons

5 Write an invitation to the party you planned in Activity 4. First, everyone will write his or her name on a piece of paper and put it in a box. Then each student will draw a name and send his or her invitation to that person. Use a lot of color on your invitation and remember to include all the necessary information.

6 Ihr möchtet der Lehrerin/dem Lehrer etwas schenken. Macht eine Liste von Geschenkideen! Dann sprecht darüber, was ihr schenken möchtet. Fragt alle in der Gruppe, was sie schenken wollen. Wie sind ihre Ideen? Toll oder blöd?

7

ROLLENSPIEL

Get together with two or three classmates and role-play the following situation:

Each group picks one type of store you have learned about so far, (**Metzgerei, Modegeschäft, Schreibwarenladen . . .**). Write it on a card, and put the cards in a box. One person from each group draws a card from the box. Your group has just been hired by the store you drew to write some commercials to help boost sales for the holidays. Write a commercial to convince people to buy the items at your store as gifts. Suggest people in the family to give the gifts to. (You will have to be pretty persuasive in order to convince people to buy gifts at a **Metzgerei**!) Bring in props and perform your commercial in front of the class.

Can you use the telephone in Germany? (p. 274)

1 If you were calling someone in Germany, how would you
   a. say who you are
   b. ask to speak to someone
   c. say hello to the person you wanted to speak with
   d. say goodbye

2 If you were answering the phone in Germany, how would you
   a. identify yourself   b. ask the caller to wait a minute

3 How would you tell someone how to use a public telephone to make a call? (Use **zuerst, dann, danach,** and **zuletzt.**)

Can you invite someone to a party and accept or decline? (p. 277)

4 How would a friend invite you to his or her birthday party on Saturday evening at 8:00?

5 How would you respond if
   a. you can come
   b. you can't come because a relative is coming to visit
   c. you can't come because you are going to a concert
   d. you can't come because you have to do your homework

Can you talk about birthdays and express good wishes? (p. 278)

6 How would you ask a friend when he or she has a birthday?

7 How would your friend respond if he or she has a birthday on
   a. May 29   b. March 9   c. February 16   d. July 7

8 How would you express good wishes for the following occasions?
   a. birthday   b. Christmas   c. Hanukkah

Can you discuss gift ideas? (p. 282)

9 How would you ask a friend what he or she is getting another friend for his or her birthday? How might your friend respond?

10 How would you tell a friend that you are going to give these items to various relatives for their birthdays?

a.
mein Vater

b.
meine Tante

c.
meine Oma

d.
mein Bruder

ERSTE STUFE
USING THE TELEPHONE IN GERMANY

telefonieren   *to call on the phone*
anrufen (sep)   *to call*
der Apparat, -e   *telephone*
das Telefon, -e   *telephone*
der Hörer, -   *receiver*
die Telefonzelle -n
   telephone booth

die Telefonnummer, -n   *telephone number*
Münzen einstecken (sep)   *to insert coins*
abheben (sep)   *to pick up (the phone)*
auflegen (sep)   *to hang up (the phone)*
die Nummer wählen   *to dial the number*

besetzt   *busy*
Einen Moment, bitte!   *Just a minute, please.*
Hier (ist) ...   *This is ...*
Hier bei ...   *The ... residence*
Kann ich bitte ... spechen?   *Can I please speak to...?*
Auf Wiederhören!   *Goodbye!*
Wiederhören!   *Bye!*

ZWEITE STUFE
INVITING SOMEONE TO A PARTY

einladen (sep)   *to invite*
   er/sie lädt ... ein   *he/she invites*

ACCEPTING OR DECLINING
Natürlich!   *Certainly!*

TALKING ABOUT BIRTHDAYS AND EXPRESSING GOOD WISHES

der Geburtstag, -e   *birthday*

Ich habe am ... Geburtstag.   *My birthday is on...*
Wann hast du Geburtstag?   *When is your birthday?*
am ersten (1.), zweiten (2.), dritten (3.), usw.   *on the first, second, third, etc....*
Alles Gute zum Geburtstag!   *Happy Birthday!*
Herzlichen Glückwunsch zum Geburtstag!   *Best wishes on your birthday!*

der Feiertag, -e   *holiday*
   Weihnachten   *Christmas*
   Fröhliche Weihnachten!   *Merry Christmas!*
   Chanukka   *Hanukkah*
   Frohes Chanukka-Fest!   *Happy Hanukkah!*
   Ostern   *Easter*
   Frohe Ostern!   *Happy Easter!*
   der Muttertag   *Mother's Day*
   Alles Gute zum Muttertag!   *Happy Mother's Day!*
   der Vatertag   *Father's Day*
   Alles Gute zum Vatertag!   *Happy Father's Day!*

DRITTE STUFE
DISCUSSING GIFT IDEAS

schenken   *to give (a gift)*
geben   *to give*
   er/sie gibt   *he/she gives*
die Geschenkidee, -n   *gift idea*
das Geschenk, -e   *gift*
   die Praline, -n   *fancy chocolate*
   die Armbanduhr, -en   *(wrist) watch*
   der Kalender, -   *calendar*
   der Blumenstrauß, ¨e   *bouquet of flowers*

das Poster, -   *poster*
die CD, -s   *compact disc*
das Parfüm, -e   *perfume*
der Schmuck   *jewelry*
deinem Vater   *to/for your father*
meinem Vater   *to/for my father*
deiner Mutter   *to/for your mother*
meiner Mutter   *to/for my mother*

PRONOUNS, DATIVE CASE
ihm   *to/for him*
ihr   *to/for her*

ARTICLES, DATIVE CASE
dem   *the (masc.)*
der   *the (fem.)*

OTHER USEFUL WORDS
wahrscheinlich   *probably*
vielleicht   *maybe*
verschieden   *different*

12
Die Fete

① So, was möchtet ihr trinken?

Teenagers in German-speaking countries like to get together and have parties with their friends. A lot of work goes into getting ready for a party, but sometimes the preparation is half the fun. What do you do to prepare for a party? Do you buy new clothes? Clean your house? Buy or cook special foods? If you are in a German-speaking country and want to prepare for a party, there are many things you will need to discuss.

In this chapter you will

- offer help and explain what to do; ask where something is located and give directions
- make plans and invite someone to come along; talk about clothing; discuss gift ideas
- describe people and places; say what you would like and whether you do or don't want more; talk about what you did

And you will

- listen to conversations at a party
- read some German recipes
- write a description of your kitchen and living room
- find out what people in German-speaking countries do to get ready for parties

② Es gibt noch viel Bratwurst.

③ Der Tomatensalat sieht lecker aus!

Los geht's!

Die Geburtstagsfete

Look at the pictures that accompany the story.
What big event is taking place in the story?
What preparations are being made for this event?
Who is helping?

Nicole Andreas Thomas Sabine

Mutter Vater Martin

---

①

Nicoles Freunde sind da. Sie wollen ihr helfen.

ANDREAS So, Nicole, was können wir für dich tun?

NICOLE Zuerst muß ich einkaufen gehen. Wer will mitkommen? Ich muß zum Supermarkt.

ANDREAS Wir beide können ja mit den Rädern fahren.

NICOLE Lieb von dir! Aber wir müssen so viel einkaufen. Die Mutti fährt uns mit dem Auto hin. — Aber du kannst mitkommen, wenn du willst.

ANDREAS Klar!

---

②

THOMAS Und was mache ich?

NICOLE Thomas, du kannst dem Vati im Garten helfen, und dann müssen wir noch das Gemüse waschen.

ANDREAS Okay! Wir können das ja machen, wenn wir zurückkommen.

---

③

Nicole und Andreas kommen vom Einkaufen zurück.

VATER Was habt ihr mitgebracht? Oh, die Bratwurst sieht gut aus! Hm ... ganz frisch. Und, was habt ihr sonst noch?

NICOLE Wir haben noch Eier, Mehl, Zucker ... Andreas und ich, wir backen dann einen Kuchen.

VATER Schön!

KAPITEL 12 Die Fete

Die Fete beginnt. Martin kommt.

NICOLE Vati! Das ist Martin!

VATER Hallo, Martin! Herzlich willkommen bei uns!

MARTIN Guten Tag! Vielen Dank für die Einladung!

VATER Schon gut! Wir freuen uns, wenn wir einmal im Jahr Nicoles Freunde zu uns einladen können. — Was willst du trinken? — Andreas, willst du Martin etwas zu trinken geben? Ich muß zum Grill.

ANDREAS Okay, Martin, was möchtest du denn haben?

NICOLE Die Bowle schmeckt gut.

MARTIN Gut! Dann probier' ich die Bowle.

ANDREAS Prost!

MARTIN — Hm, die ist wirklich gut!

MUTTER So, wer möchte was? Es gibt Kartoffelsalat, Krautsalat, Gurkensalat, Tomatensalat ... Thomas? Möchtest du Kartoffelsalat?

THOMAS Ja, bitte! — Die Wurstbrote sehen auch ganz lecker aus!

MUTTER Nimm doch gleich zwei! — Und eine Brezel!

THOMAS Okay. — Wo ist denn der Kuchen?

MUTTER Pst! Der Kuchen kommt erst nachher.

THOMAS Ach so!

Was für eine Überraschung! Vielen, vielen Dank!

Andenken - Souvenir
aus Berlin
die Geschenkidee
Tel.:(030) 345 93 98

1 Was passiert hier?

Do you understand what is happening in the story? Check your comprehension by answering these questions. Don't be afraid to guess.

1. Why are Nicole's friends at her house? What does Nicole tell them they can do to help?
2. Why does Nicole need **Eier, Mehl,** and **Zucker**?
3. Why does Nicole's mother tell Thomas to keep his voice down?
4. What do you think might happen next in the story?

2 Welche Beschreibung paßt zu welcher Person?

Match each person from the story with the most appropriate description.

1. Martin
2. Thomas
3. Nicole
4. Andreas
5. Nicoles Vater

a. geht mit Nicole einkaufen.
b. hilft Nicoles Vater im Garten und fragt Nicole, wo der Kuchen ist.
c. bekommt heute einen Geburtstagskuchen.
d. lädt ihre Freunde zur Fete ein, geht einkaufen und bäckt den Kuchen.
e. findet es super, daß Nicoles Freunde kommen, steht am Grill und grillt die Bratwurst.

3 Nacherzählen

Put the sentences in logical order to make a brief summary of the story.

1. Andreas, Sabine und Thomas kommen vorbei, um Nicole zu helfen.

Andreas gibt Martin etwas zu trinken.

Zuerst gehen Andreas und Nicole zum Supermarkt, und Thomas hilft Nicoles Vater im Garten.

Als letzter kommt der Martin.

Später am Nachmittag kommen die Gäste.

Es gibt Bowle zu trinken, und es gibt viel zu essen: Kartoffelsalat, Tomatensalat, Krautsalat, Gurkensalat und Bratwurst.

Nach dem Essen bringen Nicole und Thomas den Geburtstagskuchen, und die Freunde singen «Happy Birthday!»

4 Und ihr?

Du und dein Partner habt heute abend eine Fete. Was gibt's zu essen? Und zu trinken? Macht eine Liste! Schreibt alles auf, was ihr braucht! Dein Partner sagt dir, was er bringt, dann sagst du ihm, was du bringst. Dann besprich mit deinem Partner, wen ihr eingeladen habt und wer kommt!

BEISPIEL   PARTNER   Ich bringe ... mit. Was bringst du?
                   DU   Ich bringe ...
           PARTNER   Und wen lädst du ein?
                   DU   Ich lade ... ein.

ERSTE STUFE

Offering help and explaining what to do; asking where something is located and giving directions

SO SAGT MAN DAS!

Schon bekannt

Offering help and explaining what to do

You are having a party! Your friends come over to help you get things ready.

A friend might ask:

Kann ich etwas für dich tun?

or

Was kann ich für dich tun?

You could respond:

Du kannst für mich das Geschirr spülen.

Geh bitte einkaufen! Hol ein Pfund Bratwurst und 10 Semmeln! Kauf die Bratwurst beim Metzger und die Semmeln beim Bäcker!

5 Hör gut zu!

Nicole hat viel zu tun, denn sie muß alles für die Fete vorbereiten. Schau ihre Arbeitsliste an! Hör dir das Gespräch gut an und schreib auf, was jede Person macht, um Nicole zu helfen!

Schon bekannt
Ein wenig Grammatik

The preposition **für** is always followed by an accusative case form: **Kannst du für mich 200 Gramm Aufschnitt kaufen?** See page 329 to review the accusative pronouns. To review **du**-commands, see page 333. If you need to review the forms of **können**, see page 332.

> *Arbeitsliste für die Fete*
> *Müll sortieren*
> *Rasen mähen*
> *Staub saugen*
> *Fenster putzen*
> *Zimmer aufräumen*
> *Tisch decken*
> *Geschirr spülen*
> *Einkaufen gehen — Tomaten, Brot, Semmeln, Bratwurst, Hackfleisch, Eier, Mehl, Zucker, Äpfel, Orangen, Kartoffeln, Mineralwasser, Cola kaufen*

6 Du hast eine Fete!

a. Heute abend hast du eine Fete für eine Freundin. Schreib einen Einkaufszettel und eine Arbeitsliste!

b. Dein Partner fragt dich, wie er dir helfen kann. Sag ihm, was er für dich kaufen und machen kann! Sag deinem Partner auch, wo er die Lebensmittel kaufen soll! Dann tauscht ihr die Rollen aus!

Spätzle and Apfelküchle are specialties of Baden-Württemberg. Spätzle ("little sparrow" in the local dialect) are thick, round noodles made by spreading dough onto a board, then cutting it into small strips or pieces, and dropping them into boiling water.

Apfelküchle is a dessert made of apple slices dipped in a pancake batter and fried. The apples are then sprinkled with sugar and cinnamon. Apfelküchle is often served with vanilla sauce or vanilla ice cream.

Apfelküchle
Für 4 Portionen

200 g Mehl
3 Eier
1/4 l Milch
1 Prise Salz
4 möglichst säuerliche Äpfel (groß)
1 Zitrone
1 EL Zucker
1 EL Zimt
Butterschmalz zum Ausbacken

Käsespätzle
Für 4 Personen

400 g Mehl
2 Eier
etwas Salz
1/8 - 1/4 l Wasser
(oder Milch verdünnt)
1 EL Öl
200 g Emmentaler
4 Zwiebeln
50 g Butter
1 Spatzenbrett

7 Soll ich backen oder kochen?

Some friends are coming over for dinner. You and your partner are planning to make **Apfelküchle** and **Spätzle**, two popular southern German dishes. Each of you pick one recipe. Tell your partner what to buy for your recipe and how much. Then switch roles.

WORTSCHATZ

(die) Zwiebel **(die) Zitrone**

(das) Öl

das Salz
der Zimt *cinnamon*
das Butterschmalz *shortening*

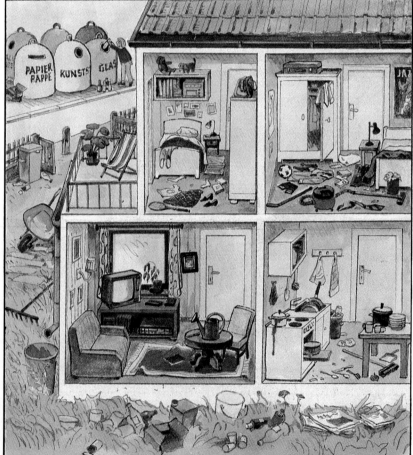

8 Am nächsten Tag

What a party! You and your friends had a great time last night, but now it's time to clean up the mess. You also promised your parents that you would do some other things around the house. Look at the picture of the house on the right and tell your partner what he or she can do to help. Then switch roles.

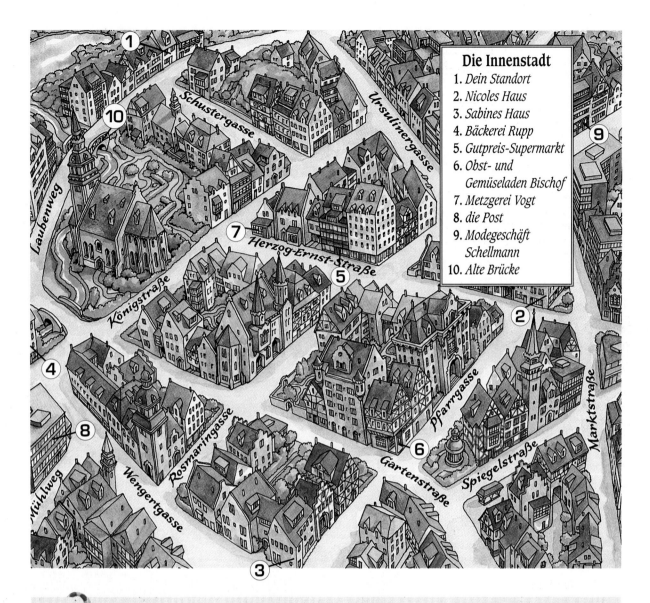

Die Innenstadt
1. *Dein Standort*
2. *Nicoles Haus*
3. *Sabines Haus*
4. *Bäckerei Rupp*
5. *Gutpreis-Supermarkt*
6. *Obst- und Gemüseladen Bischof*
7. *Metzgerei Vogt*
8. *die Post*
9. *Modegeschäft Schellmann*
10. *Alte Brücke*

SO SAGT MAN DAS !

Schon bekannt

Asking where something is located and giving directions

If your friend asks you to pick up a few things at the butcher shop, you might first have to ask someone:

Weißt du, wo die Metzgerei ist?

The response might be:

In der Herzog-Ernst-Straße.

After you leave the house, you realize that you don't know how to get to **Herzog-Ernst-Straße.**

You ask a passer-by:

Entschuldigung! Wie komme ich zur Metzgerei?

The response might be:

Gehen Sie geradeaus bis zur Schustergasse, dann nach rechts, dann die nächste Straße nach links.

9 Hör gut zu!

Following Nicole's party on Saturday, Sabine has invited everyone over on Sunday afternoon for a little get-together. Listen as both Sabine and Nicole give directions over the phone from where you are (**dein Standort**) to their houses. Write each set of instructions so that you know how to get to both parties. Check your directions on the map to see if you got them right.

die nächste Straße nach ...   nach links

nach rechts   an der Ampel nach ...

bis zum ...platz   geradeaus   bis zur ...straße

die (erste, zweite...) Straße nach...

Schon bekannt
Ein wenig *Grammatik*

See pages 335 and 330 to review the forms of **wissen** and word order following **wissen**. To review formal commands, see page 333.

10 Wie komm' ich zurück?

You are at the **Bäckerei Rupp** and your partner is at Nicole's house. Tell your partner how to get to the bakery. Then switch roles: Now you're at Sabine's house, and your partner will give you directions to the **Modegeschäft Schellman**.

11 Ihr habt Hunger

Du und deine Partnerin, ihr seid bei Sabine. Ihr habt Hunger. Wähl zwei von den folgenden Lebensmitteln aus und erzähl deiner Partnerin, wo sie die kaufen kann und wie sie dahin kommt. Schau auf den Stadtplan auf Seite 299!

When you are learning or reviewing vocabulary, remember to use the word or phrase in a sentence or conversation that gives it meaning. For example, when trying to learn the phrase **zur Bäckerei**, use it in an imaginary conversation:

— **Wie komme ich zur Bäckerei? Ich muß Brot kaufen.**
— **Die nächste Straße nach links.**

Mußt du zu Hause helfen?

You've already discovered how German students like to spend their free time, and you know that they enjoy planning and going to parties. However, life isn't all fun! Often before they go out or meet with their friends, they have to help around the house. What chores do you think German students have to do? Make a list of chores that the following German students might mention. Then read the interviews.

LANDESKUNDE

Heide,
Berlin

„Ich muß zweimal in der Woche die Toilette saubermachen, und dann ab und zu halt den Geschirrspüler ausräumen oder die Küche wischen und halt mein Zimmer aufräumen."

Monika,
Berlin

„Also, ich muß fast jeden Tag den Mülleimer runter-bringen und ab und zu mal Waschmaschine an, Waschmaschine aus, Wäsche aufhängen ... Dann ab und zu Staub saugen, wischen—also wir haben in der Küche so Fliesen *(tiles)* und—aber meistens, wenn meine Eltern keine Zeit dazu haben. Abwaschen muß ich nicht, also, wir haben einen Geschirrspüler."

Silvana,
Berlin

„Zu Hause helf' ich meistens so beim Ab-waschen, Spülma-schine ausräumen, oder die Wäsche aufhängen oder abnehmen, zusammen-legen, immer so, was anfällt."

Gerd,
Bietigheim

„Ich saug' halt ab und zu Staub, räum' die Spülma-schine aus, bring' den Müll raus, hol' halt teilweise Getränke und so, mäh' manchmal den Rasen — kommt ganz darauf an."

A. 1. Make a list of the chores that are mentioned by each of the students. Do they have chores in common? How do the chores they mention compare to those you listed before reading the interviews?

2. Which of these students do the same kinds of things that you do at home?

3. Which of the chores mentioned do you like or dislike? Give a reason in English.

B. You and your friends probably have chores to do at home. Make a list in German, indicat-ing what you have to do and for whom, and report it to your class. Keep track of which chores your classmates do. How do the chores that American students do at home compare to those of German students? Write a brief essay in which you discuss this question point-ing out the differences and similarities.

Making plans and inviting someone to come along; talking about clothing; discussing gift ideas

SO SAGT MAN DAS!

Schon bekannt

Making plans and inviting someone to come along

There are many times when you will want to make plans with your friends and invite them to go places with you.

You could say:

> **Ich will um halb drei ins Einkaufszentrum gehen, Klamotten kaufen.
> Willst du mitkommen?** *or* **Kommst du mit?**

Your friend might accept:

> **Ja gern!** *or*
> **Super! Ich komme gern mit!**

Or decline and give a reason:

> **Das geht leider nicht, denn ich muß am Nachmittag die Hausaufgaben machen.**

WORTSCHATZ

THOMAS **Wohin willst du gehen? Was willst du tun?**
SABINE **Ich will ...**

die Stadt besichtigen

in den Park gehen

in den Zoo gehen

Schlittschuh laufen

joggen

ein Brettspiel spielen

Schon bekannt
Ein wenig Grammatik

See page 332 to review the forms of **wollen** and **müssen**. In German the conjugated verb in a main clause of a statement is always in second position. If there is a second verb, it is at the end of the sentence or clause and is in the infinitive. To review German word order, see page 330.

12 Hör gut zu!

A youth magazine recently interviewed four teens in the German-speaking countries about what they like to do in their free time. Match each person interviewed with the activity below that best fits that person's interests.

1. ... in den Zoo gehen
2. ... jeden Tag joggen
3. ... Brettspiele spielen, z. B., Monopoly®
4. ... die Altstadt besichtigen

13 Jugendzentrum in Bietigheim

Du und dein Partner, ihr seid Austauschschüler in der Stadt Bietigheim. Heute besucht ihr das Jugendzentrum. Schaut auf die Tafel, dann wählt vier Tätigkeiten, die ihr zwei gern macht, und sagt, wann ihr diese Tätigkeiten machen könnt.

Tennis spielen	14⁰⁰-15³⁰
Joggen	12¹⁵-13¹⁵
Schach spielen	13⁰⁰-17⁰⁰
Tanzunterricht	16⁰⁰-17⁰⁰
Schwimmen	14⁰⁰-16³⁰
Film „Der mit dem Wolf tanzt"	12⁰⁰-14¹⁵
Basteln	15⁴⁵-17⁴⁵
Karten spielen (Skat)	13⁴⁵-15³⁰
Gitarrenunterricht	14³⁰-15³⁰
Zeichenunterricht	17⁰⁰-18⁰⁰
Basketballturnier	13⁰⁰-14³⁰

14 Willst du mitkommen?

a. Schau die Fotos an und lies den Text! Dann beantworte die Fragen!

1. Was spielen die Jungen hier?
2. Wo spielen sie?
3. Warum nennt (to name) man den Sport „Polo mit Eskimorolle"?
4. Glaubst du, daß dieser Sport Spaß macht?
5. Möchtest du „Polo mit Eskimorolle" spielen? Warum oder warum nicht?

b. Hast du Freizeitinteressen, die so ungewöhnlich sind, wie „Polo mit Eskimorolle"? Mach eine Liste mit drei Aktivitäten, die du gern machst, und lad dazu deinen Partner ein! Tauscht dann die Rollen aus!

Kein Sport für Wasserscheue: Manchmal muß man mit dem Kopf ins Wasser. In der Fachsprache heißt das „Eskimorolle".

Wo ist der Ball? Besonders geschickte Spieler führen ihn mit ihrem Paddel unter Wasser.

Wo ist das Tor? Der Ball muß zwei Meter über dem Wasser in einen Korb.

SO SAGT MAN DAS!

Talking about clothing

You might have the following conversation with the salesperson in a clothing store:

VERKÄUFERIN:	DU:
Haben Sie einen Wunsch?	Ich brauche einen Pulli, in Gelb, bitte! Oh, und ich suche auch ein T-Shirt. Der Pulli dort drüben sieht sehr fesch aus. Ich probiere ihn mal an.
Wie paßt er? Nicht zu lang oder zu eng?	Nein, überhaupt nicht. Er paßt prima, und er gefällt mir.
Ja, er sieht phantastisch aus.	Wirklich?
Wirklich!	Ja, das finde ich auch. Ich nehme ihn.

15 Hör gut zu!

Heute gibt es viele neue Modegeschäfte in Bietigheim. Leute in einem Eiscafé sprechen über diese Geschäfte. Welches Gespräch paßt zu welchem Schaufenster?

a.

b.

c.

d.

WORTSCHATZ

aus **Seide**	*made of silk*
aus **Baumwolle**	*made of cotton*
aus **Leder**	*made of leather*
gestreift	*striped*
gepunktet	*polka-dotted*

16 Du hast einen Laden

Make a window display for a clothing store. Either draw the items of clothing or cut pictures out of magazines and newspapers, then add price tags to your items. Name your store and write an advertisement for it. Look at the C & A ad on page 304 for ideas.

17 Was bekommen Sie?

You are looking for one of the items to the right in a clothing store. Your partner is the salesclerk. Find out if his or her store has the exact item you want. Find out the cost and where the item is located in the store. Then switch roles.

Schon bekannt
Ein wenig *G*rammatik

To review the nominative and accusative pronouns, see page 329. To review the definite and indefinite articles in the nominative and accusative cases, see pages 326–327.

SO SAGT MAN DAS!

Discussing gift ideas

Schon bekannt

In **Kapitel 11** you learned to talk about giving gifts on special occasions.

A friend might ask:	You might respond:
Was schenkst du deinem Bruder zum Geburtstag?	**Ich schenke ihm eine Armbanduhr.**
Und was schenkst du deiner Kusine zu Weihnachten?	**Ich schenke ihr ein Buch.**

---

18 Besondere Geschenke

Unten sind ein paar typische Geschenke aus Deutschland und der Schweiz. Schau dir die Geschenke an. Dann erzähl deinem Partner, wem du sie schenkst (z.B. dem Vater, der Mutter). Dann erzählt dir dein Partner, wem er was schenkt.

die Kuckucksuhr   der Krug

das Poster   ein Stück von der Berliner Mauer   die Armbanduhr

Schon bekannt
Ein wenig *G*rammatik

Do you remember the dative pronouns **ihm** (*to him*) and **ihr** (*to her*) and the definite articles **dem** and **der**? Don't forget the dative endings for **dein** and **mein**.

masculine	feminine
dein-⎱ em	dein-⎱ er
mein-⎰	mein-⎰

Describing people and places; saying what you would like and whether you do or don't want more; talking about what you did

SO SAGT MAN DAS!

Schon bekannt

Describing people and places

You will probably meet people at parties who will ask you about yourself, your friends, and your family.

Someone might ask:

> **Woher kommst du, Lisa?**
> **Und wo wohnst du jetzt?**
>
> **Ist das deine Schwester?**
>
> **Und was machst du in deiner Freizeit?**
> **Wer ist denn Michael?**
> **Wie sieht er aus?**

You might respond:

> **Aus Kalifornien.**
> **Ich wohne jetzt in Berlin, in der Schönleinstraße.**
> **Ja, das ist meine Schwester. Sie heißt Jennifer.**
>
> **Ich spiele oft Schach mit Michael.**
> **Mein Freund.**
> **Er hat lange, braune Haare und grüne Augen und er hat eine Brille.**

You'll also want to be able to describe places, like your own room:

> **Mein Zimmer, das ist wirklich toll! Die Möbel sind echt schön, das Bett sogar ganz neu, ja und auch der Schreibtisch. Dann habe ich auch eine Couch. Die Farbe, na ja, das Grün ist nicht sehr schön, aber sonst ist die Couch wirklich sehr bequem.**

Schon bekannt
Ein wenig *Grammatik*

When you refer to people and places, you will use the nominative pronouns **er, sie, es,** and **sie** (pl), for example, **Das ist mein Vater. Er heißt Gerd.** To review these pronouns, look at page 329. To review possessives like **mein** and **dein**, see page 327.

19 Berühmte Leute

Cut out magazine photos of two famous people and bring them to class. Place the photos in a container. Each student will take out a photo. Describe the person in the photo you picked with as much detail as possible so that your partner can guess who it is. Switch roles.

20 Auf einer Fete

Dein Freund hat eine Fete, und du bist eingeladen. Du möchtest auf der Fete andere Leute kennenlernen (*meet*). Mach eine Liste mit acht Fragen, z.B. **Wo wohnst du? Was machst du in deiner Freizeit?** Frag deine Partnerin, und schreib ihre Antworten auf! Dann tauscht ihr die Rollen aus.

21 **Deine Partnerin vorstellen** *Introducing your partner*

Heute tagt (*meets*) der Deutsch-Club. Du mußt deine Partnerin vorstellen. Erzähl der Klasse alles, was du über deine Partnerin weißt! (Verwende Information von Übung 20.)

Welche Möbel habt ihr im Wohnzimmer?

Wir haben ...

ein Sofa
einen Tisch
    aus Holz
    aus Kunststoff
eine Lampe

einen Teppich

einen Sessel

rund
eckig *(with corners)*
modern

Und in der Küche gibt es ...
einen Eßtisch

einen Kühlschrank

einen Herd

einen Ofen

ein Spülbecken

22 **Beschreib den Raum!**

Beschreib deinem Partner die Möbel im Wohnzimmer! Frag ihn, wie er die Möbel findet! Sag ihm, wie du die Möbel findest! Jetzt beschreibt dein Partner die Möbel in der Küche.

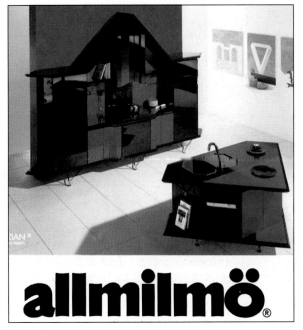

allmilmö®

23 **Für mein Notizbuch**

Beschreib dein Wohnzimmer und deine Küche! Was für Möbel gibt es da? Wie sehen diese Möbel aus? Du kannst auch eine Skizze machen.

SO SAGT MAN DAS!

Saying what you would like and whether you do or don't want more

Schon bekannt

When eating at a friend's house, you may be asked
by your host:

You could respond:

> **Was möchtest du trinken?**

> **Ich möchte eine Limo, bitte!**

Later your host might ask if you want more of something:

> **Möchtest du noch etwas?**
> **Und noch eine Semmel?**

> **Ja, bitte! Noch einen Saft.**
> **Nein, danke! Keine Semmel mehr.**

Schon bekannt
Ein wenig *G*rammatik

To review the **möchte** forms, see page 332. To review the use of **kein ... mehr**, see page 327.

---

24 Auf einer Geburtstagsfete

Spiel mit zwei oder drei Klassenkameraden die folgende Szene vor der Klasse: Ihr seid auf einer Geburtstagsfete. Ein Schüler spielt den Gastgeber (*host*). Er fragt die Gäste, was sie essen und trinken möchten. Später sagen die Gäste, wie das Essen schmeckt. Dann fragt der Gastgeber, wer noch etwas möchte.

25 Eine Imbißstube in Bietigheim

Du besichtigst heute mit zwei Klassenkameraden die Stadt Bietigheim. Ihr habt Hunger und wollt etwas essen. Schaut auf die Speisekarte und schreibt ein Gespräch! Was gibt es zu essen? Was bestellt ihr? Was kostet das Essen? Wie schmeckt das Essen? Wollt ihr noch mehr?

SO SAGT MAN DAS!

Schon bekannt

Talking about what you did

You will often want to describe to friends or family what you did in the past, for example, last week or over the weekend.

A friend might ask:

> **Was hast du am Wochenende gemacht?**

Your response might be:

> **Am Samstag war ich in der Innenstadt. Zuerst habe ich Klamotten gekauft, dann war ich im Supermarkt, danach im Eiscafé mit Andreas, und zuletzt bei Andreas zu Hause. Am Sonntag war ich die ganze Zeit zu Hause. Am Nachmittag habe ich gelesen, und am Abend habe ich ein Video gesehen. Danach haben Antje, Jörg und ich über Filme und Musik gesprochen.**

26 Hast du ein schönes Wochenende gehabt?

Frag deine Partnerin, was sie am Wochenende gemacht hat! Dann fragt dich deine Partnerin. Verwende die Vorschläge (*suggestions*) hier rechts.

> Wo warst du am Wochenende?
> im Kaufhaus
> beim Bäcker
> zu Hause
> bei Freunden
> in der Stadt
> im Konzert

> Was hast du gemacht?
> gekauft?
> gelesen?
> gesehen?
> Worüber habt ihr gesprochen?

AUSSPRACHE

Richtig aussprechen / Richtig lesen

A. To review the following sounds, say the sentences below after your teacher or after the recording.

1. The letter **w**: The letter **w** is always pronounced like the *v* in the English word *vent*.
   Weißt du, wann Werners Geburtstag ist? Am Mittwoch?

2. The letter **v**: The letter **v** sounds like the *f* in the English word *fence*.
   Volker hat viele Fische und findet immer mehr.

3. The letter **j**: The letter **j** is pronounced the same as the *y* in the English word *you*.
   Die Julia besucht Jens im Juli, nicht Juni.

4. The letters **ä** and **e**: The letters **ä** and **e** are pronounced as short vowels when followed by two consonants. When followed by one consonant or the letter h the **ä** and **e** are usually pronounced as long vowels.
   Ich finde den Sessel häßlich. Er gefällt mir nicht.
   Peter kauft Käse. Das Mädchen mäht den Rasen.

Richtig schreiben / Diktat

B. Write down the sentences that you hear.

ZUM LESEN

Mahlzeit!

LESETRICKS

Combining reading strategies You can often derive the main idea of a text by looking at visual clues and format, and then searching for cognates and words you already know. In trying to figure out the meaning of unknown words, look at the context in which they occur. Often the surrounding text will give you clues about the meaning of the unknown word.

1. Judging by their form, what kinds of texts are these? What kinds of expressions do you expect to find in them? List in English the words and expressions you would find in typical recipes at home.

2. Recalling what you know about cognates and compound words, what do the following words mean in English?
   gefüllte Eier
   Kartoffelsalat
   Mandelkuchen
   (**Mandeln**=*almonds*)

3. Since German recipes often use infinitives in the directions, you need to look at the end of the sentences to determine what to do with the ingredients. Make an educated guess about the meaning of the verbs in these phrases.

   1. mit Salz und Pfeffer **abschmecken**
   2. die Eier **halbieren**
   3. die Dotter **herausnehmen**
   4. Essig **dazugeben**
   5. Speck in kleine Würfel **schneiden**
   6. mit feingehackter Zwiebel **anrösten**

   a. *take out*
   b. *season*
   c. *brown lightly*
   d. *halve*
   e. *cut*
   f. *add*

KARTOFFELSALAT MIT SPECK

1 Pfd. gekochte Kartoffeln —50 g Speck — 1 Zwiebel — 3 Eßlöffel Essig — Salz — Pfeffer — 4 Eßlöffel Brühe

Kartoffeln in Scheiben schneiden. Warmhalten. Etwas Speck in kleine Würfel schneiden und mit feingehackter Zwiebel anrösten. Essig dazugeben und die Kartoffeln und den Speck mit Salz und Pfeffer abschmecken. Die heiße Fleischbrühe dazugeben.

GEFÜLLTE EIER

MANDELKUCHEN

150 g Butter oder Margarine — 200 g Zucker — 1 Päckchen Vanillin-Zucker — 5 Eier — 3 Tropfen Bittermandelöl — 100 g Weizenmehl — 50 g Maisstärke — 1 Teelöffel Backpulver

Aus den Zutaten einen Rührteig bereiten, dann 150 g Mandeln, gemahlen und 150 g Schokoladenstücke unterheben und alles in eine gefettete Kastenform füllen.
Bei 175 Grad etwa 60-70 Minuten backen.

MANDELKUCHEN

GEFÜLLTE EIER

Hartgekochte Eier, nach Bedarf — Butter — Salz — feingehackte Kräuter (Thymian, Majoran, Basilikum, Estragon)

Die Eier halbieren, die Dotter herausnehmen und in einer Schüssel mit der Butter, dem Salz und den feingehackten Kräutern gut verrühren. Die Masse wieder in die Eihälften füllen.

4. Scan the lists of ingredients. How are most of the ingredients measured? How does that compare to recipes in the United States?

5. What ingredients will you need to make the deviled eggs? What do you think **Kräuter** means? *(Hint: look at the words in parentheses that follow.)*

6. What ingredients will you need to make **Kartoffelsalat**? How does this differ from the way you would make potato salad?

7. What steps will you need to follow to make the **Kartoffelsalat**?

8. What ingredients will you need to make the **Mandelkuchen**? What do you think **Bittermandelöl** is?

9. What cooking temperature is given for the cake? The baking temperature for electric ovens is 175°. This number is much lower than the usual temperature needed for baking cakes. How can you explain this? (Remember what you learned in **Kapitel 7** about how temperature is measured in German-speaking countries.)

10. What are the steps in making deviled eggs?

11. Assume you are in Germany, and you have been asked to bring your favorite food to a party, along with the recipe. Choose something that is not too complicated to make and write out the recipe.

ANWENDUNG

1 You will hear five different conversations taking place at Martin's party. Listen and decide which of the five topics below belongs with which conversation.

    a. Filme   **b.** Musik   **c.** Essen   **d.** Sport   **e.** Schule

2 Wer ist deine Lieblingsperson? Schreib alles über deine Lieblingsperson in dein Notizbuch. Wer ist diese Person? Wie alt ist sie? Wo wohnt sie? Wie sieht diese Person aus? Was macht diese Person in der Freizeit? Was für Interessen hat sie?

3 a. Use the illustrations below to plan a weekend in Bietigheim and perhaps a trip to the nearby city of Stuttgart. First use the captions as clues to decide which activity is shown in each photo. Then write in German three activities that look interesting.

Im Restaurant

Musikpavillon
im Kurpark
Bad Cannstatt

Maurischer Garten
in der Wilhelma

Königstraße:
Stuttgarter
Innenstadt

Badepark Ellental —
das Freizeitvergnügen
im Sommer

Schlittschuhlaufen
in der Eissporthalle

Das große Reitturnier

b. Get together with a partner and invite him or her to come with you. Your partner will want to know exactly when you're going. Then he or she will accept, or decline and give a reason, for example: **Nein, danke! Ich schwimme nicht gern.** or **Ich kann nicht. Ich muß noch aufräumen.**

c. After you have agreed on at least three things to do together, write the activities and next to each, write a time expression telling when or in what order you will do them. Share your plans with the class.

4 Du gehst bald zu einem Familientreffen (*family reunion*). Du willst den Verwandten etwas schenken. Was schenkst du ihnen? Zum Beispiel, was schenkst du deinem Onkel? Und deiner Kusine? Erzähl es deinem Partner! Danach sagt er dir, was er schenkt.

5 You are taking a day trip to Stuttgart and would like to visit some interesting places. Go to the information center and find out how to get to the following places. Your partner will give you directions at the information counter.

  1. ins Theater in der Altstadt
  2. zum Rathaus
  3. zum Alten Schloß
  4. zur tri-bühne

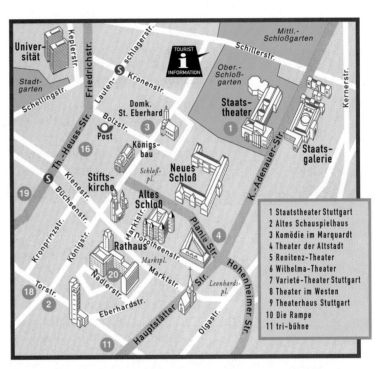

1 Staatstheater Stuttgart
2 Altes Schauspielhaus
3 Komödie im Marquardt
4 Theater der Altstadt
5 Renitenz-Theater
6 Wilhelma-Theater
7 Varieté-Theater Stuttgart
8 Theater im Westen
9 Theaterhaus Stuttgart
10 Die Rampe
11 tri-bühne

6 **R O L L E N S P I E L**

Everyone writes the name of the store that he or she created in Activity 16 on page 305 on a slip of paper and puts it into a small box. Draw out five stores. The people whose stores were chosen will line up at the front of the class with their store windows and play the **Verkäufer.** Bring in old clothing for the customers to try on. The rest of the class will divide into pairs and take turns visiting the stores on the **Einkaufsstraße.** When you are finished, draw more store names and continue your shopping spree. Remember to ask the salesperson about color and price. Try the clothes on and discuss the fit. Comment on your friend's clothing when he or she tries something on.

Can you offer help and explain what to do? (p. 297)

1 How would you offer to help a classmate do some chores around the house?

2 How would he or she respond if he or she needed you to
- **a.** pick up clothes
- **b.** clean the windows
- **c.** go to the store
- **d.** buy some tomatoes

Can you ask directions and say where something is located? (p. 299)

3 How would you tell a classmate how to get to school from your house? How would you tell him or her where your school is located?

Can you make plans and invite someone to come along? (p. 302)

4 How would your friend invite you to go to a concert at 8:30 on Saturday evening? How would you respond if
- **a.** you accept
- **b.** you decline because you're going to a movie at 8:00

Can you talk about clothes in a clothing store? (p. 304)

5 Write a conversation you would have with a salesperson in a clothing store. Talk about particular items of clothing, price, color, fit, and make some comments about how the clothing looks on you.

Can you discuss gift ideas? (p. 305)

6 How would you tell a classmate what you plan to give two family members for their birthdays?

Can you describe people and places? (p. 306)

7 How would you describe your partner: how he or she looks, his or her interests, and where he or she lives?

8 How would you describe your living room and your kitchen?

Can you say what you would like and that you do or don't want more? (p. 307)

9 How would you say that you do or don't want more of the following items?
- **a.** eine Semmel
- **b.** ein Apfel
- **c.** ein Apfelsaft
- **d.** ein Käsebrot

Can you talk about what you did? (p. 309)

10 How would a friend ask you what you did last weekend? How would you respond telling where you were, what you bought, what movies you saw, or what books you read?

WORTSCHATZ

ERSTE STUFE
INGREDIENTS FOR A RECIPE

das Salz *salt*
das Öl *oil*
die Zwiebel, -n *onion*
die Zitrone, -n *lemon*
der Zimt *cinnamon*
das Butterschmalz *shortening*

ZWEITE STUFE
MAKING PLANS

die Stadt besichtigen *to visit the city*
in den Park gehen *to go to the park*
in den Zoo gehen *to go to the zoo*
Schlittschuh laufen *ice skate*
joggen *to jog*
ein Brettspiel spielen *to play a board game*

TALKING ABOUT CLOTHING

die Seide *silk*
 aus Seide *made of silk*
die Baumwolle *cotton*
 aus Baumwolle *made of cotton*
das Leder *leather*
 aus Leder *made of leather*
gestreift *striped*
gepunktet *polka-dotted*

DRITTE STUFE
DESCRIBING PLACES

im Wohnzimmer *in the living room*
 das Sofa, -s *sofa*
 der Tisch, -e *table*
  aus Holz *made of wood*
  aus Kunststoff *made of plastic*
die Lampe, -n *lamp*
der Teppich, -e *carpet*
der Sessel, - *armchair*
die Küche, -n *kitchen*
 in der Küche *in the kitchen*
der Eßtisch, -e *dining table*
der Kühlschrank, ̈-e *refrigerator*
der Herd, -e *stove*
der Ofen, ̈ *oven*
das Spülbecken, - *sink*
rund *round*
eckig *with corners*
modern *modern*

WORTSCHATZ *dreihundertfünfzehn* 315

SUMMARY OF FUNCTIONS

Functions are probably best defined as the ways in which you use a language for specific purposes. When you find yourself in specific situations, such as in a restaurant, in a grocery store, or at school, you will want to communicate with those around you. In order to do that, you have to "function" in the language so that you can be understood: you place an order, make a purchase, or talk about your class schedule.

Such functions form the core of this book. They are easily identified by the boxes in each chapter that are labeled SO SAGT MAN DAS! These functions are the building blocks you need to become a speaker of German. All the other features in the chapter—the grammar, the vocabulary, even the culture notes—are there to support the functions you are learning.

Here is a list of the functions presented in this book and the German expressions you will need in order to communicate in a wide range of situations. Following each function is the chapter and page number where it was introduced.

SOCIALIZING

Saying hello Ch. 1, p. 21

Guten Morgen!
Guten Tag!
Morgen! ⎫
Tag! ⎭ *shortened forms*
Hallo! ⎫
Grüß dich! ⎭ *informal*

Saying goodbye Ch. 1, p. 21

Auf Wiedersehen!
Wiedersehen! *shortened form*
Tschüs! ⎫
Tschau! ⎬ *informal*
Bis dann! ⎭

Offering something to eat and drink Ch. 3, p. 70

Was möchtest du trinken?
Was möchte *(name)* trinken?
Was möchtet ihr essen?

Responding to an offer Ch. 3, p. 70

Ich möchte *(beverage)* trinken.
Er/Sie möchte im Moment gar nichts.
Wir möchten *(food/beverage)*, bitte.

Saying please Ch. 3, p. 72

Bitte!

Saying thank you Ch. 3, p. 72

Danke!
Danke schön!
Danke sehr!

Saying you're welcome Ch. 3, p. 72

Bitte!
Bitte schön!
Bitte sehr!

Giving compliments Ch. 5, p. 127

Der/Die/Das *(thing)* sieht *(adjective)* aus!
Der/Die/Das *(thing)* gefällt mir.

Responding to compliments Ch. 5, p. 127

Ehrlich?
Wirklich?
Nicht zu *(adjective)*?
Meinst du?

Starting a conversation Ch. 6, p. 145

Wie geht's? ⎫
Wie geht's denn? ⎭ *Asking how someone is doing*

Sehr gut! ⎫
Prima!
Danke, gut!
Gut!
Danke, es geht.
So lala. ⎬ *Responding to Wie geht's?*
Nicht schlecht.
Nicht so gut.
Schlecht.
Sehr schlecht.
Miserabel. ⎭

Making plans Ch. 6, p. 150

Was willst du machen?   Ich will *(activity)*.
Wohin will *(person)* gehen?   Er/Sie will in(s) *(place)* gehen.

Ordering food and beverages Ch. 6, p. 154

Was bekommen Sie?   Ich bekomme *(food/beverage)*.
Ja, bitte?
Was essen Sie?   Ein(e)(n) *(food)*, bitte.
Was möchten Sie?   Ich möchte *(food/beverage)*, bitte.
Was trinken Sie?   Ich trinke *(beverage)*.
Was nimmst du?   Ich nehme *(food/beverage)*.
Was ißt du?   Ich esse *(food)*.

Talking about how something tastes
Ch. 6, p. 156

Wie schmeckt's?	Gut!
	Prima!
	Sagenhaft!
	Der/die/das *(food/beverage)* schmeckt lecker!
	Der/die/das *(food/beverage)* schmeckt nicht.
Schmeckt's?	Ja, gut!
	Nein, nicht so gut.
	Nicht besonders.

Paying the check   Ch. 6, p. 156

Hallo!
Ich will/möchte zahlen.
Das macht (zusammen) *(total)*.
Stimmt schon!

Extending an invitation   Ch. 7, p. 174; Ch. 11, p. 277

Willst du *(activity)*?
Wir wollen *(activity)*. Komm doch mit!
Möchtest du mitkommen?
Ich habe am *(day/date)* eine Party. Ich lade dich ein. Kannst du kommen?

Responding to an invitation   Ch. 7, p. 174; Ch. 11, p. 277

Ja, gern!
Toll! Ich komme gern mit.
Aber sicher!   ] accepting
Natürlich!
Das geht nicht.   ] declining
Ich kann leider nicht.

Expressing obligations   Ch. 7, p. 174

Ich habe keine Zeit. Ich muß *(activity)*.

Offering help   Ch. 7, p. 179

Was kann ich für dich tun?
Kann ich etwas für dich tun?   ] asking
Brauchst du Hilfe?
Gut! Mach' ich!   agreeing

Asking what you should do   Ch. 8, p. 198

Was soll ich für dich tun?	Du kannst für mich *(chore)*.
Wo soll ich *(thing/things)* kaufen?	Beim (Metzger/Bäcker). In der/Im *(store)*.
Soll ich *(thing/things)* in der/im *(store)* kaufen?	Nein, das kannst du besser in der/im *(store)* kaufen.

Telling someone what to do   Ch. 8, p. 199

Geh bitte *(action)*!
(Thing/Things) holen, bitte!

Getting someone's attention   Ch. 9, p. 222

Verzeihung!
Entschuldigung!

Offering more   Ch. 9, p. 230

Möchtest du noch etwas?
Möchtest du noch ein(e)(n) *(food/beverage)*?
Noch ein(e)(n) *(food/beverage)*?

Saying you want more   Ch. 9, p. 230

Ja, bitte. Ich nehme noch ein(e)(n) *(food/beverage)*.
Ja, bitte. Noch ein(e)(n) *(food/beverage)*.
Ja, gern.

Saying you don't want more   Ch. 9, p. 230

Nein, danke! Ich habe keinen Hunger mehr.
Nein, danke! Ich habe genug.
Danke, nichts mehr für mich.
Nein, danke, kein(e)(n) *(food/beverage)* mehr.

Using the telephone   Ch. 11, p. 274

Hier *(name)*.
Hier ist *(name)*.
Ich möchte bitte *(name)* sprechen.
Kann ich bitte *(name)* sprechen?   ] starting a conversation
Tag! Hier ist *(name)*.
Wiederhören!
Auf Wiederhören!   ] ending a conversation
Tschüs!

Talking about birthdays   Ch. 11, p. 278

Wann hast du Geburtstag?	Ich habe am *(date)* Geburtstag.
	Am *(date)*.

Expressing good wishes   Ch. 11, p. 278

Alles Gute zu(m)(r) *(occasion)*!
Herzlichen Glückwunsch zu(m)(r) *(occasion)*!

EXCHANGING INFORMATION

Asking someone his or her name and giving yours   Ch. 1, p. 22

Wie heißt du?	Ich heiße *(name)*.
Heißt du *(name)*?	Ja, ich heiße *(name)*.

Asking and giving someone else's name   Ch. 1, p. 22

Wie heißt der Junge?	Der Junge heißt *(name)*.
Heißt der Junge *(name)*?	Ja, er heißt *(name)*.
Wie heißt das Mädchen?	Das Mädchen heißt *(name)*.
Heißt das Mädchen *(name)*?	Nein, sie heißt *(name)*.

Asking and telling who someone is   Ch. 1, p. 23

Wer ist das?   Das ist der/die *(name)*.

Asking someone his or her age and giving yours   Ch. 1, p. 25

Wie alt bist du?   Ich bin *(number)* Jahre alt.
Ich bin *(number)*.
(Number).
Bist du schon *(number)*?   Nein, ich bin *(number)*.

Asking and giving someone else's age   Ch. 1, p. 25

Wie alt ist der Peter?   Er ist *(number)*.
Und die Monika? Ist
sie auch *(number)*?   Ja, sie ist auch *(number)*.

Asking someone where he or she is from and telling where you are from   Ch. 1, p. 28

Woher kommst du?   Ich komme aus *(place)*.
Woher bist du?   Ich bin aus *(place)*.
Bist du aus *(place)*?   Nein, ich bin aus *(place)*.

Asking and telling where someone else is from   Ch. 1, p. 28

Woher ist *(person)*?   Er/sie ist aus *(place)*.
Kommt *(person)* aus
(place)?   Nein, sie kommt aus *(place)*.

Talking about how someone gets to school   Ch. 1, p. 30

Wie kommst
du zur Schule?   Ich komme mit der/dem *(mode of transportation)*.

Kommt Ahmet zu
Fuß zur Schule?   Nein, er kommt auch mit der/dem *(mode of transportation)*.

Wie kommt
Ayla zur Schule?   Sie kommt mit der/dem *(mode of transportation)*.

Talking about interests   Ch. 2, p. 46

Was machst du in
deiner Freizeit?   Ich *(activity)*.
Spielst du *(sport/
instrument/game)*?   Ja, ich spiele *(sport/
instrument/game)*.
Nein, *(sport/instrument/
game)* spiele ich nicht.
Was macht *(name)*?   Er/Sie spielt *(sport/
instrument/game)*.

Saying when you do various activities   Ch. 2, p. 53

Was machst du nach
der Schule?   Am Nachmittag *(activity)*.
Am Abend *(activity)*.
Und am Wochenende?   Am Wochenende *(activity)*.
Was machst du im
Sommer?   Im Sommer *(activity)*.

Talking about where you and others live   Ch. 3, p. 69

Wo wohnst du?   Ich wohne in *(place)*.
In *(place)*.
Wo wohnt der/die *(name)*?   Er/Sie wohnt in *(place)*.
In *(place)*.

Describing a room   Ch. 3, p. 75

Der/Die/Das *(thing)* ist alt.
Der/Die/Das *(thing)* ist kaputt.
Der/Die/Das *(thing)* ist klein, aber ganz bequem.
Ist *(thing)* neu?   Ja, er/sie/es ist neu.

Talking about family members   Ch. 3, p. 78

Ist das dein(e)
(family member)?   Ja, das ist mein(e)
(family member).

Und dein(e) *(family
member)*? Wie heißt er/sie?   Er/Sie heißt *(name)*.
Wo wohnen deine *(family
members)*?   In *(place)*.

Describing people   Ch. 3, p. 80

Wie sieht *(person)* aus?   Er/sie hat *(color)* Haare
und *(color)* Augen.

Talking about class schedules   Ch. 4, p. 98

Welche Fächer hast du?   Ich habe *(classes)*.
Was hast du am *(day)*?   *(Classes)*.
Was hat die Katja am *(day)*?   Sie hat *(classes)*.
Welche Fächer habt ihr?   Wir haben *(classes)*.
Was habt ihr nach der Pause?   Wir haben *(classes)*.
Und was habt ihr am Samstag?   Wir haben frei!

Using a schedule to talk about time   Ch. 4, p. 99

Wann hast du *(class)*?   Um *(hour)* Uhr *(minutes)*.
Was hast du um
(hour) Uhr?   *(Class)*.
Was hast du von
(time) bis *(time)*?   Ich habe *(class)*.

Sequencing events   Ch. 4, p. 101

Welche Fächer
hast du am *(day)*?   Zuerst hab' ich *(class)*, dann
(class), danach *(class)*, und
zuletzt *(class)*.

Talking about prices   Ch. 4, p. 107

Was kostet *(thing)*?   Er/sie kostet nur *(price)*.
Was kosten *(things)*?   Sie kosten *(price)*.
Das ist (ziemlich) teuer!
Das ist (sehr) billig!
Das ist (sehr) preiswert!

Pointing things out   Ch. 4, p. 108

Wo sind die *(things)*?   Schauen Sie!
Dort!
Sie sind dort drüben!
Sie sind da hinten.
Sie sind da vorn.

Expressing wishes when shopping   Ch. 5, p. 122

Was möchten Sie?   Ich möchte ein(e)(n) *(thing)*
                          sehen, bitte.
                          Ich brauche ein(e)(n) *(thing)*.
Was bekommen Sie?   Ein(e)(n) *(thing)*, bitte.
Haben Sie
  einen Wunsch?   Ich suche ein(e)(n) *(thing)*.

Describing how clothes fit   Ch. 5, p. 125

Es paßt prima.
Es paßt nicht.

Talking about trying on clothes   Ch. 5, p. 131

Ich probiere den/die/das *(item of clothing)* an.
Ich ziehe den/die/das *(item of clothing)* an.

If you buy it: *If you don't:*
Ich nehme es.   Ich nehme es nicht.
Ich kaufe es.   Ich kaufe es nicht.

Telling time   Ch. 6, p. 146

Wie spät ist es jetzt?   Es ist *(time)*.
Wieviel Uhr ist es?   Es ist *(time)*.

Talking about when you do things   Ch. 6, p. 146

Wann gehst du *(activity)*?   Um *(time)*.
Um wieviel Uhr *(action)* du?   Um *(time)*.
Und du? Wann *(action)* du?   Um *(time)*.

Talking about how often you do things   Ch. 7, p. 178

Wie oft *(action)* du?   (Einmal) in der Woche.
Und wie oft
  mußt du *(action)*?   Jeden Tag.
                              Ungefähr (zweimal) im Monat.

Explaining what to do   Ch. 7, p. 179

Du kannst für mich *(action)*.

Talking about the weather   Ch. 7, p. 183

Wie ist das Wetter heute?   Heute regnet es.
                              Wolkig und kühl.
Wie ist das Wetter
  morgen?   Sonnig, aber kalt.
Regnet es heute?   Ich glaube schon.
Schneit es am Abend?   Nein, es schneit nicht.
Wieviel Grad haben wir
  heute?   Ungefähr 10 Grad.

Talking about quantities   Ch. 8, p. 202

Wieviel *(food item)*
  bekommen Sie?   500 Gramm *(food item)*.
                              100 Gramm, bitte.

Asking if someone wants anything else   Ch. 8, p. 203

Sonst noch etwas?
Was bekommen Sie noch?
Haben Sie noch einen Wunsch?

Saying that you want something else   Ch. 8, p. 203

Ich brauche noch ein(e)(n) *(food/beverage/thing)*.
Ich bekomme noch ein(e)(n) *(food/beverage/thing)*.

Telling someone you don't need anything else   Ch. 8, p. 203

Nein, danke.
Danke, das ist alles.

Giving a reason   Ch. 8, p. 206

Jetzt kann ich nicht, weil ich *(reason)*.
Es geht nicht, denn ich *(reason)*.

Saying where you were   Ch. 8, p. 207

Wo warst du heute morgen?   Ich war *(place)*.
Wo warst du gestern?   Ich war *(place)*.

Saying what you bought   Ch. 8, p. 207

Was hast du gekauft?   Ich habe *(thing)* gekauft.

Talking about where something is located   Ch. 9, p. 222

Verzeihung, wissen Sie, wo
  der/die/das *(place)* ist?   In der Innenstadt.
                                  Am *(place name)*.
                                  In der *(street name)*.
Wo ist der/die/das *(place)*?   Es tut mir leid. Das
                                  weiß ich nicht.
Entschuldigung! Weißt du,
  wo der/die/das *(place)* ist?   Keine Ahnung! Ich bin
                                  nicht von hier.

Asking for directions   Ch. 9, p. 226

Wie komme ich zu(m)(r) *(place)*?
Wie kommt man zu(m)(r) *(place)*?

Giving directions   Ch. 9, p. 226

Gehen Sie geradeaus bis zu(m)(r) *(place)*.
Nach rechts/links.
Hier rechts/links.

Talking about what there is to eat and drink   Ch. 9, p. 229

Was gibt es hier
  zu essen?   Es gibt *(foods)*.
Und zu trinken?   Es gibt *(beverage)* und auch
                     (beverage).

Talking about what you did in your free time   Ch. 10, p. 260

Was hast du *(time
  phrase)* gemacht?   Ich habe
                         (person/thing) gesehen.
                         (book, magazine, etc.)
                         gelesen.
                         mit *(person)* über *(subject)*
                         gesprochen.

Discussing gift ideas, Ch. 11, p. 282

Schenkst du (person)
ein(e)(n) (thing)
zu(m)(r) (occasion)? Nein, ich schenke ihm/ihr
ein(e)(n) (thing).

Was schenkst du (person)
zu(m)(r) (occasion)? Ich weiß noch nicht. Hast
du eine Idee?

Wem schenkst du
den/die/das (thing)? Ich schenke (person)
den/die/das (thing).

EXPRESSING ATTITUDES AND OPINIONS

Asking for an opinion Ch. 2, p. 55; Ch. 9, p. 232

Wie findest du (thing/activity/place)?

Expressing your opinion Ch. 2, p. 55; Ch. 9, p. 232

Ich finde (thing/activity/place) langweilig.
(Thing/Activity/Place) ist Spitze!
(Activity) macht Spaß!
Ich finde es toll, daß ...
Ich glaube, daß ...

Agreeing Ch. 2, p. 56; Ch. 7, p. 179

Ich auch!
Das finde ich auch!
Stimmt!
Gut! Mach' ich!

Disagreeing Ch. 2, p. 56

Ich nicht!
Das finde ich nicht!
Stimmt nicht!

Commenting on clothes Ch. 5, p. 125

Wie findest du den/die/
das (clothing item)? Ich finde ihn/sie/es
(adjective).
Er/Sie/Es gefällt mir (nicht).

Expressing uncertainty, not knowing Ch. 5, p. 125; Ch. 9, p. 222

Ich bin nicht sicher.
Ich weiß nicht.
Keine Ahnung!

Expressing regret Ch. 9, p. 222

Es tut mir leid.

EXPRESSING FEELINGS AND EMOTIONS

Asking about likes and dislikes Ch. 2, p. 48; Ch. 4, p. 102; Ch. 10, p. 250

Was (action) du gern?
(Action) du gern?
Magst du (things/activities)?
Was für (things/activities) magst du?

Expressing likes Ch. 2, p. 48; Ch. 4, p. 102; Ch. 10, p. 250

Ich (action) gern.
Ich mag (things/activities).
(Thing/Activities) mag ich (sehr/furchtbar) gern.

Expressing dislikes Ch. 2, p. 48; Ch. 10, p. 250

Ich (action) nicht so gern.
Ich mag (things/action) (überhaupt) nicht.

Talking about favorites Ch. 4, p. 102

Was ist dein
Lieblings(category)? Mein Lieblings(category)
ist (thing).

Responding to good news Ch. 4, p. 104

Toll!
Das ist prima!
Nicht schlecht.

Responding to bad news Ch. 4, p. 104

Schade!
So ein Pech!
So ein Mist!
Das ist sehr schlecht!

Expressing familiarity Ch. 10, p. 252

Kennst du
(person/place/thing)? Ja, sicher!
Ja, klar! or
Nein, den/die/das kenne
ich nicht.
Nein, überhaupt nicht.

Expressing preferences and favorites Ch. 10, p. 253

(Siehst) du gern ...? Ja, aber ... (sehe) ich lieber.
Und am liebsten (sehe) ich ...

(Siehst) du lieber
... oder ...? Lieber ... Aber am liebsten
(sehe) ich ...

Was (siehst) du
am liebsten? Am liebsten (sehe) ich ...

ADDITIONAL VOCABULARY

This list includes additional vocabulary that you may want to use to personalize activities. If you can't find the words you need here, try the German–English and English–German vocabulary sections beginning on page 340.

SPORT UND INTERESSEN
(SPORTS AND INTERESTS)

angeln *to fish*
Baseball spielen *to play baseball*
Brettspiele spielen *to play board games*
fotografieren *to take photographs*
Gewichte heben *lift weights*
Handball spielen *to play handball*
joggen *to jog*
kochen *to cook*
malen *to paint*
Münzen sammeln *to collect coins*
nähen *to sew*
radfahren *to ride a bike*
reiten *to ride (a horse)*
Rollschuh laufen *to roller skate*
segeln *to sail*
Skateboard fahren *to ride a skateboard*
Ski laufen *to (snow) ski*
stricken *to knit*
Tischtennis spielen *to play table tennis*
Videospiele spielen *to play video games*

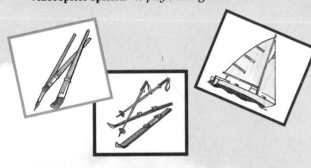

INSTRUMENTE
(INSTRUMENTS)

die Blockflöte, -n *recorder*
das Cello (Violoncello), -s *cello*
die Flöte, -n *flute*
die Geige, -n *violin*
die Harfe, -n *harp*
die Klarinette, -n *clarinet*
der Kontrabaß, (pl) Kontrabässe *double bass*
die Mandoline, -n *mandolin*
die Mundharmonika, -s *harmonica*
die Oboe, -n *oboe*
die Posaune, -n *trombone*
das Saxophon, -e *saxophone*
das Schlagzeug, -e *drums*
die Trompete, -n *trumpet*
die Tuba, (pl) Tuben *tuba*

GETRÄNKE   (BEVERAGES)

die Limo, - *lemon-flavored drink*
ein Glas Milch *a glass of milk*
ein Glas Tee *a glass of tea*
eine Tasse, -n Kaffee *a cup of coffee*

SPEISEN   (FOODS)

die Ananas, - *pineapple*
der Apfelstrudel, - *apple strudel*
die Banane, -n *banana*
die Birne, -n *pear*
der Chip, -s *potato chip*
der Eintopf *stew*
die Erdbeere, -n *strawberry*
die Erdnußbutter *peanut butter*
das Gebäck *baked goods*
die Gurke, -n *cucumber*
die Himbeere, -n *raspberry*
der Joghurt, - *yogurt*
die Karotte, -n *carrot*
die Marmelade, -n *jam, jelly*
die Mayonnaise *mayonaise*
die Melone, -n *melon*
das Müsli *muesli (cereal)*
die Nuß, (pl) Nüsse *nut*
die Orange, -n *orange*
das Plätzchen, - *cookie*
die Pommes frites (pl) *french fries*
der Spinat *spinach*
die Zwiebel, -n *onion*

MÖBEL *(FURNITURE)*

das Bild, -er *picture*
der Computer, - *computer*
die Lampe, -n *lamp*
der Sessel, - *armchair*
das Sofa, -s *sofa*
der Teppich, -e *carpet, rug*
der Tisch, -e *table*
der Vorhang, ̈e *curtain*

FAMILIE *(FAMILY)*

der Halbbruder, ̈ *half brother*
die Halbschwester, -n *half sister*
der Stiefbruder, ̈ *stepbrother*
die Stiefmutter, ̈ *stepmother*
die Stiefschwester, -n *stepsister*
der Stiefvater, ̈ *stepfather*

FÄCHER *(SCHOOL SUBJECTS)*

Algebra *algebra*
Band *band*
Chemie *chemistry*
Chor *chorus*
Französisch *French*
Hauswirtschaft *home economics*
Informatik *computer science*
Italienisch *Italian*
Japanisch *Japanese*
Orchester *orchestra*
Russisch *Russian*
Spanisch *Spanish*
Sozialkunde *social studies*
Werken *shop*
Wirtschaftskunde *economics*

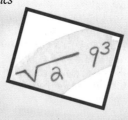

KLEIDUNGSSTÜCKE *(CLOTHING)*

der Anzug, ̈e *suit*
der Badeanzug, ̈e *swimsuit*
der Blazer, - *blazer*
das Halstuch, ̈er *scarf*
der Handschuh, -e *glove*
der Hut, ̈e *hat*
die Krawatte, -n *tie*
der Mantel, ̈ *coat*
die Mütze, -n *cap*
die Sandalen (pl) *sandals*
der Schal, -s *shawl*
die Strumpfhose, -n *panty hose*
die Weste, -n *vest*

FARBEN *(COLORS)*

beige *beige*
bunt *colorful*
gepunktet *polka-dotted*
gestreift *striped*
golden *gold*
lila *purple*
orange *orange*
rosa *pink*
silbern *silver*
türkis *turquoise*

HAUSARBEIT *(HOUSEWORK)*

das Auto polieren *to polish the car*
das Auto waschen *to wash the car*
den Fußboden kehren *to sweep the floor*
den Müll wegtragen *to take out the trash*
putzen *to clean*
Staub wischen *to dust*
saubermachen *to clean*
die Wäsche waschen *to do the laundry*
    trocknen *to dry*
    aufhängen *to hang*
    legen *to fold*
    bügeln *to iron*
    einräumen *to put away*

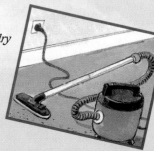

HAUSTIERE (PETS)

die Eidechse, -n *lizard*
der Fisch, -e *fish*
der Frosch, ¨e *frog*
der Hamster, - *hamster*
der Hase, -n *hare*
der Kanarienvogel, ¨ *canary*
die Maus, ¨e *mouse*
das Meerschweinchen, - *guinea pig*
der Papagei, -en *parrot*
das Pferd, -e *horse*
die Schildkröte, -n *turtle*
die Schlange, -n *snake*
das Schwein, -e *pig*
der Vogel, ¨ *bird*

WETTER (WEATHER)

feucht *damp*
gewittrig *stormy*
halbbedeckt *partly cloudy*
heiter *bright*
kühl *cool*
neblig *foggy*
nieslig *drizzly*
trüb *murky*
windig *windy*

IN DER STADT
(PLACES AROUND TOWN)

die Brücke, -n *bridge*
die Bücherei, -en *library*
der Flughafen, (pl) Flughäfen *airport*
das Fremdenverkehrsamt, (pl) Fremdenverkehrsämter
   tourist office
der Frisiersalon, -s *beauty shop*
das Krankenhaus, (pl) Krankenhäuser *hospital*
der Park, -s *park*
die Polizei *police
   station*
der Zoo, -s *zoo*

ZUM DISKUTIEREN
(TOPICS TO DISCUSS)

die Armut *poverty*
die Gesundheit *health*
der Präsident *the president*
die Politik *politics*
die Reklame *advertising*
die Umwelt *the environment*
das Verbrechen *crime*
der Wehrdienst *military service*
der Zivildienst *alternate service*

GESCHENKIDEEN
(GIFT IDEAS)

das Bild, -er *picture*
die Kette, -n *chain*
der Ohrring, -e *earring*
die Puppe, -n *doll*
das Puppenhaus, ¨er *dollhouse*
der Ring, -e *ring*
... aus Silber *made of silver*
... aus Gold *made of gold*
die Schokolade *chocolate*
das Spielzeug, -e *toy*

ERDKUNDE (GEOGRAPHY)

Here are some terms you will find on German-language maps:

LÄNDER (STATES)

Most of the states in the United States (**die Vereinigten Staaten**) have the same spelling in German that they have in English. Listed below are those states that have a different spelling.

Kalifornien	California
Neumexiko	New Mexico
Nordkarolina	North Carolina
Norddakota	North Dakota
Südkarolina	South Carolina
Süddakota	South Dakota

STAATEN (COUNTRIES)

Ägypten	Egypt
Argentinien	Argentina
Brasilien	Brazil
Indien	India
Indonesien	Indonesia
Kanada	Canada
Mexiko	Mexico
Rußland	Russia
die Vereinigten Staaten	The United States

KONTINENTE (CONTINENTS)

Afrika	Africa
die Antarktis	Antarctica
Asien	Asia
Australien	Australia
Europa	Europe
Nordamerika	North America
Südamerika	South America

MEERE (BODIES OF WATER)

der Atlantik	the Atlantic
der Golf von Mexiko	the Gulf of Mexico
der Indische Ozean	the Indian Ocean
das Mittelmeer	the Mediterranean
der Pazifik	the Pacific
das Rote Meer	the Red Sea
das Schwarze Meer	the Black Sea

GEOGRAPHICAL TERMS

der Breitengrad	latitude
die Ebene, -n	plain
der Fluß, (pl) Flüsse	river
das ... Gebirge	the ... mountains
die Grenze, -n	border
die Hauptstadt, ¨-e	capital
der Kontinent, -e	continent
das Land, ¨-er	state
der Längengrad	longitude
das Meer, -e	ocean, sea
der Nordpol	the North Pole
der See, -n	lake
der Staat, -en	country
der Südpol	the South Pole
das Tal, ¨-er	valley

DEUTSCHE NAMEN *(GERMAN NAMES)*

Some German names are listed in the **Vorschau,** but here are some additional ones that you will hear when you visit a German-speaking country.

MÄDCHEN *(GIRLS)*

Andrea	Gabriele (Gabi)	Marta
Angela, Angelika	Gertrud (Trudi(e))	Martina
Anja	Gisela	Meike
Anna	Grete	Michaela
Anneliese	Gudrun	Monika
Annette	Hannelore	Nicole
Antje	Heidi/Heidemarie	Petra
Barbara	Heike	Regina
Bärbel	Helga	Renate
Beate	Hilde	Roswitha
Birgit	Hildegard	Rotraud
Brigitte	Ilse	Sabine
Britta	Ina	Sara
Christa	Inge	Silke
Christiane	Ingrid	Simone
Christine	Irmgard	Stephanie
Claudia	Jennifer	Susanne
Connie	Julie	Silvia
Cordula	Jutta	Tanja
Dorothea	Karin	Ulrike (Uli)
Dorothee	Katharina	Ursel
Elfriede	Katja	Ursula (Uschi)
Elisabeth (Lisa)	Katrin	Ute
Elke	Kirstin	Veronika
Erika	Liselotte (Lotte)	Waltraud
Eva	Marie	

JUNGEN *(BOYS)*

Alexander	Hans-Georg	Martin
Andreas	Hans-Jürgen	Mathias
Axel	Hartmut	Max
Bernd(t)	Hauke	Michael
Bernhard	Heinrich	Norbert
Bruno	Heinz	Otto
Christian	Heinz-Dieter	Patrick
Christoph	Helmar	Paul
Daniel	Helmut	Peter
Detlev(f)	Ingo	Philipp
Dieter	Jan	Rainer (Reiner)
Dietmar	Jens	Ralf
Dirk	Joachim	Reinhard
Eberhard	Jochen	Reinhold
Erik	Johann	Rolf
Felix	Johannes	Rudi
Frank	Jörg	Rüdiger
Franz	Josef	Rudolf
Friedrich	Jürgen	Sebastian
Fritz	Karl	Stefan (Stephan)
Georg	Karl-Heinz	Thomas
Gerd	Klaus	Udo
Gerhard	Konrad	Ulf
Gottfried	Kurt	Ulrich (Uli)
Gregor	Lars	Uwe
Günter	Lothar	Volker
Gustav(f)	Lutz	Werner
Hannes	Manfred	Wilhelm (Willi)
Hans	Markus	Wolfgang

GRAMMAR SUMMARY
NOUNS AND THEIR MODIFIERS

In German, nouns (words that name a person, place, or thing) are grouped into three classes or genders: masculine, feminine, and neuter. All nouns, both persons and objects, fall into one of these groups. There are words used with nouns that signal the class of the noun. One of these is the definite article. In English there is one definite article: *the*. In German, there are three, one for each class: **der, die,** and **das**.

THE DEFINITE ARTICLE

SUMMARY OF DEFINITE ARTICLES

	NOMINATIVE	ACCUSATIVE	DATIVE
Masculine	der	den	dem
Feminine	die	die	der
Neuter	das	das	dem
Plural	die	die	den

When the definite article is combined with a noun, a noun phrase is formed. Noun phrases that are used as subjects are in the nominative case. Nouns that are used as direct objects or the objects of certain prepositions (such as **für**) are in the accusative case. Nouns that are indirect objects, the objects of certain prepositions (such as **mit, bei**), or the objects of special verbs that you will learn about in Level 2, are in the dative case. Below is a summary of the definite articles combined with nouns to form noun phrases.

SUMMARY OF NOUN PHRASES

	NOMINATIVE	ACCUSATIVE	DATIVE
Masculine	der Vater der Ball	den Vater den Ball	dem Vater dem Ball
Feminine	die Mutter die Kassette	die Mutter die Kassette	der Mutter der Kassette
Neuter	das Mädchen das Haus	das Mädchen das Haus	dem Mädchen dem Haus

THE INDEFINITE ARTICLE

Another type of word that is used with nouns is the *indefinite article:* **ein, eine, ein** in German, *a, an* in English. There is no plural form of **ein**.

SUMMARY OF INDEFINITE ARTICLES

	NOMINATIVE	ACCUSATIVE	DATIVE
Masculine	ein	einen	einem
Feminine	eine	eine	einer
Neuter	ein	ein	einem
Plural	—	—	—

THE NEGATING WORD KEIN

The word **kein** is also used with nouns and means *no, not,* or *not any*. Unlike the **ein**-words, **kein** has a plural form.

	NOMINATIVE	ACCUSATIVE	DATIVE
Masculine	kein	keinen	keinem
Feminine	keine	keine	keiner
Neuter	kein	kein	keinem
Plural	keine	keine	keinen

THE POSSESSIVES

These words also modify nouns and tell you *whose* object or person is being referred to (*my* car, *his* book, *her* mother). These words have the same endings as **kein**.

SUMMARY OF POSSESSIVES

	BEFORE MASCULINE NOUNS			BEFORE FEMININE NOUNS		BEFORE NEUTER NOUNS		BEFORE PLURAL NOUNS	
	Nom	Acc	Dat	Nom & Acc	Dat	Nom & Acc	Dat	Nom & Acc	Dat
my	mein	meinen	meinem	meine	meiner	mein	meinem	meine	meinen
your	dein	deinen	deinem	deine	deiner	dein	deinem	deine	deinen
his	sein	seinen	seinem	seine	seiner	sein	seinem	seine	seinen
her	ihr	ihren	ihrem	ihre	ihrer	ihr	ihrem	ihre	ihren

Other possessive adjectives that you will learn more about in Level 2 are

unser	*our*
euer	*your* (informal, plural)
ihr	*their*
Ihr	*your* (formal)

NOUN PLURALS

Noun class and plural forms are not always predictable. Therefore, you must learn each noun together with its article (**der, die, das**) and with its plural form. As you learn more nouns, however, you will discover certain patterns. Although there are always exceptions to these patterns, you may find them helpful in remembering the plural forms of many nouns.

Most German nouns form their plurals in one of two ways: some nouns add endings in the plural; some add endings and/or change the sound of the stem vowel in the plural, indicating the sound change with the umlaut (¨). Only the vowels **a, o, u,** and the diphthong **au** can take the umlaut. If a noun has an umlaut in the singular, it keeps the umlaut in the plural. Most German nouns fit into one of the following five plural groups.

1. Nouns that do not have any ending in the plural. Sometimes they take an umlaut.
   NOTE: There are only two feminine nouns in this group: **die Mutter** and **die Tochter**.

der Bruder, die Brüder	der Schüler, die Schüler	das Fräulein, die Fräulein
der Lehrer, die Lehrer	der Vater, die Väter	das Mädchen, die Mädchen
der Onkel, die Onkel	die Mutter, die Mütter	das Poster, die Poster
der Mantel, die Mäntel	die Tochter, die Töchter	das Zimmer, die Zimmer

2. Nouns that add the ending -e in the plural. Sometimes they also take an umlaut.
   NOTE: There are many one-syllable words in this group.

der Bleistift, die Bleistifte	der Sohn, die Söhne	das Jahr, die Jahre
der Freund, die Freunde	die Stadt, die Städte	das Spiel, die Spiele
der Paß, die Pässe		

3. Nouns that add the ending -er in the plural. Whenever possible, they take an umlaut, i.e., when the noun contains the vowels **a, o,** or **u,** or the diphthong **au. NOTE:** There are no feminine nouns in this group. There are many one-syllable words in this group.

das Buch, die Bücher	das Haus, die Häuser
das Fach, die Fächer	das Land, die Länder

4. Nouns that add the ending -en or -n in the plural. These nouns never add an umlaut.
   NOTE: There are many feminine nouns in this group.

der Herr, die Herren	die Klasse, die Klassen	die Tante, die Tanten
der Junge, die Jungen	die Karte, die Karten	die Wohnung, die Wohnungen
die Briefmarke, die Briefmarken	der Name, die Namen	die Zahl, die Zahlen
die Familie, die Familien	der Vetter, die Vettern	die Zeitung, die Zeitungen
die Farbe, die Farben	die Küche, die Küchen	
die Frau, die Frauen	die Schwester, die Schwestern	

   Feminine nouns ending in -**in** add the ending -**nen** in the plural.

die Freundin, die Freundinnen	die Verkäuferin, die Verkäuferinnen
die Lehrerin, die Lehrerinnen	

5. Nouns that add the ending -s in the plural. These nouns never add an umlaut. **NOTE:** There are many words of foreign origin in this group.

der Kuli, die Kulis	das Auto, die Autos
die Kamera, die Kameras	das Hobby, die Hobbys

SUMMARY OF PLURAL ENDINGS

Group	1	2	3	4	5
Ending:	-	-e	-er	-(e)n	-s
Umlaut:	sometimes	sometimes	always	never	never

PRONOUNS

PERSONAL PRONOUNS

		NOMINATIVE	ACCUSATIVE	DATIVE
Singular				
1st person		ich	mich	mir
2nd person		du	dich	dir
3rd person	*m.*	er	ihn	ihm
	f.	sie	sie	ihr
	n.	es	es	ihm
Plural				
1st person		wir	uns	uns
2nd person		ihr	euch	euch
3rd person		sie	sie	ihnen
you (formal, sing. & pl.)		Sie	Sie	Ihnen

DEFINITE ARTICLES AS DEMONSTRATIVE PRONOUNS

The definite articles can be used as demonstrative pronouns, giving more emphasis to the sentences than the personal pronouns **er, sie, es**. Note that these demonstrative pronouns have the same forms as the definite articles:

Wer bekommt *den* Cappucino? *Der* ist für mich.

	NOMINATIVE	ACCUSATIVE
Masculine	der	den
Feminine	die	die
Neuter	das	das
Plural	die	die

INTERROGATIVES

INTERROGATIVE PRONOUNS

	PEOPLE		THINGS	
Nominative	wer?	*who?*	was?	*what?*
Accusative	wen?	*whom?*	was?	*what?*
Dative	wem?	*to, for whom?*		

OTHER INTERROGATIVES

wann?	*when?*	wie viele?	*how many?*	welche?	*which?*
warum?	*why?*	wo?	*where?*	was für (ein)?	*what kind of (a)?*
wie?	*how?*	woher?	*from where?*	(eine)	
wieviel?	*how much? how many?*	wohin?	*to where?*	(einen)	

WORD ORDER

POSITION OF VERBS IN A SENTENCE

*The conjugated verb is in **first** position in:*	yes/no *questions (questions that do not begin with an interrogative)* **Trinkst du Kaffee?** **Spielst du Tennis?** **Möchtest du ins Konzert gehen?** *both formal and informal commands* **Kommen Sie bitte um 2 Uhr!** **Geh doch mit ins Kino!**
*The conjugated verb is in **second** position in:*	*statements with normal word order* **Wir spielen heute Volleyball.** *statements with inverted word order* **Heute spielen wir Volleyball.** *questions that begin with an interrogative* **Wohin gehst du?** **Woher kommst du?** **Was macht er?**
*The conjugated verb is in **second** position and the infinitive or past participle is **final** in:*	*statements with modals* **Ich möchte heute ins Kino fahren.** *statements in conversational past* **Ich habe das Buch gelesen.**
*The conjugated verb is in **final** position in:*	*clauses following the verb **wissen*** **Ich weiß, wo das Hotel ist.** *clauses that begin with **weil** or **daß*** **Ich gehe nicht ins Kino, weil ich kein Geld habe.** **Ich glaube, daß er Rockmusik gern hört.**

NOTE: In Level 2 you will learn more about word order in clauses with modals and verbs with separable prefixes:

Ich komme morgen nicht, weil ich zu Hause helfen muß.
Ich weiß nicht, wer heute morgen angerufen hat.

POSITION OF **NICHT** IN A SENTENCE

To negate the entire sentence, as close to end of sentence as possible:	Er fragt seinen Vater		nicht.
Before a separable prefix:	Ich rufe ihn	nicht	an.
Before any part of a sentence you want to negate, contrast, or emphasize:	Er kommt	nicht	heute. (Er kommt morgen.)
Before part of a sentence that answers the questions **wo?**	Ich wohne	nicht	in Berlin.

VERBS

PRESENT TENSE VERB FORMS

		REGULAR	**-eln** VERBS	STEM ENDING WITH **t/d**	STEM ENDING WITH **s/ß**
INFINITIVES		**spiel -en**	**bastel -n**	**find -en**	**heiß -en**
PRONOUNS		stem + ending	stem + ending	stem + ending	stem + ending
I	ich	spiel -e	bastl -e	find -e	heiß -e
you	du	spiel -st	bastel -st	find -est	heiß -t
he	er				
she	sie }	spiel -t	bastel -t	find -et	heiß -t
it	es				
we	wir	spiel -en	bastel -n	find -en	heiß -en
you (plural)	ihr	spiel -t	bastel -t	find -et	heiß -t
they	sie	spiel -en	bastel -n	find -en	heiß -en
you (formal)	Sie	spiel -en	bastel -n	find -en	heiß -en

NOTE: There are important differences between the verbs in the above chart:

1. Verbs ending in **-eln** (**basteln, segeln**) drop the **e** of the ending **-eln** in the **ich**-form: **ich bastle, ich segle** and add only **-n** in the **wir-, sie-, and Sie**-forms. These forms are always identical with the infinitive: **basteln, wir basteln, sie basteln, Sie basteln.**

2. Verbs with a stem ending in **d** or **t,** such as **finden,** add an **e** before the ending in the **du**-form (**du findest**) and the **er-** and **ihr**-forms (**er findet, ihr findet**).

3. All verbs with stems ending in an **s**-sound (**heißen**) add only -t in the **du**-form: **du heißt.**

VERBS WITH A STEM-VOWEL CHANGE

There are a number of verbs in German that change their stem vowel in the **du-** and **er/sie-** forms. A few verbs, such as **nehmen** (*to take*), have a change in the consonant as well. You cannot predict these verbs, so it is best to learn each one individually. They are usually irregular only in the **du-** and **er/sie-** forms.

	e → i			e → ie		a → ä	
	essen	geben	nehmen	lesen	sehen	fahren	einladen
ich	esse	gebe	nehme	lese	sehe	fahre	lade ein
du	ißt	gibst	nimmst	liest	siehst	fährst	lädst ein
er, sie	ißt	gibt	nimmt	liest	sieht	fährt	lädt ein
wir	essen	geben	nehmen	lesen	sehen	fahren	laden ein
ihr	eßt	gebt	nehmt	lest	seht	fahrt	ladet ein
sie	essen	geben	nehmen	lesen	sehen	fahren	laden ein
Sie	essen	geben	nehmen	lesen	sehen	fahren	laden ein

SOME IMPORTANT IRREGULAR VERBS: HABEN, SEIN, WISSEN

	haben	sein	wissen
ich	habe	bin	weiß
du	hast	bist	weißt
er, sie	hat	ist	weiß
wir	haben	sind	wissen
ihr	habt	seid	wißt
sie	haben	sind	wissen
Sie	haben	sind	wissen

MODAL (AUXILIARY) VERBS

The verbs **können, müssen, sollen, wollen, mögen** (and the **möchte**-forms) are usually used with an infinitive at the end of the sentence. If the meaning of that infinitive is clear, it can be left out: **Du mußt sofort nach Hause!** (**Gehen** is understood and omitted.)

	können	müssen	sollen	wollen	mögen	möchte
ich	kann	muß	soll	will	mag	möchte
du	kannst	mußt	sollst	willst	magst	möchtest
er, sie	kann	muß	soll	will	mag	möchte
wir	können	müssen	sollen	wollen	mögen	möchten
ihr	könnt	müßt	sollt	wollt	mögt	möchtet
sie	können	müssen	sollen	wollen	mögen	möchten
Sie	können	müssen	sollen	wollen	mögen	möchten

VERBS WITH SEPARABLE PREFIXES

Some verbs have separable prefixes: prefixes that separate from the conjugated verbs and are moved to the end of the sentence.

	INFINITIVE: aussehen
ich sehe ... aus	Ich sehe heute aber sehr schick aus!
du siehst ... aus	Du siehst heute sehr fesch aus!
er/sie/es sieht ... aus	Sieht sie immer so modern aus?
	Sieht dein Zimmer immer so unordentlich aus?
wir sehen ... aus	Wir sehen heute sehr lustig aus.
ihr seht ... aus	Ihr seht alle so traurig aus.
sie sehen ... aus	Sie sehen sehr schön aus.
Sie sehen ... aus	Sie sehen immer so ernst aus.

Here are the separable-prefix verbs you learned in Level 1.

abheben	anziehen	einkaufen
abräumen	auflegen	einladen
anprobieren	aufräumen	einstecken
anrufen	aussehen	mitkommen

COMMAND FORMS

Regular Verbs	gehen	kommen
Persons you address with **du** (singular) with **Sie** (sing & pl)	Geh! Gehen Sie!	Komm! Kommen Sie!

Separable-prefix Verbs	mitkommen	anrufen	einladen	anziehen	ausgehen
	Komm mit! Kommen Sie mit!	Ruf an! Rufen Sie an!	Lad ein! Laden Sie ein!	Zieh an! Ziehen Sie an!	Geh aus! Gehen Sie aus!

Stem-changing Verbs	essen	nehmen	geben	sehen	fahren
	Iß! Essen Sie!	Nimm! Nehmen Sie!	Gib! Geben Sie!	Sieh! Sehen Sie!	Fahr! Fahren Sie!

NOTE: The vowel changes e → i and e → ie are maintained in the **du**-form of the command. The umlaut vowel change a → ä does not occur in the command form.

EXPRESSING FUTURE TIME

You can use the present tense with a time expression to talk about events that will take place in the future:

> **Wir fahren morgen nach Berlin.**

> **Am Wochenende besuche ich meine Großeltern.**

PAST TENSE VERB FORMS

In this book, you learned the following verbs to express past time:

WEAK VERBS		STRONG VERBS	
PRESENT TENSE FORM	PAST TENSE FORM	PRESENT TENSE FORM	PAST TENSE FORM
Er macht das. Sie kauft das.	Er hat das gemacht. Sie hat das gekauft.	Er spricht oft. Sie sieht das nicht. Du liest gern.	Er hat oft gesprochen. Sie hat das nicht gesehen. Du hast gern gelesen.

In addition you learned the simple past form of the verb **sein**:

THE SIMPLE PAST OF SEIN

ich	**war**
du	**warst**
er, sie	**war**
wir	**waren**
ihr	**wart**
sie	**waren**
Sie (formal)	**waren**

THE CONVERSATIONAL PAST

In Level 2 you will learn more about how to express past events. In general, German verbs are divided into two groups: weak verbs and strong verbs. Weak verbs usually follow a regular pattern, as do the English verb forms *play, played, has played*. In German, weak verbs add a **ge-** and a **-t** to the verb stem to form the past participle. Strong verbs usually have irregularities, like the English verb forms *run, ran, has run* and *go, went, has gone*. Look at the past tense verb forms chart above and compare the present tense forms of the verbs on the left with the past tense forms on the right. As a rule of thumb, verbs that are irregular (stem-changing verbs) in the present tense are irregular, or strong, in the past tense.

In Level 1 you have learned that **haben** is used as the helping verb with the past participle. In Level 2 you will also learn some verbs that use **sein** as their helping verb, such as the verb **gehen** in the following example:

> **Ich gehe oft ins Kino.**   **Ich bin gestern ins Kino gegangen.**

PRINCIPAL PARTS OF THE VERBS PRESENTED IN LEVEL 1*

This list includes all verbs included in the **Wortschatz** sections of this textbook. Both strong and weak verbs, including verbs with separable prefixes, stem-vowel changes, and other irregularities are listed. Though most of the verbs in this list form the conversational past with **haben**, a few of the verbs you have learned take **sein** in the present perfect tense. You will work with these verbs and learn more about them in Level 2.

STRONG VERBS

INFINITIVE	PRESENT (stem vowel change and/or seperable prefix)	PAST PARTICIPLE	MEANING
abheben	hebt ab	abgehoben	to lift (the receiver)
anrufen	ruft an	angerufen	to call up
anziehen	zieht an	angezogen	to put on (clothes)
aussehen	sieht aus	ausgesehen	to look, appear
bekommen	bekommt	bekommen	to get, receive
einladen	lädt ein	eingeladen	to invite
essen	ißt	gegessen	to eat
fahren	fährt	(ist) gefahren	to drive, ride
finden	findet	gefunden	to find
geben	gibt	gegeben	to give
gefallen	gefällt	gefallen	to like, be pleasing to
gehen	geht	(ist) gegangen	to go
gießen	gießt	gegossen	to pour; to water
haben	hat	gehabt	to have
heißen	heißt	geheißen	to be called
helfen	hilft	geholfen	to help
kommen	kommt	(ist) gekommen	to come
lesen	liest	gelesen	to read
mitkommen	kommt mit	(ist) mitgekommen	to come along
nehmen	nimmt	genommen	to take
scheinen	scheint	geschienen	to shine
schreiben	schreibt	geschrieben	to write
schwimmen	schwimmt	(ist) geschwommen	to swim
sehen	sieht	gesehen	to see
sein	ist	(ist) gewesen	to be
sprechen	spricht	gesprochen	to speak
trinken	trinkt	getrunken	to drink
tun	tut	getan	to do
wissen	weiß	gewußt	to know

*The past participles in this chart are for reference only. Most of them will be taught in Level 2.

WEAK VERBS

abräumen	räumt ab	abgeräumt	to clear away
anprobieren	probiert an	anprobiert	to try on
auflegen	legt auf	aufgelegt	to hang up (receiver)
aufräumen	räumt auf	aufgeräumt	to pick up/clean room
basteln	bastelt	gebastelt	to do arts and crafts
besichtigen	besichtigt	besichtigt	to sight see
besuchen	besucht	besucht	to visit
brauchen	braucht	gebraucht	to need
decken	deckt	gedeckt	to set (the table)
füttern	füttert	gefüttert	to feed
einkaufen	kauft ein	eingekauft	to shop
einstecken	steckt ein	eingesteckt	to insert (coin)
glauben	glaubt	geglaubt	to believe
holen	holt	geholt	to get
hören	hört	gehört	to hear
kaufen	kauft	gekauft	to buy
kennen	kennt	*gekannt	to know
kosten	kostet	gekostet	to cost
machen	macht	gemacht	to do or make
mähen	mäht	gemäht	to mow
meinen	meint	gemeint	to think, be of the opinion
passen	paßt	gepaßt	to fit
putzen	putzt	geputzt	to clean
regnen	regnet	geregnet	to rain
sagen	sagt	gesagt	to say
sammeln	sammelt	gesammelt	to collect
schauen	schaut	geschaut	to look (at)
schenken	schenkt	geschenkt	to give (a gift)
schmecken	schmeckt	geschmeckt	to taste
sortieren	sortiert	sortiert	to sort
spielen	spielt	gespielt	to play
spülen	spült	gespült	to wash dishes
suchen	sucht	gesucht	to look for
tanzen	tanzt	getanzt	to dance
telefonieren	telefoniert	telefoniert	to call (on the phone)
verbringen	verbringt	*verbracht	to spend time
wählen	wählt	gewählt	to dial
wandern	wandert	(ist) gewandert	to hike
wohnen	wohnt	gewohnt	to live
zahlen	zahlt	gezahlt	to pay
zeichnen	zeichnet	gezeichnet	to draw

*Although weak, these verbs have a vowel change in the past participle.

GUIDE TO PRONUNCIATION FEATURES

Learning to pronounce new and different sounds can be one of the most challenging aspects of learning a new language. You must first learn to hear new sounds. Then you have to learn to use your tongue, lips, jaw, and facial muscles in new ways to produce the sounds. Pronunciation can also be a very important aspect of learning a language; poor pronunciation can often interfere with communication. Although it is not necessary to learn to speak "like a native," it is important that you learn to make the sounds in order to communicate clearly and effectively.

The pronunciation features treated in this book are intended to be as helpful as possible. The descriptions of the German sound system used throughout this book focus on spelling and how different letters or letter combinations are usually pronounced. The **Aussprache** sections are meant to familiarize you with the German sound system, to help you recognize individual sounds when they occur, and to enable you to "sound out" new words and pronounce them correctly. Luckily, in German there is a much closer relationship between spelling and pronunication than there is in English. There are, of course, exceptions, and for the most conspicuous ones, we have provided examples to remind you that these pronunciation rules are usually true, but not always.

Whenever possible, a familiar sound in an English word is compared to the German sound being introduced. All German sounds are designated by bold faced print, and all English sounds are designated by italics. For sounds not occurring in English, we have provided brief descriptions of how to produce the sounds. In general, German vowels require more tension in the facial muscles and less movement of the tongue than English. The vowels usually do not glide, which means the sounds are more pure or continuous.

The thought of learning a whole new sound system might be intimidating at first, but practice will be your key to success. Here are some hints that might make learning pronunciation seem a little easier:

Don't be afraid to guess the pronunciation of an unfamiliar German word!
In general, German words are pronounced just like they are written. By looking at the spelling of a German word you can often guess the pronunciation. Regardless of whether you are dealing with a short word, like **Katze,** or a much longer word, such as **Donaudampfschiffahrtsgesellschaftskapitän,** you should be able to sound out the word using the spelling as a guide.

Don't be afraid to make pronunciation mistakes!
Learning a foreign language takes time, and you are going to make some mistakes along the way. Making German sounds requires the use of different facial muscles and, just like riding a bike, it takes practice to get it right.

Pronunciation and dictation exercises are found at the end of the **Dritte Stufe** in each chapter. The symbols within slashes below, for example /e/, are from the *International Phonetic Alphabet* and represent sounds.

CHAPTER	PAGE	LETTER/COMBINATION	IPA SYMBOL	EXAMPLE
Ch. 1	p. 33	the long vowel ä	/e/	Mädchen
		the long vowel e	/e/	zehn
		the long vowel ü	/y/	Grüß
		the long vowel ö	/ø/	hören
		the letter w	/v/	wer
		the letter v	/f/	vier
Ch. 2	p. 57	the vowel combination ie	/i/	spielen
		the diphthong ei	/ai/	schreiben
		the letter j	/j/	Junge
		the letter z	/ts/	zur
Ch. 3	p. 81	the long vowel o	/o/	Obst
		the long vowel u	/u/	Stuhl
		the letter s	/z/	sieben
		the letter s	/s/	Preis
		the letters ss	/s/	müssen
		the letter ß	/s/	Straße
Ch. 4	p. 109	the diphthong eu	/ɔy/	teuer
		the diphthong äu	/ɔy/	Verkäufer
		the diphthong au	/au/	bauen
		the final b	/p/	gelb
		the final d	/t/	Rad
		the final g	/k/	sag
Ch. 5	p. 133	the short vowel i	/ɪ/	schick
		the short vowel ä	/ɛ/	lässig
		the short vowel e	/ɛ/	Bett
		the long vowel a	/a/	haben
		the letter combination sch	/ʃ/	Schule
		the letter combination st	/ʃt/	Stiefel
		the letter combination sp	/ʃp/	Spitze
Ch. 6	p. 157	the letter combination ch	/ç/	ich
		the letter combination ch	/x/	doch
		the letter r	/r/	rund
		the final er	/ɐ/	super

CHAPTER	PAGE	LETTER/ COMBINATION	IPA SYMBOL	EXAMPLE
Ch. 7	p. 185	the short vowel **o**	/ɔ/	wolkig
		the short vowel **u**	/ʊ/	uns
		the letter **l**	/l/	Lehrer
		the letter combination **th**	/t/	Mathe
		the letter combination **pf**	/pf/	Pfennig
Ch. 8	p. 209	the short vowel **ö**	/œ/	können
		the short vowel **ü**	/Y/	Stück
		review diphthong **ei**	/ai̯/	Eier
		review vowel combination **ie**	/i/	wieder
		review letter **z**	/ts/	Zeit
Ch. 9	p. 233	review long vowel **ü**	/y/	für
		review long vowel **ö**	/ø/	blöd
		review letter **s**	/z/	Senf
		review letter **s**	/s/	es
		review letters **ss**	/s/	besser
		review letter **ß**	/s/	Spaß
Ch. 10	p. 261	review short vowel **o**	/ɔ/	Onkel
		review long vowel **o**	/o/	Oma
		review short vowel **u**	/ʊ/	Gruppe
		review long vowel **u**	/u/	Musik
		review combination **ch**	/ç/	Pech
		review combination **ch**	/x/	Buch
Ch. 11	p. 285	review **r**	/r/	Bruder
		review **er**	/ɐ/	meiner
		review long vowel **a**	/a/	Vater
		review diphthong **eu**	/ɔy/	heute
		review diphthong **äu**	/ɔy/	Verkäufer
		review diphthong **au**	/au̯/	Strauß
Ch. 12	p. 309	review letter **w**	/v/	weiß
		review letter **v**	/f/	viel
		review letter **j**	/j/	Juli
		review short vowel **ä**	/ɛ/	häßlich
		review short vowel **e**	/ɛ/	Sessel
		review long vowel **ä**	/e/	Käse
		review long vowel **e**	/e/	dem

GERMAN-ENGLISH VOCABULARY

This vocabulary includes almost all words in this textbook, both active (for production) and passive (for recognition only). Active words and phrases are practiced in the chapter and are listed in the **Wortschatz** section at the end of each chapter. You are expected to know and be able to use active vocabulary. An entry in black, heavy type indicates that the word or phrase is active. All other words—some in the opening dialogs, in exercises, in optional and visual material, in the **Landeskunde, Zum Lesen** and **Kann ich's wirklich?** sections—are for recognition only. The meaning of these words and phrases can usually be understood from the context or may be looked up in this vocabulary.

With some exceptions, the following are not included: proper nouns, forms of verbs other than the infinitive, and forms of determiners other than the nominative.

Nouns are listed with definite article and plural form, when applicable. The numbers in the entries refer to the chapter where the word or phrase first appears or where it becomes an active vocabulary word. Vocabulary from the preliminary chapter is followed by a page reference only.

The following abbreviations are used in this vocabulary: adj (adjective), pl (plural), pp (past participle), sep (seperable-prefix verb), sing (singular), and conj (conjunction).

A

ab *from, starting at,* 4; ab und zu *now and then,* 10
der Abend, -e *evening,* 2; **am Abend** *in the evening,* 2; jeden Abend *every evening,* 10
abends *evenings,* 6
der Abenteuerfilm, -e *adventure movie,* 10
aber *but,* 3; Aber sicher! *Sure!,* 11
abheben (sep) *to pick up,* 11; **den Hörer abheben** *to pick up the receiver,* 11
abräumen (sep) *to clean up, clear off,* 7; **den Tisch abräumen** *to clear the table,* 7
abschmecken (sep) *to taste,* 12
abwaschen (sep) *to wash up,* 12
Ach *Oh!,* 2; **Ach ja!** *Oh yeah!,* 1; Ach so! *Oh, I see!,* 1; Ach was! *Give me a break!,* 5; Ach wo! *Oh no!,* 4
acht *eight,* 1
achten *to pay attention (to),* 11
Achtung! *Attention!,* 6
achtzehn *eighteen,* 1
achtzig *eighty,* 3
der Ackerbau *agriculture,* 6
der Actionfilm, -e *action movie,* 10
das Adreßbuch, ⸚er *address book,* 11
ähnlich *similar,* 11
die Ahnung: Keine Ahnung! *I have no idea!,* 9
aktiv *active,* 12
die Aktivität, -en *activity,* 12
aktuell *current,* 5
die Algebra *algebra,* 4
alle *all, everyone,* 2

allein *alone,* 8
aller *of all,* 8
allerdings *admittedly,* 7
alles *everything,* 2; **Das ist alles.** *That's all.* 8; Alles klar! *O.K.!,* 10; **Alles Gute zum Geburtstag!** *Best wishes on your birthday!,* 11; **Alles Gute zum Muttertag!** *Happy Mother's Day!,* 11
allgemein *general,* 4; im allgemeinen *in general,* 10
der Alptraum, ⸚e *nightmare,* 10
als *as,* 6; als letzter *the last,* 12
also *well then,* 2; Also, auf geht's! *Well, let's go!,* 9; **Also, einfach!** *That's easy.* 1
alt *old,* 3; **Wie alt . . .** *How old . . . ,* 1
älter *older,* 3
das Altpapier *recycled paper,* 7
die Altstadt, ⸚e *historical part of downtown,* 12
am=an dem *at the,* 2; **am ...platz** *on ... Square,* 9; **am Abend** *in the evening,* 2; **am ersten (Juli)** *on the first (of July),* 11; **am liebsten** *most of all,* 10; Am liebsten sehe ich Krimis. *I like detective movies the best.,* 10; **am Montag** *on Monday,* 4; **am Nachmittag** *in the afternoon,* 2; **am Wochenende** *on the weekend,* 2
der Amerikaner, - *American (male),* 9
die Amerikanerin, -nen *American (female),* 9
amerikanisch *American (adj),* 8

die Ampel, -n *traffic light,* 9; an der Ampel *at the traffic light,* 9; **bis zur Ampel** *until you get to the traffic light,* 9
amtlich *official,* 9
an *to, at,* 4; an der Ampel *at the traffic light,* 9; ansonsten *otherwise,* 11; an welchem Tag? *on which day?,* 11
die Ananas, - *pineapple,* 8
das Andenken, - *souvenir,* 11
andere *other,* 2
ändern *to change,* 9
anfallen (sep): alles was anfällt *anything that comes up,* 12
angefangen (pp) *started,* 7
angeln *to fish,* 10
anprobieren (sep) *to try on,* 5
anrösten *to brown,* 12
anrufen (sep) *to call* (phone), 11; Ruf mal an! *Give me a call!,* 11
anschauen (sep) *to look at,* 6
ansehen (sep) *to look at,* 9
ansonsten *otherwise,* 11
anstrengend *exhausting,* 7
die Antwort, -en *answer,* 1
antworten *to answer,* 2
der Anwalt, ⸚e *lawyer,* 10
die Anwendung, -en *application,* 1
die Anzeige, -n *ad,* 10
anziehen (sep) *to put on, wear,* 5
der Anzug, ⸚e *suit,* 5
der Apfel, ⸚ *apple,* 8
der Apfelkuchen, - *apple cake,* 6
das Apfelküchle, - *(see p. 298),* 12
der Apfelsaft, ⸚e *apple juice,* 3; **ein Glas Apfelsaft** *a glass of apple juice,* 3

der Apfelstrudel, - *apple strudel*, 8
der Apparat, -e *telephone*, 11
der April *April*, 7
die Arbeit *work*, 7
die Arbeitsliste, -n *work list*, 12
ärgerlich *annoying*, 6
die Armbanduhr, -en *wristwatch*, 11
der Ärmel, - *sleeve*, 5
der Ast, ‑e *branch*, 8
    auch *also*, 1; **Ich auch.** *Me too.*, 2
    auf *on; to*, 1; *Also, auf geht's! Well, let's go!*, 9; **auf dem Land** *in the country*, 3; **auf dem Weg** *on the way*, 6; **auf der Straße** *on the street*, 9; **auf einer Fete** *at a party*, 12; **auf englisch** *in English*, 10; **auf Schritt und Tritt** *all the time*, 10; **Auf Wiederhören!** *Goodbye! (on the telephone)*, 11; **Auf Wiedersehen!** *Goodbye!*, 1; auf deutsch *in German*, 9; auf der rechten Seite *on the right (hand) side*, 9
aufdringlich *pushy*, 7
der Aufdruck, -e *design*, 5
    aufhängen (sep) *to hang up*, 12; **die Wäsche aufhängen** *to hang up the laundry*, 7
    aufhören (sep) *to stop*, 3
    auflegen (sep) *to hang up (the telephone)*, 11; **den Hörer auflegen** *to hang up (the receiver)*, 11
die Aufnahme, -n *admittance*, 2
    aufpassen: **Paß auf!** *Watch out!*, 6; **Paßt auf!** *Pay attention!*, p. 8
    aufräumen (sep) *to clean up*, 7; **mein Zimmer aufräumen** *to clean my room*, 7; **meine Klamotten aufräumen** *to pick up my clothes*, 7
der Aufschnitt *cold cuts*, 8
das Auge, n *eye*; **blaue (grüne, braune) Augen** *blue (green, brown) eyes*, 3
der August *August*, 7
    aus *from*, 1; *made of*, 9; **aus Baumwolle** *made of cotton*, 12; **aus Holz** *made of wood*, 12; **aus Kunststoff** *made of plastic*, 12; **aus Leder** *made of leather*, 12; **aus Seide** *made of silk*, 12
    ausbacken (sep) *to bake until done*, 12
der Ausdruck, ‑e *expression*, p. 8
    ausgeben (sep) *to spend (money)*, 8
    ausgehen (sep) *to go out*, 11
der Ausländer, - *foreigner*, 9

ausleihen (sep) *to rent*, 10
auspacken (sep) *to unpack*, 8
ausräumen (sep) *to clean, clear out*, 12; **den Geschirrspüler ausräumen** *to unload the dishwasher*, 12
ausreichend *sufficient, passing (grade)*, 4
die Aussage, -n *statement*, 9
    aussehen (sep) *to look like, to appear*, 3; **der Rock sieht ... aus.** *The skirt looks...*, 5; **er/sie sieht aus** *he/she looks like*, 5; **Wie sieht er aus?** *What does he look like?*, 3; **Wie sehen sie aus?** *What do they look like?*, 3
    außerdem *in addition*, 7
    außerhalb *outside of*, 6
    aussprechen (sep) *to pronounce*, 1; richtig aussprechen *to pronounce correctly*, 1
die Ausstellung, -en *exhibit*, 10
der Austauschschüler, - *exchange student*, 9
die Auswahl *selection*, 11
    auswählen (sep) *to select*, 4
das Auto, -s *car*, 1; **Auto fahren** *to drive (a car)*, 9; **mit dem Auto** *by car*, 1

B

    backen *to bake*, 8
der Bäcker, - *baker*, 8; **beim Bäcker** *at the baker's*, 8
die Bäckerei, -en *bakery*, 8
das Backpulver *baking powder*, 12
das Bad, ‑er *pool*, 12
    baden *to swim*, 6; **baden gehen** *to go swimming*, 6
der Badepark, -s *park with swimming facilities*, 12
der Bahnhof, ‑e *train station*, 9
    bald *soon*, 11
der Ball, ‑e *ball*, 12
der Ballon, -s *balloon*, 11
die Banane, -n *banana*, 3
die Bank, -en *bank*
das Basilikum *basil*, 12
das Basisstück, -e *basic item*, 5
der Basketball, ‑e *basketball*, 2
    basteln *to do crafts*, 2
    bauen *to build*, 5
die Baumwolle *cotton*, 12; **aus Baumwolle** *made of cotton*, 12
    bayrisch *Bavarian (adj)*, 9
    beantworten *to answer*, 9
der Becher, - *cup*, 6
der Bedarf *need*, 12
    bedeuten *to mean*, 10; **Was bedeutet ... ?** *What does...mean?*, p. 8
    bedruckt *printed*, 5

befriedigend *satisfactory (grade)*, 4
    beginnen *to begin*, 11
    begleiten *to accompany*, 9
    begonnen (pp) *begun*, 10
    begrüßen *to greet*, 1
    behalten *to keep*, 6
    bei *at*, 1; **bei meinen Freunden** *at my friends'*, 10; **beim Bäcker** *at the baker's*, 8; **beim Metzger** *at the butcher's*, 8; **Hier bei ...** *The ...residence.*, 11
    beide *both*, 5
    beim=bei dem *at the*, 2
das Beispiel, -e *example, model*, p. 5; **zum Beispiel** *for example*, 10
    bekannt *familiar*, 12
der Bekannte *acquaintance (male)*, 7
    bekommen *to get, to receive*, 5; **ich bekomme ...** *I'll have...*, 6; **Was bekommen Sie?** *What would you like?*, 5; *What will you have?* 6
    belegen: mit Tomaten belegen *to top with tomatoes*, 8
    beliebt *popular*, 6
die Belletristik *fiction*, 10
    bemalt *painted*, 11
die Bemerkung, -en *remark*, 4
    benutzen *to use*, 11
    Benutzung, -en *use*, 4
    bequem *comfortable*, 3
die Beratung, -en *advice*, 11
    bereit *ready*, 10
    bereiten *to prepare*, 12
der Berg, -e *mountain*, 10
der Bericht, -e *report*, 10
der Berliner, - *here: jelly-filled roll*, 9
die Berliner (pl) *residents of Berlin*, 9
    berühmt *famous*, 7
    beschäftigt *occupied, busy*, 8
    beschattet *tailed, shadowed*, 10
    beschreiben *to describe*, 9
die Beschreibung, -en *description*, 12
    besetzt *busy (telephone)*, 11
    besichtigen *to visit, to sightsee*, 9; **die Stadt besichtigen** *to visit the city*, 12
    besonder *special*, 7
    besonders *especially*, 8; **Nicht besonders.** *Not really.* 6; **besonders gern** *especially like*, 10
    besprechen *to discuss*, 12
    besser *better*, 8
    best *best*, 1
    bestimmt *certainly, definitely*, 5
    bestreuen *to sprinkle*, 8
    besuchen *to visit*, 2; **Freunde besuchen** *to visit friends*, 2
das Bett, -en *bed*, 3; **das Bett machen** *to make the bed*, 7
die Beurteilung, -en *evaluation*, 4
der Beutel, - *bag*, 8

bevor *before*, 2
bewohnbar *inhabitable*, 3
die Bewölkung *cloudiness*, 7
bieten: anbieten (sep) *to offer*, 7
das Bild, -er *picture*, 11
billig *cheap*, 4
bin: ich bin *I am*, 1
die Biologie (Bio) *biology*, 4
die Biologielehrerin, -nen *biology teacher (female)*, 1
die Birne, -n *pear*, 8
bis *until*, 1; Bis bald! *See you soon!*, 9; **Bis dann!** *Till then! See you later!*, 1; **bis zum ...platz** *until you get to ... Square*, 9; **bis zur ...straße** *until you get to ... Street*, 9; **bis zur Ampel** *until you get to the traffic light*, 9
bist: du bist *you are*, 1
bitte *please*, 3; **Bitte?** *Excuse me?*, 1; **Bitte (sehr, schön)!** *You're (very) welcome!*, 3; **Bitte?** *Yes? Can I help you?*, 5
bißchen: ein bißchen *a little*, 5; **ein bißchen mehr** *a little more*, 8;
blättrig *flaky*, 8
blau *blue*, 3; **in Blau** *in blue*, 5
bleiben *to stay*, 7
der Bleistift, -e *pencil*, 4
der Blick, -e *view*, 7
blöd *dumb*, 2
blond *blonde*, 3
bloß *only*, 4
der Blouson, -s *short jacket*, 5
die Blume, -n *flower*, 7; **die Blumen gießen** *to water the flowers*, 7
das Blumengeschäft, -e *florist shop*, 8
der Blumenkohl *cauliflower*, 8
der Blumenstrauß, ⁼e *bouquet of flowers*, 11
die Bluse, -n *blouse*, 5
blutig *bloody*, 10
die Bockwurst, ⁼e *bockwurst*, 6
die Bowle, -n *punch*, 12
die Bratkartoffeln (pl) *fried potatoes*, 6
die Bratwurst, ⁼e *bratwurst*, 8
brauchen *to need*, 5; **ich brauche ...** *I need...*, 5; **ich brauche noch ...** *I also need...*, 8
die Brauerei, -en *brewery*, 7
braun *brown*, 3; **in Braun** *in brown*, 5
das Brettspiel, -e *board game*, 2; **ein Brettspiel spielen** *to play a board game*, 12
die Brezel, -n *pretzel*, 8
die Brezenstange, -n *pretzel stick*, 8
der Brief, -e *letter*, 2
die Briefmarke, -n *stamp*, 2;

Briefmarken sammeln *to collect stamps*, 2
die Brille, -n *a pair of glasses*, 3
bringen *to bring*, 1
das Brot, -e *bread*, 8; **Ich habe Brot gekauft.** *I bought bread.*, 8
das Brötchen, - *hard roll*, 8
der Bruder, ⁼ *brother*, 3
die Brühe, -n *broth*, 12
brutal *brutal, violent*, 10
brutalste *the most brutal*, 10
das Buch, ⁼er *book*, 4
die Buchhandlung, -en *bookstore*, 10;
buchstabieren *to spell aloud*, 1
bügeln *to iron*, 7
der Bummel *stroll*, 9
das Bundesland, ⁼er *federal state (German)*, 1
bunt *colorful*, 6
der Bus, -se *bus*, 1; **mit dem Bus** *by bus*, 1
die Butter *butter*, 8
das Butterschmalz *shortening*, 12

C

das Café, -s *café*, 6; **in ein Café/ins Café gehen** *to go to a/the café*, 6
der Cappuccino, -s *cappuccino*, 6
die CD, -s *compact disc*, 11
der Champignon, -s *mushroom*, 8
die Chance, -n *chance*, 10
Chanukka *Hanukkah*, 11; **Frohes Chanukka-Fest!** *Happy Hanukkah!*, 11
charmant *charming*, 3
die Chemie *chemistry*, 4
chic *smart (looking)*, 12
der Chor, ⁼e *choir*, 4
die Clique, -n *clique*, 10
der Club, -s *club*, 2
die Cola, -s *cola*, 3
die Comics (pl) *comic books*, 2; **Comics sammeln** *to collect comics*, 2
die Couch, -en *couch*, 3
der Cousin, -s *cousin (male)*, 3
die Currywurst, ⁼e *curry sausage*, 6

D

da *there*, 1; da drüben *over there*, 4; **da hinten** *there in the back*, 4; **da vorn** *there in the front*, 4
dabei *with*, 4
das Dach, ⁼er *roof*, 7
dafür *for it*, 5
dahin *there*, 10
die Dame, -n *lady*, 5
damenhaft *ladylike*, 5
damit *with it; so that*, 7
danach *after that*, 4

Danke! *thank you!*, 3; **Danke (sehr, schön)!** *Thank you (very much)!*, 3
dann *then*, 4
darauf *on it*, 12
darüber *about it*, 5
das *the* (n); *that*, 1; **Das ist ...** *That's...*, 1; **Das ist alles.** *That's all.*, 8; **Das sind...** *These are...* (with plurals), 3
daß *that* (conj), 9; **ich finde es gut/schlecht, daß ...** *I think it's good/bad that...*, 9; **ich finde, daß ...** *I think that...*, 9; ich glaube, daß ... *I think that...*, 9
dasselbe *the same*, 11
dauern *to last*, 9
dazugeben *to add*, 12
decken: den Tisch decken *to set the table*, 7
dein *your*, 3; **deinem Vater** *to, for your father*, 11; **deiner Mutter** *to, for your mother*, 11
dem *the* (masc, neuter, dat case), 11
den *the* (masc, acc case), 5
denken *to think*, 3
denn (particle), 1; 6
denn *because, for* (conj), 8
der *the* (m), 1; *to the* (fem, dat case), 11
des *of the*, 4
desillusioniert *disillusioned*, 10
deutsch *German* (adj), 9
Deutsch *German* (language), p. 4; (school subject), 4; **Ich habe Deutsch.** *I have German.*, 4
der Deutsche, -n *German (male)*, 2
die Deutsche *German (female)*, 2
die Deutschen (pl) *German people*, 2
der Deutschlehrer, - *German teacher (male)*, 1
die Deutschlehrerin, -nen *German teacher (female)*, 1
der Dezember *December*, 7
dich *you* (acc), 7
die *the*, 1
der Dienstag *Tuesday*, 4
dies- *this, these*, 2
das Diktat, -e *dictation*, 1
der Dinosaurier, - *dinosaur*, 10
dir *to you*, 3
direkt *direct(ly)*, 6
der Dirigent, -en *conductor (music)*, 6
die Disko, -s *disco*, 6; **in eine Disko gehen** *to go to a disco*, 6
diskutieren *to discuss*, 10
DM = Deutsche Mark *German mark* (monetary unit), 4
doch (particle), 6
Doch! *Oh yes!*, 2

der **Donnerstag** *Thursday*, 4
donnerstags *Thursdays*, 6
doof *dumb*, 10
dort *there*, 4; **dort drüben** *over there*, 4;
die Dose, -n *can*, 7
das Dotter, - *egg yolk*, 12
drei *three*, 1
dreimal *three times*, 7
dreißig *thirty*, 3
dreiundzwanzig *twenty-three*, 3
dreizehn *thirteen*, 1
drin *in it*, 9
dritte *third*, 8
du *you* (sing), 2
dumm *dumb, stupid*, 10
dunkelblau *dark blue*, 5; **in Dunkelblau** *in dark blue*, 5
durch *through*, 9; *divided by*, 3
der Durst *thirst*, 6

E

eben (particle), 5
echt *real, really*, 5
eckig *with corners*, 12
ehrlich *honestly*, 5
das Ei, -er *egg*, 8
der Eierkuchen, - 9
eigen *own* (adj), 10
eigentlich *actually*, 5
die Eigentumswohnung, -en *condominium*, 3
ein *a, an*, 3; **ein paar** *a few*, 3; **eine Eins (Zwei, Drei, Vier, Fünf, Sechs)** (German grades), 4
einen *a, an* (masc, acc case), 5; **Einen Pulli in Grau, bitte.** *A sweater in gray, please.*, 5
einfach *simple, easy*, 1; **Also, einfach!** *That's easy!*, 1
das Einfamilienhaus, -er *single-family house*, 3
einfarbig *solid color*, 5
eingeladen (pp) *invited*, 11
eingelegt (pp) *docked (boat)*, 9
einige *some*, 9
der Einkauf, -e *purchase*, 8
einkaufen *to shop*, 8; **einkaufen gehen** *to go shopping*, 8
der Einkaufsbummel *shopping trip*, 8
das Einkaufszentrum, die Einkaufszentren *shopping center*, 6; **ins Einkaufszentrum gehen** *to go to the shopping center/mall*, 6
der Einkaufszettel, - *shopping list*, 8
einladen (sep) *to invite*, 11; **er/sie lädt ... ein** *he/she invites*, 11
die Einladung, -en *invitation*, 11

einmal *once*, 7
eins *one*, 1; **eine Eins** *an A*
der Eintritt *admission*, 2
einundzwanzig *twenty-one*, 3
einverstanden *agreed*, 8
der Einwohner, - *inhabitant*, 6
die Einwohnerzahl, -en *population*, 1
einzeln *single individual*, 7
der Einzelpassagier, -e *individual passenger*, 9
das Eis *ice cream*, 6; *ice*, 7; **ein Eis essen** *to eat ice cream*, 6
der Eisbecher, - *a dish of ice cream*, 6
die Eissporthalle, -n *skating rink*, 12
EL=Eßlöffel, - *tablespoon*, 8
die Elektronik *electronics*, 7
die Elektrotechnik *electrical engineering*, 10
elf *eleven*, 1
Eltern (pl) *parents*, 3
der Emmentaler *Emmentaler (cheese)*, 12
das Ende *end*, 5
endgültig *final*, 10
eng *tight*, 5
engagiert *occupied*, 10
die Engländer (pl) *English people*, 1
der Engländer, - *English person (male)*, -
die Engländerin, -nen *English person (female)*, -
englisch *English* (adj), 4; **auf englisch** *in English*, 10
Englisch *English* (school subject), 4; *(language)*, 8
entscheiden *to decide*, 9; sie entscheidet sich für *she decides on*, 11
entschließen *to decide*, 9
Entschuldigung! *Excuse me!*, 9
er *he*, 2; *it*, 3
das Erdbeereis *strawberry ice cream*, 9
die Erdbeere, -n *strawberry*, 8
der Erdbeerkuchen, - *strawberry cake*, 8
die Erdkunde *geography*, 4
die Erdnußbutter *peanut butter*, 8
erfüllen *to fulfill*, 7
ergänzen *to complete*, 9
erkennen *to recognize*, 10
erklären *to explain*, 5
ermittelt von *compiled by*, 10
ernst: im Ernst? *seriously?*, 10
erst *first*, 6
ersten: **am ersten (Juli)** *on the first (of July)*, 11
erwarten *to expect*, 12
erwecken *to awaken*, 10
erweisen *to grant*, 10
erzählen *to tell*, 10; Erzähl weiter! *Keep on talking!*, 10
es *it*, 3

essen *to eat*, 3; **er/sie ißt** *he/she eats*, 6
der Essig *vinegar*, 12
der Eßlöffel, - *tablespoon*, 8
der Eßtisch, -e *dining table*, 12
der Estragon *tarragon*, 12
etwa *approximately*, 12
etwas *something*, 7; **Sonst noch etwas?** *Anything else?*, 8
euch *you* (pl, acc case), 7
europäisch *European* (adj), 10
die Europareise, -n *trip to Europe*, 11

F

das Fach, -er *school subject*, 4
der Fächer, - *fan*, 11
die Fachsprache, -n *technical lingo*, 12
fahren *to go, ride, drive (using a vehicle)*, 9; **er/sie fährt** *he/she drives*, 9; **in die Stadt fahren** *to go downtown (by vehicle)*, 11; **wir fahren Rad** *we're riding bikes*, 10
der Fahrpreis, -e *fare*, 4
die Fahrpreisermäßigung, -en *reduced fare*, 4
das Fahrrad, -er *bicycle*, 7
die Fahrt, -en *drive* 2; **Auto fahren** *to drive (a car)*, 9
fällen *to fall*, 4
falsch *false*, 11
die Familie, -en *family*, 3
das Familienmitglied, er *family member*, 4
das Familientreffen, - *family reunion*, 12
Fang mit ... an! *Begin with...*, 9
das Fantasybuch, -er *fantasy book*, 10
der Fantasyfilm, -e *fantasy film*, 10
der Fantasyroman, -e *fantasy novel*, 10
die Farbe, -n *color*, 5; **Wir haben das in allen Farben.** *We have that in all colors.*, 5
fast *almost*, 12
faul *lazy*, 7
der Februar *February*, 7
fehlen *to be missing*, 4; **Was fehlt hier?** *What's missing?*, 5
feiern *to celebrate*, 11
der Feiertag, -e *holiday*, 11
feiertags *holidays*, 10
feingehackt *finely chopped*, 12
die Feinmechanik *precision mechanics*, 10
das Fenster, - *window*, p. 8; **die Fenster putzen** *to clean the windows*, 7
die Ferien (pl) *vacation*, 1
das Ferngespräch, -e *long distance call*, 11

das Fernsehen *television*, 2; **Fernsehen schauen** *to watch television*, 2; im Fernsehen *on television*, 5

die Fernsehsendung, -en *television show*, 9

fertig *finished*, 7

fesch *stylish, smart*, 5

das Fest, -e *festivity*, 11

die Fete, -n *party*, 5; auf einer Fete *at a party*, 12

feurig *fiery*, 6

der Film, -e *movie*, 10; **einen Film sehen** *to see a movie*, 6

die Filmart, -en *type of movie*, 10

der Filmverleih, -e *movie rental*, 10

finden *to think of*, 2; **Das finde ich auch.** *I think so, too.*, 2; **Das finde ich nicht.** *I disagree.*, 2; **ich finde es gut/schlecht, daß ...** *I think it's good/bad that...*, 9; **ich finde (Tennis) ...** *I think (tennis) is...*, 2; **Ich finde den Pulli stark!** *The sweater is awesome!*, 5; **Ich finde es toll!** *I think it's great!*, 9; **Wie findest du (Tennis)?** *What do you think of (tennis)?*, 2

die Firma, die Firmen *firm, company*, 9

der Fisch, -e *fish*, 8

die Fläche, -n *surface, area*, 1

die Flasche, -n *bottle*, 7

das Fleisch *meat*, 8

die Fleischbrühe, -n *meat broth*, 12

die Fliese, -n *tile*, 12

die Flöte, -n *flute*, 2

die Floßfahrt, -en *rafting trip*, 9

der Fluß, ⁼sse *river*, 1

folgende *following*, 9

die Form, -en *form*, 5

das Foto, -s *photo*, 3

das Fotoalbum, die Fotoalben *photo album*, 3

das Fotogeschäft, -e *photo store*, 9

die Frage, -n *question*, 1

fragen *to ask*, 9

Französisch *French* (school subject), 4

Frau *Mrs.*, 1

die Frau, -en *woman*, 3

frei: Wir haben frei. *We are off (out of school).*, 4

freilich *of course*, 9

der Freitag *Friday*, 4

freitags *Fridays*, 6

freiwillig *voluntary*, 7

der Freiwillige, -n *volunteer*, 4

die Freizeit *free time, leisure time*, 2

das Freizeitinteresse *free time interest*, 12

der Freizeitpark, -s *amusement park*, 10

das Freizeitvergnügen, - *enjoyment of leisure time*, 12

die Fremdsprache, -n *foreign language*, 4

die Freude, -n *joy, happiness*, 11

freuen *to be happy, glad*, 7; **Freut mich!** *It's a pleasure!*, 8

Sie freut sich darüber. *She is happy about it.*, 11; wir freuen uns *we're very happy, pleased*, 12

der Freund, -e *friend (male)*, 2; **Freunde besuchen** *to visit friends*, 2

der Freundeskreis, -e *peer group*, 9

die Freundin, -nen *friend (female)*, 1

freundlich *friendly*, 9

frisch *fresh*, 8

froh *happy*, 11

fröhlich *happy, cheerful*, 11

die Frucht, ⁼e *fruit*, 8

das Fruchteis *ice cream with fruit*, 6

der Frühling *spring* (season), 2; **im Frühling** *in the spring*, 2

führen *to lead*, 12

füllen *to fill*, 12

fünf *five*, 1

fünfundzwanzig *twenty-five*, 3

fünfzehn *fifteen*, 1

fünfzig *fifty*, 3

für *for*, 7

Für wen? *For whom?*, 7

furchtbar *terrible, awful*, 5; **furchtbar gern** *to like a lot*, 10

fürs=für das *for the*, 2

der Fuß, ⁼e *foot*, 1; **zu Fuß** *on foot*, 1

der Fußball *soccer*, 2; **Ich spiele Fußball.** *I play soccer.*, 2

füttern *to feed*, 7; **die Katze füttern** *to feed the cat*, 7

G

ganz *really, quite* 3

ganz *not broken*, 4; *whole*, 9; **die ganze Zeit** *the whole time*, 12; **Ganz einfach!** *Quite simple!*, 9; **Ganz klar!** *Of course!*, 4

gar (particle), 3; **gar nicht gern** *not to like at all*, 10

die Garderobe, -n *wardrobe*, 5

der Garten, ⁼ *yard, garden*, 9

der Gast, ⁼e *guest*, 12

der Gastgeber, - *host*, 12

das Gebäude, - *building*, 7

geben *to give*, 11; **er/sie gibt** *he/she gives*, 11; **Was gibt es hier zu essen?** *What is there to eat here?*, 9; **Was gibt's?** *What's up?*, 1

geboren *born*, 4

gebrüht *simmered*, 8

gebucht *booked*, 9

gebunden *bound*, 10

das Geburtsdatum (pl -daten) *date of birth*, 4

die Geburtsstadt, ⁼e *place of birth*, 6

der Geburtstag, -e *birthday*, 11; **Alles Gute zum Geburtstag!** *Best wishes on your birthday!*, 11; **Herzlichen Glückwunsch zum Geburtstag!** *Best wishes on your birthday!*, 11; **Ich habe am ... Geburtstag.** *My birthday is on...*, 11

das Geburtstagsgeschenk, -e *birthday present*, 8

die Geburtstagskarte, -n *birthday card*, 11

der Geburtstagskuchen, - *birthday cake*, 12

gefährdet *endangered*, 11

gefahren (pp) *driven*, 10

gefährlich *dangerous*, 9

gefallen *to be pleasing, to like*, 5; **Er/Sie/Es gefällt mir.** *I like it.*, 5; **Sie gefallen mir.** *I like them.*, 5

gefettet *oiled*, 12

gefüllt *filled*, 12

gegenseitig *reciprocal(ly)*, 5

gegessen (pp) *eaten*, 9

gehackt *chopped*, 8

gehen *to go*, 2; **Das geht nicht.** *That won't work.*, 7; **Es geht.** *It's okay.*, 6; **nach Hause gehen** *to go home*, 3; **Geht er noch?** *Is it still working?*, 4; **Wie geht's (denn)?** *How are you?*, 6

gekauft (pp) *bought*, 8; **Ich habe Brot gekauft.** *I bought bread.*, 8; **Was hast du gekauft?** *What did you buy?*, 8

geknotet *knotted*, 5

gekocht *cooked*, 12

gelb *yellow*, 4; **in Gelb** *in yellow*, 5

das Geld *money*, 4

gelesen (pp) *read*, 10; **Was hast du gelesen?** *What did you read?*, 10

gemacht (pp) *done*, 10; **Was hast du am Wochenende gemacht?** *What did you do on the weekend?*, 10

gemahlen *ground*, 12

gemalt *painted*, 11

gemeinsam *common*, 11

gemischt *mixed*, 8

das Gemüse *vegetables*, 8; **im Obst- und Gemüseladen** *at the produce store*, 8
der Gemüseladen, ⁼ *produce store*, 8
genau *exact(ly)*, 6; genauer lesen *reading for detail*, 6
genießen *to enjoy*, 6
genug *enough*, 9; **Ich habe genug.** *I have enough.*, 9
geöffnet *open*, 6
gepunktet *polka-dotted*, 12
gerade *just*, 8
geradeaus *straight ahead*, 9; Fahren Sie geradeaus! *Drive straight ahead.*, 9
das Gericht, -e *dish* (food), 6
gern (machen) *to like (to do)*, 2; **gern haben** *to like*, 4; **Gern geschehen!** *My pleasure!*, 9; **nicht gern (machen)** *to not like (to do)*, 2; **nicht so gern** *not to like very much*, 2; Siehst du gern Horrorfilme? *Do you like to watch horror movies?*, 10; **besonders gern** *especially like*, 10
gesagt (pp) *said*, 10
gesalzen *salted*, 8
das Geschäft, -e: ein Geschäft machen *to make a deal*, 7
geschehen: **Gern geschehen!** *My pleasure!*, 9
das Geschenk, -e *gift*, 11
die Geschenkidee, -n *gift idea*, 11
der Geschenkladen, ⁼ *gift shop*, 11
die Geschenkliste, -n *gift list*, 11
die Geschenkwaren (pl) *gifts*, 9
die Geschichte *history*, 4
geschickt *clever, talented*, 12
das Geschirr (pl) *dishes*, 7; **das Geschirr spülen** *to wash the dishes*, 7
der Geschirrspüler, - *dishwasher*, 12; den Geschirrspüler ausräumen *to unload the dishwasher*, 12
geschlossen *closed*, 10
der Geschmack *taste*, 8
die Geschwister (pl) *brothers and sisters*, 3
gesehen (pp) *seen*, 10; **Was hast du gesehen?** *What did you see?*, 10
gesetzt *sat*, 10
das Gespräch, -e *conversation*, 7
die Gesprächsnotiz, -en *message*, 11
gesprochen (pp) *spoken*, 10; **Worüber habt ihr gesprochen?** *What did you (pl) talk about?*, 10; Worüber sprichst du mit deinen Freunden? *What do you talk about with your friends?*, 10

die Geste, -n *gesture*, 7
gestern *yesterday*, 8; **gestern abend** *yesterday evening*, 8;
gestreift *striped*, 12
gesund *healthy*, 8
das Getränk, -e *beverage*, 11
gewachsen *grown*, 8
gewinnen *to win*, 2
das Gewitter, - *thunderstorm*, 7
gewöhnlich *usually*, 11
das Gewürz, -e *spice*, 8
gewürzt *spiced*, 8
gießen *to water*, 7; **die Blumen gießen** *to water the flowers*, 7
die Gitarre, -n *guitar*, 2
Gitarrenklänge *guitar music*, 6
gitterförmig *criss cross*, 8
das Glas, ⁼er *glass*, 3; **ein Glas Apfelsaft** *a glass of apple juice*, 3; **ein Glas (Mineral) Wasser** *a glass of (mineral) water*, 3; **ein Glas Tee** *a glass of tea*, 6
die Glatze, -n *bald head*, 3; **eine Glatze haben** *to be bald*, 3
glauben *to believe*, 2; **ich glaube I think**, 2; ich glaube, daß ... *I think that...*, 9; Ich glaube schon. *I believe so.*, 7
gleich *equal*, 3; *same*, 10
das Glück *luck*, 4; **So ein Glück!** *What luck!*, 4
der Glücksklee *clover* (symbol for good luck), 11
das Glücksschwein, -e *good luck pig* (symbol for good luck), 11
das Golf *golf*, 2
der Grad *degree(s)*, 7; **zwei Grad** *two degrees*, 7; **Wieviel Grad haben wir?** *What's the temperature?*, 7
das Gramm *gram*, 8
grau *gray*, 3; **in Grau** *in gray*, 5
grausam *cruel*, 10
groß *big*, 3
die Größe, -n *size*, 5
die Großeltern (pl) *grandparents*, 3
die Großmutter (Oma), ⁼ *grandmother*, 3
der Großvater (Opa), ⁼ *grandfather*, 3
grün *green*, 3; **in Grün** *in green*, 5
das Grundstück, -e *piece of land*, 3
grüner *greener*, 8
die Gruppe, -n *group*, 10
der Gruselroman, -e *horror novel*, 10
grüßen: **Grüß dich!** *Hi!*, 1
gültig *valid*, 4
die Gültigkeit *validity*, 6
günstig *advantageous; low-priced*, 4
die Gurke, -n *cucumber*, 8
der Gürtel, - *belt*, 5

gut *good*, 4; **Gut!** *Good! Well!*, 6; **Gut! Mach' ich!** *Okay, I'll do that!*, 7; **Alles Gute!** *Best wishes*, 11
der Gutschein, -e *gift certificate*, 11
das Gymnasium, die Gymnasien (German secondary school), 4
das Gyros *gyros*, 9

H

das Haar, -e *hair*, 3
haben *to have*, 4; **er/sie hat** *he/she has*, 4; **gern haben** *to like*, 4; **Haben Sie das auch in Rot?** *Do you also have that in red?*, 5
das Hackfleisch *ground meat*, 8
der Haferbrei *oatmeal*, 9
das Hähnchen, - *chicken*, 8
halb *half*, 6; **halb (eins, zwei, usw.)** *half past (twelve, one, etc.)*, 6
der Halbbruder, ⁼ *half brother*, 3
halbieren *to halve*, 12
das Halbjahr, -e *half a year*, 4
die Halbschwester, -n *half sister*, 3
die Hälfte, -n *half*, 12
Hallo! *Hi! Hello!*, 1
der Hals, ⁼e *neck*, 8
das Halstuch, ⁼er *scarf*, 11
halt *(particle)*, 6
halten *to hold*, 7
der Hamster, - *hamster*, 7
der Handball *handball*, 2
häßlich *ugly*, 3
der Hauptbahnhof, ⁼e *main train station*, 4
hauptsächlich *mainly*, 6
die Hauptstadt, ⁼e *capital*, 1
das Haus, ⁼er *house*, 3; **zu Hause sein** *to be at home*, 6; **nach Hause gehen** *to go home*, 3; **zu Hause helfen** *to help at home*, 7
die Hausarbeit, -en *chores*, 7
die Hausaufgaben (pl) *homework*, 2; **Hausaufgaben machen** *to do homework*, 2
der Haushalt, -e *household*, 7
das Haustier, -e *pet*, 3
die Hauswirtschaft *home economics*, 4
He! *Hey!*, 1
das Heft, -e *notebook*, 4
heiß *hot*, 7
heißen *to be called*, 1; **er heißt** *his name is*, 1; **ich heiße** *my name is*, 1; **sie heißt** *her name is*, 1; **Wie heißt das Mädchen?** *What's the girl's name?*, 1; **Heißt sie ...?** *Is her name ...?*, 1; **Wie heißt der Junge?** *What's the boy's name?*, 1; **Wie heißt du?** *What's your name?*, 1

helfen *to help,* 7; **zu Hause helfen** *to help at home,* 7
hell *light,* 5
hellblau *light blue,* 5; **in Hellblau** *in light blue,* 5
hellgrau *light gray,* 5
hellgrün *light green,* 5
das Hemd, -en *shirt,* 5
herausnehmen *to take out,* 12
der Herbst *fall* (season), 2; **im Herbst** *in the fall,* 2
der Herd, -e *stove,* 12
Herr *Mr.,* 1
herzlich: Herzliche Grüße! *Best regards!,* 1; **Herzlich willkommen bei uns!** *Welcome to our home!,* 12; **Herzlichen Glückwunsch zum Geburtstag!** *Best wishes on your birthday!,* 11
heute *today,* 7; **heute morgen** *this morning,* 8; **heute nachmittag** *this afternoon,* 8; **heute abend** *tonight, this evening,* 7
hier *here,* 3; **Hier bei ...** *The... residence.,* 11; **Hier ist ...** *This is...,* 11; **hier vorn** *here in front,* 5
hierher *over here,* 11
die Hilfe, -n *help,* 7
hin *to,* 8
hinten *back there,* 4; **da hinten** *there in the back,* 4
das Hobbybuch, ¨er *hobby book,* 10
hoch *high,* 10
hochbegabt *very talented,* 10
hoffen *to hope,* 9
holen *to get, fetch,* 8
das Holz *wood,* 12; **aus Holz** *out of wood,* 12
der Honig *honey,* 8
hören *to hear,* 1; **Hör gut zu!** *Listen carefully,* p. 6; **Hört zu!** *Listen!,* p. 8; **Musik hören** *to listen to music,* 2
der Hörer, - *receiver,* 11; **den Hörer abheben** *to pick up the receiver,* 11; **den Hörer auflegen** *to hang up (the telephone),* 11
der Horrorfilm, -e *horror movie,* 10
die Hose, -n *pants,* 5
das Hotel, -s *hotel,* 9
hübsch *pretty,* 5
das Hufeisen, - *horse shoe,* 11
der Hund, -e *dog,* 3
hundert *a hundred,* 3
der Hunger *hunger,* 9

I

ich *I,* 2; **Ich auch.** *Me too.,* 2; **Ich nicht.** *I don't.; Not me.,* 2

die Idee, -n *idea,* 9
ihm *to, for him* (masc, neuter, dat case), 11
ihn *it, him* (masc, acc case), 5
ihnen *them* (pl, dat case), 12
Ihnen *you* (formal, dat case), 5
ihr *her* (poss adj), 3
ihr *their* (poss adj), 2
ihr *to, for her* (fem, dat case), 11
ihr *you* (pl, subj pron), 2
im=in dem *in the,* 1; **im Fernsehen** *on television,* 5; **im Frühling** *in the spring,* 2; **im Herbst** *in the fall,* 2; **im Januar** *in January,* 7; **im Kino** *at the movies,* 10; **im Konzert** *at the concert,* 10; **(einmal) im Monat** *(once) a month,* 7; **im Sommer** *in the summer,* 2; **im Supermarkt** *at the supermarket,* 8; **im Winter** *in the winter,* 2
der Imbißstand, ¨e *snack stand,* 6
die Imbißstube, -n *snack bar,* 9
immer *always,* 7
in *in,* 1; **in Blau** *in blue,* 5; **in Braun** *in brown,* 5; **in Gelb** *in yellow,* 5; **in Grau** *in gray,* 5; **in Grün** *in green,* 5; **in Hellblau** *in light blue,* 5; **in Rot** *in red,* 5; **in Schwarz** *in black,* 5; **in Weiß** *in white,* 5
der Individualist, -en *individualist,* 9
die Industrie, -n *industry,* 1
die Informatik *computer science,* 4
die Information, -en *information,* 10
der Ingenieur, -e *engineer,* 10
die Innenstadt, ¨e *downtown,* 5; **in der Innenstadt** *in the city, downtown,* 9
ins=in das *in the, into the,* 2; *to the,* 6
die Insel, -n *island,* 6
insgesamt *all together,* 8
das Instrument, -e *instrument,* 2
interessant *interesting,* 2
das Interesse, -n *interest,* 2; **Hast du andere Interessen?** *Do you have any other interests?,* 2
interessieren *to interest,* 10
irgend- *any,* 11
irgend etwas *anything,* 6
irgendwann *anytime,* 11
irgendwelch- *some,* 8
irgendwie *somehow,* 8
ist: er/sie/es ist *he/she/it is,* 1; **sie ist aus** *she's from,* 1

J

ja *yes,* 1; **Ja klar!** *Of course!,* 1
die Jacke, -n *jacket,* 5

das Jahr, -e *year,* 1; **Ich bin ... Jahre alt.** *I am...years old.,* 1
der Januar *January,* 7; **im Januar** *in January,* 7
die Jeans, - *jeans,* 5
die Jeans-Tasche, -n *denim school bag,* 4
jed- *every,* 5; **jeden Abend** *every evening,* 10; **jeden Tag** *every day,* 7
jeglich- *any,* 8; **jeglicher Art** *every kind,* 9
jetzt *now,* 1
joggen *to jog,* 12
der Jogging-Anzug, ¨e *jogging suit,* 5
der Joghurt *yogurt,* 8
das Joghurteis *yogurt ice cream,* 8
die Jugend *youth,* 10
der Jugendclub, -s *youth club,* 9
der Jugendliche, -n *young adult,* 7
das Jugendzentrum, die Jugendzentren *youth center,* 12
der Juli *July,* 7
jung *young,* 10
der Junge, -n *boy,* 1
der Juni *June,* 7

K

der Kaffee *coffee,* 8; **eine Tasse Kaffee** *a cup of coffee,* 6
der Kaiser, - *emperor,* 6
der Kaiserschmarren (Austrian and southern German dish), 8
das Kalb, ¨er *veal,* 8
der Kalender, - *calendar,* 11
die Kalorie, -n *calorie,* 8
kalt *cold,* 7
der Kanal, ¨e *canal,* 1
das Kaninchen, - *rabbit,* 7
die Kanzlei, -en *law office,* 10
das Kapitel, - *chapter,* 1
kaputt *broken,* 3
die Kapuze, -n *hood (of coat),* 5
die Karte, -n *card,* 2
das Kartenspiel, -e *card game,* 2
die Kartoffel, -n *potato,* 8
der Kartoffelsalat, -e *potato salad,* 12
der Käse, - *cheese,* 8
das Käsebrot, -e *cheese sandwich,* 6
der Käsekuchen, - *cheese cake,* 6
die Kasse, -n *cashier,* 10
die Kassette, -n *cassette,* 4
die Kastagnette, -n *castanet,* 11
der Kasten, - *box, container,* 9
die Kastenform, -en *bread pan,* 12
die Katze, -n *cat,* 3; **die Katze füttern** *to feed the cat,* 7
kaufen *to buy,* 5
das Kaufhaus, ¨er *department store,* 5
kegeln *to bowl,* 10

kein *no, none, not any,* 9; **Ich habe keine Zeit.** *I don't have time.,* 7; **Ich habe keinen Hunger mehr.** *I'm not hungry any more.,* 9; **kein(en) ... mehr** *no more...,* 9; **Kein Problem!** *No problem!,* 11; **Keine Ahnung!** *I have no idea!,* 9; Nein danke, keinen Kuchen mehr. *No thanks. No more cake.,* 9; **Ich möchte kein(e)(en) ... mehr.** *I don't want another....,* 9

der Keks, -e *cookie,* 3; **ein paar Kekse** *a few cookies,* 3

der Kellner, - *waiter,* 6

kennen *to know, be familiar or acquainted with,* 10

kennenlernen *to get to know,* 12

die Kerze, -n *candle,* 11

das Kilo=Kilogramm, - *kilogram,* 8

das Kind, -er *child,* 8

die Kinderkirche *Sunday school,* 8

das Kino, -s *cinema,* 6; **im Kino** *at the movies,* 10; **ins Kino gehen** *to go to the movies,* 6

die Kinokarte, -n *movie ticket,* 9

das Kinoprogramm, -e *movie guide,* 10

die Kirche, -n *church,* 9

die Kirschtorte, -n *cherry cake,* 10

die Kiwi, -s *kiwi,* 8

die Klamotten (pl) *casual term for clothes,* 5; **meine Klamotten aufräumen** *to pick up my clothes,* 7

Klar! *sure,* 2; *clear,* 9; Alles klar! *O.K.!,* 10; **Ja, klar!** *Of course!* 1

Klasse! *Great! Terrific!,* 2

die Klasse, -n *grade level,* 4

die Klassenarbeit, -en *test, exam,* 4

der Klassenkamerad, -en *classmate,* 3

das Klassenzimmer, - *classroom,* p. 8

der Klassiker, - *classicist,* 11

klassisch *classical,* 10

das Klavier, -e *piano,* 2; **Ich spiele Klavier.** *I play the piano.,* 2

das Kleid, -er *dress,* 5

klein *small,* 3

die Kleinigkeit, -en *small thing,* 11

klug *clever,* 9

die Knoblauchzehe, -n *garlic clove,* 8

der Knochen, - *bone,* 8

kochen *to cook,* 2

kommen *to come,* 1; **er kommt aus** *he's from,* 1; **ich komme** *I come,* 1; **ich komme aus** *I'm from,* 1; **Komm doch mit!** *Why don't you come along?,* 7; Komm mit nach ... *Come along to...,* 1; es kommt ganz darauf an *it really depends,* 12; **sie kommen aus** *they're from,* 1; **sie kommt aus** *she's from,* 1; **Wie komme**

ich zum (zur) ... ? *How do I get to...?,* 9; **Wie kommst du zur Schule?** *How do you get to school?,* 1; Wie kommt man dahin? *How do you get there?,* 9

die Komödie, -n *comedy,* 10

der Komponist, -en *composer,* 11

die Konditorei, -en *confectioner's,* 8

können *to be able to,* 7; **Kann ich bitte Andrea sprechen?** *Could I please speak with Andrea?,* 11; Kann ich's wirklich? *Can I really do it?,* 1; **Was kann ich für dich tun?** *What can I do for you?,* 7; **Kann ich etwas für dich tun?** *Can I do something for you?,* 7

das Kontingent, -e *allotment,* 9

das Konzert, -e *concert,* 6; **im Konzert** *at the concert,* 10; **ins Konzert gehen** *to go to a concert,* 6

der Kopf, ⸚e *head,* 1

der Kopfsalat, -e *head lettuce,* 8

der Korb, ⸚e *basket,* 7

kosten *to cost,* 4; **Was kostet ... ?** *How much does...cost?,* 4

köstlich *delicious,* 8

das Kotelett, -s *cutlet,* 8

die Kräuter (pl) *herbs,* 12

kriegen *to get,* 10

der Kriegsfilm, -e *war movie,* 10

der Krimi, -s *detective movie,* 10

der Krug, ⸚e *jug,* 12

die Kruste, -n *crust,* 8

die Küche, -n *kitchen,* 12; **in der Küche** *in the kitchen,* 12

der Kuchen, - *cake,* 3; **ein Stück Kuchen** *a piece of cake,* 3

die Kugel, -n *scoop (of ice cream),* 6

kühl *cool,* 7

kühler *cooler,* 7

der Kühlschrank, ⸚e *refrigerator,* 12

die Kuckucksuhr, -en *cookoo clock,* 12

der Kuli, -s *ballpoint pen,* 4

kulturell *cultural,* 10

der Kümmel *caraway,* 8

die Kunst, ⸚e *art,* 4

der Kunststoff, -e: **aus Kunststoff** *out of plastic,* 12

der Kurpark, -s *spa park,* 12

kurz *short,* 3

die Kusine, -n *cousin (female),* 3

L

lachen *to laugh,* 11

der Laden, ⸚ *store,* 8; **im Obst- und Gemüseladen** *at the produce store,* 8

die Lampe, -n *lamp,* 12

das Land, ⸚er *country,* 3; **auf dem Land** *in the country,* 3

die Landeshauptstadt, ⸚e *state capital,* 1

lang *long,* 3

länger *longer,* 7

der Langlauf *cross country,* 9

langweilig *boring,* 2

lässig *casual,* 5

die Last, -en *burden,* 7

das Latein *Latin,* 4

laufen *to run,* 2; Rollschuh laufen *to roller skate,* 9; **Schlittschuh laufen** *to ice skate,* 12

das Leben, - *life,* 10

die Lebensmittel (pl) *groceries,* 8

die Leber *liver,* 9

der Leberkäs (see p. 229), 9

lecker *tasty, delicious,* 6

das Leder *leather,* 12; **aus Leder** *made of leather,* 12

legen *to put, lay,* 8

leger *casual,* 5

der Lehrer, - *teacher (male),* 1

die Lehrerin, -nen *teacher (female),* 1

leicht *easy,* 10

leid: Es tut mir leid. *I'm sorry.,* 9

leider *unfortunately,* 7; **Ich kann leider nicht.** *Sorry, I can't.,* 7

das Leinen *linen,* 5

die Lektüre *reading,* 10

lernen *to study, learn,* 8

lesen *to read,* 10; **er/sie liest** *he/she reads,* 10; richtig lesen *to read correctly,* 1

der Leserbrief, -e *letter to the editor,* 9

der Lesetrick, -s *reading trick,* 1

letzt- *last,* 8; **letzte Woche** *last week,* 8; **letztes Wochenende** *last weekend,* 8

die Leute (pl) *people,* 9

das Licht, -er *light,* p. 8

lieb *nice,* 7

lieber (mögen) *to prefer,* 10; Ich sehe Komödien lieber. *I like comedies better.,* 10

Liebe(r) ... *Dear...,* 1

der Liebesfilm, -e *romance,* 10

der Liebesroman, -e *romance novel,* 10

Lieblings- *favorite,* 4

das Lieblingsessen, - *favorite food,* 4

liebsten: am liebsten *most of all,* 10

das Lied, -er *song,* 10

liegen *to lie,* 1

lila *purple,* 5

die Limo, -s (Limonade, -n) *lemon drink,* 6

link *left, left hand,* 10; **nach links** *to the left,* 9; auf der linken Seite *on the left (side),* 9

der Linseneintopf, ⸚e *lentil soup,* 9

die Liste, -n *list,* 10

der Liter, - *liter,* 8

locker *loose, easy going,* 5

logisch *logical*, 4
los: Los geht's! *Let's start!*, 1; Was ist los? *What's happening?*, 5
die Lust: Lust haben *to feel like*, 7
lustig *funny*, 10
lustigste *funniest*, 10

M

machen *to do*, 2; **Das macht (zusammen) ...** *That comes to...*, 6; **Gut! Mach' ich!** *Okay, I'll do that!*, 7; **Machst du Sport?** *Do you play sports?*, 2; **Macht nichts!** *It doesn't matter!* 4; **die Hausaufgaben machen** *to do homework*, 2
das Mädchen, - *girl*, 1
mähen *to mow*, 7; **den Rasen mähen** *to mow the lawn*, 7
die Mahlzeit, -en *meal*, 8
der Mai *May*, 7; **im Mai** *in May*, 7
die Maisstärke *corn starch*, 12
der Majoran *majoram*, 12
mal (particle), 6; (short for **einmal**) *once*, 9
malen *to paint*, 2
man *one, you (in general), people*, 1
manchmal *sometimes*, 7
der Mandelkuchen, - *almond cake*, 12
die Mandel, -n *almond*, 12
mangelhaft *unsatisfactory* (grade), 4
der Mann, ⸚er *man*, 3
der Mantel, ⸚ *coat*, 5
die Margarine *margarine*, 12
der Marienkäfer, - *lady bug*, 11
die Mark, - *mark (German monetary unit)*, 4
der Markt, ⸚e *market*, 6
der Marktplatz, ⸚e *market square*, 9
die Marmelade, -n *jam, jelly*, 8
der März *March*, 7; **im März** *in March*, 7
der Maschinenbau *machine building industry*, 10
die Masse, -n *mass*, 12
die Mathearbeit, -en *math test*, 4
die Mathematik (Mathe) *math*, 4
die Matheprüfung, -en *math exam*, 6
die Mauer, -n *wall*, 12
die Maultaschen (pl) (Southern German dish), 9
Mau Mau (card game), 2
die Maus, ⸚e *mouse*, 7
das Meer, -e *ocean*, 6
das Meerschweinchen, - *guinea pig*, 7
das Mehl *flour*, 8
mehr *more*, 2; **Ich habe keinen Hunger mehr.** *I'm not hungry anymore.*, 9
die Mehrwegflasche, -n *refund bottle*, 7

mein *my*, 3; **meinem Vater** *to, for my father*, 11; **meiner Mutter** *to, for my mother*, 11
meinen: **Meinst du?** *Do you think so?*, 5
die Meinung, -en *opinion*, 2
meisten *most*, 9
meistens *mostly*, 5
die Melone, -n *melon*, 3
der Mensch, -en *person*, 7; Mensch! *Oh man!*, 2
das Messer, - *knife*, 10
der Metzger, - *butcher*, 8; **beim Metzger** *at the butcher's*, 8
die Metzgerei, -en *butcher shop*, 8
mich *me*, 7
die Milch *milk*, 8
mild *mild*, 8
die Million, -en *million*, 7
das Mineralwasser *mineral water*, 3
minus *minus*, 3
die Minute, -n *minute*, 8
mir *to me*, 3
miserabel *miserable*, 6
der Mist: **So ein Mist!** *That stinks! What a mess!*, 4
mit *with, by*, 1; **mit Brot** *with bread*, 6; **mit dem Auto** *by car*, 1; **mit dem Bus** *by bus*, 1; **mit dem Moped** *by moped*, 1; **mit dem Rad** *by bike*, 1; **mit der U-Bahn** *by subway*, 1; **mit Senf** *with mustard*, 9; **mit Zitrone** *with lemon*, 6
mitarbeiten (sep) *to work with*, 7
mitgebracht (pp) *brought with*, 12
die Mithilfe *cooperation*, 7
mitkommen (sep) *to come along*, 7
mitnehmen (sep) *to take with*, 10
der Mitschüler, - *classmate (male)*, 1
die Mitschülerin, -nen *classmate (female)*, 1
der Mittag *noon*, 8
die Mittagspause, -n *midday break*, 9
die Mitternacht *midnight*, 10
mittler- *middle*, 6
der Mittwoch *Wednesday*, 4; **am Mittwoch** *on Wednesday*, 4
die Möbel (pl) *furniture*, 3
möchten *would like to*, 3; **Ich möchte ... sehen.** *I would like to see...*, 5; **Was möchtest du essen?** *What would you like to eat?*, 3; **Ich möchte noch ein(e)(en) ...** *I'd like another...*, 9; **Ich möchte kein(e)(en) ... mehr.** *I don't want another...*, 9
die Mode, -n *fashion*, 10
das Modegeschäft, -e *clothing store*, 5
der Modekenner, - *fashion expert*, 5
modern *modern*, 12

modisch *fashionable*, 5
mogeln *to cheat*, 2
mögen *to like, care for*, 10
möglich *possible*, 4
möglichst ... *as...as possible*, 12
der Moment, -e *moment*, 3; **Einen Moment, bitte!** *Just a minute, please.*, 11; **im Moment gar nichts** *nothing at the moment*, 3
der Monat, -e *month*, 7; **(einmal) im Monat** *(once) a month*, 7
das Monster, -s *monster*, 1
der Montag *Monday*, 4; **am Montag** *on Monday*, 4
das Moped, -s *moped*, 1; **mit dem Moped** *by moped*, 1
morgen *tomorrow*, 7
der Morgen, - *morning*, 2; **Guten Morgen!** *Good morning!*, 1; **Morgen!** *Morning!*, 1
der Müll *trash*, 7; **den Müll sortieren** *to sort the trash*, 7
der Mülleimer, - *trash can*, 12
die Münchner (pl) *residents of Munich*, 9
mündlich *oral*, 4
die Münze, -n *coin*, 11; **Münzen einstecken** *to insert coins*, 11
das Museum, die Museen *museum*, 9
die Musik *music*, 2; **klassische Musik** *classical music*, 10; **Musik hören** *to listen to music*, 2
das Musikprogramm, -e *music program*, 10
das Müsli *muesli*, 8
müssen *to have to*, 7; **ich muß** *I have to*, 7
die Mutter, ⸚ *mother*, 3
die Mutti *mom*, 3
der Muttertag *Mother's Day*, 11; **Alles Gute zum Muttertag!** *Happy Mother's Day!*, 11

N

Na? *Well?*, 2; Na ja. *Oh well*, 5; na dann *well then*, 9; Na klar! *Of course!*, 5
nach *after*, 2; **nach der Schule** *after school*, 2; **nach links** *to the left*, 9; **nach rechts** *to the right*, 9; **nach der Pause** *after the break*, 4; **nach Hause gehen** *to go home*, 3
die Nachbarschaft *neighborhood*, 8
nacherzählen *to retell*, 3
nachfolgend- *following*, 7
nachher *later, afterwards*, 3
die Nachhilfe *tutoring*, 7
die Nachhilfestunde, -n *tutoring lesson*, 7

der Nachmittag, -e *afternoon*, 2; **am
    Nachmittag** *in the afternoon*, 2
nächste *next*, 6; **die nächste
    Straße** *the next street*, 9
die Nacht, ⸚e *night*, 6
die Nähe: **in der Nähe** *nearby*, 3
der Name, -n *name*, 1
der Namenstag, -e *name day*, 11
    naß *wet*, 7
    Natürlich! *Certainly!*, 11
    nehmen *to take*, 5; **er/sie nimmt**
    he/she takes, 5; **ich nehme ...**
    I'll take..., 5; **Nehmt ein Stück
    Papier!** *Take out a piece of
    paper.*, p. 8
    nein *no*, 1
    nennen *to name*, 5
    nett *nice*, 2
    neu *new*, 3
    neun *nine*, 1
    neunundzwanzig *twenty-nine*, 3
    neunzehn *nineteen*, 1
    neunzig *ninety*, 3
    neuste *newest*, 10
    nicht *not*, 2; **Nicht besonders.**
    Not really., 6; **nicht gern haben**
    to dislike, 4; **nicht schlecht** *not
    bad*, 4; **Ich nicht.** *I don't.*, 2;
    Nicht zu lang? *Not too long?*, 5
    nichts *nothing*, 2; **Nichts,
    danke!** *Nothing, thank you!*,
    3; **Nichts mehr, danke!**
    Nothing else, thanks!, 9
    nie *never*, 7
    noch *yet, still*, 2; **Haben Sie
    noch einen Wunsch?** *Would
    you like anything else?*, 8; **Ich
    brauche noch ...** *I also need...*,
    8; **Möchtest du noch etwas?**
    Would you like something else?,
    9; **noch ein** *more, another*, 9;
    Noch einen Saft? *Another
    glass of juice?*, 9; **Noch etwas?**
    Anything else?, 9; **Ich möchte
    noch ein(e)(en) ...** *I'd like
    another...*, 9
    normalerweise *usually*, 10
die Note, -n *grade*, 4
das Notizbuch, ⸚er *notebook*, 1
der November *November*, 7; **im
    November** *in November*, 7
die Nudelsuppe, -n *noodle soup*, 6
    null *zero*, 1
die Nummer, -n *number*, 1
    nun *now*, 6
    nur *only*, 4

O

ob *whether* (conj), 9
oben *upstairs; up there*, 3
das Obst *fruit*, 3

der Obst- und Gemüseladen, ⸚ *fresh
    produce store*, 8; **im Obst- und
    Gemüseladen** *at the produce
    store*, 8
der Obstkuchen, - *fruit cake*, 8
der Obstsalat, -e *fruit salad*, 8
    obwohl *although* (conj), 7
    oder *or*, 1
der Ofen, ⸚ *oven*, 12
    öffnen: Öffnet eure Bücher auf
    Seite ... ! *Open your books to
    page...*, p. 8
    oft *often*, 7
    ohne *without*, 5
    Oje! *Oh no!*, 6
der Oktober *October*, 7; **im Oktober**
    in October, 7
das Öl, -e *oil*, 12
die Oma, -s *grandmother*, 3
der Onkel, - *uncle*, 3
der Opa, -s *grandfather*, 3
die Oper, -n *opera*, 10
die Optik *optics*, 10
die Orange, -n *orange*, 3
der Orangensaft *orange juice*, 3
das Orchester, - *orchestra*, 4
    organisieren *to organize*, 11
die Originalfassung, -en *original
    version*, 10
der Ort, -e *place, location*, 9
das Ostern *Easter*, 11; **Frohe Ostern!**
    Happy Easter, 11
    österreichisch *Austrian* (adj), 9

P

das Paar, -e *pair*, 5;
    paar: ein paar *a few*, 3
das Päckchen, - *packet*, 12
das Paddel, - *paddle*, 12
die Pailletten (pl) *beads*, 5
das Papier *paper*, p. 8
der Paprika *bell pepper*, 8
das Parfüm, -e *perfume*, 11
der Park, -s *park*, 12; **in den Park
    gehen** *to go to the park*, 12
der Partner, - *partner (male)*, p. 7
die Partnerin, -nen *partner (female)*, 6
der Passant, -en *passer-by*, 9
    passen *to fit*, 5; **der Rock paßt
    prima!** *The skirt fits great!*, 5;
    Was paßt zusammen? *What
    goes together?*, 1; aufpassen:
    Paßt auf! *Pay attention!*, p. 8;
    Paß auf! *Watch out!*, 6
    passieren: Was passiert hier?
    What's happening here?, 1
die Pastellfarben (pl) *pastel colors*, 5
die Pause, -n *break*, 4; **nach der
    Pause** *after the break*, 4
das Pech *bad luck*, 4; **So ein Pech!**
    Bad luck!, 4

die Perle, -n *bead*, 5
die Person, -en *person*, 3
    persönlich *personally*, 11
der Pfadfinder, - (similar to Boy
    Scout), 6
    Pfd.=Pfund *pound*, 8
der Pfeffer *pepper*, 12
der Pfennig, - (smallest unit of
    German currency; 1/100 of a
    mark), 4
die Pflaume, -n *plum*, 8
    pflegen *to do regularly*, 9
die Pflicht, -en *duty*, 7
der Pflichtunterricht *mandatory
    class*, 4
das Pfund, - (Pfd.) *pound*, 8
    phantasievoll *imaginative*, 10
    phantastisch *fantastic*, 3
die Physik *physics*, 4
    pikant *spicy*, 8
der Pilz, -e *mushroom*, 6
die Pizza, -s *pizza*, 6
der Plan, ⸚e *plan*, 6
    planen *to plan*, 6
die Planung, -en *planning*, 10
der Platz, ⸚e *place, spot*, 1; **am
    ...platz** *on ... Square*, 9; **bis
    zum ...platz** *until you get to ...
    square*, 9
der Pokalsieg, -e *victory*, 9
die Politik *politics*, 10
    populär *popular*, 11
    populärste *most popular*, 11
das Portemonnaie, -s *wallet*, 8
die Portion, -en *portion*, 12
die Post *post office*, 9
das Poster, - *poster*, 11
die Postkarte, -n *postcard*, 1
die Praline, -n *fancy chocolate*, 11
der Präsident, -en *president*, 9
der Preis, -e *price*, 4
das Preisplakat, -e *poster with prices*, 8
    preiswert *reasonably priced*, 4;
    Das ist preiswert. *That's a
    bargain.*, 4
    Prima! *Great!*, 1; **Prima Idee!**
    Great idea!, 7
die Prise, -n: **eine Prise Salz** *a pinch
    of salt*, 12
    probieren *to try* (with foods), 9
das Problem, -e *problem*, 8
    Prost! *Cheers!*, 12
das Prozent, - *percent*, 5
die Prüfungsvorbereitung, -en *prepa-
    ration for a test*, 7
    Pst! *Ssh!*, 12
der Pulli, -s (Pullover, -) *pullover,
    sweater*, 5
das Putenschnitzel, - *turkey cutlets*, 8
    putzen *to clean*, 7; **die Fenster
    putzen** *to wash the windows*, 7
das Putzmittel, - *cleaning agent*, 7

Q

der Quadratkilometer, - *square kilometer*, 1
die Qualität *quality*, 5
der Quark (milk product), 8
Quatsch! *Nonsense!*, 7

R

das Rad, ⸚er *bike*, 1; **mit dem Rad** *by bike*, 1; Wir fahren Rad. *We're riding bikes.*, 10
radeln *to ride a bike*, 7
radfahren *to ride a bike*, 2
der Radiergummi, -s *eraser*, 4
das Radieschen, - *radish*, 8
das Radio, -s *radio*, 11
der Rasen, - *lawn*, 7; **den Rasen mähen** *to mow the lawn*, 7
raten: Rate! *Guess!*, 2; Rate mal! *Guess!*, 1
das Rathaus, ⸚er *city hall*, 9
der Rechner, - *calculator*, 4
recht: Du hast recht! *You're right!*, 4
recht- *right, right hand*, 7; **nach rechts** *to the right*, 9
die Rechtschreibung *spelling*, 8
reden *to talk*, 5
reduziert *reduced*, 5
das Regal, -e *bookcase*, 3
die Regel, -n *rule*, 2
regelmäßig *regularly*, 7
der Regen *rain*, 7
die Regie *director (of a film)*, 10
regnen: Es regnet. *It's raining.*, 7
regnerisch *rainy*, 7
das Reich, -e *empire*, 6
reich *rich*, 8
die Reihe, -n *row*, 10
der Reim, -e *rhyme*, 11
rein *pure*, 6
das Reisebüro, -s *travel agency*, 9
reiten *to ride horseback*, 2
das Reitturnier, -e *riding tournament*, 12
die Religion, -en *religion* (school subject), 4
das Restaurant, -s *restaurant*, 9
richtig *correct(ly)*, 1
riechen *to smell*, 8
Riesen- *gigantic*, 8
der Rock, ⸚e *skirt*, 5
die Rolle, -n *role*, 9
der Rollschuh, -e *roller skate*, 2
die Rollschuhbahn, -en *roller skating course*, 9
Rollschuh laufen *to roller skate*, 9; ich laufe Rollschuh *I roller skate*, 9
der Roman, -e *novel*, 10
der Rosenkohl *Brussel sprouts*, 9

S (first column continued)

die Rosine, -n *raisin*, 8
rot *red*, 3; **in Rot** *in red*, 5
Ruhe! *Quiet!*, 4
der Ruhetag, -e *day of rest*, 6
der Rührteig, -e *batter*, 12
rund *round*, 12
runter *down*, 3

S

das Sachbuch, ⸚er *non-fiction book*, 10
die Sache, -n *thing*, 5
der Saft, ⸚e *juice*, 3
saftig *juicy*, 6
der Saftstand, ⸚e *juice stand*, 9
sagen *to say*, 2; Sag, ... *Say...*, 1; **Sag mal ...** *Say...*, 2; so sagt man das *here's how you say it*, 1; Was sagst du dazu? *What do you say to that?*, 9; **Was sagt der Wetterbericht?** *What does the weather report say?*, 7; Wie sagt man ... auf deutsch? *How do you say...in German?*, p. 8;
sagenhaft *great*, 6
sagte *said*, 10
die Sahne *cream*, 8
die Saison, -s *season*, 5
der Salat, -e *lettuce*, 8; *salad*, 12
das Salz *salt*, 12
sammeln *to collect*, 2; **Comics sammeln** *to collect comics*, 2; **Briefmarken sammeln** *to collect stamps*, 2
der Samstag *Saturday*, 4; **am Samstag** *on Saturdays*, 4
der Sänger, - *singer (male)*, 10
die Sängerin, -nen *singer (female)*, 10
der Satz, ⸚e *sentence*, 1; Sätze bauen *to form sentences*, 1
sauberer *cleaner*, 7
saubermachen *to clean*, 12
sauer *annoyed*, 2
säuerlich *sour*, 12
saugen: Staub saugen *to vacuum*, 7
das Schach *chess*, 2
Schade! *Too bad!*, 4
die Schale, -n *serving dish*, 8
schauen *to look*, 2; **Schau!** *Look!*, 4; Schau mal! *Take a look!*, 1; **Schauen Sie!** (formal) *Look!*, 4; Schaut auf die Tafel! *Look at the board!*, 12; **Fernsehen schauen** *to watch television*, 2
der Schauer, - *(rain) shower*, 7
das Schaufenster, - *store window*, 12
der Schauspieler, - *actor*, 10
die Schauspielerin, -nen *actress*, 10

S (third column)

die Scheibe, -n *slice*, 8
scheinen *to shine*, 7; **Die Sonne scheint.** *The sun is shining.*, 7
schenken *to give (a gift)*, 11; **Schenkst du deinem Vater einen Kalender zum Geburtstag?** *Are you giving your father a calendar for his birthday?*, 11; **Was schenkst du deiner Mutter?** *What are you giving your mother?*, 11
scheußlich *hideous*, 5
schick, chic *smart (looking)*, 5
schimpfen *to complain*, 7
der Schinken *ham*, 6
das Schlagzeug *drums; percussion*, 2
schlecht *bad(ly)*, 4
der Schlittschuh, -e *ice skate*, 12; **Schlittschuh laufen** *to ice skate*, 12
das Schloß, die Schlösser *castle*, 12
schmalzig *corny, mushy*, 10
schmecken: **Schmeckt's?** *Does it taste good?*, 6; **Wie schmeckt's?** *How does it taste?*, 6
der Schmuck *jewelry*, 11
der Schnee *snow*, 7
schneien: **Es schneit.** *It's snowing.*, 7
schneiden *to cut*, 8
schnell *fast*, 7
das Schnitzel, - *schnitzel*, 9
das Schokoladeneis *chocolate ice cream*, 6
die Schokoladenstücke (pl) *pieces of chocolate*, 12
schon *already*, 1; schon bekannt *already known*, 2; Schon gut! *That's okay!*, 1
schön *pretty, beautiful*, 3
schöner *more beautiful, prettier*, 5
schönste *most beautiful*, 5
der Schornsteinfeger, - *chimney sweep*, 11
der Schrank, ⸚e *cabinet*, 3
schreiben *to write*, 2; richtig schreiben *to write correctly*, 1; Schreibt euren Namen auf! *Write down your names.*, p. 8; Schreib ... auf! *Write down...!*, 12
der Schreibtisch, -e *desk*, 3
der Schreibwarenladen, ⸚ *stationery store*, 4
schriftlich *written*, 4
der Schritt, -e *step*, 10; auf Schritt und Tritt *all the time*, 10
die Schule, -n *school*, 4; **nach der Schule** *after school*, 2; **Wie kommst du zur Schule?** *How do you get to school?*, 1

der Schüler, - *pupil, student (male)*, 3
die Schülerin, -nen *pupil, student (female)*, -
der Schülerausweis, -e *student I.D.*, 4
der Schulhof, ⸚e *school yard*, 4
das Schuljahr, -e *school year*, 4
die Schulsachen (pl) *school supplies*, 4
die Schultasche, -n *schoolbag*, 4
die Schulter, -n *shoulder*, 8
die Schüssel, -n *bowl*, 12
der Schutzumschlag, ⸚e *dust jacket (on a book)*, 10
schwarz *black*, 3; in Schwarz *in black*, 5
das Schwein, -e *pig*, 8
der Schweinebraten, - *pork roast*, 8
das Schweinschnitzel, - *pork cutlet*, 9
die Schweinshaxe, -n *pork shank*, 7
das Schweinswürstel, - *little pork sausage*, 8
schwer *difficult, hard*, 11
die Schwester, -n *sister*, 3
das Schwimmbad, ⸚er *swimming pool*, 6; ins Schwimmbad gehen *to go to the (swimming) pool*, 6
schwimmen *to swim*, 2
der Science-fiction-Film, -e *science fiction movie*, 10
sechs *six*, 1
sechsundzwanzig *twenty-six*, 3
sechzehn *sixteen*, 1
sechzig *sixty*, 3
der See, -n *lake*, 1
die See *sea*, 4
segeln *to go sailing*, 2
sehen *to see*, 10; Am liebsten sehe ich Krimis. *I like detective movies the best.*, 10; er/sie sieht *he/she sees*, 10; einen Film sehen *to see a movie*, 6
sehenswert *worth seeing*, 9
sehr *very*, 2; Sehr gut! *Very well!*, 6
seid: ihr seid *you (pl) are*, 1
die Seide, -n *silk*, 12; aus Seide *made of silk*, 12
sein *to be*, 1; er ist *he is*, 1; er ist aus *he's from*, 1; ich bin aus *I am from*, 1; sie sind *they are*, 1; sie sind aus *they're from*, 1; du bist *you are*, 1
sein *his*, 3
seit *since, for*, 10
die Seite, -n *page*, 6; *side*, 9; auf der rechten Seite *on the right (hand) side*, 9
selber *myself*, 7
selbst *yourself*, 7
Selbstgemachtes *homemade*, 11
selten *seldom*, 7

die Semmel, -n *roll*, 8
der Senf *mustard*, 6; mit Senf *with mustard*, 9
sensationell *sensational*, 10
separat *separate*, 7
der September *September*, 7
der Sessel, - *armchair*, 12
setzen *to sit down*, 6; Setzt euch! *Sit down!*, p. 8
die Shorts *pair of shorts*, 5
sich *oneself*, 5
Sicher! *Certainly!*, 3; Ich bin nicht sicher. *I'm not sure.*, 5
sichern *to secure*, 9
sie *she*, 2
sie (pl) *they*, 2
Sie *you* (formal), 2
sie *it* (with objects), 3
sie (pl) *they* (with objects), 3; *them* (with objects), 5
sieben *seven*, 1
siebenundzwanzig *twenty-seven*, 3
siebzehn *seventeen*, 1
siebzig *seventy*, 3
sind: sie sind *they are*, 1; Sie (formal) sind *you are*, 1; wir sind *we are*, 1
singen *to sing*, 10
sitzen *to be sitting*, 10
Skat (German card game), 2
Ski laufen *to ski*, 2
so *so, well, then*, 2; so groß wie *as big as*, 6; so lala *so so*, 6; so oft wie möglich *as often as possible*, 10; so sagt man das *here's how you say it*, 1
sobald *as soon (as)*, 10
die Socke, -n *sock*, 5
das Sofa, -s *sofa*, 12
sollen *should, to be supposed to*, 8
der Sommer *summer*, 2; im Sommer *in the summer*, 2
sommerleicht *summery (clothing)*, 5
das Sonderangebot, -e *sale*, 4
sondern *but*, 5
die Sonne *sun*, 7
sonnig *sunny*, 7
der Sonntag *Sunday*, 4
sonntags *Sundays*, 8
sonst *otherwise*, 2; ansonsten *otherwise*, 11; Sonst noch etwas? *Anything else?*, 8
die Sorge, -n *worry*, 8
sorgen *to care (for), to take care of*, 6
sortieren *to sort*, 7; den Müll sortieren *to sort the trash*, 7
soviel *as much*, 9
sowieso *anyway*, 5
Sozialkunde *social studies*, 4

Spanisch *Spanish* (class), 4; (language), 10
spannend *exciting, thrilling*, 10
der Spargel *asparagus*, 8
sparsam *thrifty*, 7
der Spaß *fun*, 2; Hat es Spaß gemacht? *Was it fun?*, 10; (Tennis) macht keinen Spaß. *(Tennis) is no fun.*, 2; (Tennis) macht Spaß. *(Tennis) is fun.*, 2; Viel Spaß! *Have fun!*, 9
spät *late*, 6; Wie spät ist es? *What time is it?*, 6
später *later*, 2
das Spätprogramm, -e *late show*, 10
das Spatzenbrett, -er (cutting board to make Spätzle), 12
die Spätzle (pl) (see p. 298), 12
der Speck *bacon*, 12
die Speisekarte, -n *menu*, 6
spektakulärste *most spectacular*, 10
die Spezialität, -en *specialty*, 9
das Spiel, -e *game*, 10
spielen *to play*, 2; Ich spiele Fußball. *I play soccer.*, 2; Ich spiele Klavier. *I play the piano.*, 2; Spielst du ein Instrument? *Do you play an instrument?*, 2
der Spieler, - *player*, 12
der Spießbraten, - *roast*, 6
der Spinat *spinach*, 9
Spitze! *Super!*, 2
die Spitzenqualität *top quality*, 8
sponsern *to sponsor*, 10
spontan *spontaneous(ly)*, 9
der Sport *sports*, 2; *physical education*, 4; Machst du Sport? *Do you play sports?*, 2
die Sportart, -en *type of sport*, 9
die Sporthalle, -n *indoor gym*, 6
sportlich *sportive*, 5
die Sportmode *sportswear*, 9
die Sprache, -n *language*, 5
sprechen: sprechen über *to talk about, discuss*, 10; er/sie spricht über *he/she talks about*, 10; Kann ich bitte Andrea sprechen? *Could I please speak with Andrea?*, 11
das Spülbecken, - *sink*, 12
spülen *to wash*, 7; das Geschirr spülen *to wash the dishes*, 7
die Spülmaschine, -n *dishwasher*, 12; die Spülmaschine ausräumen *to unload the dishwasher*, 12
die Stadt, ⸚e *city*, 9; in der Stadt *in the city*, 3; in die Stadt fahren *to go downtown (by vehicle)*, 11; in die Stadt gehen *to go downtown*, 6

das Stadtmuseum *city museum*, 9
der Stadtplan, -̈e *city map*, 9
stark *great, awesome*, 5
der Staub *dust*, 7; **Staub saugen** *to vacuum*, 7
stehen: Steht auf! *Stand up!*, p. 8; Wie steht's mit dir? *How about you?*, 10
der Stehimbiß, -sse *fast food stand*, 9
stellen *to put*, 10
die Stereoanlage, -n *stereo*, 3
der Stiefbruder, -̈ *stepbrother*, 3
der Stiefel, - *boot*, 5
die Stiefmutter, -̈ *stepmother*, 3
die Stiefschwester, -n *stepsister*, 3
der Stiefvater, -̈ *stepfather*, 3
stimmen *to be correct*, 3; **Stimmt (schon)!** *Keep the change.*, 6; **Stimmt!** *That's right! True!*, 2; **Stimmt nicht!** *Not true!; False!*, 2
stimmungsvoll *full of atmosphere*, 6
das Stirnband, -̈er *headband*, 5
die Straße, -n *street*, 9; **auf der Straße** *on the street*, 9; **bis zur ...straße** *until you get to ... Street*, 9; **die erste (zweite, dritte) Straße** *the first (second, third) street*, 9; **in der ...straße** *on ... Street*, 3
der Streifen, - *stripe*, 5
streng *strict*, 7
das Stück, -e *piece*, p. 8; **ein Stück Kuchen** *a piece of cake*, 3
die Stufe, -n *level*, 1
der Stuhl, -̈e *chair*, 3
die Stunde, -n *hour*, 9
der Stundenplan, -̈e *class schedule*, 4
suchen *to look for, search for*, 5; **ich suche ...** *I'm looking for...*, 5
super *super*, 2
der Supermarkt, -̈e *supermarket*, 8; **im Supermarkt** *at the supermarket*, 8
süß *sweet*, 8
die Süßspeise, -n *dessert*, 9
das Süßwarengeschäft, -e *candy store*, 11
die Szene, -n *scene*, 9

T

die Tafel, -n *(chalk)board*, p. 8; Geht an die Tafel! *Go to the board*, p. 8
der Tag, -e *day*, 2; eines Tages *one day*, 10; **Guten Tag!** *Hello!*, 1; **Tag!** *Hello!*, 1; **jeden Tag**

every day, 7
täglich *daily*, 10
die Tante, -n *aunt*, 3
tanzen *to dance*, 2; **tanzen gehen** *to go dancing*, 6
das Taschengeld *pocket money*, 7
der Taschenrechner, - *pocket calculator*, 4
die Tasse, -n *cup*, 3; **eine Tasse Kaffee** *a cup of coffee*, 6
tauschen *to switch, trade*, 9; Tauscht die Rollen aus! *Switch roles.*, 8
die Technik *technology*, 4
der Tee *tea*, 3; **ein Glas Tee** *a (glass) cup of tea*, 6
der Teelöffel (TL) *teaspoon*, 8
der Teig *dough*, 8
teilweise *partly*, 12
das Telefon, -e *telephone*, 11
telefonieren *to call*, 11
die Telefonnummer, -n *telephone number*, 11
die Telefonzelle, -n *telephone booth*, 11
der Teller, - *plate*, 11
Tennis *tennis*, 2
der Teppich, -e *carpet*, 12
teuer *expensive*, 4
der Teufel, - *devil*, 10
der Text, -e *text*, 12
das Theater, - *theater*, 9; ins Theater gehen *to go to the theater*, 12
das Theaterstück, -e *(stage) play*, 10
das Thema, die Themen *topic*, 10
der Thymian *thyme*, 12
das Tier, -e *animal*, 7
der Tisch, -e *table*, 7; **den Tisch abräumen** *to clear the table*, 7; **den Tisch decken** *to set the table*, 7
Tischtennis *table tennis*, 2
der Titel, - *title*, 10
Tja ... *Hm...*, 2
tödlich *deadly*, 10
die Toilette, -n *toilet*, 12
toll *great, terrific*, 2; Ich finde es toll! *I think it's great!*, 9
die Tomate, -n *tomato*, 8
das Tor, -e *gate*, 12
die Torte, -n *layer cake*, 8
das Training *training*, 1
die Traube, -n *grape*, 8
der Traumjob, -s *dream job*, 10
traurig *sad*, 10
traurigste *saddest*, 10
der Treff *meeting place*, 10
treffen *to meet*, 9
treiben: Ich treibe Sport. *I do sports.*, 9

trinken *to drink*, 3
trocken *dry*, 7
die Trompete, -n *trumpet*, 2
der Tropfen, - *drop*, 12
trotzdem *nevertheless*, 5
trüb *overcast*, 7
Tschau! *Bye! So long!*, 1
Tschüs! *Bye! So long!*, 1
das T-Shirt, -s *T-shirt*, 5
tun *to do*, 7; **Es tut mir leid.** *I'm sorry.*, 9
die Tür, -en *door*, p. 8
der Turnschuh, -e *sneaker, athletic shoe*, 5
tust: du tust *you do*, 9
die Tüte, -n *bag*, 5
typisch *typical*, 7

U

die U-Bahn=Untergrundbahn *subway*, 1; **mit der U-Bahn** *by subway*, 1
die U-Bahnstation, -en *subway station*, 9
üben *to practice*, p. 9
über *about*, 4
überhaupt: überhaupt nicht *not at all*, 5; **überhaupt nicht gern** *strongly dislike*, 10
überließ *left (to someone else)*, 10
die Überraschung, -en *surprise*, 12
übertreffen *to outdo, surpass*, 5
übrigens *by the way*, 3
die Übung, -en *exercise*, 11
Uhr *o'clock*, 1; **um 8 Uhr** *at 8 o'clock*, 4; **um ein Uhr** *at one o'clock*, 6; **Wieviel Uhr ist es?** *What time is it?*, 6
die Uhrzeit *time (of day)*, 6
um *at*, 1; *around*, 9; **um 8 Uhr** *at 8 o'clock*, 4; **um ein Uhr** *at one o'clock*, 6; **Um wieviel Uhr?** *At what time?*, 6
die Umfrage, -n *survey*, 1
umgeben *to surround*, 10
umhören *to listen around*, 7
die Umrechnungstabelle, -n *conversion table*, 5
umsteigen *to change lines (on a bus, subway, etc.)*, 4
die Umwelt *environment*, 10
unbedingt *absolutely*, 11
unbequem *uncomfortable*, 3
und *and*, 1
unfreundlich *unfriendly*, 11
ungefähr *about, approximately*, 7
ungenügend *unsatisfactory (grade)*, 4
ungewöhnlich *unusual*, 12
unheimlich *incredibly, incredible*, 8
die Uni, -s (Universität, -en), *university*, 2

unlogisch *illogical*, 4
die Unordnung *disorder*, 8
unregelmäßig *irregularly*, 8
uns *us*, 7
unser *our*, 4
unten *below, downstairs*, 10
unter *below, under*, 8
unterbrechen *to interrupt*, 10
unterhalten *to entertain*, 11
unterheben *to fold in*, 12
die Unterrichtsveranstaltung, -en
school-sponsored activity, 4
die Unterschrift, -en *signature*, 4
unterstützen *to support*, 10
unterwegs *on the way*, 10
usw. = und so weiter *etc., and so forth*, 10

V

die Vanille *vanilla*, 6
das Vanilleeis *vanilla ice cream*, 6
der Vater, ¨ *father*, 3; **deinem Vater** *to, for your father*, 11; **meinem Vater** *to, for my father*, 11
der Vatertag *Father's Day*, 11; **Alles Gute zum Vatertag!** *Happy Father's Day!*, 11
verabreden *to make a date*, 6
die Veranstaltung, -en *event*, 10
verbringen *to spend (time)*, 10; **Wie verbringst du deine Freizeit?** *How do you spend your free time?*, 10
verdienen *to earn*, 7
verdünnt *diluted*, 12
der Verein, -e *club*, 9
verfeinern *to improve*, 8
die Vergünstigung, -en *benefit*, 10
der Verkauf *sale*, 6
der Verkäufer, - *sales clerk (male)*, 4
die Verkäuferin, -nen *sales clerk (female)*, 4
der Verlag, -e *publishing house*, 7
verlegt: auf (time expression) verlegt *postponed until*, 6
verlieren *to lose*, 2
vermeiden *to avoid*, 7
verrühren *to blend*, 12
der Vers, -e *verse*, 11
verschenkt *given away*, 11
verschieden *different*, 11
versteckt: versteckte Sätze *hidden sentences*, 3
versuchen *to try*, 10
verteilen *to distribute*, 8
der Verwandte, -n *relative (male)*, 11
die Verwandte, -n *relative (female)*, 11
verwenden *to use*, 10
Verzeihung! *Excuse me!*, 9
das Video, -s *video cassette*, 10
das Videospiel, -e *video game*, 2

die Viehzucht *cattle raising*, 6
viel *a lot, much*, 2; Viel Spaß! Have fun!, 9; **viel zu** *much too*, 5;
viele *many*, 2; viele Grüße *best regards*, 9; **Vielen Dank!** *Thank you very much!*, 9
die Vielfalt *diversity*, 5
vielleicht *probably*, 11
vier *four*, 1
viermal *four times*, 7
das Viertel, - *quarter*, 6; **Viertel nach** *a quarter after*, 6; **Viertel vor** *a quarter till*, 6
vierundzwanzig *twenty-four*, 3
vierzehn *fourteen*, 1
vierzig *forty*, 3
der Vogel, ¨ *bird*, 7
Volleyball *volleyball*, 2
das Vollkornbrot, -e *whole grain bread*, 8
die Vollkornsemmel, -n *whole grain roll*, 9
vom=von dem *from the*, 8
von *of*, 1; *from*, 3; **von 8 Uhr bis 8 Uhr 45** *from 8:00 until 8:45*, 4
vor *before*, 1; *in front of*, 9; vor allem *especially*, 9; **zehn vor ... ten till...**, 6
voraus *in advance*, 9
vorbeigehen *to go by*, 7
vorbeikommen *to come by*, 9
vorbeigekommen *came by*, 8
vorbereiten *to prepare*, 12
die Vorbereitung, -en *preparation*, 12
vorgestern *day before yesterday*, 8
der Vormittag *before noon*, 2
vorn *ahead*, 4; hier vorn *here in front*, 5; **da vorn** *there in the front*, 4
der Vorort, -e *suburb*, 3; **ein Vorort von** *a suburb of*, 3
der Vorschlag, ¨e *suggestion*, 12
vorstellen *to introduce*, 1
die Vorstellung, -en *introduction*, 10
die Vorwahlnummer, -n *area code*, 11
die Vorzeit, -en *pre-history*, 10

W

wählen *to choose*, 10; **die Nummer wählen** *to dial the (telephone) number*, 11
das Wahlpflichtfach, ¨er *required elective*, 4
Wahnsinn! *Crazy!*, 11
wahr *true*, 11
während *while*, 6
wahrscheinlich *probably*, 11
der Walnußkern, -e *walnut*, 8
wandern *to hike*, 2

wann? *when?*, 2; **Wann hast du Geburtstag?** *When is your birthday?*, 11
war: ich war *I was*, 8; **Ich war beim Bäcker.** *I was at the baker's.*, 8
die Ware, -n *ware*, 5
waren: wir waren *we were*, 8; **sie waren** *they were*, 8; **Sie (formal) waren** *you were*, 8
warm *warm*, 7
warmhalten *to keep warm*, 12
warst: du warst *you were*, 8; **Wo warst du?** *Where were you?*, 8
wart: ihr wart *you (plural) were*
warten *to wait*, 2; ich warte auf *I'm waiting for*, 10
warum? *why?*, 7
was? *what?*, 1; Was ist los? *What's up?*, 4; Was gibt's? *What's up?*, 1; Was ist das? *What is that?*, p. 8; **Was noch?** *What else?*, 2
was für? *what kind of?*, 10; **Was für Filme magst du gern?** *What kind of movies do you like?*, 10; **Was für Musik hörst du gern?** *What kind of music do you like?*, 10
die Wäsche *laundry*, 12; die Wäsche aufhängen *to hang up the laundry*, 7
die Waschmaschine, -n *washing machine*, 12
das Wasser *water*, 3; **ein Glas (Mineral)Wasser** *a glass of (mineral) water*, 3
wasserscheu *afraid of water*, 12
der Wecken, - *roll*, 8
weg *away*, 7
der Weg, -e: den Weg zeigen *to give directions*, 9
wegbringen *to take away*, 7
weggebracht (pp) *taken away*, 7
der Weichkäse, - *soft cheese*, 8
das Weihnachten *Christmas*, 11; **Fröhliche Weihnachten!** *Merry Christmas!*, 11
weil *because* (conj), 8
weiß *white*, 3; **in Weiß** *in white*, 5
die Weißwurst, ¨e (southern German sausage specialty), 9
weit *far*, 3; *wide*, 5; **weit von hier** *far from here*, 3
weiter *farther*, 7
das Weizenmehl *wheat flour*, 12
welch- *which*, 4; an welchem Tag? *on which day?*, 11; **Welche Fächer hast du?** *Which subjects do you have?*, 4

die Welt *world*, 8
   wem? *to whom?, for whom?*, 11
   wen? *whom?*, 7; **Wen lädst du ein?** *Whom are you inviting?*, 12
   wenden *to turn (to)*, 9
   wenig *few*, 7
   wenn *when, if* (conj), 5
   wer? *who?*, 1; **Wer ist das?** *Who is that?*, 1
die Werbung *advertisement*, 4
   werden *to become*, 5
   Werken *shop* (school subject), 4
die Weste, -n *vest*, 5
der Western, - *western* (movie), 10
das Wetter *weather*, 7; **Wie ist das Wetter?** *How's the weather?*, 7
der Wetterbericht, -e *weather report*, 7
   wichtig *important*, 7
   wie? *how?*, 1; **Wie alt bist du?** *How old are you?*, 1; **Wie bitte?** *Excuse me?*, 8; **Wie blöd!** *How stupid!*, 4; **wie oft?** *how often?*, 7
   wieder *again*, 9
   Wiederhören *Bye!* (on the telephone), 11; **Auf Wiederhören!** *Goodbye!* (on the telephone), 11
   Wiedersehen! *Bye!*, 1; **Auf Wiedersehen!** *Goodbye!*, 1
   wiederverwertet *reused*, 7
   wiegen *to weigh*, 8
das Wiener (Würstchen), - *sausage*, 6
   wieviel? *how much?*, 8; **Wieviel Grad haben wir?** *What's the temperature?*, 7; **Wieviel Uhr ist es?** *What time is it?*, 6
   willkommen: Herzlich willkommen bei uns! *Welcome to our home!*, 12
   windig *windy*, 7
der Winter *winter*, 2; **im Winter** *in the winter*, 2
   wir *we*, 2
   wird *becomes*, 7
   wirklich *really*, 5
die Wirkung, -en *effect*, 8
   wischen *to mop*, 12
   wissen *to know* (a fact, information, etc.), 9; **Das weiß ich nicht.** *That I don't know.*, 9; **Ich weiß nicht.** *I don't know.*, 5; **Weißt du noch?** *Do you still remember?*, 7; **Weißt du, wo das Museum ist?** *Do you know where the museum is?*, 9
   witzig *funny*, 10
   wo? *where?*, 1

   wobei *in doing so, in the process of*, 7
die Woche, -n *week*, 6; **(einmal) in der Woche** *(once) a week*, 7
das Wochenende, -n *weekend*, 2; **am Wochenende** *on the weekend*, 2
die Wochenendheimfahrerin, -nen *student (female) who goes home on weekends*, 3
   woher? *from where?*, 1; **Woher bist du?** *Where are you from?*, 1; **Woher kommst du?** *Where are you from?*, 1
   wohin? *where (to)?*, 6; Wohin geht's? *Where are you going?*, 7
das Wohlergehen *welfare*, 8
   wohnen *to live*, 3; **Wo wohnst du?** *Where do you live?*, 3
die Wohnung, -en *apartment*, 3
das Wohnzimmer, - *living room*, 12; **im Wohnzimmer** *in the living room*, 12
der Wolf, ⸚e *wolf*, 12
   wolkig *cloudy*, 7
   wollen *to want (to)*, 6
die Wollwurst, ⸚e *(southern German sausage specialty)*, 8
das Wort, ⸚er *word*, 2
das Wörterbuch, ⸚er *dictionary*, 4
der Wortschatz *vocabulary*, 1
   worüber? *about what?*, 10; **Worüber habt ihr gesprochen?** *What did you (pl) talk about?*, 10; Worüber sprichst du mit deinen Freunden? *What do you talk about with your friends?*, 10
   wunderbar *wonderful*, 4
der Wunsch, ⸚e *wish*, 5; **Haben Sie einen Wunsch?** *May I help you?*, 5; **Haben Sie noch einen Wunsch?** *Would you like anything else*, 8
   würde *would*, 10
   würdest: du würdest *you would*, 7
der Würfel, - *cube*, 12
die Wurst, ⸚e *sausage*, 8
das Wurstbrot, -e *bologna sandwich*, 6
das Würstchen, - *sausage link*, 9

Z

   z.B.=zum Beispiel *for example*, 10
   zahlen *to pay*, 6; **Hallo! Ich möchte/will zahlen!** *The check please!*, 6

die Zahlen (pl) *numbers*, p. 9
   zart *tender*, 8
   zehn *ten*, 1
   zeichnen *to draw*, 2
die Zeichnung, -en *drawing*, 6
   zeigen *to show*, 3; den Weg zeigen *to give directions*, 9
die Zeile, -n *line*, 11
die Zeit *time*, 4; die ganze Zeit *the whole time*, 12; **Ich habe keine Zeit.** *I don't have time.*, 7
die Zeitschrift, -en *magazine*, 10
die Zeitung, -en *newspaper*, 10
das Zeug *stuff*, 4
das Zeugnis, -se *report card*, 4
das Ziel, -e *goal*, 2
   ziemlich *rather*, 4
das Zimmer, - *room*, 3; **mein Zimmer aufräumen** *to clean my room*, 7
der Zimt *cinnamon*, 12
die Zitrone, -n *lemon*, 12; **mit Zitrone** *with lemon*, 6
der Zitronensaft, ⸚e *lemon juice*, 8
der Zoo, -s *zoo*, 12; **in den Zoo gehen** *to go to the zoo*, 12
   zu *too*, 5; *to*, 7; **zu Fuß** *on foot*, 1; **zu Hause** *at home*, 3; **zu Hause helfen** *to help at home*, 7; zu Hause sein *to be at home*, 6
die Zubereitung, -en *preparation (of food)*, 8
der Zucker *sugar*, 8
   zuerst *first*, 4
der Zug, ⸚e *train*, 4
   zuhören *to listen*, p. 6
   zuletzt *last of all*, 4
   zum = zu dem *to the*, 2; zum Beispiel *for example*, 10
   zur = zu der *to the*, 1
   zurück *back*, 4
   zurückbekommen *to get back*, 4
   zurückkommen *to come back*, 12
   zusammen *together*, 2
   zusammenlegen *to fold (the wash)*, 12
   zusammentun *to join*, 11
der Zuschauer, - *viewer*, 7
die Zutaten (pl) *ingredients*, 8
   zwanzig *twenty*, 1
   zwei *two*, 1
   zweimal *twice*, 7
   zweite *second*, 4; **am zweiten... ** *on the second...*, 11
   zweiundzwanzig *twenty-two*, 3
die Zwiebel, -n *onion*, 12
   zwischen *between*, 9
   zwölf *twelve*, 1
   zynisch *cynical(ly)*, 10

ENGLISH-GERMAN VOCABULARY

This vocabulary includes all of the words in the **Wortschatz** sections of the chapters. These words are considered active—you are expected to know them and be able to use them.

Idioms are listed under the English word you would be most likely to look up. German nouns are listed with definite article and plural ending, when applicable. The number after each German word or phrase refers to the chapter in which it becomes active vocabulary. To be sure you are using the German words and phrases in the correct context, refer to the chapters in which they appear.

The following abbreviations are used in the vocabulary: sep (separable-prefix verb), pl (plural), acc (accusative), dat (dative), masc (masculine), and poss adj (possessive adjective).

A

a, an *ein(e)*, 3
about *ungefähr*, 7
action movie *der Actionfilm, -e*, 10
actor *der Schauspieler, -*, 10
actress *die Schauspielerin, -nen*, 10
adventure movie *der Abenteuerfilm, -e*, 10
after *nach*, 2; **after school** *nach der Schule*, 2; **after the break** *nach der Pause*, 4
after that *danach*, 4
afternoon *der Nachmittag, -e*, 2; **in the afternoon** *am Nachmittag*, 2
again *wieder*, 9
along: Why don't you come along! *Komm doch mit!*, 7
already *schon*, 1
also *auch*, 1; **I also need...** *ich brauche noch ...*, 8
always *immer*, 7
am: I am *ich bin*, 1
and *und*, 1
another *noch ein*, 9; **I don't want any more....** *Ich möchte kein(e)(en) ... mehr.*, 9; **I'd like another....** *Ich möchte noch ein(e)(en) ...*, 9
anything: Anything else? *Sonst noch etwas?*, 8
appear *aussehen (sep)*, 5
apple *der Apfel, ∵*, 8
apple cake *der Apfelkuchen, -*, 6
apple juice *der Apfelsaft, ∵*, 3; **a glass of apple juice** *ein Glas Apfelsaft*, 3
approximately *ungefähr*, 7
April *der April*, 7
are: you are *du bist*, 1; (formal) *Sie sind*, 1; (pl) *ihr seid*, 1; **we are** *wir sind*, 1
armchair *der Sessel, -*, 12
art *die Kunst*, 4
at: at 8 o'clock *um 8 Uhr*, 4; **at one o'clock** *um ein Uhr*, 6; **at the**

baker's *beim Bäcker*, 8; **at the butcher's** *beim Metzger*, 8; **at the produce store** *im Obst- und Gemüseladen*, 8; **at the supermarket** *im Supermarkt*, 8; **At what time?** *Um wieviel Uhr?*, 6
August *der August*, 7
aunt *die Tante -n*, 3
awesome *stark*, 5; **The sweater is awesome!** *Ich finde den Pulli stark!*, 5
awful *furchtbar*, 5

B

bad *schlecht*, 4; **badly** *schlecht*, 6; **Bad luck!** *So ein Pech!*, 4
baker *der Bäcker, -*, 8; **at the baker's** *beim Bäcker*, 8
bakery *die Bäckerei, -en*, 8
bald: to be bald *eine Glatze haben*, 3
ballpoint pen *der Kuli, -s*, 4
bank *die Bank, -en*, 9
bargain: that's a bargain *das ist preiswert*, 4
basketball *Basketball*, 2
be *sein*, 1; **I am** *ich bin*, 1; **you are** *du bist*, 1; **he/she is** *er/sie ist*, 1; **we are** *wir sind*, 1; (pl) **you are** *ihr seid*, 1; (formal) **you are** *Sie sind*, 1; **they are** *sie sind*, 1
be able to *können*, 7
be called *heißen*, 1
beautiful *schön*, 3
because *denn, weil*, 8
bed *das Bett, -en*, 3; **to make the bed** *das Bett machen*, 7
believe *glauben*, 9
belt *der Gürtel, -*, 5
best: Best wishes on your birthday! *Herzlichen Glückwunsch zum Geburtstag!*, 11
better *besser*, 8
big *groß*, 3
bike *das Fahrrad, ∵er*, 1; **by bike** *mit dem Rad*, 1

biology *Bio (die Biologie)*, 4
biology teacher (female) *die Biologielehrerin, -nen*, 1
birthday *der Geburtstag, -e*, 11; **Best wishes on your birthday!** *Herzlichen Glückwunsch zum Geburtstag!*, 11; **Happy Birthday!** *Alles Gute zum Geburtstag!*, 11; **My birthday is on....** *Ich habe am ... Geburtstag.*, 11; **When is your birthday?** *Wann hast du Geburtstag?*, 11
black *schwarz*, 3; **in black** *in Schwarz*, 5
blond *blond*, 3
blouse *die Bluse, -n*, 5
blue *blau*, 3; **blue (green, brown) eyes** *blaue (grüne, braune) Augen*, 3; **in blue** *in Blau*, 5
board game *das Brettspiel, -e*, 12
bologna sandwich *das Wurstbrot, -e*, 6
book *das Buch, ∵er*, 4
bookcase *das Regal -e*, 3
boot *der Stiefel, -*, 5
boring *langweilig*, 2
bought *gekauft*, 8; **I bought bread.** *Ich habe Brot gekauft.*, 8
bouquet of flowers *der Blumenstrauß, ∵e*, 11
boy *der Junge, -n*, 1
bread *das Brot, -e*, 8
break *die Pause, -n*, 4; **after the break** *nach der Pause*, 4
broken *kaputt*, 3
brother *der Bruder, ∵*, 3; **brothers and sisters** *die Geschwister (pl)*, 3
brown *braun*, 3; **in brown** *in Braun*, 5
brutal *brutal*, 10
bus *der Bus, -se*, 1; **by bus** *mit dem Bus*, 1
busy (telephone) *besetzt*, 11
but *aber*, 3
butcher shop *die Metzgerei, -en*, 8; **at the butcher's** *beim Metzger*, 8

butter *die Butter*, 8
buy *kaufen*, 5; **What did you buy?**
Was hast du gekauft?, 8
by: by bike *mit dem Rad*, 1; **by bus**
mit dem Bus, 1; **by car** *mit dem
Auto*, 1; **by moped** *mit dem Moped*,
1; **by subway** *mit der U-Bahn*, 1
Bye! *Wiedersehen! Tschau! Tschüs!*, 1;
(on the telephone) *Wiederhören!*, 11

C

cabinet *der Schrank, ⸚e*, 3
café *das Café, -s*, 6; **to the café** *ins
Café*, 6
cake *der Kuchen, -*, 3; **a piece of
cake** *ein Stück Kuchen*, 3
calendar *der Kalender, -*, 11
call *anrufen (sep), telefonieren*, 11
can *können*, 7
capital *die Hauptstadt, ⸚e*, 1
car *das Auto, -s*, 1; **by car** *mit dem
Auto*, 1
cards *Karten*, 2
care for *mögen*, 10
carpet *der Teppich, -e*, 12
cassette *die Kassette, -n*, 4
casual *lässig*, 5
cat *die Katze, -n*, 3; **to feed the cat**
die Katze füttern, 7
Certainly! *Natürlich!*, 11; *Sicher!*, 3
chair *der Stuhl, ⸚e*, 3
change: Keep the change! *Stimmt
(schon)!*, 6
cheap *billig*, 4
check: The check please! *Hallo! Ich
möchte/will zahlen!*, 6
cheese *der Käse, -*, 8
cheese sandwich *das Käsebrot, -e*, 6
chess *Schach*, 2
chicken *das Hähnchen, -*, 8
Christmas *das Weihnachten, -*, 11;
Merry Christmas! *Fröhliche
Weihnachten!*, 11
church *die Kirche, -n*, 9
cinammon *der Zimt*, 12
cinema *das Kino, -s*, 6
city *die Stadt, ⸚e*, 9; **in the city** *in
der Stadt*, 3
city hall *das Rathaus, ⸚er*, 9
class schedule *der Stundenplan, ⸚e*, 4
classical music *klassische Musik*, 10
clean: to clean the windows *die
Fenster putzen*, 7; **to clean up my
room** *mein Zimmer aufräumen
(sep)*, 7
clear: to clear the table *den Tisch
abräumen (sep)*, 7
clothes (casual term for) *die
Klamotten (pl)*, 5; **to pick up my
clothes** *meine Klamotten aufräumen (sep)*, 7

cloudy *wolkig*, 7
coffee *der Kaffee*, 8; **a cup of coffee**
eine Tasse Kaffee, 6
coin *die Münze, -n*, 11
cold *kalt*, 7
cold cuts *der Aufschnitt*, 8
collect *sammeln*, 2; **to collect comics**
Comics sammeln, 2, **to collect
stamps** *Briefmarken sammeln*, 2
color *die Farbe, -n*, 5
come *kommen*, 1; **I come** *ich
komme*, 1; **That comes to....** *Das
macht (zusammen) ...*, 6; **to come
along** *mitkommen (sep)*, 7
comedy *die Komödie, -n*, 10
comfortable *bequem*, 3
comics *die Comics*, 2; **to collect
comics** *Comics sammeln*, 2
compact disc *die CD, -s*, 11
concert *das Konzert, -e*, 6; **to go to a
concert** *ins Konzert gehen*, 6
cookie *der Keks, -e*, 3; **a few cookies**
ein paar Kekse, 3
cool *kühl*, 7
corners: with corners *eckig*, 12
corny *schmalzig*, 10
cost *kosten*, 4; **How much does...
cost?** *Was kostet ... ?*, 4
cotton *die Baumwolle*, 12; **made of
cotton** *aus Baumwolle*, 12
couch *die Couch, -en*, 3
country *das Land, ⸚er*, 3; **in the
country** *auf dem Land*, 3
cousin (female) *die Kusine, -n*, 3;
cousin (male) *der Cousin, -s*, 3
crime drama *der Krimi, -s*, 10
cruel *grausam*, 10

D

dance *tanzen*, 2; **to go dancing**
tanzen gehen, 6
dark blue *dunkelblau*, 5; **in dark
blue** *in Dunkelblau*, 5
day *der Tag, -e*, 1; **day before yesterday** *vorgestern*, 8; **every day**
jeden Tag, 7; **day before yesterday**
vorgestern, 8
December *der Dezember*, 7
definitely *bestimmt*, 5
degree *der Grad, -*, 7
Delicious! *Lecker!*, 6
desk *der Schreibtisch, -e*, 3
detective movie *der Krimi, -s*, 10
dial *wählen*, 11; **to dial the number**
die Nummer wählen, 11
dictionary *das Wörterbuch, ⸚er*, 4
different *verschieden*, 11
dining table *der Eßtisch, -e*, 12
directly *direkt*, 4
disagree: I disagree. *Das finde ich
nicht.*, 2

disco *die Disko, -s*, 6; **to go to a
disco** *in eine Disko gehen*, 6
dishes *das Geschirr*, 7; **to wash the
dishes** *das Geschirr spülen*, 7
dislike *nicht gern haben*, 4; **strongly
dislike** *überhaupt nicht gern*, 10
do *machen*, 2; *tun*, 7; **do crafts**
basteln, 2; **do homework** *die
Hausaufgaben machen*, 2; **Do you
have any other interests?** *Hast
du andere Interessen?*, 2; **Do you
need help?** *Brauchst du Hilfe?*, 7;
Do you play an instrument?
Spielst du ein Instrument?, 2; **Do
you play sports?** *Machst du
Sport?*, 2; **Do you think so?**
Meinst du?, 5; **Does it taste good?**
Schmeckt's?, 6; **What did you do
on the weekend?** *Was hast du am
Wochenende gemacht?*, 10
dog *der Hund, -e*, 3
done *gemacht*, 10
downtown *die Innenstadt*, 9; **to go
downtown** *in die Stadt gehen*, 6
draw *zeichnen*, 2
dress *das Kleid, -er*, 5
drink *trinken*, 3
drive *fahren*, 9; **he/she drives** *er/sie
fährt*, 9
dry *trocken*, 7
dumb *blöd*, 2; *doof, dumm*, 10

E

Easter *das Ostern, -*, 11; **Happy
Easter!** *Frohe Ostern!*, 11
easy *einfach*, 1; **That's easy!** *Also,
einfach!*, 1
eat *essen*, 3; **he/she eats** *er/sie ißt*,
6; **to eat ice cream** *ein Eis essen*, 6
egg *das Ei, -er*, 8
ehrlich *honestly*, 5
eight *acht*, 1
eighteen *achtzehn*, 1
eighty *achtzig*, 3
eleven *elf*, 1
enough *genug*, 9
environment *die Umwelt*, 10
eraser *der Radiergummi, -s*, 4
especially *besonders*, 6; **especially
like** *besonders gern*, 10
evening *der Abend*, 1; **in the
evening** *am Abend*, 2
every: every day *jeden Tag*, 7
exciting *spannend*, 10
Excuse me! *Entschuldigung!,
Verzeihung!*, 9
expensive *teuer*, 4
eye *das Auge, -n*, 3; **blue (green,
brown) eyes** *blaue (grüne,
braune) Augen*, 3

F

fall *der Herbst*, 2; **in the fall** *im Herbst*, 2
family *die Familie*, *-n*, 3
fancy chocolate *die Praline*, *-n*, 11
fantasy novel *der Fantasyroman*, *-e*, 10
far *weit*, 3; **far from here** *weit von hier*, 3
fashion *die Mode*, 10
father *der Vater*, ∻, 3; **to, for your father** *deinem Vater*, 11; **to, for my father** *meinem Vater*, 11
Father's Day *der Vatertag*, 11; **Happy Father's Day!** *Alles Gute zum Vatertag!*, 11
favorite *Lieblings-*, 4
February *der Februar*, 7
feed *füttern*, 7; **to feed the cat** *die Katze füttern*, 7
fetch *holen*, 8
few: a few *ein paar*, 3; **a few cookies** *ein paar Kekse*, 3
fifteen *fünfzehn*, 1
fifty *fünfzig*, 3
five *fünf*, 1
first *erst-*, 11; **first of all** *zuerst*, 4; **on the first of July** *am ersten Juli*, 11; **the first street** *die erste Straße*, 9
fit *passen*, 5; **The skirt fits great!** *Der Rock paßt prima!*, 5
flower *die Blume*, *-n*, 7; **to water the flowers** *die Blumen gießen*, 7
foot: on foot (I walk) *zu Fuß*, 1
for *für*, 7; *denn* (conj), 8
forty *vierzig*, 3
four *vier*, 1
fourteen *vierzehn*, 1
for whom? *für wen?*, 8
free time *die Freizeit*, 2
fresh *frisch*, 8
fresh produce store *der Obst- und Gemüseladen*, ∻, 8
Friday *der Freitag*, 4
friend (male) *der Freund*, *-e*, 1; **(female)** *die Freundin*, *-nen*, 1; **to visit friends** *Freunde besuchen*, 2
from *aus*, 1; *von*, 4; **from 8 until 8:45** *von 8 Uhr bis 8 Uhr 45*, 4
from where? *woher?*, 1; **I'm from** *ich bin (komme) aus*, 1; **Where are you from?** *Woher bist (kommst) du?*, 1
front: there in the front *da vorn*, 4
fruit *das Obst*, 8; **a piece of fruit** *Obst*, 3
fun *der Spaß*, 2; **(Tennis) is fun.** *(Tennis) macht Spaß.*, 2; **(Tennis) is no fun.** *(Tennis) macht keinen Spaß.*, 2
funny *lustig*, 10
furniture *die Möbel* (pl), 3

G

garden(s) *der Garten*, ∻, 9
geography *die Erdkunde*, 4
German mark (German monetary unit) *DM = Deutsche Mark*, 4
German teacher (male) *der Deutschlehrer*, *-*, 1; **(female)** *die Deutschlehrerin*, *-nen*, 1
get *bekommen*, 4; *holen*, 8
gift *das Geschenk*, *-e*, 11
gift idea *die Geschenkidee*, *-n*, 11
girl *das Mädchen*, *-*, 1
give *geben*, 11; **he/she gives** *er/sie gibt*, 11
give (a gift) *schenken*, 11
glass *das Glas*, ∻er, 3; **a glass (cup) of tea** *ein Glas Tee*, 6; **a glass of (mineral) water** *ein Glas (Mineral)Wasser*, 3; **a glass of apple juice** *ein Glas Apfelsaft*, 3
glasses: a pair of glasses *eine Brille*, *-n*, 3
go *gehen*, 2; **to go home** *nach Hause gehen*, 3
golf *Golf*, 2
good *gut*, 4; **Good!** *Gut!*, 6
Good morning! *Guten Morgen! Morgen!*, 1
Goodbye! *Auf Wiedersehen!*, 1; **(on the telephone)** *Auf Wiederhören*, 11
grade *die Note*, *-n*, 4
grade level *die Klasse*, *-n*, 4
grades: a 1, 2, 3, 4, 5, 6 *eine Eins, Zwei, Drei, Vier, Fünf, Sechs*, 4
gram *das Gramm*, *-*, 8
grandfather *der Großvater (Opa)*, ∻, 3
grandmother *die Großmutter (Oma)*, ∻, 3
grandparents *die Großeltern* (pl), 3
grape *die Traube*, *-n*, 8
gray *grau*, 3; **in gray** *in Grau*, 5
Great! *Prima!*, 1; *Sagenhaft!*, 6; *Klasse! Toll!*, 2
green *grün*, 3; **in green** *in Grün*, 5
groceries *die Lebensmittel* (pl), 8
ground meat *das Hackfleisch*, 8
group *die Gruppe*, *-n*, 10
guitar *die Gitarre*, *-n*, 2
gyros *das Gyros*, *-*, 9

H

hair *die Haare* (pl), 3
half *halb*, 6; **half past (twelve, one, etc.)** *halb (eins, zwei, usw.)*, 6
hang up (the telephone) *auflegen* (sep), 11

Hanukkah *Chanukka*, 11; **Happy Hanukkah!** *Frohes Chanukka Fest!*, 11
have *haben*, 4; **he/she has English** *er/sie hat Englisch*, 4; **I have German.** *Ich habe Deutsch.*, 4; **I have no classes on Saturday.** *Am Samstag habe ich frei.*, 4; **I'll have...** *Ich bekomme ...*, 6
have to *müssen*, 7; **I have to** *ich muß*, 7
he *er*, 2; **he is** *er ist*, 1; **he's from** *er ist (kommt) aus*, 1
hear *hören*, 2
Hello! *Guten Tag! Tag! Hallo! Grüß dich!*, 1
help *helfen*, 7; **to help at home** *zu Hause helfen*, 7
her *ihr* (poss adj), 3; **her name is** *sie heißt*, 1
hideous *scheußlich*, 5
hike *wandern*, 2
him *ihn*, 5
his *sein* (poss adj), 3; **his name is** *er heißt*, 1
history *die Geschichte*, 4
hobby book *das Hobbybuch*, ∻er, 10
holiday *der Feiertag*, *-e*, 11
homework *die Hausaufgabe*, *-n*, 2; **to do homework** *Hausaufgaben machen*, 2
horror movie *der Horrorfilm*, *-e*, 10
horror novel *der Gruselroman*, *-e*, 10
hot *heiß*, 7
hotel *das Hotel*, *-s*, 9
how much? *wieviel?*, 8; **How much does. . . cost?** *Was kostet ... ?*, 4
how often? *wie oft?*, 7
how? *wie?*, 1; **How are you?** *Wie geht's (denn)?*, 6; **How do I get to...?** *Wie komme ich zum (zur) ... ?*, 9; **How do you get to school?** *Wie kommst du zur Schule?*, 1; **How does it taste?** *Wie schmeckt's?*, 6; **How old are you?** *Wie alt bist du?*, 1; **How's the weather?** *Wie ist das Wetter?*, 7
hunger *der Hunger*, 9
hungry: I'm hungry. *Ich habe Hunger.*, 9; **I'm not hungry any more.** *Ich habe keinen Hunger mehr.*, 9

I

I *ich*, 2; **I don't.** *Ich nicht.*, 2
ice *das Eis*, 7
ice cream *das Eis*, 6; **a dish of ice cream** *ein Eisbecher*, 6
ice skate *Schlittschuh laufen*, 12
idea: I have no idea! *Keine Ahnung!*, 9
imaginative *phantasievoll*, 10

in *in*, 2; **in the afternoon** *am Nachmittag*, 2; **in the city** *in der Stadt*, 3; **in the country** *auf dem Land*, 3; **in the evening** *am Abend*, 2; **in the fall** *im Herbst*, 2; **in the kitchen** *in der Küche*, 12; **in the living room** *im Wohnzimmer*, 12; **in the spring** *im Frühling*, 2; **in the summer** *im Sommer*, 2; **in the winter** *im Winter*, 2

insert *einstecken*, 11; **to insert coins** *Münzen einstecken* (sep), 11

instrument *das Instrument, -e*, 2; **Do you play an instrument?** *Spielst du ein Instrument?*, 2

interesting *interessant*, 2

interest *das Interesse, -n*, 2; **Do you have any other interests?** *Hast du andere Interessen?*, 2

invite *einladen* (sep), 11; **he/she invites** *er/sie lädt ... ein*, 11

is: he/she is *er/sie ist*, 1

it *er, es, sie*, 3; *ihn*, 5

J

jacket *die Jacke, -n*, 5

January *der Januar*, 7; **in January** *im Januar*, 7

jeans *die Jeans, -*, 5

jewelry *der Schmuck*, 11

jog *joggen*, 12

jogging suit *der Jogging-Anzug, ⸚e*, 5

juice *der Saft, ⸚e*, 3

July *der Juli*, 7

June *der Juni*, 7

just: Just a minute, please. *Einen Moment, bitte.*, 11

K

keep: Keep the change! *Stimmt (schon)!*, 6

kilogram *das Kilo, -*, 8

kitchen *die Küche, -n*, 12; **in the kitchen** *in der Küche*, 12

know (a fact, information, etc.) *wissen*, 9; **I don't know.** *Ich weiß nicht.*, 5

know (be familiar or acquainted with) *kennen*, 10

L

lamp *die Lampe, -n*, 12

last *letzt-*, 8; **last of all** *zuletzt*, 4; **last week** *letzte Woche*, 8; **last weekend** *letztes Wochenende*, 8

Latin *Latein*, 4

lawn *der Rasen, -*, 7; **to mow the lawn** *den Rasen mähen*, 7

layer cake *die Torte, -n*, 8

---

leather *das Leder*, 12; **made of leather** *aus Leder*, 12

left: to the left *nach links*, 9

lemon *die Zitrone, -n*, 12

lemon drink *die Limo, -s*, 3

lettuce *der Salat*, 8

light blue *hellblau*, 5; **in light blue** *in Hellblau*, 5

like *gern haben*, 4; *mögen*, 10; **I like it.** *Er/Sie/Es gefällt mir.*, 5 **I like them.** *Sie gefallen mir.*, 5; **like an awful lot** *furchtbar gern*, 10; **not like at all** *gar nicht gern*, 10; **not like very much** *nicht so gern*, 5

like (to do) *gern (machen)*, 2; **to not like (to do)** *nicht gern (machen)*, 2

listen (to) *hören*, 2; *zuhören*, p. 6

liter *der Liter, -*, 8

little *klein*, 3; **a little** *ein bißchen*, 5; **a little more** *ein bißchen mehr*, 8

live *wohnen*, 3

living room: in the living room *im Wohnzimmer*, 12

long *lang*, 3

look *schauen*, 2; **Look!** *Schauen Sie!*, 4

look for *suchen*, 5; **I'm looking for** *ich suche*, 5

look like *aussehen* (sep), 5; **he/she looks like** *er/sie sieht ... aus*, 5; **The skirt looks....** *Der Rock sieht ... aus.*, 5; **What do they look like?** *Wie sehen sie aus?*, 3; **What does he look like?** *Wie sieht er aus?*, 3

lot: a lot *viel*, 2

luck: Bad luck! *So ein Pech!*, 4; **What luck!** *So ein Glück!*, 4

M

made: made of cotton *aus Baumwolle*, 12; **made of leather** *aus Leder*, 12; **made of plastic** *aus Kunststoff*, 12; **made of silk** *aus Seide*, 12; **made of wood** *aus Holz*, 12

magazine *die Zeitschrift, -en*, 10

make *machen*, 2; **to make the bed** *das Bett machen*, 7

man *der Mann, ⸚er*, 3

many *viele*, 2

March *der März*, 7

mark *die Mark, -*, 4

market square *der Marktplatz, ⸚e*, 9

math *Mathe (die Mathematik)*, 4

may: May I help you? *Haben Sie einen Wunsch?*, 5

May *der Mai*, 7

maybe *vielleicht*, 11

me *mich*, 7; **Me too.** *Ich auch.*, 2

meat *das Fleisch*, 8

mess: What a mess! *So ein Mist!*, 4

---

milk *die Milch*, 8

mineral water *das Mineralwasser*, 3

minute: Just a minute, please. *Einen Moment, bitte.*, 11

miserable *miserabel*, 6

modern *modern*, 12

moment *der Moment, -e*, 3

money *das Geld*, 4

month *der Monat, -e*, 7

moped *das Moped, -s*, 2; **by moped** *mit dem Moped*, 1

more *mehr*, 9

morning *der Morgen*, 1; **Morning!** *Morgen!*, 1

most of all *am liebsten*, 10

mother *die Mutter, ⸚*, 3

Mother's Day *der Muttertag*, 11; **Happy Mother's Day!** *Alles Gute zum Muttertag!*, 11

movie *der Film, -e*, 10; **to go to the movies** *ins Kino gehen*, 6

movie theater *das Kino, -s*, 6

mow *mähen*, 7; **to mow the lawn** *den Rasen mähen*, 7

Mr. *Herr*, 1

Mrs. *Frau*, 1

much *viel*, 2; **much too** *viel zu*, 5

museum *das Museum, die Museen*, 9

music *die Musik*, 2; **to listen to music** *Musik hören*, 2

mustard *der Senf*, 6; **with mustard** *mit Senf*, 6

my *mein*, 3; **my name is** *ich heiße*, 1; **to, for my father** *meinem Vater*, 11 **to, for my mother** *meiner Mutter*, 11

N

name *der Name, -n*, 1; **her name is** *sie heißt*, 1; **his name is** *er heißt*, 1; **my name is** *ich heiße*, 1; **What's the boy's name?** *Wie heißt der Junge?*, 1; **What's the girl's name?** *Wie heißt das Mädchen?*, 1; **What's your name?** *Wie heißt du?*, 1

nearby *in der Nähe*, 3

need *brauchen*, 5; **I need** *ich brauche*, 5

never *nie*, 7

new *neu*, 3

newspaper *die Zeitung, -en*, 10

next: the next street *die nächste Straße*, 9

nine *neun*, 1

nineteen *neunzehn*, 1

ninety *neunzig*, 3

no *kein*, 9; **No more, thanks!** *Nichts mehr, danke!*, 9

non-fiction book *das Sachbuch, ⸚er*, 10

none *kein*, 9

noodle soup *die Nudelsuppe, -n*, 6
not *nicht*, 2; **not at all** *überhaupt nicht*, 5; **not like at all** *gar nicht gern*, 10; **Not really.** *Nicht besonders.*, 6; **Not too long?** *Nicht zu lang?*, 5
not any *kein*, 9
notebook *das Notizbuch*, 1; *das Heft, -e*, 4
nothing *nichts*, 3; **nothing at the moment** *im Moment gar nichts*, 3; **Nothing, thank you!** *Nichts, danke!*, 3
novel *der Roman, -e*, 10
November *der November*, 7
now *jetzt*, 1; *nun*, 6
number *die (Telefon)nummer*, 11; **to dial the number** *die Nummer wählen*, 11

O

o'clock: **at 8 o'clock** *um 8 Uhr*, 4; **at one o'clock** *um ein Uhr*, 6
October *der Oktober*, 7
Of course! *Ja klar!*, 1; *Ganz klar!*, 4
often *oft*, 2
Oh! *Ach!*, 1; **Oh yeah!** *Ach ja!*, 1
oil *das Öl*, 12
Okay! I'll do that! *Gut! Mach' ich!*, 7; **It's okay.** *Es geht.*, 6
old *alt*, 3; **How old are you?** *Wie alt bist du?*, 1
on: **on ... Square** *am ...platz*, 9; **on ... Street** *in der ...straße*, 3; **on foot (I walk)** *zu Fuß*, 1; **on Monday** *am Montag*, 4; **on the first of July** *am ersten Juli*, 11; **on the weekend** *am Wochenende*, 2
once *einmal*, 7; *mal*, 9; **once a month** *einmal im Monat*, 7; **once a week** *einmal in der Woche*, 7
one *eins*, 1
one hundred *hundert*, 3
onion *die Zwiebel, -n*, 12
only *bloß, nur*, 1
opera *die Oper, -n*, 10
orange juice *der Orangensaft, ⁒e*, 3
other *andere*, 2
oven *der Ofen, ⁒*, 12
over there *dort drüben*, 4; **over there in the back** *da hinten*, 4
overcast *trüb*, 7

P

pants *die Hose, -n*, 5
parents *die Eltern* (pl), 3
park *der Park, -s*, 12; **to go to the park** *in den Park gehen*, 12
pencil *der Bleistift, -e*, 4

people *die Leute* (pl), 9
perfume *das Parfüm*, -, 11
pet *das Haustier, -e*, 3
physical education *der Sport*, 4
piano *das Klavier, -e*, 2; **I play the piano** *Ich spiele Klavier.*, 2
pick up *aufräumen* (sep), 7; **to pick up my clothes** *meine Klamotten aufräumen*, 7; **to pick up the telephone** *abheben* (sep), 11
piece *das Stück, -e*, 3; **a piece of cake** *ein Stück Kuchen*, 3; **a piece of fruit** *Obst*, 3
pizza *die Pizza, -s*, 6
plastic *der Kunststoff, -e*, 12; **made of plastic** *aus Kunststoff*, 12
play *spielen*, 2; **I play soccer.** *Ich spiele Fußball.*, 2; **I play the piano.** *Ich spiele Klavier.*, 2; **to play a board game** *ein Brettspiel spielen*, 12
please *bitte*, 3
pleasure: **My pleasure!** *Gern geschehen!*, 9
pocket calculator *der Taschenrechner, -*, 4
politics *die Politik*, 10
polka-dot *gepunktet*, 12
post office *die Post*, 9
poster *das Poster, -*, 11
potato *die Kartoffel, -n*, 8
pound *das Pfund, -*, 8
prefer *lieber (mögen)*, 10
pretty *hübsch*, 5; *schön*, 3
pretzel *die Brezel, -n*, 8
probably *wahrscheinlich*, 11
produce store *der Obst- und Gemüseladen, ⁒*, 8; **at the produce store** *im Obst- und Gemüseladen*, 8
Pullover *der Pulli, -s*, 5
put on *anziehen* (sep), 5

Q

quarter: **a quarter after** *Viertel nach*, 6; **a quarter to** *Viertel vor*, 6

R

railroad station *der Bahnhof, ⁒e*, 9
rain *der Regen*, 7; **It's raining** *Es regnet.*, 7
rainy *regnerisch*, 7
rather *ziemlich*, 4
read *lesen*, 10; **he/she reads** *er/sie liest*, 10; **What did you read?** *Was hast du gelesen?*, 10
really *ganz*, 3; *echt*, 5; **Not really.** *Nicht besonders.*, 6
receive *bekommen*, 4
receiver *der Hörer, -*, 11
red *rot*, 3; **in red** *in Rot*, 5

refrigerator *der Kühlschrank, ⁒e*, 12
religion *die Religion, -en*, 4
residence: **The ... residence** *Hier bei ...*, 11
right: **to the right** *nach rechts*, 9
roll *die Semmel, -n*, 8
romance *der Liebesfilm, -e*, 10; **romance novel** *der Liebesroman, -e*, 10
room *das Zimmer, -*, 3; **to clean up my room** *mein Zimmer aufräumen* (sep), 7
round *rund*, 12

S

sad *traurig*, 10
salt *das Salz*, 12
Saturday *der Samstag*, 4
sausage *die Wurst, ⁒e*, 8
say *sagen*, 1; **Say!** *Sag mal!*, 2; **What does the weather report say?** *Was sagt der Wetterbericht?*, 7
school *die Schule, -n*, 4; **after school** *nach der Schule*, 2; **How do you get to school?** *Wie kommst du zur Schule?*, 1
school subject *das Fach, ⁒er*, 4
school supplies *die Schulsachen* (pl), 4
schoolbag *die Schultasche, -n*, 4
science fiction movie *der Science-fiction-Film, -e*, 10
search (for) *suchen*, 4
second *zweit-*, 11; **the second street** *die zweite Straße*, 9
see *sehen*, 10; **he/she sees** *er/sie sieht*, 10; **See you later!** *Bis dann!*, 1; **to see a movie** *einen Film sehen*, 6; **What did you see?** *Was hast du gesehen?*, 10
sensational *sensationell*, 10
September *der September*, 7
set *decken*, 7; **to set the table** *den Tisch decken*, 7
seven *sieben*, 1
seventeen *siebzehn*, 1
seventy *siebzig*, 3
she *sie*, 2; **she is** *sie ist*, 1; **she's from** *sie ist (kommt) aus*, 1
shine: **the sun is shining** *die Sonne scheint*, 7
shirt *das Hemd, -en*, 5
shop *einkaufen* (sep), 8; **to go shopping** *einkaufen gehen*, 8
short *kurz*, 3
shortening *das Butterschmalz*, 12
shorts: **pair of shorts** *die Shorts, -*, 5
should *sollen*, 8
silk *die Seide*, 12; **made of silk** *aus Seide*, 12

singer (female) *die Sängerin, -nen*, 10

singer (male) *der Sänger, -*, 10

sink *das Spülbecken, -*, 12

sister *die Schwester, -n*, 3; **brothers and sisters** *die Geschwister* (pl), 3

six *sechs*, 1

sixteen *sechzehn*, 1

sixty *sechzig*, 3

size *die Größe, -n*, 5

skirt *der Rock, ⸚e*, 5

small *klein*, 3

smart (looking) *fesch, schick, chic*, 5

snack bar *die Imbißstube, -n*, 9

sneaker *der Turnschuh, -e*, 5

snow *der Schnee*, 7; **It's snowing** *Es schneit.*, 7

so *so*, 2; **So long!** *Tschau! Tschüs!*, 1; **so so** *so lala*, 6

soccer *der Fußball*, 2; **I play soccer.** *Ich spiele Fußball.*, 2

sock *die Socke, -n*, 5

soda: **lemon-flavored soda** *die Limo, -s (die Limonade, -n)*, 3

sofa *das Sofa, -s*, 12

something *etwas*, 7

sometimes *manchmal*, 7

song *das Lied, -er*, 10

sorry: **I'm sorry.** *Es tut mir leid.*, 9; **Sorry, I can't.** *Ich kann leider nicht.*, 7

sort *sortieren*, 7; **to sort the trash** *den Müll sortieren*, 7

spend (time) *verbringen*, 10

sports *der Sport*, 2; **Do you play sports?** *Machst du Sport?*, 2

spring *der Frühling*, 2; **in the spring** *im Frühling*, 2

square *der Platz, ⸚e*, 9; **on ... Square** *am ...platz*, 9

stamp *die Briefmarke, -n*, 2; **to collect stamps** *Briefmarken sammeln*, 2

state: **German federal state** *das Bundesland, ⸚er*, 1

stereo *die Stereoanlage -n*, 3

stinks: **That stinks!** *So ein Mist!*, 4

store *der Laden, ⸚*, 8

storm *das Gewitter, -*, 7

stove *der Herd, -e*, 12

straight ahead *geradeaus*, 9

street *die Straße, -n*, 9; **on ... Street** *in der ...straße*, 3

striped *gestreift*, 12

stupid *blöd*, 5

subject (school) *das Fach, ⸚er*, 4; **Which subjects do you have?** *Welche Fächer hast du?*, 4

suburb *der Vorort, -e*, 3; **a suburb of** *ein Vorort von*, 3

subway *die U-Bahn*, 1; **by subway** *mit der U-Bahn*, 1

subway station *die U-Bahnstation, -en*, 9

sugar *der Zucker*, 8

summer *der Sommer*, 2; **in the summer** *im Sommer*, 2

sun *die Sonne*, 7; **the sun is shining** *die Sonne scheint*, 7

Sunday *der Sonntag*, 4

sunny *sonnig*, 7

Super! *Spitze!, Super!*, 2

supermarket *der Supermarkt, ⸚e*, 8; **at the supermarket** *im Supermarkt*, 8

supposed to *sollen*, 8

sure: **I'm not sure.** *Ich bin nicht sicher.*, 5

sweater *der Pulli, -s*, 5

swim *schwimmen*, 2; **to go swimming** *baden gehen*, 6

swimming pool *das Schwimmbad, ⸚er*, 6; **to go to the (swimming) pool** *ins Schwimmbad gehen*, 6

T

T-shirt *das T-Shirt, -s*, 5

table *der Tisch, -e*, 12; **to clear the table** *den Tisch abräumen* (sep), 7; **to set the table** *den Tisch decken*, 7

take *nehmen*, 5; **he/she takes** *er/sie nimmt*, 5; **I'll take** *ich nehme*, 5

talk about *sprechen über*, 10; **he/she talks about** *er/sie spricht über*, 10 **What did you (pl) talk about?** *Worüber habt ihr gesprochen?*, 10

taste *schmecken*, 6; **Does it taste good?** *Schmeckt's?*, 6; **How does it taste?** *Wie schmeckt's?*, 6

Tasty! *Lecker!*, 6

tea *der Tee*, 6; **a glass (cup) of tea** *ein Glas Tee*, 6

teacher (male) *der Lehrer, -*, 1; (female) *die Lehrerin, -nen*, 1

telephone *das Telefon, -e, der Apparat, -e*, 11; **pick up the telephone** *abheben* (sep), 11

telephone booth *die Telefonzelle, -n*, 11

telephone number *die Telefonnummer, -n*, 11

television *das Fernsehen*, 2; **to watch TV** *Fernsehen schauen*, 2

temperature: **What's the temperature?** *Wieviel Grad haben wir?*, 7

ten *zehn*, 1

tennis *Tennis*, 2

terrible *furchtbar*, 5

terrific *Klasse, prima, toll*, 2

thank *danken*, 3; **Thank you (very much)!** *Danke (sehr, schön)!*, 3; *Vielen Dank!*, 9; **Thank you!** *Danke!*, 3

that *daß* (conj), 9; **That's all.** *Das ist alles.*, 8; **That's...** *Das ist ...*, 1

the *das, der, die*, 1; *den* (masc, acc), 5; *dem* (masc, neuter, dat), 11

theater *das Theater, -*, 9

then *dann*, 4

there *dort*, 4

they *sie*, 2; **they are** *sie sind*, 1; **they're from** *sie sind (kommen) aus*, 1

think: **Do you think so?** *Meinst du?*, 5; **I think** *ich glaube*, 2; **I think (tennis) is...** *Ich finde (Tennis) ...*, 2; **I think so too.** *Das finde ich auch.*, 2; **I think it's good/bad that....** *Ich finde es gut/schlecht, daß ...*, 9; **I think that...** *Ich finde, daß ...*, 9 **What do you think of (tennis)?** *Wie findest du (Tennis)?*, 2

third *dritte*, 9

thirteen *dreizehn*, 1

thirty *dreißig*, 1

this: **this afternoon** *heute nachmittag*, 8; **This is...** *Hier ist ...* (on the telephone), 11; **this morning** *heute morgen*, 8

three *drei*, 1

three times *dreimal*, 7

thrilling *spannend*, 10

Thursday *der Donnerstag*, 4

tight *eng*, 5

till: **ten till two** *zehn vor zwei*, 6

time *die Zeit*, 4; **At what time?** *Um wieviel Uhr?*, 6; **I don't have time.** *Ich habe keine Zeit.*, 7; **What time is it?** *Wie spät ist es?, Wieviel Uhr ist es?*, 6

to, for her *ihr*, 11

to, for him *ihm*, 11

today *heute*, 7

tomato *die Tomate, -n*, 8

tomorrow *morgen*, 7

tonight *heute abend*, 7

too *zu*, 5; **Too bad!** *Schade!*, 4

tour *besichtigen*, 12; **to tour the city** *die Stadt besichtigen*, 12

train station *der Bahnhof, ⸚e*, 9

trash *der Müll*, 7; **to sort the trash** *den Müll sortieren*, 7

true: **Not true!** *Stimmt nicht!*, 2; **That's right! True!** *Stimmt!*, 2

try *probieren*, 9

try on *anprobieren* (sep), 5

Tuesday *der Dienstag*, 4

twelve *zwölf*, 1

twenty *zwanzig*, 1

twenty-one *einundzwanzig*, 3; (see p. 79 for numbers 21-29)

twice *zweimal*, 7

two *zwei*, 1

U

ugly *häßlich*, 3
uncle *der Onkel*, -, 3
uncomfortable *unbequem*, 3
unfortunately *leider*, 7; Unfortunately I can't. *Leider kann ich
   nicht.*, 7
until: from 8 until 8:45 *von 8 Uhr
   bis 8 Uhr 45*, 4; until you get to ...
   Square *bis zum ...platz*, 9; until
   you get to ... Street *bis zur
   ...straße*, 9; until you get to the
   traffic light *bis zur Ampel*, 9
us *uns*, 7

V

vacuum *Staub saugen*, 7
vegetables *das Gemüse*, 8
very *sehr*, 2; Very well! *Sehr gut!*, 6
video cassette *das Video*, -s, 10
violent *brutal*, 10
visit *besuchen*, 2; to visit friends
   Freunde besuchen, 2
volleyball *Volleyball*, 2

W

want (to) *wollen*, 6
war movie *der Kriegsfilm*, -e, 10
warm *warm*, 7
was: I was *ich war*, 8; I was at the
   baker's. *Ich war beim Bäcker.*, 8;
   he/she was *er/sie war*, 8
wash *spülen*, 7; to wash the dishes
   das Geschirr spülen, 7
watch *schauen*, 2; to watch TV
   Fernsehen schauen, 2; Watch out!
   Paß auf! 6
water: to water the flowers *die
   Blumen gießen*, 7
water *das Wasser*, 3; a glass of
   (mineral) water *ein Glas
   (Mineral)Wasser*, 3
we *wir*, 2
wear *anziehen* (sep), 5

weather *das Wetter*, 7; How's the
   weather? *Wie ist das Wetter?*, 7;
   What does the weather report say?
   Was sagt der Wetterbericht?, 7
Wednesday *der Mittwoch*, 4
week *die Woche*, -n, 7
weekend *das Wochenende*, -n, 2; on
   the weekend *am Wochenende*, 2
weigh *wiegen*, 8
were: Where were you? *Wo warst
   du?*, 8; we were *wir waren*, 8;
   they were *sie waren*, 8; (pl) you
   were *ihr wart*, 8; (formal) you
   were *Sie waren*, 8
western (movie) *der Western*, -, 10
wet *naß*, 7
what? *was?*, 2; What can I do for
   you? *Was kann ich für dich tun?*,
   7; What else? *Noch etwas?*, 9
what kind of? *was für?*, 10; What
   kind of movies do you like? *Was
   für Filme magst du gern?*, 10; What
   kind of music do you like? *Was
   für Musik hörst du gern?*, 10; What
   will you have? *Was bekommen
   Sie?*, 6
when? *wann?*, 2
where? *wo?*, 1; Where are you
   from? *Woher bist (kommst) du?*, 1
where (to)? *wohin?*, 6
which *welch-*, 4
white *weiß*, 3; in white *in Weiß*, 5
who? *wer?*, 1; Who is that? *Wer ist
   das?*, 1
whole grain roll *die Vollkornsemmel*,
   -n, 9
whom *wen*, 7; *wem*, 11
why? *warum?*, 8; Why don't you
   come along! *Komm doch mit!*, 7
wide *weit*, 5
window *das Fenster*, -, 7; to clean
   the windows *die Fenster putzen*, 7
winter *der Winter*, 2; in the winter
   im Winter, 2

with *mit*, 6; with bread *mit Brot*, 6;
   with corners *eckig*, 12; with
   lemon *mit Zitrone*, 6; with mustard *mit Senf*, 9
woman *die Frau*, -en, 3
wood: made of wood *aus Holz*, 12
work: That won't work. *Das geht
   nicht.*, 7
would like (to) *möchten*, 3; I would
   like to see.... *Ich möchte ... sehen.*,
   5; What would you like to eat?
   Was möchtest du essen?, 3; What
   would you like? *Was bekommen
   Sie?*, 5; Would you like anything
   else? *Haben Sie noch einen
   Wunsch?*, 8
wristwatch *die Armbanduhr*, -en, 11
write *schreiben*, 2

Y

year *das Jahr*, -e, 1; I am...years old.
   Ich bin ... Jahre alt., 1
yellow *gelb*, 5; in yellow *in Gelb*, 5
yes *ja*, 1; Yes? *Bitte?*, 5
yesterday *gestern*, 8; yesterday
   evening *gestern abend*, 8; the day
   before yesterday *vorgestern*, 8
you *du*, 2; you are *du bist*, 1; (pl)
   you are *ihr seid*, 1; (formal) you
   are *Sie sind*, 1
you (formal) *Sie*, 2
you (plural) *ihr*, 2
you (pl, acc pronoun) *euch*, 7
you (acc pronoun) *dich*, 7
you're (very) welcome! *Bitte (sehr,
   schön)!*, 3
your *dein*, 3; to, for your father
   deinem Vater, 11; to, for your
   mother *deiner Mutter*, 11

Z

zoo *der Zoo*, -s, 12; to go to the zoo
   in den Zoo gehen, 12

GRAMMAR INDEX

NOTE: For a summary of the grammar presented in this book see pages 326–336.

ABBREVIATIONS

acc	*accusative*	dir obj	*direct object*	prep	*preposition*
comm	*command*	indir obj	*indirect object*	pres	*present*
conv past	*conversational past*	inf	*infinitive*	pron	*pronoun(s)*
dat	*dative*	interr	*interrogative*	ques	*question(s)*
def	*definition*	nom	*nominative*	sep pref	*separable prefix*
def art	*definite article*	pers	*person*	sing	*singular*
indef art	*indefinite article*	plur	*plural*	subj	*subject*

A

accusative case: def art, p. 123; indef art, p. 123; p. 230; third pers pron, sing, p. 128; third pers pron, plur, p. 180; first and second pers pron, p. 180; following **für**, p. 180; p. 297; following **es gibt**, p. 229

article: *see* definite article, indefinite articles

anziehen: pres tense forms of, p. 131

aussehen: pres tense forms of, p. 132

C

case: *see* nominative case, accusative case, dative case

class: def, p. 24

command forms: **du**-commands, p. 200; p. 297; **Sie**-commands, p. 227

conjunctions: **denn** and **weil**, p. 206; **daß**, p. 232

D

dative case: introduction to, p. 283; following **mit**, p. 283; word order with, p. 284; *see also* indirect objects

definite article: to identify class, p. 24; p. 74; acc, p. 123; dat, p. 283

direct object: def, p. 123; *see also* accusative case

direct object pronouns: p. 128; p. 180

du-commands: p. 200; p. 297

E

ein: nom, p. 72; acc, p. 123; p. 230

ein-words: **mein(e)**, **dein(e)**, p. 78; acc, p. 230; **kein**, p. 231; dat, p. 283

es gibt: p. 229

essen: pres tense forms of, p. 155

F

fahren: pres tense forms of, p. 227

für: prep followed by acc, p. 180; p. 297

formal form of address, p. 50

future: use of **morgen** and present tense for, p. 183

G

gefallen: p. 125; p. 132

H

haben: pres tense forms, p. 100

I

indefinite articles: **ein**, nom, p. 72; acc, p. 123; p. 230

indirect object: def, p. 283; *see also* dative case

indirect object pronouns: p. 283

infinitive: use with **wollen**, p. 150; use with **müssen**, p. 175; in final position following modals, p. 302

interrogative pronouns: nom form **wer**, p. 23; acc form **wen**, p. 180; dat form **wem**, p. 283

interrogatives: **wo, woher, wie**, p. 23; **was**, p. 48; **worüber**, p. 259

K

kein: p. 231; p. 307

können: pres tense of, p. 179; p. 297

L

lesen: pres tense forms of, p. 259

Lieblings-: p. 102

M

möchte-forms: pres tense, p. 71; p. 155; p. 308

modal auxiliary verbs: **möchte**-forms, p. 71; **wollen**, p. 150; **müssen**, p. 175; **können**, p. 179; **sollen**, p. 199; **mögen**, p. 250

mögen: pres tense forms of, p. 250

müssen: pres tense forms of, p. 175; p. 302

ACKNOWLEDGMENTS [continued from page ii]

Hilton Hotel: Advertisement, "Kulinarische Highlights Im München City Hilton."

Immobilien: Advertisement, "Immobilien T. Kurcz," from *Südwest Presse: Schwäbisches Tagblatt,* July 14, 1990.

Institut Rosenberg: Advertisement, "Institut Rosenberg," from *Süddeutsche Zeitung,* July 10–11, 1993, p. 40.

IVT-Immobiliengesellschaft der Volksbank Tübingen mbH & Co.: "Auf dem Lande" and "2-Zi.-Eigentumswohnung" from "Immobilienverbund-Volksbanken Raiffeisenbanken" from *Südwest Presse: Schwäbisches Tagblatt,* Tübingen, July 14, 1990.

Jahreszeiten Verlag GmbH: "DAS WEISSE HEMD" from *Petra,* May 1992, p. 52.

K+L Ruppert: Advertisements, "Kurz Und Gut!" and "Qualitäts-Garantie."

Kabarett Mon Marthe: Text and photograph to "Reiner Kröhnert," from *Kabarett Mon Marthe: Das Programm bis Juni 1993.*

Karsten Jahnke Konzertdirektion: Advertisement of upcoming concert tours from *Konzerte: Karsten Jahnke Präsentiert Konzertübersicht 1993,* no. 248.

Kriegbaum Aktuell: Advertisement, "Stark Reduziert!," from *Südwest Presse: Schwäbisches Tagblatt,* Tübingen, June 27, 1990.

Liberty Diskothek Café: Advertisement, "Liberty Diskothek Café," from *in münchen,* no. 30/31, July 25–August 7, 1991.

Mädchen: Recipe, "Pizzateig," from *Mädchen,* March 1993, no. 13, p. 62.

Messe Stuttgart Kongress-U. Tagungsbüro.: "Hanns-Martin-Schleyer-Halle" from *Veranstaltungskalender der Messe Stuttgart: Programm,* March *1992.*

Müller Brot: Advertisements, "Der Mensch ist, wie er ißt" and "HOTLINE."

Neuen Zürcher Zeitung: Advertisements, "The Addams Family," "Das verlorene Halsband der Taube," "JFK," "Little Man Tate," and "Prince of Tides," from *Neuen Zürcher Zeitung,* Zurich, March 3, 1992, no. 52, p. 16.

OK-PUR: From "MTV News" and "OK-PUR TAGESTIP: The Romeos" from *OK-PUR,* June 22, 1993.

Quick-Schuh GmbH & Co. KG, Mainhausen: "Stundenplan" (class schedule) from *Quick-Schuh.*

QUICK Verlag GmbH: Advertisement, "Milchbars," from *QUICK,* August 8, 1991, no. 33. Copyright © 1991 by QUICK Verlag GmbH.

Dr. Rall GmbH, Reutlingen: Advertisement, "Tübingen-Lustnau Am Herrlesberg," from *Südwest Presse: Schwäbisches Tagblatt,* Tübingen, July 14, 1990.

Sator Werbe-Agentur: Advertisement, "Bahrenfelder Forstaus," from *Hotels und Restaurants 93/94,* Hamburg Das Tor zur Welt.

Hartmut Schmid: Game, "Schach," from *Südwest Presse: Schwäbisches Tagblatt,* Tübingen, July 13, 1990.

Schneider & Händle, Werbeagentur Deutschland: Advertisement, "Der mit dem Wolf tanzt," from *1. Ludwigsburger: Sommernachts Open-Air-Kino,* text by Frank Schneider, illustration by Gernot Händle.

Schwäbisches Tagblatt: Advertisement, "UNI Sommerfest," from *Südwest Presse: Schwäbisches Tagblatt,* Tübingen, June 23, 1990.

Spar Öst Warenhandels-AG: From flyer, "Spar Supermarkt: NEUERÖFFNUNG, July 1, 1993."

Stadt Bietigheim-Bissingen, Presseamt und Stadtarchiv: Captions from *Stadt Bietigheim-Bissingen.*

Südwest Presse: Advertisement, "Eninger Hot Jazz Festival," *Schwäbisches Tagblatt,* Tübingen, June 23, 1990.

Tiefdruck Schwann-Bagel GmbH: Adaption of advertisement, "Hobby," from *JUMA Das Jugendmagazin,* 2/90, p. 47, February 1990. Advertisement, "Mode '91" from *JUMA Das Jugendmagazin,* 3/91, p. 31, July 1991. "Christoph, 12," "Nils, 19 Jahre," from *JUMA Das Jugendmagazin,* 4/91, pp. 7 and 22, October 1991. Pictures & captions from "Polo mit Eskimorolle" from *JUMA Das Jugendmagazin,* 1/92, pp. 2–3, January 1992. "Traumhaus" from *JUMA Das Jugendmagazin,* 1/92, p. 16, January 92. "...in Dänemark," from *JUMA Das Jugendmagazin,* 3/92, p. 42, July 1992. "Geschenke," "Hallo Heiko!," "Hallo Sven!," "Hallo Tina!," "Im Geschenkladen sucht," "Im Supermarkt läuft Ben," and "Stefan wird Im Schreibwarengeschäft," from *JUMA Das Jugendmagazin,* 2/93, pp. 21, 23, 38, 39, 40, and 42, April 1993.

Turner Broadcasting: Advertisement, "The Wall," from *Der besondere Film.*

United International Pictures GmbH: Advertisement, "Jurassic Park," from *Kino Magazin,* February 1993.

Verkehrsamt Stuttgart: Captions from *Stuttgart.*

Verlag DIE ABENDZEITUNG, GmbH & Co. KG: Movie advertisements, "Beethoven," "Mein Vetter Winnie," "Vater der Braut," from *Abendzeitung,* May 1992, p. 34. Movie advertisement, "Schtonk," from *Abendzeitung,* June 4, 1992, p. 31.

Verlag Mohr, Georg Siebeck, publisher: Advertisement, "Wohnung," from *Südwest Presse: Schwäbisches Tagblatt,* Tübingen, July 14, 1990.

VIPP Video: "Video Hits" from *Bravo,* 44/1991, p. 67, October 1991.

PHOTOGRAPHY CREDITS

Abbreviations used: (t) top, (c) center, (b) bottom, (l) left, (r) right, (i) inset.

FRONT COVER: (bl) Nawrocki Stock Photo, Inc., **BACK COVER:** (tl) Fridmar Damm/Leo de Wys, Inc., (tr) David Frazier Photolibrary, **FRONT AND BACK COVER COLLAGE:** HRW Photo by Andrew Yates

Chapter Opener photos: Scott Van Osdol

All photographs by George Winkler/Holt, Rinehart and Winston, Inc. except:

TABLE OF CONTENTS: Page v(bl), vi(tl), vi(cl), vi(bl), vii(br), viii(cr), viii(bl), viii(br), ix(b), x(tl), x(c), x(b), xi(t), xi(b), xii(tl),xii(cl), xii(cr), xii(b), (all) Michelle Bridwell/Frontera Fotos.

Preliminary Chapter: (background), (all) Eric Beggs. Page 1(tl), 1(tc), Westlight; 1(tr), FPG International; 4(tl), DPA Photoreporters; 4(tr), Westlight; 4(cl), Robert Young Pelton/Westlight; 4(bl), Dallas & John Heaton/Westlight; 4(br), Westlight; 5(tl), 5(c), 5(br), Bettmann Archive; 5(tr), AP/Wide World Photos, Inc.; 5(b), Archive Photo; 7(tl), 7(tr), Michelle Bridwell/Frontera Fotos; 10(cl), 10(b), AP/Wide World Photos, Inc.; 10(tr), I. George Bilyk.

UNIT ONE: Page 12–13, Jose Fuste Raga/The Stock Market; 14(tl), Kaki/Helga Lade/Peter Arnold, Inc.; 14(c), D. Assmann/Helga Lade/Peter Arnold, Inc. **Chapter One:** Page 20, 21(tl), 21(bl), 21(br), Michelle Bridwell/Frontera Fotos; 21(tr), Viesti Associates, Inc.; 28, Michelle Bridwell/Frontera Fotos; 34–35(background), Courtesy of Lufthansa German Airlines, New York; 35(bl), 36, HRW Photo. **Chapter Two:** Page 41(b), Michelle Bridwell/Frontera Fotos; 44, HRW Photo by Michelle Bridwell; 47, HRW Photo by Richard Hutchings; 48, Harbrace Photo by Oscar Buitrago; 51, (all) Michelle Bridwell/Frontera Fotos; 58(t), Comstock; 61, (all) Viesti Associates, Inc. **Chapter Three:** Page 69(tl), 69(bli), 69(bci), 69(bri), Michelle Bridwell/Frontera Fotos; 69(br), Viesti Associates, Inc.; 70(l), PhotoEdit; 70(cl), 70(cr), Viesti Associates, Inc.; 76, (all) Michelle Bridwell/Frontera Fotos; 76(tl), Courtesy of Scandinavia Contemporary Interiors/Michelle Bridwell/Frontera Fotos; 77(top row), Viesti Associates, Inc.; 77(second row), (2,3,4) Viesti Associates, Inc.; 77(third row), (5) Viesti Associates, Inc.; 77(fourth row), (all), 85, 86, (all) Michelle Bridwell/Frontera Fotos.

UNIT TWO: Page 88, 89, 90, (all) R. Robert/Helga Lade/Peter Arnold, Inc. **Chapter Four:** Page 93(b), 107(t), (all) Michelle Bridwell/Frontera Fotos; 107(b), HRW Photo by Michelle Bridwell. **Chapter Five:** Page 125, 129, 131, (all) Michelle Bridwell/Frontera Fotos; 131(l), Courtesy of Texas Clothier/Michelle Bridwell/Frontera Fotos; 137, David Vance/The Image Bank. **Chapter Six:** Page 158–159(background), Rolf Nobel/Visum.

UNIT THREE: Page 164, 165, Comstock. **Chapter Seven:** Page 173(top row), (1,2) Michelle Bridwell/Frontera Fotos; 173(second row), (1,2,3) Michelle Bridwell/Frontera Fotos; 173(third row), (4) Viesti Associates, Inc.; 183, (all) PhotoEdit; 186, 187(tl), Viesti Associates, Inc.; 187(b), Michelle Bridwell/Frontera Fotos; 188 (5), Michelle Bridwell/Frontera Fotos. **Chapter Eight:** Page 193(tr), 194(tl), Michelle Bridwell/Frontera Fotos; 197(top left panel), (all) Michelle Bridwell/Frontera Fotos; 197(right panel: top), Michelle Bridwell/Frontera Fotos; 197(right panel: bottom), HRW Photo by Sam Dudgeon; 197(center panel), HRW Photo by Sam Dudgeon; 197(bottom panel), (1) Viesti Associates, Inc.; (2), HRW Photo by Sam Dudgeon; (3,4t), Viesti Associates, Inc.; (4b), HRW Photo by Sam Dudgeon; (5), Viesti Associates, Inc.; (6t), HRW Photo by Sam Dudgeon; (6b), Viesti Associates, Inc.; 198(tr), Viesti Associates, Inc. **Chapter Nine:** Page 226(t), 226(b), composite photographs, Munich Square: George Winkler; people: Michelle Bridwell/Frontera Fotos; 232, Thomas Kanzler/Viesti Associates, Inc.; 237(top row) (2,3) Michelle Bridwell/Frontera Fotos; 237(bottom row) (1), Michelle Bridwell/Frontera Fotos.

UNIT FOUR: Page 240–241(background), 242(tl), S.K./Helga Lade/Peter Arnold, Inc. **Chapter Ten:** Page 249(top row), (all) Motion Picture & TV Photo Archive; 249(center row) (l) Motion Picture & TV Photo Archive; 249(c), 249(r), Everett Collection; 249(bottom row), (all) Motion Picture & TV Photo Archive; 251, Marko Shark; 256, 259, (all) Michelle Bridwell/Frontera Fotos; 260, Thomas Kanzler/Viesti Associates, Inc. **Chapter Eleven:** Page 268, 269, (all) Michelle Bridwell/Frontera Fotos; 281(t), Courtesy of Wicks & Sticks/Michelle Bridwell/Frontera Fotos; 281(top row), (1) Michelle Bridwell/Frontera Fotos; (2) Viesti Associates, Inc.; (3) Michelle Bridwell/Frontera Fotos; (4) Viesti Associates, Inc.; (5) Michelle Bridwell/Frontera Fotos; 281(bottom row), 283, 285, 288, (all) Michelle Bridwell/Frontera Fotos. **Chapter Twelve:** Page 300(top row), (r) Michelle Bridwell/Frontera Fotos; 300(bottom row), (l) Viesti Associates, Inc.; 303(tr), 310(background), 310(t), 310(b), 311(c), (all) Michelle Bridwell/Frontera Fotos.

ILLUSTRATION AND CARTOGRAPHY CREDITS

Beier, Ellen: 9

Böhm, Eduard: 45, 46, 49, 71, 72, 106, 113, 121, 155, 175, 181, 199, 202, 231, 254, 278, 279, 298, 305, 307

Carlson, Susan: xviii, 2, 3

Cooper, Holly: i, v, vi, viii, x, xii, xiv, 6, 22, 60, 71, 77, 97, 99, 121, 124, 125, 132, 133, 136, 138, 145, 156, 157, 160, 175, 190, 199, 228, 265, 304, 305

Kell, Leslie: 11, 146, 225, 236, 265

Krone, Mike: 279, 284, 290, 299

Maryland Cartographics: 1, 13, 89, 165, 241

McLeod, George: 22, 23, 30, 49, 70, 74, 108, 148, 174, 181, 223, 289, 302

Piazza, Gail: 45, 53, 80, 100

Rummonds, Tom: 8, 37, 84, 126, 127, 145, 149, 179, 180, 184, 200, 208, 273, 274

Rushing, Riki: 225, 313

Williamson, Reagan: 27

Wilson, John: 221, 223, 238